The Hollow Crown

THE PENGUIN HISTORY OF BRITAIN

I: DAVID MATTINGLY Roman Britain: 100–409

II: ROBIN FLEMING Anglo-Saxon Britain: 410–1066

III: DAVID CARPENTER The Struggle for Mastery: Britain 1066–1284*

IV: MIRI RUBIN The Hollow Crown:
A History of Britain in the Late Middle Ages*

V: SUSAN BRIGDEN New Worlds, Lost Worlds: Britain 1485–1603*

VI: MARK KISHLANSKY A Monarchy Transformed: Britain 1603–1714*

VII: LINDA COLLEY A Wealth of Nations? Britain 1707–1815

VIII: DAVID CANNADINE At the Summit of the World: Britain 1800–1906

IX: PETER CLARKE Hope and Glory: Britain 1901–2000, 2nd edition*

* already published

MIRI RUBIN

The Hollow Crown

A History of Britain in the Late Middle Ages

ALLEN LANE
an imprint of
PENGUIN BOOKS

ALLEN LANE

Published by the Penguin Group

Penguin Books Ltd, 80 Strand, London WC2R ORL, England
Penguin Group (USA) Inc., 375 Hudson Street, New York, New York 10014, USA
Penguin Books Australia Ltd, 250 Camberwell Road, Camberwell, Victoria 3124, Australia
Penguin Books Canada Ltd, 10 Alcorn Avenue, Toronto, Ontario, Canada M4V 3B2
Penguin Books India (P) Ltd, 11 Community Centre, Panchsheel Park, New Delhi – 110 017, India
Penguin Group (NZ), cnr Airborne and Rosedale Roads, Albany, Auckland 1310, New Zealand
Penguin Books (South Africa) (Pty) Ltd, 24 Sturdee Avenue, Rosebank 2196, South Africa

Penguin Books Ltd, Registered Offices: 80 Strand, London WC2R ORL, England

www.penguin.com

First published 2005
1

Set in 10.75/13.75 pt Monotype Sabon
Typeset by Rowland Phototypesetting Ltd, Bury St Edmunds, Suffolk
Printed in England by Clays Ltd, St Ives plc

ISBN 0–713–99066–X

Contents

List of Illustrations		vii
Preface		ix
Editorial Note		xiii
Maps		xv
	Introduction	1
1	Famine and Deposition, 1307–1330	17
2	Plague and War, 1330–1377	57
3	An Empty Land and its King, 1377–1399	116
4	Usurpation and the Challenges to Order, 1399–1422	173
5	'For the world was that time so strange', 1422–1461	224
6	Little England and a Little Peace, 1462–1485	275
	Epilogue	319
	Genealogical Table	323
	An Essay on Further Reading	325
	Index	355

List of Illustrations

Photographic acknowledgements are given in parentheses.

1. Zodiac Man, British Library Egerton 2572, fol. 50v (British Library)
2. Edward III granting the Black Prince the principality of Aquitaine (Bridgeman Art Library)
3. Women throwing corn to hens and chickens, British Library Additonal 42130, fol. 166v (British Library)
4. Virgin and Child, Eaton Bishop Church (Eaton Bishop Church/Bridgeman Art Library)
5. Bamburgh Castle (Corbis)
6. Effigy of the Black Prince, Canterbury Cathedral (Canterbury Cathedral/Corbis)
7. Battle of Crécy, British Library Cotton Nero E II, fol. 152v (British Library)
8. Effigy of Walter de Helyon, Much Marcle Church (Much Marcle Church/photograph by kind permission of David Mocatta)
9. Death of Wat Tyler, British Library Royal 18 E I, fol. 175 (Bridgeman Art Library)
10. Frontispiece to Chaucer's manuscript of *Troilus and Criseyde*, Cambridge, Corpus Christi College, Manuscript 61, fol. 1v (Master and Fellows of Corpus Christi College, Cambridge)
11. Wilton Diptych, National Gallery (by kind permission of the National Gallery of London/Corbis)
12. Richard II receiving the Earl of Northumberland, British Library Harley 1319, fol. 37v (British Library)
13. Henry Bolingbroke claiming the throne, British Library Harley 1319, fol. 57 (British Library)

14. Effigies of Henry IV and Queen Joan of Navarre on their tomb in Canterbury Cathedral (Bridgeman Art Library)
15. Duke of Clarence effigy, St Michael's Chapel, Canterbury Cathedral (Corbis)
16. Henry V with the English poet Thomas Hoccleve (Corbis)
17. Battle of Agincourt, Lambeth Palace Library 6, fol. 243 (Bridgeman Art Library)
18. The Duke of Bedford worshipping Saint George, British Library Additional 18850, fol. 256 (British Library)
19. Thomas Mac William Burke, MS 1440 fol. 21v (The Board of Trinity College Dublin)
20. Henry VI gives the Earl of Shrewsbury the sword of the Constable of France, British Library Royal 15 E 6, fol. 405 (British Library)
21. Manchester misericord, Manchester Cathedral (Manchester Cathedral and Manchester University Art History Department)
22. King's College Chapel, Cambridge (Corbis)
23. Parchment illustrated with historical passages from the life of Edward IV and his pedigree, British Library Harley 7353 (Bridgeman Art Library)
24. Image of a clandestine marriage, British Library Royal 6 E 6, fol. 286v (British Library)
25. Obverse of a rose-noble of Edward IV (Bridgeman Art Library)
26. Wenhaston Doom, St Peter's Church, Wenhaston (Rector and Churchwardens of St Peter's, Wenhaston and Blythweb Ltd, http://www.wenhaston.ws)

Preface

The first history book I ever bought was Dorothy Stenton's volume of the Pelican History of England. Although in paperback it was an expensive treat for a poor undergraduate in Jerusalem in the 1970s. To the pleasure of buying it was added the thrill of rummaging through the shelves of the most old-fashioned of scholarly bookshops, Ludwig Mayer's. Since then much has come and gone, in Jerusalem, in my life, in our book-buying habits, and in the practice of history. Like that much treasured book, *The Hollow Crown* aims to share historical reflection, discovery and enthusiasm with those who love and cherish history, but who have not made it their vocation. It is the product of the quarter-century of my life as a historian, but it is not for historians alone. The French have an excellent term to describe the intended audience – *le grand publique* – the great public, the many who devote some of their leisure to reading and visiting, and finally asking: How did we get here? How have we become what we think we are? How different are we from those who lived before us? What may we choose to learn and what to discard from the dizzying range of human experience which history reveals?

I say this book is not primarily for historians, or even history students, but it could not have been made without the incorporation of the intelligence, diligence and commitment of hundreds of workers in the historical fields: academic historians, historians of art, students of medieval literature, miners of archaeological remains. While writing *The Hollow Crown* I came to realize just how many historians there are in Britain today outside the universities: people who research and publish excellent scholarship while preserving archives, teaching in schools, guarding historic sites, curating in museums; how many continue to study and write long after retirement, or during years at home while caring for children.

The main, and perhaps sole, frustration arising from the writing of this book has been the impossibility of acknowledging debts in footnote form. I aim to do justice to the most heavily used sources in the Essay on Further Reading at the end of this book, and have listed all sources in a full bibliography which is available on-line at http://www.history.qmul.ac.uk/staff/rubinbiblio.html. My reading and research at the Cambridge University Library was graciously supported by the assistance of Colin Clarkson, Lucas Elkin, Michael Fuller, Neil Hudson, Andrew Kennedy and Morag Law.

I name here with pleasure those who generously provided material as yet unpublished or who answered queries: Caroline Barron, Jim Bolton, Chris Briggs, Christopher Fletcher, Ian Forrest, Harold Fox, Barbara Hanawalt, Katie Hawks, Richard Helmholz, Brian Patrick McGuire, Marygold Norbye, Mark Ormrod, Danna Piroyanski, Ivan Polancec, Richard Smith, Craig Taylor, Anne de Windt and Edwin de Windt. As to the many friends who helped me along the years – over cups of coffee and tea in the Cambridge University Library or the British Library, at meetings and seminars and conferences – they know how grateful I am, and what fun it has been to make history together.

Some people must be mentioned by name. My young colleagues, whom I have seen grow from brilliant and blushing graduate students to confident and creative scholars – Anthony Bale, Chris Briggs, Christopher Fletcher, Ian Forrest, Julian Luxford, Ruth Nisse, Danna Piroyanski, Max Satchell, Phillip Schofield, David Stone, Marianne Turner, Anna Whitelock – have kept me alert and abreast of their exciting ways of making history. I am delighted to thank, for his formative intellectual gifts, Richard Smith, who presides over the buoyant study of British rural societies; Mark Bailey, who combines subtle understanding of landscape with the best that economic history has to offer; Paul Binki, who knows English medieval art in all its forms as no other does, and is passionate and generous too; John Watts, who, together with the late and sorely lamented Simon Walker, has brought new grace and vision to the study of late medieval politics; Mark Ormrod, who always reminds us that Britain is part of Europe, and toils at the long history of state formation; Christopher Dyer, who has made the feeding, clothing and housing of medieval British people a central historical preoccupation, with a combination of erudition and common sense; Richard Britnell, who explores the creative forces of medieval exchange and town life; Paul Strohm and David Wallace, who have taught me how to read texts historically; Ira Katznelson, who excels in using contemporary politics as a historian's tool, without shame; and Rees Davies, a luminous practitioner of *histoire totale*, a supportive friend and shining example in all my endeavours.

At Queen Mary, University of London, I am surrounded by wonderful examples of innovation in British History. My move from Oxford to London in 2000 brought me into touch with a wonderful new group of colleagues and friends. With some I run the European History Seminar – David Carpenter (the author of the volume preceding my own in this series), David D'Avray, Sophie Page, Brigitte Resl and Nigel Saul. From them and from the seminar's alert and lively participants I have learned much that is offered in this book.

Thanks to Joan Stedman Jones I have come to know Herefordshire and the Marches well. She and Christopher Walbank, both lovers of everything historical, have served as my intelligent lay readers, and have contributed meaningfully to the book's improvement. Christopher Brooke, Shulamith Shahar, Jon Parry and Gareth Stedman Jones turned their formidable historical minds to my draft; they read the volume closely and with the commitment of real friends. They indicated delicately points for improvements and have thus become partners in the book. My son Joseph Stedman Jones is the best possible companion on the trips and walks which have contributed to the making of this book.

I live in a very historically minded household. My partner is a historian, his son studies history, and our son, Joseph, once told me – after a visit to Castle Acre in Norfolk – that he is keen on castles and priories almost in equal measure. When he was six years old Joseph developed a passion for Shakespeare through viewing the History Plays, directed by Michael Boyd during the 2001 season of the Royal Shakespeare Company. Most mothers would consider this passion a blessing – and I definitely did – but it also dramatized the weight of history, story and drama, which we all carry with us when approaching any area of history, above all late medieval British history. I have acknowledged this fact by letting Shakespeare in so he doesn't haunt us so much; his words will accompany us through each chapter, the ghost at the feast, less voracious, I hope, for having been allocated a space at the table.

I am grateful to David Cannadine for having chosen me for this task, and to Simon Winder, my editor at Penguin. Simon has read every word with the incision and sympathy of the talented historian that he is. I greatly enjoyed Penguin's support towards publication: Janet Tyrrell's editorial touch, Alison Hennessey's care for images, and Elisabeth Merriman's attentive coordination.

Writing this book feels like a homecoming – for I live in Britain, far from Chicago where I was born and Jerusalem where I was nurtured. This book is a gift to all those who have made Britain feel like home.

Editorial Note

Several decisions have been taken in this book in order to facilitate the presentation of source material and familiarize the reader with the places and people discussed. In most cases personal names are offered in a modern English-language version, as are place-names; these are followed by the name of the county in which they are currently situated. Titles of books are given in their original language and spelling and are followed by an English translation. Sums of money are rendered in pounds (£), shillings (s.) and pence (d.), but occasionally the accounting term 'mark', which was equivalent to two-thirds of a pound, is used when the original document did so. I have translated most original sources, but have made use of a published modern translation of Chaucer's work and a standard edition of Shakespeare's poetry: Geoffrey Chaucer, *The Canterbury Tales*, trans. David Wright, Oxford, 1986; William Shakespeare, *The Collected Works*, ed. Stanley Wells, Gary Taylor, John Jowett and William Montgomery, Oxford, first edn 1966.

Miri Rubin
Cambridge, September 2004

Maps

1. The counties of England   xvi
2. The units of governance in Wales   xvii
3. The counties and regions of Ireland   xviii
4. France in the Hundred Years War: the fourteenth century   xix
5. France in the Hundred Years War: the fifteenth century   xx

The counties of England

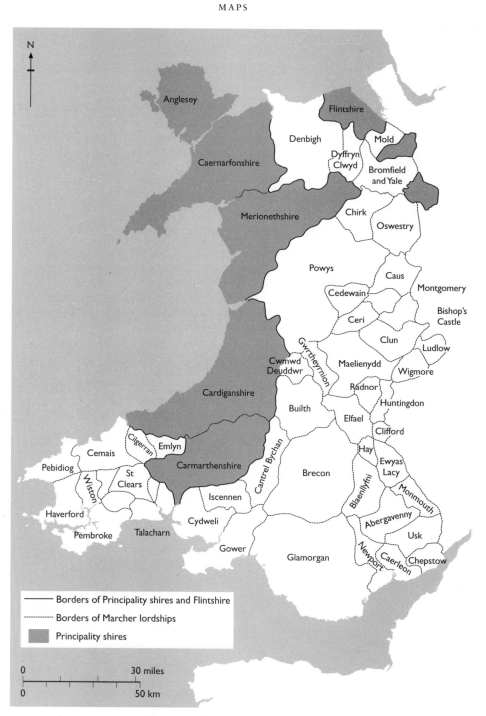

The units of governance in Wales

The counties and regions of Ireland

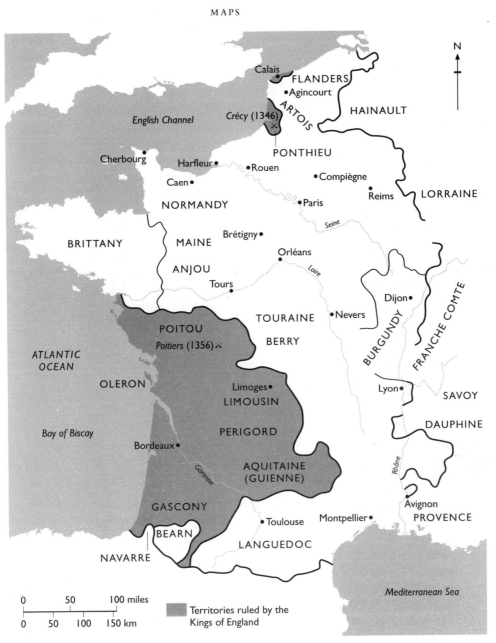

France in the Hundred Years War: the fourteenth century

N

Calais
Agincourt (1415) ✕
FLANDERS
ARTOIS

English Channel
•Crécy

PICARDY

Cherbourg
Harfleur•
•Rouen
•Compiègne
Caen•
Reims

NORMANDY
•Paris

BRITTANY
Brétigny•
Seine

MAINE
Orléans•
Domrémy•

ANJOU Tours
BERRY

Chinon•
NEVERS DUCHY
OF
TOURAINE
Nevers•
BURGUNDY

POITOU
•Poitiers
BOURBON

TERRITORY OF
THE FRENCH KING

OLERON
Limoges•

LIMOUSIN

ATLANTIC
OCEAN

Bay of Biscay
DAUPHINE

Bordeaux•
AUVERGNE

AQUITAINE

GASCONY
Garonne

Rhône

Avignon
ARMAGNAC
PROVENCE

•Toulouse

BEARN
LANGUEDOC

TOULOUSE

Loire

Mediterranean Sea

| 0 | 50 | 100 miles |
| 0 | 50 | 100 | 150 km |

English conquests

Loyal to the Duke of Burgundy

France in the Hundred Years War: the fifteenth century

Introduction

Some 5–6 million people lived in Britain around the year 1300. These men and women, young and old, were born and bred towards the end of a mighty phase of population growth, almost two centuries of extension of cultivation to new lands, decades which witnessed a vitalization of agrarian life and commercial exchange. This trend affected the whole of Europe. It meant that by 1300 there were some 1,500 market towns of varying sizes in England and Wales, a third of them in East Anglia. To such towns peasants brought their surplus produce, in them artisans organized workshops and produced goods that both peasants and town-dwellers could hope to buy. There were also some 10,000–15,000 mills – moved by water everywhere and in the north-east also by wind – which marked villages with their familiar shapes and accompanying millponds. The dramatic rise in Europe's agrarian productivity, together with its population growth, in the century and a half before 1300 meant that those who held great estates and vast tracts of land were motivated towards improvement and better management, towards higher productivity of cash-crops: corn, barley, wheat – and wool. Wool was the prime export of England and Wales, some 40,000 sacks a year being produced from around 10 million sheep. All these were marketed in England and abroad, fetching good prices and high returns.

England and Wales, Scotland and Ireland were part of an integrated European system of exchange with two obvious foci – in the Mediterranean, and in the North Sea and the Baltic. The wool produced in Britain at the beginning of our period was worked into cloth in the Low Countries, where the dyes to colour them were also grown: weld, which provided the yellow hue, around Lille, madder for red around Ypres and Bruges, and woad leaves for blue, south of Ghent. It was widely appreciated that the rivers Humber, Thames and Severn formed Britain's crucial communication system, allowing ready access to much of the country. There were eighty-nine ports in the British Isles. By 1300 those travelling to one of them – Hull or York, Poole or Dublin – encountered specialized structures on the waterfronts, in sea ports and river ports: warehouses, wharfs, inns, customs halls, with planking and provisions for removal of refuse, as well as customary arrangements for the hire of packing and loading hands. The Cinque Ports of the south-east gained special privileges in return for mustering vessels and transporting kings and armies. Those who chose to travel by road used a system which included iron-age ridgeways, partially paved Roman roads and Anglo-Saxon cartways, and forded rivers on bridges maintained by lords since the Norman conquest.

England's manors were transformed in this period into market-oriented enterprises. To benefit from the possibilities of exchange, landlords used all their customary privileges, and above all the control of the un-free peasantry: control of their marriages, and access to some of their labour and much of the produce of their tenancies. The intensification of agricultural production took many forms, which differed by region: in movement from food grain to drink grain, in the rearing of dairy animals for meat, in the use of draught horses rather than oxen, and in the planting of legumes on lands while fallow. On the whole, before 1350 most manors were organized for the production of crops; after the Black Death pastoral husbandry became more attractive, since it was less labour-intensive. The wealth generated by manorial production and trade in agricultural goods allowed landlords to experiment with their lifestyle and comforts. The earliest surviving manor house, of c.1300, is at Little Wenham (Suffolk). It was built of brick, in Flemish style, and stands near the other important building of the manor, the parish church. But there were regions which were almost entirely pastoral: in Wales, Yorkshire, the Cotswolds. There were vast expanses of land which remained uncultivated. Thornbury Manor was the glory of the Clare earls of Gloucester, 10,000 acres in size, but at the beginning of our period only half of it was cultivated; the rest was woodland and marsh, a possible pocket of malaria in the Severn wetlands.

There were some very large cities in England around the year 1300: London with a population of 100,000, York with 13,000, Coventry and Norwich around 10,000. Hundreds of small towns dotted the countryside in England and parts of Wales, Ireland and Scotland. These formed a central feature of life by 1300: there were 50 towns of over 2,000 inhabitants, and some 650 with populations of 300–2,000. Smallholders grew crops to feed their families, but they also produced for the market. Around 40 per cent of grain was sold in markets, to which it was transported by stewards of estates selling surplus, by rectors of parishes, who collected tithes in kind from parishioners, and by peasants themselves. Such marketing provided the foodstuffs for some 200,000 families who worked in towns and cities and who did not produce most of their own food. Towns needed meat, and wood for heat and light; we find butchers and chandlers in even very small towns such as Kimbolton (Cambridgeshire), Alnwick (Northumberland) or Halesowen (Worcestershire). Attempts at town-creation sometimes failed; Brentford (Warwickshire) and Newburgh (Staffordshire) never quite thrived. While the spread of commercial possibilities is impressive, some areas such as Devon and Cornwall had relatively few towns. Most towns retained many traces of the rural life which flowed through them: these names have endured in Sheep Streets in the Cotswolds, as well as in lanes named after geese, hogs and dogs.

Vast tracts of the countryside, between a third and a quarter in England, were forest: forest by physical character and forest in legal status. For this landscape acquired its own legal character, with an array of forest officials – established already by the Anglo-Norman kings – who enforced the exclusive rights of kings and lords to timber and fruit, game and wildlife. Their powers were great; they could search homes and persons, seeking incriminating remains – a skin, some offal. And where officials held great powers there was the temptation to bribe and be bribed. It is not surprising that some of the most evocative and enduring ballads, plays and songs in English have the forest as their stage, forest officials and poachers as their characters.

In forests – Dartmoor, the Forest of Dean, Epping – unusual and interesting communities developed. They benefited from the demand generated by the occasional presence of the royal or aristocratic households nearby, as well as from a varied habitat. The town of Brill, for example, was the centre of manufacture and exchange in Bernwood Forest (Buckinghamshire), and in it some of the finest domestic pottery was produced – cooking pots, skillets, herring dishes – perhaps inspired by the needs of the neighbouring royal parties, and exported throughout the east Midlands. A subtle understanding of the uses of trees guided rhythms of planting. Timber was used for the ubiquitous fires of cooking, heating and industry. Ash wood was preferred for its regular flame, over sparking chestnut, or conifers with their smoky resin; beech's even heat was good for industry and cooking. Oak was the backbone for durable construction of houses and ships.

There was a great intimacy between people and the local landscape, the main stage for most people's lives. The countryside offered some gifts, like the colour of its vegetation, or the texture of its soil. Some of this backdrop changed with the seasons, and so people used holly and ivy at Christmastime, willows for Palm Sunday processions, hawthorns for May Day and roses for the summer feast of Corpus Christi. Herbals contain fine and careful drawings of leaves, fruit and list their properties, for cooking and the preparation of cures as well as of poisons. This knowledge was practical, but it could also be turned into a poetic celebration: the abundant carving of leaves on the capitals of the chapter-house columns at Southwell Minster (Nottinghamshire) displays excellent craftsmanship, based on finely drawn models, and expresses the desire to exhibit talent while celebrating the diverse genius of Creation.

Fleeting leaves were thus set to endure in solid stone. The most enduring colours of the landscape were of the rocks from which building and carving stone was cut: the dark and crystalline stone of Cumbria, or the warm-tinted light stone of Yorkshire, which then changes into the dark stone of the Pennines and, further east, the iron-rich brown stone of Northamptonshire. In the many river valleys the rich combination of water, stone and leaf produced settings such as Swinbrook, a village of golden Cotswold stone, at the rise of the river Windrush, with willows on each bank.

Few peasants held holdings sufficient for their subsistence – which required about thirty acres – and therefore many serfs and the members of their families offered their labour to others. English villages in particular contained a high proportion of members who held only very small amounts of land. So tenants laboured on seigneurial lands – often known as demesne lands – for a daily wage often paid in a combination of coin, produce and food rations. In the east of England substantial tenants were more common than elsewhere, and they sometimes employed their less fortunate neighbours. When such hard-pressed smallholders failed to thrive, their better-off neighbours were able and keen to buy their lands. In those parts of Ireland settled by English colonizers from the later twelfth century, tenants held large tenancies in free tenure and traded in the produce of wool and hides.

By the beginning of our period the trend of growth and extension had reached its peak in many regions, and was probably being reversed in some. Population growth meant that many rural tenants could not provide land for their sons and daughters. The demand for land sometimes inspired cooperation between landlords and peasant communities: reclamation of land in the Welland marshes (Kent) and in the Somerset Levels, drainage in Holland (Lincolnshire) and the building and maintenance of sea defences. As competition for land intensified, relations between peasants and their lords became acrimonious. Episodes of rancour and violence against the demands of lords multiplied in the decades which precede our point of departure.

These lords were rarely met or confronted in person: about a third of English manors were held by religious institutions, which were represented by stewards, laymen accountable to an abbey, cathedral or priory. Great magnates held about a quarter of the land, and were also represented by administrators, whose presence and influence were most intensive on estates in Wales and Ireland. Conversely, the fortunes of some families such as the Despensers or the Mortimers were intimately bound up with the holding of lands in the Marches with all the authority and the access to armed men that this situation allowed. The fortunes of all those involved in rural life – the landlords who benefited from the marketing of agricultural produce, the serfs who worked to produce food, the local worthies who supervised agrarian work on estates – were affected by the devastation of the Great Famine of 1315–22, with which this book begins. The landscape and their minds alike were marked by the loss and destruction caused by a run of years which produced nothing but rain and mud.

Politics were linked to patterns of land-holding in rural areas, and to trading wealth and office-holding in towns. Land-holding defined men's access to county and parish politics, as well as to office-holding on behalf of magnates or the crown. Their role as jurors in local administrative frames – the county, and its subdivision, the hundred – was paramount in dispensing justice. Marks of their status and ambition were as locally situated as were their lands. Sir Simon de Drayton chose to be represented after death in the glass of his parish church of Lowick (Northamptonshire) in a position of homage. This image evoked the web of obligations by which his land was held, and on which his authority over the lives of tens of parishioners was based. He contributed to the rebuilding of the parish church; he served as representative in parliament eleven times, and as commissioner of array three times.

His deterrent power sometimes turned into outright violence: he was accused of abducting a woman, gouging out her eyes and cutting out her tongue. His family continued to maintain and adorn this fine church. Sir Ralph Greene of Drayton (d.1415) hired craftsmen from Derbyshire to make the tomb chest with brasses which can still be seen, with the effigies of himself, his wife and two dogs. For all the influence and power to subordinate that men like the Greenes had in their locality, this was by no means a society marked by deference alone. A lord was 'good' as long as he earned loyalty; if he acted badly – as Sir Simon may have done – opinion could be reversed quite swiftly, and with it the loyalty of politically active free men. The period produced its iconic figures of charismatic leaders in the name of utopian equality. John Ball, who preached during the uprising of 1381, echoed scripture to support a demand for political change: 'In Christ Jesus there is neither Jew nor Greek, there is neither bond nor free.'

The deterrent power represented by a man of violence, such as Simon de Drayton, benefited his dependants, but it also contained the seeds of destruction when the peace based on reciprocities between peers and neighbours was shattered. The law, as well as sermons and romance literature, aimed to curb the violent prerogative of such men. A much-cited maxim from antiquity – a reworking of Aristotle and Juvenal – claimed that true nobility is proven in good actions and character, rather than by bloodline alone. It called for courtliness, largesse, loyalty and prowess in privileged men and women. A truly noble person was free and autonomous, but also servile to a set of moral maxims, and ultimately to God. Yet the competitive nature of knightly pursuits was always apparent: in the bearing of certain names and titles, in rich attire, in the carrying of weapons, in a residence sometimes adorned by protective defences against imagined attacks – moats, gates, towers – and in the ever-present accompaniment of grooms, squires and dogs. While thousands of men considered themselves knights, only tens of families were of magnate status with constant and enduring roles in national and international politics.

At all degrees of gentility families and individuals were bound through interlocking notions of good lordship; and while lordship could be won, it could also be lost. The terms which determined and expressed these changes may be called a political culture. This political culture acknowledged the king, the product of dynastic succession, around whom claims to enjoy and administer several territories were realized.

These claims were enacted and tested in every locality, as with the 13,000 communities defined as villages for the purpose of taxation in 1334. The political system touched every village with an average of some 400 heads around 1334 (and 200 a century later). In each such village tens of men were involved in public life through law enforcement, regulation of communal resources (meadows, rivers full of fish, the grain remaining in harvested fields for gleaning), through by-laws, in offices such as juror or churchwarden or assessor, or reeve of the manor. Great regional magnates created the overarching frame of trust in the law, the royal law enforced by and for local people. Thus assured, communities allowed local men – those most trustworthy, most prosperous, most sensible, most vociferous – to participate in the many interactions to which their communities were subject. For they were answerable to customs of the manor, by-laws of their village, the canon law of the church, for the crimes committed in their hundred, to the court of their country, and in the Marches to the peculiar institutions of peace-making which these distinctive regions developed. There was much governance. Many institutions and their working depended then, as ours still do, on the charisma of those who made them work.

Land and the lives tied to it were held and managed by – apart from the great religious institutions – royal administrators on behalf of the crown, and a few tens of magnates. Upon these few depended the effectiveness of the kingdom as a war-state. These men represented exalted families and landed interests accumulated over decades and centuries, through royal grant, through purchase, through marriage and through conquest. Magnates' spheres of influence were immense, for in their persons and households many aspects of the state were embodied: the operation of the law, leadership in times of war, protection against invaders in border areas, preferment for all those lesser free men and women who held lands and positions from them. Magnates held a whole array of offices, titles and honours as keepers of royal parks, protectors of the North or Welsh Marches and lieutenants of Ireland or Gascony. In addition to the magnates were bishops, whose estates were as vast, but who were free from the imperative of dynastic succession, although they too preferred and promoted members of their families and households. Since marriage was prohibited to priests, their contribution to their families' fortunes was made through diplomacy and administration: they contracted marriages, negotiated for truces and treaties. They also devised fiscal pathways which enabled kings and magnates to fight wars and protect the joint enterprise of England, Ireland, Wales, Gascony – the enterprise which may be called Britain, for it certainly concerned more than England, though it was British in different ways at different times.

English or British or French? *The Hollow Crown* deals with people whose affinities ranged from the Orkneys to the Pyrenees, who lived in lowland zones like most of England, and in highlands like north-west England, Wales and the Western Isles. The kings who ruled this empire were dynasts who spoke French most of the time and who had each a different set of loyalties and experiences. Edward II, for example, had a French wife and a French mother and a Gascon best friend; Edward III a French mother and Flemish wife; Richard II a Bohemian wife and later a French wife; Henry IV crusaded in Lithuania; Henry V grew up as a very Welsh prince, as Edward II had done; Henry VI was a boy-king of France; Richard III grew up in France and Yorkshire; and Henry VII hardly knew England at all before 1485. All these men and those around them felt comfortable speaking in French, some did in English, and most recognized another language – Flemish, Welsh, Gascon. They diverged greatly in formative influences yet participated similarly in a European aristocratic culture.

Personal and group identity is best thought of as a cluster of attributes and associations including aspects of age, gender, region, occupation, experience and training. Areas of identity are always heightened when they seem most different. The Anglo-Irish thought more about their Englishness than did those who lived in the Midlands, and they worked hard to acquire up-to-date political intelligence, just as they diligently commissioned copies of formative English literature, such as *Piers Plowman* or the devotional image-poem *The Charter of Christ*. Northern clerks promoted to posts in the royal chancery felt their Yorkshire sympathies acutely and gathered in regional groups of sociability and institutions for mutual help. Welsh students at Oxford dwelt for safety and amity in specific hostels, and then in a college – Jesus College – which still boasts its Welsh connection. Unmarried women created their minute religious group for the maintenance of a light in the church of Ashburton (Devon), as did the 'bachelors' of Bassingbourn (Cambridgeshire) and Boxford (Suffolk). A regional dialect was most clearly noted when heard among another region's cadences. Language came to stand for homeland, and people enjoyed the creation of occasions for enacted nostalgia. Free men and women were expert at the work of association, of creating intimate and meaningful groups – such as the group of pilgrims so brilliantly conjured by Chaucer – treasured equally for those they included, and for those they excluded: in fraternities, Inns of Court, guilds, workshops, town councils, orders of chivalry. These were creations of tentative amity and support against the world's bewildering diversity, marking *us* out from *them*.

The coming together in groups for the creation of enduring monuments to success, virtue and good taste had a profound effect on social provision, and on the fabric within which people worshipped and worked. Throughout our period people increasingly chose collective frames for efforts in religion and commemoration, in chantries for perpetual prayer on behalf of self, spouse or kin. King, bishops and aristocrats, civil servants and occasionally townsmen founded academic colleges at Cambridge or Oxford from the early fourteenth century, and grammar schools followed in the fifteenth. While hundreds of leper houses and small hospitals were founded in the twelfth and thirteenth centuries, later provision for the poor was considered most effective when provided in supervised almshouses, mostly parish-related. The almshouse at Ewelme (Oxfordshire), founded by the Duke and Duchess of Suffolk in 1437, is a carefully designed, lavishly built and closely regulated institution for thirteen poor men and two priests, and can still be seen today. It was a charitable institution for destitute men but also one which generated commemorative prayer in perpetuity. Many such charitable institutions, like academic colleges, survived the Reformation, and endured with lands and buildings for generations, to inspire such works as Anthony Trollope's *The Warden*.

As the efforts at consolidation and association were at work in local frames, Englishness is far harder to identify than the many local intersections and borrowings between regions which characterized life in the late medieval British state. Government provided coin, the law, weights and measures, and defined military goals to be achieved with the support of taxes. But the world into which these services and capacities were inserted was greatly varied. Thus Anglo-Irish magnates delighted in Irish music, poetry and the technology of war; the lords of the Marches married Welsh women; Shropshire merchants gathered and sold Welsh wool; East Anglian churches displayed Flemish-style stained glass; and London poets delighted audiences with seemingly archaic alliterative verse borrowed from the Midlands. Englishness may be perceived in a style of governance. The choice or duty to emulate it was an aspect of political hegemony: the exchequers of Dublin, Berwick and Caernarfon were meant to function 'come est fait en Angleterre', 'as done in England'.

Everywhere the universal Christian story was a palimpsest of accumulations and innovations achieved over centuries. Perhaps identity is best understood and perceived by us as a particular set of habits and expectations, an aesthetic which sets apart an English crucifix from an Italian one; a set of family structures, which set apart English families – with late marriage and few children – from Welsh ones; expectations in relations of men and women which set apart property-holding English widows from Welsh ones who did not inherit. It may be perceived in the affinity felt towards the instruments of law and the operation of administration: free people used the English law knowingly in England, but common law was not available to remedy the grievances of Welsh people, who used *brehon* law for private affairs, while clerks and priests and bishops maintained a parallel system of canon law informed by principles of Roman law. Women acted fully in ecclesiastical courts, where they were allowed to give full expression to grievances and disappointment in marital life, but they acted in common law only through proctors and lawyers. Law created communities and individual expectation, and some of the stories which this book tells reflect the fluctuating degree of trust which people had for the law at different stages of our journey.

This book will introduce you to the world whose triumphs and tribulations inspired the brilliant re-enactment of Shakespeare's history plays and also a comedy, *The Merry Wives of Windsor*. Shakespeare was no historian; the centuries which lay between his lifetime and those of the Plantagenet, Lancastrian, Yorkist and early Tudor kings – and of their subjects – created a meaningful historical distance. Yet he was an astute student of rule and rulership, and himself lived in turbulent times, during which dynasty, loyalty, faction and religious identity were harshly tested in all regions of Britain, in the lives of people of all ranks and situations.

The Hollow Crown provides an entry into this world. Shakespeare is just one exceptional example of the use which Tudor writers and thinkers made of the late Middle Ages as the source of cautionary tales about rule, misrule and the vagaries of fortune. Shakespeare read such accounts and poetically dramatized historical figures, sometimes inventing physical traits, at other times rearranging chronology. The following chapters will describe and narrate the fall of kings. However, it does so with an eye for the varying repercussions which regime change had on the life and livelihood, security and sensibility of the wide range of soldiers and farmers, merchants and craftsmen, men and women in rural and urban communities ruled by the kings of England, who were also the kings of Wales and Ireland, dukes of Aquitaine and counts of Ponthieu. Shakespeare's often arresting visions will help us reflect on the nature of historical memory and its contribution to local, regional and national identities.

Pauses to think about memory will occur at a number of points in the book. Alongside the struggle for material security – food production, travel, exchange, taxation, warfare, nurture – and alongside the efforts involved in survival and betterment, people carried memory with them, within themselves. Memory was contained in every aspect of the built and tilled and shaped environment. People used churches, many of which had been built in the twelfth century, to which aisles were added in the thirteenth, great altarpieces in the fourteenth, and windows and rood-screens often in the fifteenth. They worshipped in build-ings that were sometimes very ancient – like the vast Saxon church of the parishioners of Brixworth (Northamptonshire), or St Botolph's, Hadstock (Essex), with its Saxon door. Most frequently they met in buildings which were a patchwork of many stages of construction and decoration, like Kilpeck (Herefordshire) with its unique blend of assertive Anglo-Norman shape in distinctive local pink sandstone and stylized indigenous carving. In these edifices memories of alliances and long-standing dynastic claims were crafted into stained-glass windows, painting of arms, tombs, banners, even cushions. A hectic culture of heraldic display drew the participation of parish gentry and magnates alike, as well as of townsmen, bishops and university colleges, in the adornment of buildings and the provision of furnishings.

Around half of the 9,000 parish churches of England were associated with religious houses, particularly those of the Benedictine and Augus-tinian orders. These houses collected the income from each parish – from tithes, from agricultural produce, from rents – and were obliged to supervise the upkeep of fabric and provision of pastoral care for parishioners by appointing a suitable vicar. The other half of parishes were under the patronage of magnates, gentry families or bishops, patrons who were expected to recommend candidates as rectors and vicars for the bishop's approval. In parish churches there always was –

and still is – something to look at, for such power and influence circulated through emblems. All types of patronage left their signs and marks, from elaborate tombs in and around the church, to inscriptions on the edges of windows or names carved on screens or altar railings.

Those who could not read apprehended their benefactors from the heraldic display, the signature of benefactors and patrons, who gave, and wished to be remembered. There were also less definite messages, spirited signatures of craftsmen and painters, messages in the carved ends of benches in church – a poppy, a woman, a monster – and for those who troubled to look, within the chancel, many more than the 3,400 surviving misericords, carved seats which displayed a whole array of local knowledge: proverbs, monsters, rhymes, fables, legends, in the working of chisel on wood. Old stories were elegantly told anew, to be discovered only by those who could gain access to the chancel – privileged or knowing, then as now. Such, for example, is the misericord at Chester Cathedral, carved c.1380, which depicts romantic passion in the shape of the Celtic 'wild men', or one carved ten years later at Worcester Cathedral, retelling a Norse tale of a clever daughter who became a queen. Even the Bible offered material for satire, such as the scene depicted in misericords in Ely Cathedral and in Ludlow church: Noah's wife beating her husband for upsetting the household with his impossible building plans.

Some memories were very widely shared: of famine in the 1320s, of the plague in the 1350s, 1360s and again in the 1370s and 1390s, which halved the population; some were personal and to be shared with only a few, like Edward II's memory of his executed friend Piers Gaveston, the trauma of bereavement visited on mothers and widows of the victims of war, or of civil war and rebellion. People carried within them regional memories too – of conquest in Wales, of Scottish raids in the north. Shakespeare captures well the pain and call for vengeance harboured by grieving mothers and wives in an imagined chorus of mournful women: Cicely of York (widow of Richard Duke of York, and mother of Richard III), Margaret of Anjou (widow of Henry VI and bereaved mother of Prince Edward), and Elizabeth Woodville (bereaved mother of the princes killed in the Tower). Each intoned the names of her dead, killed at the hands of her fellow women's kin.

The memory of such loss was somewhat countered by the beneficial effect of rituals of consolation, of the joys of birth and regeneration. Marriage was a gesture of reconciliation which sought to join the bodies and substances of families into new lineages, mixing the best of both, with a measure of good will, all blessed as a sacrament. Indeed, this book will end with one such marriage, that between the Earl of Richmond/Henry VII and Elizabeth of York, a union which created a new dynasty, the Tudors, with its emblem, the Tudor Rose, made of the red and white petals of Lancaster and York. Yet rituals do not work magic, and the reconciliation they can offer is most effective when participants have exhausted all other means, exhausted each other. Arranged marriages between the great could also generate lengthy lawsuits and much rancour around issues of dower, inheritance and the multi-layered, many-generational families which characterized life then, as they do today. Where Christian ritual failed to heal with love, the law of the land was invoked – law, which in its several jurisdictions occupied a steadily growing number of men, and much time and effort throughout the period covered by this book.

The shapes of outdoor spaces contained and revealed local history – the work of women, men and nature. Names of fields derived from names of long-forgotten Danes who had settled the land, or of those who had reclaimed it from forest and meadows. Even within one large estate – such as that of the Bishop of Winchester – the variety of land and landscape dictated different rhythms of husbandry: Wiltshire, Hampshire, Sussex and the downs of Wessex were chalk, north-east Wiltshire was clay, and the Hampshire basin gravel. A single estate and its many different parts encompassed and demanded differing types of expertise and experience of even neighbouring villages and villagers. Place names and field names were so local that they would have meant little to someone living even a few miles away: how many knew where 'oppermeadow' was, or 'le maltmilie', or the enclosure known as 'le Bigging', all in Clare (Suffolk)? Yet these associations were not permanent and unchanging: the names of fields could be forgotten altogether as the use of fields changed. The surveyor of a tenancy in Medland (Cornwall) on an estate of the Arundels commented c.1408 that where farmland was turned to grazing land, and hedges had been beaten down, 'the names of the fields are forgotten'. Communal space was also marked by strife, and by its outcome. The abbot of St Albans had a millstone placed at the entrance to the abbey following a dispute with the townsmen. This was to be a tangible reminder to his tenants that the abbey's monopoly over milling was not open to dispute. They in turn took particular joy in smashing it up during the uprising of

1381, when they distributed pieces of the smashed stone as so many communion wafers to the crowd of onlookers.

Historians of the lands and people ruled by the kings of England are fortunate in having plentiful sources for study. Since the late Anglo-Saxon period these lands were much governed, by kings and by the church. The land was divided into counties (shires) and dioceses, the fundamental units of state and church administration, and was subdivided too: into hundreds and wapentakes, deaneries and parishes. The records of royal administration are plentiful: court rolls, tax returns, lists compiled by commissions of array which recruited to the king's army, as well as accounts of the royal household and the returns by which sheriffs made themselves accountable to the Exchequer. Experiments in taxation resulted in some years in the imposition of a poll-tax, producing returns which listed payers by household in great detail, and which allow us to aim at approximate demographics, such as those with which this introduction began. Parliamentary rolls included petitions and the royal response to them, as well as records of treaties and diplomatic exchanges. To these can be added the thousands of cases from bishops' courts, which survive in plenty from the late fourteenth century. These dealt with marriage, defamation, heresy, failure of oaths, and more, and provide some of the most vivid sources on the life of modest villagers and townsfolk. Since church courts allowed women to bring cases, they are a rich source for female voices, as these articulated (through the mediation of a court clerk, who often translated the testimony into Latin) the complaint, or provided opinion as a witness. All these sources reflect a vast range of political, economic and social activity and reveal the life experiences of subjects, often in their own words, recorded by a clerk, when they gave depositions to courts.

Most people lived on manors organized for production and social order under manorial customs, enforced by frequently held courts. Manorial court rolls and accounts of management of manors have provided in recent decades challenging material for an intimate encounter with the rhythms of work – day in and day out – which is the experience of most people at all times. Families and their tenancies – the land allotted to them for generations by their landlord, in return for payments in kind, coin and labour – are encountered in these parchment rolls, in the full array of behaviours and inclinations. There were lazy, headstrong, loyal and enterprising, rebellious and deferential serfs. Above all, they were vigilant and aware of opportunity and interest, as changing trends and events, sometimes far away, affected them and their dependants. We will encounter them in the records of manorial rolls at marriage and death, in conflict and when making a generous bequest to a son or daughter, when directed to mend a fence or pay a fine, or go to war. Occasionally lords commissioned comprehensive surveys of their lands – a local Domesday Book – and these described and often depicted the land and other important resources: fields, meadows, mills, ponds, forest.

Some rural folk chose to leave and go on the road, seeking work in another village or town, and as they moved they gained their freedom. So towns generate other types of sources: not so scrutinizing of daily labour, but alert to the regulation of quality, price and profit. In towns men were free to associate in craft groupings and they sometimes generated records which have survived, recording internal discipline, terms of apprenticeship, codes of practices of the guilds of goldsmiths, tailors, physicians, and others.

Most of our sources are thus the product of monitoring and even punitive institutions, and they are to be used by us with care, even cunning. Those who chose a religious vocation – in the relative seclusion of monasteries or in the engaged service of parishes, dioceses, universities and schools – often produced literatures of experience and guidance. Preserved in institutional or family libraries, much of their work has survived, despite the ravages of the Reformation and its aftermath. We are extremely well informed about religious services, the teaching to the laity, the more adventurous reaches of mystical life. Like many of the records of state, those of the church were also aimed at monitoring, correction and listing.

Social and political relations, as well as spiritual thoughts and yearnings, often inspired material expression or indeed marked a landscape. *The Hollow Crown* will bring together the insights gleaned from manorial records, from descriptions of fields and meadows, the teachings of the church with the stained glass and rood-screens that imparted them, the liturgy and its setting, the family and its home, women with their belongings – books, cooking utensils, clothes – kings and the poetry of complaint of disappointed subjects. It is hard to capture the sounds, or indeed the silences, of that world, but over two turbulent and testing centuries, the capacity of its people to change and think afresh will become abundantly clear.

Do not be surprised to find that the behaviour of the people whose lives make up this book resembles what you know about the behaviour of individuals and groups in your own lifetime. History loses none of its charm and importance when we admit the similarity of certain preoccupations and relations – with material security and achievement, with sociability, with family fortunes, the tension between generations, the camaraderie of work, travel and battle. Certain kinds of people or patterns of social behaviour may seem very familiar: the awkward effects of rapid social mobility, the sycophancy which power creates and maintains, the preoccupation of rulers with their image, the desperate double standard which prevails in judgement of male and female behaviours, the mixture of pomposity and public-spiritedness which characterizes civic leaders. What is most different about them is sometimes the most ineffable and elusive: smells and sounds, the shapes of nightmares. We can sometimes catch them in niches of our own contemporary world: when visiting a pilgrimage shrine in India or in Mexico, when passing through a market of fresh produce sold by the farmers who grew it in Sicily or Sri Lanka, when hearing the street cries of food vendors, when observing the rituals in the courts of monarchs and presidents. The historian's craft is most importantly realized in guiding the reader through the recognition of the familiar and the shock of the different.

I

Famine and Deposition, 1307–1330

FAMINE

If we are to appreciate the scale of devastation which the Great Famine of 1315–22 brought to the British Isles, as it did to the whole of northern Europe, we must bring to mind calamities such as the Irish Famine, and the distress and dislocation that they generate. This is apposite even though the subsistence crisis was caused not by drought, but by unusually hard and prolonged rainfall, accompanied by sharp cold spells. These calamitous climatic conditions affected regions which had known steady population growth in the thirteenth century. Expansion had for a number of decades relocated rural families, creating new hamlets and communities with the encouragement of their lords. Tenants cultivated these increasingly marginal, poorer lands, often combining smallholding tenancies with income from labour for support of the family group. Of the 10–15 per cent of the population that perished during the Great Famine, a large proportion must have been among the landless and these precarious smallholders. Conversely, people migrated away from such devastated villages, swelling regional centres, such as Norwich, in the famine years. The social fabric was strained by horrific rumours: from reports about men and women eating dogs and horses in Northumbria, to cases of cannibalism. Those who memorialized these times adopted biblical and moralizing language and imagery. The calamities – famine, disease, raids by the Scots – were described by chroniclers as punishment for sin, while the illuminator of the Queen Mary Psalter (c.1325–6) gave pride of place to the figure of Joseph, who had wisely stocked Pharaoh's granaries before the coming of famine. Edward II's seven fat years, 1307–14, followed by seven very lean ones from 1315 to 1322, seemed to be part of a divine plan.

The famine was accompanied not by shocked economic lethargy but by frenzied activity, as poorer and needier folk sold land and livestock to their better-off neighbours, all in an attempt to gain coin and purchase ever dearer food. The many small transactions recorded in manorial courts in East Anglia reveal the anxiety of the times: the evidence of litigation over strips of land discloses not only expectations of heirs hopeful of inheriting, but the demands of creditors and arrears in rents accumulated in the years of dearth. As is often the case, credit was all but withdrawn in the years of bad harvest, to the benefit of the few who could afford to buy the lands forfeited by those forced to sell in order to buy food. The active land-market may also reflect exchanges of land from parents to sons and daughters, which anticipated inheritance, and aimed to help young families during the famine years.

To the crisis in agricultural production was added diminution in the number of livestock: sheep, pigs and cows, ducks and geese were slaughtered for food, and added to this was the high mortality among cattle and sheep due to murrain. This nasty epidemic was highly contagious and affected the cows, oxen and sheep so vital as traction animals, as sources of food, and for the production of wool. On the estates of Bolton Priory (Yorkshire) between 1319 and 1322 the number of oxen fell from 139 to 53, and of cattle from 225 to 31. The hides and wool of dead animals had to be buried, since burning was difficult in the very wet weather, a miserable task in the muddy expanses which the fields had become. Several regional economies depended upon wool: by the early fourteenth century, 40,000 sacks of wool were exported from Britain, mainly by Flemish and Italian merchants. Pastoral regions were thus doubly hit – through high corn prices and through the loss of livestock. The Welsh community of Morgannwg (Glamorgan) pleaded for relief from dues because it was left without any animals.

Beautiful barns and granaries kept food for the seigneurial family and its guests, and stored crops awaiting transfer to the market, like that built in warm Cotswold stone, at Great Coxwell. Such barns were later likened by William Morris to cathedrals, and Thomas Hardy imagined in them a true religious quality. During the famine years they were the targets of frustrated looting, and of conspiracies to empty them of their precious contents. King and parliament tried, although with limited success, to encourage the distribution of grain, and to counter speculation and buying up bread-corns before they could reach the market. Edward II wrote to men of influence, such as Richard Kellaw, Bishop of Durham, in 1316, with the request that he ensure that grain was sold and not hoarded. Parliament attempted to control the price of livestock in 1314, and of ale in 1317. Some institutions made special provisions in this emergency, for example Westminster Abbey in 1318–19, with additional distributions of grain for the poor. But most provision depended on the workings of thousands of local communities who were in the habit of vigilantly monitoring production and distribution of corn. By 1319–20 prices were stabilized in Devon through the import by sea of grain from East Anglia and Normandy.

The famine put further pressure on the internal workings of these communities. The neat provisions for communal cooperation, such as team-ploughing, which expected each member to contribute plough-beasts, collapsed as animals lay dying. Times of sowing were regulated, so that a neighbour's sprouting growths would not be trampled under the sower's foot: at Moundsmere (Hampshire) in 1327 by-laws recommended that Lent sowing be done when oak leaves were the size of mouse ears, and no later. All this careful regulation of pasturing and gleaning meant very little when crops failed to thrive, and the care taken to identify and punish offenders foundered as the familiar landscape and its makers disappeared. The intricate array of relations which supported agricultural production also deteriorated; with the famine vital services and structures suffered too. Everywhere, but above all in the north, mills are reported as being left in disrepair, standing untended because of the absence of millers, and in Lancashire and Cumbria the powerful water supplies to mills destroyed them in floods. These years saw the emergence in many areas of official commissions for the supervision of banks and sewers. Thomas of Ingoldisthorp was commissioner for the four Wiggenhall parishes on the Great Ouse upstream from King's Lynn and his report of 1319 described 'incalculable damage'. Throughout the 1320s commissioners supervised expenditure on the building of sea-dykes and the shoring-up of river-banks. Such maintenance and vigilance depended on local people, and thus a new tier of officialdom was added to existing governance: local dyke-reeves supported by a system of by-laws by which negligence to maintain banks was fined, with doubling and tripling on recurrent offences.

All this change affected the income of landlords: Canterbury Cathedral Priory, whose manors produced a surplus up to 1315, fell into deficit, which reached a shortfall of 45 per cent by 1318. Large institutional employers were also faced by growing wage-bills: the heavy waterlogged lands of champion England – that is, unenclosed and level tracts of country – required more labour if crops were to be planted in the hope of yields which might fetch the unusually high prices. In 1315 and 1316 Bury St Edmunds Abbey continued to pay its agrarian workers in bushels of wheat, food which was now much dearer than it had been in the past. Bolton Priory aimed to increase its income in these hard years by selling retirement packages to well-off pensioners, like Ranulf of Otterburn in 1314 and Adam Prophet, a local farmer, in 1317/18. The priory thus raised some £152 in two years. The management of estates and relations with tenants and labourers were supervised by reeves – who also hired carters, herdsmen, ploughmen and dairy-women, as necessary – crucial agents in the ravaged landscape.

When the weather improved slightly after 1318, and then finally after 1322, population recovered quickly and the cohort that had survived, together with its children and livestock, was better off in terms of diet and resources – a classic Malthusian pattern. In Taunton (Somerset) there was population loss of some 9.3 per cent between 1313 and 1319, but by 1330 population had recovered. Halesowen (Worcestershire) suffered a 15 per cent drop between 1315 and 1321 but experienced steady growth of 0.4 per cent a year thereafter.

Social patterns responded to the calamity with great subtlety and also remarkable speed. Earlier in the century, with pressure on land, young men married landed widows in order to establish themselves as tenants. In some regions up to half of marriages were of this type: John, son of Reginald Attepond of Redgrave (Suffolk), paid five marks for the hand of Agnes, widow of John son of Nicholas, in 1316, while only two shillings were paid for her sister's hand. After the famine rates of remarriage fell as pressure on land diminished and the prices paid for marriage of landed widows declined, as more 'companionate' marriages were made, between men and women of similar age and situation. In such marriages the bride was expected to bring with her some property: in 1312 a Derbyshire woman from a servile family brought 20s. in cash, a cow worth 10s., a dress worth 13s. 4d., and the promise of a house.

Rents and incomes recovered by the 1330s and the fruitful interdepen-dence between the villages of England and Wales and their neighbouring market towns and smaller towns was re-established. Wherever agrarian and commercial diversification had developed in the period of growth this was now a useful bulwark in the aftermath of crop failure: tin-mining in Cornwall, fishing on the eastern coast, animal-trapping in

Pickering Forest (Yorkshire), the keeping of rabbit warrens in the Breckland of East Anglia, charcoal-burning in the Forest of Inglewood (Cumbria), glasswork in the Weald of Sussex.

Crucial to recovery was the re-establishment by seigneurial households of their patterns of expenditure, which could reach thousands of pounds a year on food alone, often a third and sometimes a half of their annual incomes. Bread and ale were baked and brewed locally, and fed servants, but members of aristocratic families and their guests expected supplies of meat and fish and wine. Meat was salted and kept, but fresh meat was expected at the best tables, and it had to be hunted or bought, whatever the cost.

Most of these goods were to be acquired at local markets. The country was dotted with market towns, and it was to such small towns that much migration was directed. In them people were more likely to be known by a name of occupation than by their place of origin, which was frequently close by and shared by many others. In most small towns specialisms were rare, but manufacture of vessels and tools, building, baking and brewing, even scribal services, merely reflected the variety of skills that a well-administered manor required and rewarded, and which could be easily transferred from village to town. Manors supported the services of many such trades and skills. Bolton Priory supported a miller, carpenter, brewers, baker, smith, cook, carters; and all of these could find work in towns. Thus wheelwrights, smiths of all kinds, brewers, masons, butchers, bakers, coopers, farriers, could move easily between village and small town, facilitating trade and distribution. Such skilled workers were welcomed into small towns such as Brill in the Forest of Bernwood (Buckinghamshire), which was recognized in 1316 as a royal borough, with its prison and market, mills and fishponds, clay-pits and kilns, as well as being a royal residence. The evidence of debts among villagers further demonstrates the continuity between the work of substantial villagers and small-town enterprise: Alice Spileman claimed in 1329 that William Kembald from Walsham-le-Willows (Suffolk), as was she, owed her a bushel of wheat, some ale as well as vats, casks and bowls, all probably for use in brewing. More modest householders, like Thomas Bouzon of Woodford, near Thrapston in Northamptonshire, whose accounts have survived for the year 1328, displays this dependence on a combination of home production and additional bought goods. Flour was dispensed to his kitchen once a fortnight for big batches of baking; and every Saturday meat was bought at Higham Ferrers market, as were poultry, eggs and a variety of fish.

The greatest market of all was London. Over a third of overseas trade passed through it, requiring regulation, accommodation, and the enforcement of law and order to allow it to prosper. The growth in government in Westminster and the establishment of parliaments drew members of the political class more regularly into its orbit. Persons or corporations of importance sought to have a *pied-à-terre* in the capital: by 1311 the bishops of Hereford had a London residence, an inn, in St Mary Munthaw parish, which they occasionally leased out, but which was also used for storage of wool from their estates. Magnates such as Thomas of Lancaster, with an annual income of some £11,000 and estates all over England and Wales, also owned an inn in London, with elaborate quarters and stables, an island of self-sufficiency within the city. Even the king had a house built in Southwark in 1325, the Rosary, in Abbot's Lane. To secure the services and goods for its diverse and growing population, London government occasionally moved to break up conspiracies to defraud and developed methods for recording its acts. The first surviving London customal – a book recording the city's customs – was compiled in these decades, and in it examples of good practice in governance from other cities were preserved. The creation of such records was the product of efforts by men such as Andrew Horn, a fishmonger from Bridge Street, who was chamberlain of London in the 1320s and had extensive and direct knowledge of the practices of trade and manufacture. Such knowledge was essential if disruptive plots, like that contrived by some bakers in 1327 to bake with perforated moulding boards (hence using less dough), were to be spotted and suitably punished. Such control was necessary if London was to retain its primacy and see its share in trade grow.

THE CHALLENGES TO BRITAIN

While governance in the south was recovering from the famine, in the north this Europe-wide disaster was compounded by challenges to authority and physical ravages. By far the most menacing was the challenge from Scotland, the consequences of which also led to an invasion of Ireland and the possibility of rebellion in Wales. The collapse of Anglo-Scottish truces saw the beginning of a period of fierce raiding, mostly from Scotland into the north of England. Any notion of a linear border is anachronistic; dominions were marked by strongholds and castles, open to seizure and loss. At the northern Borders they attracted the attention and ambition of Robert Bruce, King of the Scots.

Robert Bruce succeeded in establishing his family's hegemony in 1308 following a civil war which saw him encounter and vanquish the Comyns at Invercurie, and follow this with a campaign of destruction in Buchan. At the parliament which met at St Andrews in the following year his power was solemnized in oaths of loyalty to him and to his dynasty, taken by both barons and clergy. Once the north and west of Scotland were subdued, these provided additional sources of fighting men and expertise for the warfare which was to follow. Robert Bruce now turned his attention to the lands further south, with two raids in 1311, to which there was no effective English answer. Robert Bruce announced in October 1313 that at the end of a year he would confiscate the lands of those who remained loyal to Edward II. Added to this, Stirling Castle was under siege by Edward Bruce, Robert's brother. Edward II was forced to respond. Writs for recruitment were sent out in December 1313 and recruitment in Wales began, although Edward did not have the support of the disaffected group of barons who had been challenging his actions since his accession.

Edward II mustered a great army of some 15,000 infantry and 2,500 cavalry, which marched towards Stirling. The Scottish army, some 8,000 men strong, sought to avoid an open battle outside the city – such encounters were very rare in British arenas more used to raids and skirmishes – and offered battle at Bannockburn, a hilly area just west of Stirling. An English mounted offensive, supported by infantry and archers, was devastated by the Scottish force, largely made up of infantrymen. The first day saw fierce fighting by spearmen, and the next (23–24 June) the definitive failure of heavy mounted cavalry. Although chroniclers claimed that Edward II had fought like a lion under the standard of St John of Beverley, which his father had used before him, Bannockburn was a disaster. Edward only narrowly saved his own life, and many magnates lost theirs. Governments rarely survive defeat in war, and this was to be a nemesis for Edward.

At the same time success buoyed Robert Bruce. It silenced his opponents in Scotland, attracted to him English landowners with lands either side of the Borders, and it encouraged his visions of hegemony over the north of England. This was to be maintained by ravaging the country-side, which had disastrous effects on all areas of life in the north. The chronicler John of Trokelowe, monk of St Albans Abbey, describes the events of 1315:

Meanwhile the Scots, with their forces, moved throughout the whole of Northumberland and the western parts, from Carlisle to York, slaughtering and looting without any opposition, and destroying with sword and flame whatever crossed their path. And it is known that there remained in these parts nowhere where the English could be safe, unless it was within the town of Carlisle or the borough of Newcastle upon Tyne and the priory of Tynemouth, and other towns in Northumbria which were defended with exhausting effort and at immense expense . . .

The Scottish Wars marked the north in several ways: they forced families to decide whether they were to offer allegiance to the King of England or of Scotland; they pauperized the countryside, distracted attention and deflected resources from the business of the south of England and the habitual desires of its political classes. The constant invasions and raids also took a toll of royal authority. For the kings came to depend on a heavy contribution from magnates, both in resources and in blood, and compensated those who shouldered the burden most significantly. Just as William the Conqueror had favoured the earls who settled and maintained the Marches, so great families developed out of the relative power and autonomy which the wardenships of the north entailed. The Nevilles and the Percies, whom we shall meet repeatedly in these pages, came to prominence in these years: Robert Neville was captured at Bannockburn and died during the siege of Berwick in 1319, and the Percies acquired Alnwick Castle from Archbishop Bek, of York, together with the duty of maintaining it and protecting the hinterland which depended on it. The need for wardenships of the north and of the Marches, offices created by Edward I, was to be crucial for British history for centuries, marking political power and aspiration which could make a magnate dream of kingship. The office was at once both utterly necessary and highly destabilizing to political order. Welsh leaders stood by the king in the Principality, but they also stood each man beside his own Marcher lord – as did Rhys ap Hywel who was loyal to the Earl of Hereford, Lord of Brecon, and Iorwerth ap Llywarch Lleweni to Thomas of Lancaster, Lord of Denbigh.

The long years of Edward I had set out a vision of English political hegemony with the impressive conquest of Wales and the attempts to dominate Scotland. But in the first years of Edward II's reign this level of engagement was not sustained. Cities and towns in the north were left to defend themselves: they did so by raising murage, payment for protective walls, as in Berwick, Hartlepool and Hull. Edward II's distraction in struggles with his magnates facilitated Robert Bruce's attempts to consolidate his position as King of Scotland. Bruce was not without his enemies – crucially the Earls of Buchan and Ross and Argyll – but he sought support in the lowlands, and benefited from an occasional windfall, like control of Moray in the absence of its lord. The victory at Bannockburn encouraged Bruce to create a single focus of loyalty for Scottish magnates instead of the shared loyalty to the King of England and the King of Scotland. Those who held lands from both rulers had now to choose, and they were encouraged to join an emerging alternative political vision: no longer English, but British.

The new vision of Bruce saw Scotland, Ireland and Wales as a political unit of cooperation, supported from across the channel by sympathetic French neighbours. It was to be a confederation of lordships loosely centred around kings in each of the countries. Such cooperation could realize the reclamation of territories conquered and settled by the English, from Anglesey to Ulster. Although there were peace negotiations in late 1314 between England and Scotland, these failed and so a Scottish assembly in Ayr in April 1314 produced a muster in support of an invasion of Ireland, an invasion aimed at inspiring a rising, with supporters such as Domnal O'Neill, King of the Irish in Ulster. In May 1315 Robert Bruce's brother, Edward, led a fleet to Carrickfergus in Ulster, the first stage of the campaign.

Edward Bruce promoted a plan of coordinated rejection of English rule through pressure from Scotland, Ireland and Wales. Indeed, Scottish ships captured Welsh vessels in autumn 1315, and in 1316 a rebellion led by Llewellyn Bren agitated Glamorgan. Edward II had nurtured his Welsh alliances, promoting men and awarding them royal offices, more in opposition to Marcher lords than to the unforeseen Scottish invasion. These, on the whole, stood fast. Robert Bruce attempted to mobilize Gruffydd Llwyd, a loyalist who had fought with Edward in Scotland and in Wales, leading Welsh forces. Edward II acted swiftly, responding to Welsh petitions and turning the attention of his court to discussion of the state of Welsh castles and requests from Welsh subjects. The Lincoln Parliament of 1316 agreed to respect Welsh custom and to remove restrictions on the purchase of land by Welsh people. Later that year Edward mustered some 1,500 men from north Wales, led by Sir Gruffydd Llwyd and Iorwerth ap Gruffydd. It is impressive to note just how committed Welsh leaders were to maintaining the political reciprocities achieved during Edward II's early years. Welsh royal castles were favoured as centres for mustering troops on their way to Scotland, and for exercising royal dignity and authority. Few Welsh were attracted by the rumour of Irish ascendancy and the promise of Celtic brotherly usurpation. For if Scotland and Ireland were Greater and Lesser Scotland, what was Wales to be in such a commonwealth?

Edward Bruce's campaign was a failure, and it made even harder the lives of the Irish during years of famine. In Ireland and the northern counties of England these were years of ravage and plunder, years which might otherwise have seen recovery from the famine and epidemics in these regions. Above all the West Riding and Lancashire suffered, and a variety of sources describe the depredation in all areas of life. After the fall of Berwick Castle in May 1318 several other castles simply capitulated and the Scottish force moved as if in its own land. The raids habitually began with entry into Yorkshire from the east, and exit from the west after a full sweep of manors and religious houses, small towns and villages. While the English standing army was occupied in the attempt to relieve Berwick, fortified by many able men, townsmen and rural folk, those unfit for battle were left behind to suffer the attacks. Lists from 1319 show the failure of tens of villages to pay their dues to ecclesiastical houses: the most common reason given was burning at the hand of the Scots. With the ravaging and burning of crops and buildings, there was a dramatic fall in incomes for those who owned land in the north: lay lords, ecclesiastical houses and monasteries large and small. The natural resources of the Forest of Knaresborough and the settlements of lower Wharfedale suffered in 1318/19 and then again in 1322. Durham, Northumberland and the north-west did not recover from these blows for a very long time.

The evidence of destruction appears in all areas of life in the north, and hence in several types of surviving sources. The records of Cockermouth (Cumberland) show a fall in rents in the years 1316–18 because of the raids, and the destruction of the fulling-mill. A well-endowed tenancy in Paxton-on-Tweed, including house, granaries, pasture and cottage, worth £2 16s. 8d. in time of peace, was reported as valueless in 1315. So marked was the damage done to the local economy that

Cumberland was totally exempt from taxation from 1313, a very rare concession. And the raids continued, so normal business of church officials was disrupted. The Archbishop of York wrote to priories to postpone his visitation in 1319 because of the Scottish invasion. The religious institutional terrain was shifting too: whole religious houses were dispersed because of the danger, as with Moxby nunnery in 1322 (Yorkshire). When the Bishop of Whithorn was consecrated in 1323, the Archbishop of York protested that it was an English diocese, but the pope went ahead with a Scottish confirmation. A new campaign against the Scots was being planned for 1323. Communities were assessed for their potential contributions; each village was assessed for the number of foot-soldiers it could yield, two to three men per village. So from Hemingford, near Huntingdon, Simon atte Style, Simon Everard and Henry Barber made their way north. Half of the resulting army's infantry was made up of Welshmen, a sign of a regional specialization which was to hold in future decades. But the campaign never got off the ground. Those who committed the events to memory could only blame 'English arrogance and pride'; God was using the Scots as a tool of vengeance.

While the Scottish invasion devastated the north of England, it promoted a sense of political purpose and ambition among the Scots. In 1320 a fascinating document of national self-assertion was composed by the clerks in Robert Bruce's service, a document which laid out the claim for Scottish sovereignty and the rejection of English overlordship, the Declaration of Arbroath. As is often the case in the annals of nation-making, a small group of men (here thirty-nine earls and barons) declared a claim for liberation, through the assertion of shared historical roots and moral right, and in a propitious political climate. The Declaration of Arbroath is a very elegant document. It laid the blame on Edward I:

Thus our people lived free and in peace till the noble prince Edward king of England, father of the present king, attacked our kingdom under the guise of friendship and support when it was without a head.

The signatory barons requested that the pope encourage Edward II to leave Scotland in peace.

The reality was, of course, quite different, for the north of England had much more to fear from the Scottish king than Scotland did from Edward II in the years that followed Bannockburn. Moreover, the rhetorical stance of an appeal to the pope, beautifully executed by the draftsman of the Declaration, chose to ignore the fact that at the time Bruce had been excommunicated for fourteen years, a punishment most recently renewed in January 1320. Bruce did not convince Pope John XXII, to whom the letter was directed. But the Declaration manifests the ambition which the defeat of the English at Bannockburn and the recent invasion of England had produced, which even the lacklustre aftermath of the Irish invasion did not diminish. It is a founding document of Scottish history and myth-making, as it establishes an imagined genealogy and ethnic origin for the Scottish people (tradition linked the Scots to the daughter of a Pharaoh), strengthened through the struggle against Britons, Picts, Norwegians, Danes and the English. These were claims which no English king and no English army could ignore or counter. These achievements were not only blows to the English king and his subjects, they also silenced the opposition to Bruce's dynastic hegemony.

For the English crown Ireland was a land of conquest, and hence was settled and endowed with a set of English-style institutions: parliament, dioceses, taxes, boroughs, army and royal appointees. Anglo-Irish settlement concentrated along the east coast, and the centre of administration was Dublin, where an Irish exchequer and parliament developed in parallel with those in Westminster. When Edward II was crowned in 1308, it was as King of England, Wales and Ireland. Following the ceremony, he sent a letter which included the Statute of Winchester (1285), a gesture which incorporated Ireland within the king's peace, and declared his own commitment, a bond grounded in his coronation oath. But English control was limited; it failed to penetrate the highlands of Leinster, and much of Ulster and Connacht was ruled by Irish kings. In areas of Anglo-Irish hegemony lordship was held by families who lived and ruled in symbiosis with the native Irish population. Such families attempted to keep a mixed landed estate in England and Ireland. By this period most Anglo-Irish families had decided to pursue a single course, either as absentees, or as lords permanently settled in Ireland.

The constant state of low-level warfare in Ireland, aggression which never reached pitched battles but which none the less informed all aspects of life, produced important interactions and borrowings. Following his father, Edward II mobilized the effective power of Irish light horsemen, who rode saddle-free on slightly built horses that were quite different from the heavy English war-horse. They were effective on difficult terrain, and in guerrilla action. These Irish *hobelars* formed part of the garrison of Berwick Castle in 1311/12, and helped relieve Carlisle in 1314. Such units became an established part of the Anglo-Irish army under the Lieutenant of Ireland in future decades.

Subsidies were raised from Ireland in support of the Scottish wars, and while in England notions of knight-service were becoming obsolete, they were maintained in Ireland as the basis for recruitment of local personnel. Anglo-Irish lords also used native retainers, and when these great men died they were lamented in traditional Irish song. A sense of Anglo-Irish identity emerges in adversarial conflicts over spheres of influence: Arnold Power protested to the English Bishop of Ossory at the Dublin Parliament of 1324 that Ireland, which should rightly be called the 'island of saints', was treated by newcomers as if all natives were heretics. It is not surprising that the Lieutenants of Ireland pre-ferred to bring their own armies when they took up office and treated with suspicion the Anglo-Irish political class, whose members seemed too Irish for comfort.

KING EDWARD II

'Blessed be the time that he was born, for we shall see the day, an Emperor chosen worthy of Christianity.' The birth of Edward, son of Edward, was hailed in these exultant words in the prophetic text *Adam Davy's Dream of Edward II*. He was, after all, the son of a man whose long reign and many conquests had animated the English crown and turned its territories into an empire. Like all colonization and conquest this came at a mighty price, borne by English subjects, who paid for it, and by the people of Wales, Ireland and Scotland, whose destinies were shaped by it. Edward II was not made for the level of activism and aggression that his father had maintained until his death. On their way to Scotland in 1300 father and son spent some time as guests of the Abbey of Bury St Edmunds in Suffolk, resting before the exertions of battle and seeking the traditional protection of St Edmund. Edward I left his teenage son there for a while; when he was sent for by his father, the prince was far from eager to leave.

Yet Prince Edward passed adequately through the rites of passage which prepared him for kingship. His knighting ceremony in 1306, at which many other heirs to great men were dubbed, was described by Peter Langtoft, canon of Bridlington Priory, as an Arthurian extravaganza:

> Never in Britain, since God was born,
> was there such nobleness in towns nor in cities,
> Except Caerleon in ancient times,
> When Sir Arthur the king was crowned there.

An ode written after Edward I's death in 1307 expressed the hope that Edward II would

> Be no worse a man
> Than his father, nor less in might
> To uphold the rights of poor men
> And understand well good counsel.

Edward II's dynastic security was never in question, and the machinery of state was well-oiled at his accession. At the age of fifteen Edward had been engaged to Isabella, daughter (then two years old) of Philip IV, King of France. He married her a decade later in London. He succeeded at the age of twenty-three and his coronation was a magnificent affair, celebrated after a delay to follow his marriage to Isabella. A new order of service was used: it included prayers in support of the king against his enemies, rebels and infidels. When their son was born in 1312, it was in a royal bed, secure in his future succession. Isabella was brought up in the mightiest court of Christendom, and contemporary images and comment flatter her. Her husband's seal presented her with the shields of England and of France, in a position usually reserved for the Virgin Mary. A carved stone at Beverley Minster attributes to her great beauty, while chronicles described her as 'very wise'. She was not a mere consort but a queen, with political aims and ambitions which sometimes surpassed her husband's in coherence and effect.

Almost from the start Edward II confronted the pent-up demands of the magnates of his realm. For the habits of the court in which Edward II had developed as prince and lived as king worried and distressed some of the leading political actors. Some of the earls were too old to act, and some too young, but a significant group – Lancaster, Hereford, Warwick – all close to Edward and comrades from the Scottish wars, were acute in observing the operations of political power in the new regime. Edward's choice of advisers, and his almost total abandonment of the military zone of the north – so important to the landed security of any Earl of Lancaster – created an atmosphere of anxiety and distrust. Edward's leadership ran contrary to the aspirations of a political class, and of a bureaucracy almost totally ecclesiastical, which expected and respected royal direction and reward. This concern was to animate much of the politics of the subsequent two centuries: the balance between royal autonomy and the expectation that the king act as a linchpin of good government, as the arbiter between the institutions of state, and as a sensible leader to a group of extremely powerful, autonomous and ambitious magnates.

Even as he gained the throne, Edward II's wisdom and choices were being questioned. This crystallized in 1308 around the elevation of his brother-in-arms and close friend, the Gascon Piers Gaveston, to the title of Earl of Cornwall. Edward's friendship with Gaveston gave focus to political complaints. It was believed that the king was under his sway, and hence was not ruling independently. A very intense working relationship had developed between the two men: a few contemporaries commented on Edward's 'excessive love' for Gaveston, and a generation later the court chronicler Jean Froissart described the relationship as 'sodomitic'. As in other famous political partnerships, the 'friend' attracted complaint and acted as a lightning conductor, deflecting wrath from the official holder of power, in this case the king, at least for a while. The barons resented the elevation of the king's best friend to positions of wealth – he had married the heiress Margaret of Clare – and administrative clout. On Gaveston were showered the Earldom of Cornwall, the Keepership of the Realm; he became Lieutenant of Ireland and Chamberlain and played a prominent role in the coronation. The barons requested Gaveston's exile in 1308, and the king finally acceded, with very little grace.

Political demands were animated by more than the distaste which Gaveston provoked. They reflected a desire by leading subjects for structural involvement in royal financial and military administration. In 1311 the struggle took the form of a list of demands, Ordinances, in clauses published by a group of barons, who came to be named after them as the Ordainers. They demanded to be involved in all important decision-making – such as deliberation over war – as well as in greater supervision of royal finances and in the judiciary, including collective appointment of sheriffs. The king was accused of wanton expenditure, following rumours that the crown planned to tinker with the currency.

A committee was to supervise royal receipts and their administration, and two of the five leading officers of the court – the steward and the keeper of the wardrobe – were in future to be appointed with the consent of the lords in parliament. Another clause demanded an end to persecution of men for debt. The king would submit himself to peers' advice, and respect the natural constituency of magnates as advisers and close associates. The document was thrashed out mostly among the barons, and the interests of townsmen and knights are hardly present in it.

In the barons' demands there was a tone of impatience and intolerance. The complaints and demands of these men, who had been the king's friends and intimates, reflected a tradition of baronial political activism almost a century old. Some of the clauses of the Ordinances of 1311 are reminiscent of grievances put to Edward I in 1297; others were to emerge again in the early as well as in the later years of Edward III. The political gains signalled by the Ordinances of 1311 were that the king must accept suitable counsel and consider the wishes of political constituencies. Increasingly the venue for such debate was parliament; at issue were the processes of policy-making in fiscal and judicial affairs.

Baronial political demands regarding counsel and influence on the king were bound to return to the issue of Piers Gaveston and consequently he was exiled in 1311. Edward tried to pave the way of his close friend, as he travelled to the continent in exile, by dispatching letters to the Duke of Brabant and to the King of France requesting that he be protected and received by them. Gaveston returned to the country stealthily following the birth of his daughter after Christmas 1311. Attempts to arrange for his permanent return failed, and by May 1312 the king was forced to agree to hand him to the protection of the Earl of Pembroke, thus distancing him from court but also keeping him safe. But through a subterfuge the Earl of Warwick gained access to Gaveston, and took him to Warwick Castle, where in the company of Lancaster and Arundel he held a mock trial, the verdict of which was execution for treason. Gaveston was executed at Blacklow, on the land of the Earl of Hereford, by two Welshmen of the earl's retinue, his body being pierced and then beheaded. Vindictive partisan poetry expressed the visceral delight in his unmaking, and celebrated Lancaster's achievement:

The comet of Earls shines,
I mean the Earl of Lancaster,
Who tamed him, whom nobody could tame.
Whereby the pestiferous one,
Being wounded by the blades of the Welsh,
Was disgracefully beheaded.
Blessed the hand which expunged him.

Satirical verse created a celebratory liturgy:

Celebrate my tongue, the death of Peter [Piers]
 Who destroyed England.
Whom the King, loving him above all things,
 placed over Cornwall.

While the annalist John of Trokelowe claimed that England would know no peace as long as Gaveston lived, his execution served to alienate the king, and turn him into an even more dependent figure. Edward II was devastated and resentful. On the first anniversary of Gaveston's death he petulantly showed how much decorum he wished to maintain: the Wardrobe accounts record expenditure on the services of Bernard the Fool and on a troupe of fifty-four naked dancers 'with stamping of feet in dance'. He even attempted to have his erstwhile friend canonized. In the space around him the king craved the reassurance of devotees, men beholden to him. The next to enjoy his favour were a family pair, father and son, the Despensers.

The king had been required to act and lead soon after his accession by the military challenge from Scotland. The territorial integrity of England was at stake, and this dictated shifts in the spheres of action and placement of the main political actors. The court dwelt in the north for long periods between 1310 and 1323. The logistical challenge involved in defending the north was enormous: the parliaments of 1314, 1318, 1319, 1320, May and November 1322 met at York, and the courts of King's Bench, Common Pleas and the Exchequer similarly spent long periods in the north. In forty years spanning three kings – 1298–1338 – the royal court spent half its time in the north. Royal servants were constantly packing and transferring furniture and archives and money to Yorkshire and Northumbria. In September 1320 one of the king's serjeants-at-arms was ordered to move 1,000 marks from London to Fenham Castle in Northumbria with the aid of an eight-strong guard.

Such convoys criss-crossed the country northwards, turning the north for a while into the true centre of government. This emphasis came to an end once the war with France dominated military and diplomatic effort from the 1330s. But the northern connection left its mark at the heart of government, with long-standing effects on recruitment of personnel.

In facing all these challenges the king's need for support and advice was met not only by his bishops, but by a family happy to counter received wisdom, a family as yet not part of the baronage nor a carrier of its aspirations and values. The Leicestershire Despensers occupied pride of place in the middle years of Edward II's reign, as trusted friends and as a bulwark between the king and his magnates. By 1318 Hugh Despenser, a close associate, who had fought with Edward I, and then with Edward II at Bannockburn, was granted the lucrative wardship of the heir to the Earldom of Warwick. The Despensers managed patronage and filtered information directed at the court from all parts of the country and from Gascony. Father and son worked hard at promoting court identity and royal interest in a narrow sense, but they offended the other partner in the social and political contract – the magnates, who aimed to consolidate and defend those constitutional gains made in the 1290s and in the early years of Edward II's reign. Magnates sought access to the king, and predominance in the provision of counsel. They also wished parliament rather than the court to be the venue for political deliberation.

Even as famine hit the country and the Scots invaded in the north, the country was on the verge of civil war. Thomas of Lancaster, the greatest and richest magnate of his day, had resigned as leader of the king's council in 1316, thus marking disaffection and an intention to act. The country was all but divided into two, and access to the north was blocked to royal officials. While prelates attempted to pacify, an agreement was grudgingly accepted by both sides. The Leake Treaty of July 1318 aimed at re-establishing loyalty to the king and allaying baronial anxiety about his lordship. While the parties were discussing their demands, and negotiations were still taking place, chroniclers reported a bizarre incursion. In Northampton a man was arrested – John Powderham, son of a tanner from Exeter – who made a claim to the throne as Edward's brother. One chronicler describes him as a *litteratus*, probably a clerk, who had been educated at Oxford. His claim to royal blood was through Edward I, who had removed him from his royal cradle at birth because of an injury. In the unquiet 1320s the story was elaborated into an example of Edward's deficiency: for the king gave the man a jester's club and treated the episode too lightly. The barons and the queen insisted on a trial in the king's absence, and so John Powderham was finally hanged. His dead body was left hanging, as a caution.

As a truce was secured in the north in 1320–21 unrest resurfaced in Wales and among the magnates. The baronial party – a cautious and brittle alliance – expressed its displeasure with the Despensers on their home ground in the Wye valley: in 1321 a force led by Thomas of Lancaster destroyed, sacked and killed in the Marcher lordships. Many unhappy subjects had joined Thomas of Lancaster – such as the Mortimers of Chirk and the Earl of Hereford – and lost their lands even as they brought down the Despenser lordship in the Wye valley. Despenser control had been built with the king's acceptance, and in the face of rightful heirs, such as John Lord Mowbray in the Gower. Many of the magnates of England were clearly willing to fight in order to achieve a restructuring of the royal court. For they did not aim at deposition, rather at humbling and coercing the king. Throughout 1321 Thomas Earl of Lancaster all but ruled the north; two parliaments were assembled in the summer, at Pontefract and Sherburn, at which magnates combined by oath to oppose the rule of the Despensers. Edward II mustered an army to counter the rebels, marching from Wales through Staffordshire to Yorkshire. At the crossing at Boroughbridge on 16 March 1322, the two forces faced each other: the king and the Despensers on the one hand, and Thomas Earl of Lancaster with the magnates, on the other. The bloody battle resulted in the death of the Earl of Hereford, and in the surrender of Thomas of Lancaster.

Thomas of Lancaster, the richest and most prominent magnate, the king's first cousin, was tried and executed. He was accused of treason, murder, robbery and arson, of appearing armed at parliament and of treasonous contact with the Scots. His status dictated the more decorous mode of execution, beheading by sword, rather than hanging and quartering, the usual punishment for treason. In the lands of Lancastrian affinity and sympathy he became a martyr of sorts, and the priory at Pontefract, which held his body, became a pilgrimage site. The king had triumphed, but his rule had been a sorry one, for it had witnessed perverse politics. The *Brut* chronicle lamented the state of the political nation, for as the rebels were caught, 'they were robbed, and bound like thieves. Alas, the shame and despite, that the gentle order of knighthood had there at that battle!'

Ever alert to Edward's weaknesses Robert Bruce invaded the north again in 1322, scorched its earth and harassed its people. Despite his victory over rebellious magnates, Edward II was deemed responsible for all this distress.

Following Boroughbridge a new settlement was created. It affected Wales acutely, since half of the Marcher lordships changed hands. Edward II continued to favour the patronage of Welsh gentry families in his service, and he summoned Welsh knights to parliament. But what he achieved in Wales was not reproduced elsewhere in the country and an unsettled mood is evident, as it had been during Edward I's last dozen years. Conspiracies were reported, urging people to join gangs for mutual support and protection; groups connived to defraud and to commit treason. Such a case was revealed in the course of the examination of Robert le Marescal, who was tried for murder in 1324. Among his many confessions – for he had turned king's witness – was the claim that twenty-seven men of Coventry had conspired to kill the king and the Despensers, who supported their local adversary, the Prior of Coventry. They were guided by a magician in occult rites, during which the king's wax image was pierced with a lead pin on several occasions. Why did a group of burgesses resort to magic in their struggle with the Prior of Coventry over market rights? Why, in a country so well provided with legal personnel and procedures, this desperate act? The law was evidently no longer sufficiently trusted. Only a few months after Robert was executed for his crimes, the king himself was killed.

Edward II did not manage to settle the kingdom into a clear political order which saw the smooth interaction of crown, magnates and parliament. In these years new contributions were made to the already rich literature of complaint in all the British vernaculars. Poems such as 'On the evil times of Edward II', in an east-Midlands dialect, complained about all manner of men (and men only) – priests and lawyers and physicians, court officials and judges of assizes. Natural catastrophe was linked to human misconduct and so after years of 'plenty and mirth' came those of 'hunger and dearth'. All this was a punishment from God, and a nemesis for periods of vanity and ambition, which probably allude to Edward I's reign.

Yet Edward II's example also inspired patrons to build and fund religious and educational institutions. Bishop Hothum of Ely (1316–37), whom Edward II saved from the wreck of Gaveston's household, realized the plans for the foundation of the King's Hall in Cambridge in 1317 as a training branch of the Chapel Royal; it accommodated forty boys destined for service in the royal chapel and chancery. Edward II had started something of a trend; his son Edward III amplified the institution, and hence is considered as a founder. His statue is still to be seen in the Great Court of Trinity College. His Chancellor of the Exchequer, Harvey de Stanton, founded Michaelhouse in 1324 (now part of Gonville and Caius College). In Oxford the example – part fashion, part expedient – was followed by his Treasurer, Walter de Stapledon, in Exeter College for men of Cornwall and Devon, and by Adam de Brome, at Oriel College.

A EUROPEAN COURT

The expenses of the royal court show it to have maintained a western European network with contacts of diplomacy, marriage and cultural exchange. Like his father, for most of his reign Edward II spent some £13,000 per annum, an amount which fell to £10,000 in 1323–6. Expenditure covered a wide range of activities in England, the Scottish Borders, Ireland and Gascony, and was disbursed under the knowing eye of a series of proactive treasurers. Some attempts were made to strengthen Gascon administration by establishing there a royal archive, as suggested in 1310 by the Bishop of Norwich, and the Earl of Richmond was charged with conducting an inquiry. In 1315 the royal council in Gascony petitioned the king's council to supply copies of seminal documents to support their efforts in negotiations with the French over rights, lands and castles; in 1319 it requested that some documents be checked against the originals in Westminster. The many rights through which the king's lordship in Gascony was realized – oaths of fealty, control of castles, legal determinations – had to be maintained properly, if the competing lordship of the French king, conveniently offered to Gascon subjects, was to be countered. The complicated nature of the claim to Gascony – by Edward, who was both a mighty king and a vassal of the King of France – was further enhanced after Philip V's death in 1322. For Edward II's homage for the Duchy of Aquitaine and the County of Ponthieu became due.

When Charles IV ascended the throne of France in 1322 he did not press his claim, as Edward II was occupied yet again by Scottish troubles. But in 1323, after the successful negotiation of a truce with Robert Bruce, Edward II was expected to pay him a visit in France and offer homage. While Edward II prevaricated, the situation in Gascony became unstable and in some ways lordless, for many cases awaiting resolution – above all disputes over land and inheritance – could not be resolved with a gap in the feudal chain. Edward would also lose his French fiefs if he were to remain absent. And so, as ever in Gascony when the king seemed remote, local lords pushed their claims. A *bastide*, a fortified village, at Saint-Sardos, whose building had been authorized by the parliament of Paris, was burnt by a local lord, vassal of Edward II. Between 1323 and 1325 a war broke out over this dispute, a foretaste of some of the issues over which a future war, far greater in scale and bloodier, would rage – the Hundred Years War.

Edward II had a great sense of public display and was inventive in the forms it took and the occasions on which it was deployed. He retained much from visits to France, as when he attended the sumptuous pageant of 1313 at the knighting of his brothers-in-law, the sons of Philip IV, in Paris and Boissy. Philip IV was the most important European monarch of his day, and at his death in 1314 Edward II requested that prayers for the departed be said in all churches of his realm. The business of Edward's court was managed by a vast diplomatic network, and despite its frequent itineration, this seems to have been an efficient system, assisted by the diplomatic services of a French queen. Edward relished court occasions: he revived the ceremony of royal Maundy, suspended since the days of King John.

Livery was used knowingly, for it was costly and potentially divisive; to it were also added distinctions such as placement at table and precedence in procession. Under the ordinances for the royal household of 1318 royal servants were rewarded in combinations of wage and garb: so bannerets received twenty marks in fee and livery worth sixteen marks. Inasmuch as those surrounding a lord in his household were also partisans and protectors, representing loyalty to his cause, livery always carried martial connotations. These could be reversed and used against the king. When in 1321 Marcher lords approached the king to demand the dismissal of his favourites the Despensers, Roger Mortimer of Wigmore, Humphrey Bohun Earl of Hereford and Essex, Roger Amory, and Hugh Audley the Younger – all associates of Thomas of

Lancaster – distributed distinctive livery to their knights-followers: coloured coats of armour. Those who were accused and then tried for joining the baronial force, such as Roger de Elmerugge, former sheriff of Herefordshire, who did so while in royal service, were hanged in their livery.

From his court Edward II maintained a wide range of connections and supervised the affairs of England, Wales, Ireland and Gascony. The court drew its talent from the wider British domains: Edward II's bodyguards in 1317/18 were two Welsh archers, the brothers Gough, his trumpeter in 1325 was John the Scot, who had served at his side at Boroughbridge. When possible, he used trusted bureaucrats who had served his father. One such long-standing servant in a pivotal position was Andrea Sapiti, the king's representative at the papal court of Avignon, who also negotiated important loans for the king with Italian financiers. Edward II was in constant correspondence with a number of cardinals, several of whom led the papal efforts in negotiation between England and France over Gascony. Edward II was deeply involved in governance. He came to the throne a grown man, and occupied himself with the minutiae of government. He favoured and promoted administrators, even as he seemed to need close friends loyal to none but himself. He experimented in maintaining contact with his prelates and magnates: he used writs to the clergy to inform them of diplomatic and military developments and turned to the country with requests for prayers in support of initiatives such as Queen Isabella's trip to France in 1325. His interests ranged from the state of outstanding debts to Jews who had been expelled by his father in 1290, debts which he cancelled in full in 1326, to dealing with corrupt officials in Gascony, and ordering excellent Spanish horses for his army.

TRADE AND TRAVEL

The rule of Gascony and diplomatic ties with the Low Countries and Castile together formed the backdrop for Britain's trading activities. These years also saw the steady refinement of England's place in the European wool trade, and established England's ports as stations for Castilian and Portuguese traders. Italian merchants in England were deeply involved in the wool trade; they dealt in over half of exported wool and in turn brought bullion, Mediterranean goods and exotica with them. The flow of traffic saw Portuguese ships offload cargoes of figs, raisins, leather, dyes and honey, and leave laden with broadcloths, hangings, tin, lead and Welsh cloths. All this was unprecedented in extent. The number of commercial transactions was rising dramatically, almost doubling between the 1280s and the first decade of the fourteenth century. Most wool came from Yorkshire, followed by Norfolk, Devon, Herefordshire and Derbyshire, though the Scottish wars diminished Yorkshire's portion. Regional variations developed, and were appreciated by exporters, who could choose from a range of blankets, worsteds, kerseys, russets, mendips and bluets. Edward II's government attempted to foster and favour international exchange, seeing it as benign and beneficial. Protectionist reaction can be seen only in a few specific cases, such as action against the fishing of herring off the East Anglian coast by Netherlandish fishermen.

The ability to move food and livestock across the country with relative speed and ease facilitated the commercialization of medieval England and Wales in this period. The Gough Map of the mid-fourteenth century shows five main roads linking London to all parts of the realm: to Exeter, to Bristol, to St David's, to Carlisle, and, by the Old North Road, to Yorkshire. This basic grid of communication was supported by waterways, and it enabled a person to reach London from any part within a fortnight. York to London could be made in four days, weather allowing, for flooding was a constant problem. The able-bodied could walk some 30 miles a day, and ride perhaps 40 miles. Progress was much slower when travel was encumbered. A unique drover's diary of 1323 describes in great detail the progress of John the Baker, a valet of the royal household, from Holland in Lincolnshire to Tadcaster in Yorkshire, with 19 cows and a bull, 313 ewes, 192 hoggasters (young sheep), 272 lambs and a ram, of which he and eight boys and a shepherd were in charge. On 13 May 1323 they set off, wending their way through towns and villages, picking up more livestock and help. The trip took twelve days, and involved passage of the Trent on a ferry at Littleborough.

RELIGION AND THE CHURCH

Most towns contained a dense array of religious institutions. By the early fourteenth century parishes were well established, and with them the houses of religious orders, as well as hospitals. There were twenty-two cathedral cities in England, three in Wales, twenty-three in Ireland and seventeen in Scotland, and in them the presence of clergy was highly noticeable. Pilgrims, clerks and cathedral servants mingled in cathedral precincts, which were unique in their architecture, style and the protected status of their inhabitants. Cathedrals and religious houses exercised considerable economic power over their urban neighbours. They accumulated properties and incomes through bequests left to them, but above all through planned extension of their landed estates. Thus even in the decade and a half which saw economic calamity for most in England, the Dominicans of Norwich gained at least twelve urban plots from the local land market. Religious houses were major builders and thus also employers. When fire demolished the central crossing of the great Anglo-Norman cathedral of Ely in February 1322, repair began almost immediately, producing the impressive Octagon of Ely, sumptuously decorated with sculpted arches and decorative reliefs. Such projects created demand for the craft skills of masonry, but also for the highly prized expertise of internationally renowned sculptors.

Although Protestant iconoclasm and neglect have allowed most medieval panel painting to perish, some of the finest surviving examples attest to a brilliant East Anglian school in these years. It produced works such as the Thornham Parva retable, an altarpiece which probably belonged to the Dominican house of Thetford in Suffolk c.1330. In this piece Christ, his mother and major saints – St Edmund (patron of East Anglia and of the house's founder, Edmund Gonville, Bishop of Norwich) and St Dominic – are displayed with a delicacy reminiscent of fine and small-scale manuscript illumination, and look as good as Parisian work of the period. Similar in quality and sumptuousness in the warm tones of its oil paints is the oak altar-frontal found in Kingston Lacy (Dorset), depicting a row of seated prelates alternating with saintly kings (Edmund King of East Anglia, Edward the Confessor King of England). In other regions sculpted stone screens and altar-pieces predominated, like the more modest and yet ornate rood-screen at Welsh Newton (Herefordshire) of c.1320 displaying the delicate ball-flower motif. This screen separated the chancel off from the laity but also allowed visual access to the altar through its uncluttered arched openings. In religious houses this was also a period of great musical creativity and inventiveness: early fourteenth-century psalters such as the Howard Psalter of around 1310–20 habitually include miniature illuminations, offering snapshots of monks and canons in song. So fine is the image that we can sometimes decode the motet which is being sung, the notes and words unfolding on a music roll before the singers.

The bishops seated in the Kingston Lacy frontal were the figureheads of much that had been achieved in religious instruction, patronage and intellectual work by the early fourteenth century. In England, Ireland and Wales bishops had become pivotal administrators of royal business and overseers of a complex and ambitious system of church law, liturgy and education. Each cathedral was a hub of activity, with its church courts, the synods which summoned to it the many priests of the diocese every Easter, the library of seminal and useful books in theology and church law, the schools which trained clergy, the households which administered vast estates that supported the whole enterprise. Bishops were often absentees, away on royal business, but their dual functions usually enhanced the aims of church and state: in the north bishops were crucial in attempts to secure the Borders, while the Bishops of Lincoln and Ely monitored, respectively, the workings of two of Europe's most important universities, Oxford and Cambridge. Bishops were patrons of art, innovators in technology, diplomats, and under them were appointed men increasingly trained in both Roman and canon law, members of an ecclesiastical bureaucracy. Such men had the power to regulate a wide range of human affairs: marriage and its dissolution, inheritance, sexual morality, profits and restitution, beliefs and errors, the appointment of 10,000 priests to parishes, as well as the ordination of a multitude of clerics to lower orders.

Christian life in the parish was the subject of 'micro-management' by the bishop and his staff. Visitations were meant to be annual events, but were in reality less frequent. Yet when the gaze was cast on a community and its activities, it could be intrusive. The visitation of Kent in 1327–8 showed deficiencies in fabric and provision: Ickham church had broken windows and no suitable lecterns or seats for the congregation; its parish priest was found to be married, and so another had to be instituted in his place. The rector at Westwell was also cohabiting and was thus demoted to the lower order of sexton, one which could be held by a married clerk. Well-trained priests were often attracted by the prospect of further study, or service to influential households. Bishops allowed them periods of leave, as long as these did not result in neglect of their parishes: the rector of Swanscombe in Kent was allowed, in the visitation of 1326, to go on a year's leave to serve the Countess of Pembroke.

The level of provision for parishioners depended greatly on the wealth and disposition of the religious houses or gentry families who were their patrons. Parish income was often allocated to the support of religious houses and these were obliged to provide suitable care and maintenance of the fabric of the churches. The peculiar English custom, that the rector maintained the chancel, meant that religious houses were obliged to do so in the churches appropriated to them. This provided in some cases, as in Cherry Hinton (Cambridgeshire), a great difference in quality and style between the chancel and the nave. When the system worked, it had advantages for parishioners – for example the high level of instruction enjoyed by some 300 communities in East Anglia which the Augustinian friars of Clare (Suffolk) visited regularly, providing preaching, hearing confessions and collecting alms and offerings.

By the late thirteenth century a corpus of basic Christian teachings had been composed by John Pecham, Archbishop of Canterbury, and several handbooks were created to assist priests in teaching and in further explanation of these themes. To be of widest use these texts had to be in English, and several compositions provided just that. William Shoreham, a member of the priory at Leeds (Kent), and from c.1320 the vicar of Chart Sutton parish, composed a rhymed work on a wide range of themes in catechism and devotion: the seven sacraments, prayers to the Cross, the ten commandments, the seven mortal sins, the five joys of Mary, some prayers to the Virgin Mary, and an exposition on the Trinity, Creation, Adam and Eve. In vivid Kentish dialect sound theology was conveyed:

> To wash us Christ shed his blood
> And water out of his wound.
> Hereof sprung the sacraments
> Of Holy Church worthy.

He explains what a sacrament is:

> And is to say sacrament
> a sign of a holy thing.

And the eucharist is such a sign:

> Token of it is God's body
> At church in form of bread.*

Religious instruction aimed at the knightly and aristocratic circles, often copied into books for private reading, was written in Anglo-Norman, the dialect of northern French introduced to the British Isles at the Norman Conquest. Nicholas Bozon was a Franciscan preacher and poet, who composed clever arguments for a sophisticated audience. His elegant verse sermons flattered with subtlety, as in his argument against those who claimed that the friars spread ideas about possible sins in their lively and daring sermons against sin. He demonstrated:

> When the ray of sunshine enters
> A room or chamber through the window . . .
> It catches the dust through the glass.

But that ray, he explained – preaching – does not create the invisible dust – sin; it illuminates it, distinguishing thus between right and wrong.

Such verses, easily memorized or read, were sometimes accompanied by schemes of visual representation which were similarly ambitious in telling the Christian story. At All Saints, Croughton (Northampton-shire), c.1310 the interlocking tales of the life of Mary and of Jesus's infancy were told in bands of painted scenes divided into three tiers on the south wall, and were followed on the north wall with scenes leading up to the Passion. With such aids it was easy to spread the fundamentals of a complex sacramental religion among parishioners, most of whom could neither read nor write. Such stories could even add moralizing depth for those who would reflect further through individual or group reading.

The parish served most people as the fitting place for prayer, liturgy and worship. Church law penetrated the parish through the priest's

---

* To wesschen ous cryst schedde his blod
And water out of hys wonde.
Hereof spronges þe sacremens
Of holy chyrche digne.
. . .
And his to segge sacrment
Of holy þynge signe.
. . .
Tokene þer-of his goddess bodi
At cherche ine forme of brede.

questions at confession, or the examination by the officials at visitation. The rural parish frequently coincided with the unit of work and land tenure – the manor. In small towns, it coincided with the whole settlement. In towns and cities in England (like north-west France) many small parishes coincided. The small town of Cambridge had fifteen parishes, each comprising hardly more than a street or two. Through the regulation of marriage and testamentary bequests, church law touched upon the property and material well-being of parishioners. The spheres of work and religion met in the exaction of tithes from produce, in the scrutiny of ill-gotten profits, and the requirement for restitution for illicit work. While the customs of seaboard communities regulated the reclamation of shipwrecked cargo, church law intervened here too. When in July 1313 the ship *St Mary* of Bayonne was wrecked near the cliffs of Cale Bay on the Isle of Wight, Walter de Godeston and some locals salvaged 174 tuns (casks) of wine, as well as saving the crew. Penance was imposed on Walter since the wine had belonged to a monastery in Picardy: he was, fittingly, made to build a lighthouse on top of St Katherine's Down in restitution.

Layfolk who could afford investment in religious life also created spaces for worship at home, or experimented with rigorous forms of religious experience. Longthorpe Tower outside Bedford was the residence of the Thorpe family, and in about 1330 Robert Thorpe had a vaulted solar turned into a decorated chamber, adorned with wall-paintings which still delight. Moralizing themes addressed important stages of family and personal life: the seven ages of man depict human progress from cradle to decrepitude, the occupations of the months are shown alongside the twelve apostles and the articles of faith. Here is a secular setting, one in which Christian reflection and imagery provide narrative frame and substance.

Similar in its characteristic mingling of the natural world, life experience and moral precepts is the sumptuous De Lisle Psalter, which was produced *c.*1320–30, and owned by the daughter of Robert de Lisle of Yorkshire: its prayers to the Virgin are surrounded by lively decorative scenes of country life. A similar work, the Taymouth Hours, was made for Princess Joan, daughter of Edward II and Isabella, the future bride of David Bruce, *c.*1325–35. The book may have been prepared for the occasion of her marriage, at the age of seven (to a husband aged four), as part of the Anglo-Scottish reconciliation through the Treaty of Edinburgh (1328). It includes prayers and offices for all occasions: the

Hours of the Holy Spirit, of the Trinity, of the Virgin, the Office of the Cross, for the Dead, as well as penitential psalms. Once the girl learned her Latin and French she had as good a religious compendium, in this book, as did other noblewomen of her day. It was not only noblewomen who owned such books: the Reydon Hours of c.1320–24, which is somewhat lighter in content and adorned with scenes of Christ's infancy, is also a prayerbook for all seasons, made for Alice de Reymes, wife of Sir Robert de Reydon, a Suffolk lawyer in royal service.

Such books were for most owners a gift or an inheritance to last a lifetime: precious, even sacred, and personal. People wrote in their prayerbooks, annotated, and recorded on their back-leaves important dates, affairs to remember. Time and life's course emerge from their pages, with illuminated calendars depicting all estates of women and men, all ages, people in all seasons and of all pursuits, especially rural ones. Books were not the only repositories of images; other artefacts could animate contemplation and reflection. An inventory of the belongings of Humphrey de Bohun Earl of Hereford and Essex, made between 1319 and 1322, recorded 'an image of the lady made of ivory within a closed tabernacle', as well as a small ivory image of St Katherine. The personal effects of Roger Mortimer, listed after their seizure following his execution, included an ivory image of the Virgin, which had belonged to his wife.

Books and images were prized by givers and recipients; they circulated among the living and were bequeathed by the dead, part of the intricate relations of love, memory and commemoration. With the emergence of the vogue for commemoration of the dead, old institutions became homes to new structures expressive of new styles and ideas: the twelfth-century civic chapel of St William at the north end of the Ouse Bridge in York came to house four new chantries founded by York citizens over the decade 1321–31. In these decades were established the patterns of foundation and provision which were to persist until the Reformation: each founder, man and woman, worked towards the accumulation of prayer for the benefit of souls already languishing in purgatory, and in hope of lightening the penalty which would be theirs – or that of their loved ones – after death. Death preoccupied and tantalized, and the many ghost-stories of this period demonstrate that the death of loved ones was seen not as the closing of a chapter, but as a possible link with the mysteries of the hereafter. The Welsh 'Gwidw and the prior' of c.1324 reports an imaginary exchange of questions and answers, through a prior's mediation, between Gwidw and his grieving widow, on purgatory and prayers to the dead. Conversely, a less anxious view is offered in a poem about paradise by the former monk Michael of Kildare: paradise seems too dull a place compared to his image of the land of Cockaigne, a place of gushing plenty.

Women's duties towards dead spouses, in widowhood and even within the bosom of a subsequent marriage, were an important obligation worthy of careful planning and execution. Joan, sister of Alan, Lord of Kilpeck, made an exalted second marriage to Henry, grandson of Humphrey Earl of Hereford and Essex. After Henry died at Bannockburn she undertook the planning of a suitable memorial and the provision of prayer in a prestigious Lady Chapel at Hereford Cathedral. It was decorated with wall-paintings, among them one of herself kneeling before the Virgin. Joan, who died in 1327, requested that she be buried there, as Lady Kilpeck, and to the prayers of the cathedral monks she also added the intercession of more humble folk, the inmates of God's hospital at Portsmouth. There is here a real sense of choice, an awareness of the subtly different hues of religious merit produced by different recipients, and of careful judgement as to best effect in the pursuit of prayer after death.

Death in this life could also be chosen, as did few but remarkable men and women who left their families and friends to live a solitary life. While men could become hermits in forests and caves, women were not allowed to wander freely, and so strict instructions on living the 'anchoritic' life were developed. By the fourteenth century such women were expected to undergo a ceremony of death and burial officiated by a bishop, after which they were walled into a cubicle usually attached to a parish church. Friends and community were to contribute to the support of such a person, who sometimes brought a maid with her into enclosure. While cut off from the world, a little chink allowed the anchoress to observe the liturgy within the church, and an opening allowed offerings of food to be passed into her chamber. The system was regulated by bishops, but each case was a personal drama enacted publicly. When Christine Carpenter, daughter of William the carpenter of Shere (Surrey), expressed a desire to become an anchorite in 1329, an investigation was undertaken by her parish priest and resulted in the Bishop of Winchester's approval. Christine was duly enclosed, but her choice was not a happy one, as we know from the fact that less than three years later Bishop Stratford dispatched a letter, into which was copied a dispensation which allowed Christine to return to her enclosure after she had 'left her cell inconstantly and returned to the world'. An array of styles of perfection was available to men and women, but most people found them too daunting and forbidding even to try, and settled for parish religion. Those few who chose the life of religious striving often found it too demanding, lonely or discouraging, as contemporary reports about runaway religious clearly, and sometimes tragically, attest.

LAW AND ORDER

The order imparted on manors and communities, on parishes and even on markets, was created through the parallel and interlocking work of restraint and deterrence, the working of social and moral norms together with the threat and promise of the law. It was thus deeply devastating when the king, the apex of the system of authority and law, was perceived to be out of tune with social propriety and legal probity. Robert, a member of the royal household, was able to ascribe in July 1314 the defeat at the hands of the Scots at Bannockburn to the fact that the king did not attend mass, and preferred to occupy himself with frivolous activities, such as ditch-digging. For this the man was arrested. As a messenger to Kent, Robert later complained that when he turned up with royal writs produced under the Privy Seal, people 'threw them to the ground and trampled them under foot'. He was released through the queen's intervention and the surety of the Archbishop of Canterbury, but we glimpse here the type of comment – the king is not in charge – which was exploited to justify drastic actions by ambitious opponents of Edward II, members of his own court and family.

Members of the royal household, some more and some less exalted, not only spread derision, but acted openly against the king's interest. In September 1317 Gilbert de Middleton attacked the convoy leading the bishop-elect of Durham, Louis de Beaumont – a favourite of the queen – two cardinals and other officials. On the road from Darlington to Durham, on a papal mission to Robert Bruce, these dignitaries were seized; the bishop-elect and his brother were kept at Mitford Castle for a few weeks, while the cardinals were only robbed, and allowed to make their way to Durham. This was an attack by a member of the court, who received annuities and robes from the king's hand. He was caught, tried and suffered the terrible death of a traitor.

Two contradictory trends were at work in these decades. On the one hand, a system of justice was in place, lawyers were trained, and some 200 were available in the central court of the Westminster Bench – just as some were in the Dublin court – to plead for adversaries before royal justices. These are also the decades in which regular parliaments emerged and became an expected feature of political life. On the other hand, the men whose patronage and leadership guaranteed the system's operation were at odds with their king: they suspected his competence and his ability to represent their aims in war, finance and the dispensation of patronage. An elaborate system of training and preferment solidified and made homogeneous the practices and attitudes of lawyers and judges. They were trained on the job, as Inns of Court were still a fledgling institution, first mentioned in 1329. Yet when the king's justice failed to deter and was slow to punish malefactors, people sought other means of protection.

Some differentiation between magnates and gentry was also becoming clearer; for while the barons ordained and appealed and rebelled against the king, the gentry was largely mobilized to the effort of maintaining borders and supervising the delivery of justice in intricate and innovative administrative formations. Royal officials and local communities enforced the common law and deterred malefactors. They were keepers of the peace in the shires, chosen by king and council, and they acted largely on their strength as important local landlords with local knowledge and connections to others like them. Some excellent brasses from this period portray such men – sometimes soldiers, sometimes local officers – such as that of Sir John Creke and his wife Alyne, at Westley Waterless near Cambridge, of 1325, or of Sir John d'Aubernoun the Younger, at Stoke d'Abernon (Surrey). Royal justices were not awarded salaries, but they had access to expenses for their travel, and above all benefited from royal patronage, expressed in the grants of land and of annuities.

One such royal servant was Robert of Madingley, a gentleman from the village of that name just outside Cambridge, probably one of Edward II's most assiduous royal justices. Robert held three estates in Cambridgeshire, two of which had come to him from his uncles. In the decade preceding his death in 1321 he was, among other things, a commissioner charged with enforcing the statutes for keeping of the peace in Essex and Hertfordshire, assessor of tallages (local taxes) in Cambridgeshire, and commissioner to investigate irregularities related to tax collection in Somerset. He travelled the country from Essex to Somerset, sometimes resting at his estates en route. He occasionally had to appear at Westminster, to which he sometimes travelled with his wife, well supplied with foodstuffs for the journey and sojourn, some of which were the produce of his own estates. His domestic and local base supported his service.

Another interesting example of service is Robert of Adderbury's career, which was made more dramatic through the regime changes of 1327 and 1330. He was commissioner of array as well as a keeper of the peace in 1325, following his elevation from mere local constable under Edward II. He was then charged with supervision of keepers of the peace in 1328, a position usually held by men of higher status. He reached even greater dignity under Edward III, who used him on peace commissions, and made him sheriff of Oxfordshire and Berkshire in 1333, the year in which he was also knighted. These two Roberts flourished through their local respectability and administrative skill.

In the years which saw turbulence inspired by barons, Robert of Adderbury and men like him, of essentially local importance and influence, were the ones most likely to be trusted and promoted, with tasks beyond the confines of that local circle. The aspirations and loyalties such men harboured were being mobilized in these decades through the working of parliament. Adderbury was now a knight of the shire, a man likely to be summoned to parliament to form the ranks of the Commons, which contained county representatives and those chosen to represent boroughs, who were often also members of the gentry. The Lords comprised magnates and bishops, some abbots and representatives of other ecclesiastical bodies. The clergy also acted as a group following deliberations in Convocation, a gathering headed by the Archbishop of Canterbury.

In Edward II's years parliamentary procedure was extended and tested. By the time of his son Edward III, it was a vigorous forum for fiscal and military deliberation. The most telling parliamentary document of Edward II's reign, the *Modus tenendi Parliamentum* (*The Manner of Holding Parliament*), was composed around 1322, probably by a clerk of parliament. It is a technical treatise, which was copied frequently into legal collections in later centuries, and was revived as an aspirational model by John Pym (1583–1643) in the 1640s. The

Modus sees parliament as having a number of functions. It was a venue for important trials involving peers, and for treason trials; it was the proper forum for the settling of disputes between the king's subjects; it served as a court of appeal, and attended to subjects' petitions. The *Modus* emphasizes the accountability of the institution, and its long memory: accounts were to be kept in rolls (25 cm wide), and then in files, all kept by five clerks who were paid two shillings a day. The king presided over parliament and around him, in a careful order of precedence, were his officials, his magnates and his prelates. The *Modus* both described current practices and set out principles for future change. It was used by lawyers, advisers to great men, and by kings, as parliament's prominence in political affairs steadily increased.

Petitions – from individuals, corporations and communities – highlighted unresolved court cases or conflicting claims to land, or cases touching upon royal rights. This orientation explains the prominence of justices – of King's Bench and Common Bench – on the panels which sifted through parliamentary petitions. It also explains the frequency with which local lawyers, men of no more than local renown, were elected to parliament. Finally, at parliament the king presented his demands for taxation and there the level was deliberated and the mode of collection determined.

Parliament in this period was an expanding and evolving version of a royal council with its functions of deliberation and information gathering, and its attempts to arbitrate and negotiate reconciliation between political interests. The challenges of war and administration, together with the political desires of barons and townsmen, had formed it in the thirteenth century as a forum for the hearing of grievances, and as long as the king acted as a fair arbiter he could also use it for his own ends. Parliament's role in the scrutiny of legislation was as yet a future development, but it germinated in complaints about widespread iniquities and in requests for correction. Complaints came from individuals but also from groups, both lay and clerical. Bishops were invited to attend, or rather were 'forewarned'. The clergy were never required to appear, but rather invited to do so. The archbishops of Canterbury and York held assemblies that purported to gather the clergy for consultation. The clergy too used parliament for the expression of grievances, as in the case of the clergy of Canterbury who refused to pay taxes in 1323. Several bishops and archdeacons were important royal officials, scholars and experienced diplomats; like the judges they provided professional underpinning to parliamentary deliberations.

Edward II's parliaments were royal affairs, which followed the centre of royal activity, and they had about them a quality of looseness in organization which also allowed charismatic characters to mark the proceedings. As we have already seen, several parliaments met in the north during the Scottish campaigns. In 1311 and in 1327 parliament became the tool for curbing the king, as the barons forced deliberation on royal competence and baronial grievance. Thus it may be said that Edward II summoned many parliaments, but did not always control them, since he did not command the respect of all the political constituencies to which the assembly gave voice.

THE DEPOSITION OF EDWARD II

Parliament was the scene for the last stages of Edward II's rule. Despite a decade of baronial discontent, the final opposition arose within his own family, led not by disgruntled subjects but by his own wife and son. Queen Isabella succeeded in isolating the king, following her return from France. She arrived with an invasion force, supported by the Count of Hainault, having passed from Dordrecht to Suffolk, landing on 24 September 1326, with her lover Roger Mortimer and the fourteen-year-old prince. Having the prince on their side facilitated the establishment of their party as the 'community of the realm'. London welcomed her, the king having removed himself from Westminster, retreating to Wales. There Edward II attempted to muster support; he commanded his long-time allies in Wales to raise forces, but this did not achieve much. In the Lordship of Glamorgan, near the Despensers' castle of Llantrisant, where Edward had sought refuge, he was captured. Wales was the stage for this dramatic political struggle, although the king had many loyal followers and servants there.

The disorder of his household exemplified the failure of Edward II's rule. His wife battled against him, with the support of a magnate, and his son was forced to decide which parent to follow. The kingdom was pressed, with war in Gascony since 1323 and invasions from Scotland. Parliament provided a venue for the airing of these discontents, and for the first time it enacted the scene of deposition. The heir to the throne was named 'custodian' of the realm: he was, after all, the king's flesh and blood. But his other parent consolidated her disruptive hold throughout the autumn. Eventually the king was made a prisoner and his son came to the throne and was crowned in February 1327.

Even as these events were unfolding a royal clerk, Walter of Milmete, was at work translating a text aimed at imparting wisdom to kings: *De nobilitatibus, sapientiis et prudentiis regum* (*On the Nobility, Wisdom and Prudence of Kings*). Begun in Edward II's lifetime, for the edification of his son Edward Prince of Wales, this was a translation of the book said to have been written by Aristotle for Alexander the Great. It was lavishly illustrated and included much practical advice, adapted to the contemporary English reality. The king should not take sides with factions of his magnates, it taught, and he should listen to their claims, especially those made '*in parliamentis*' (which means 'in conversations', but perhaps, already, meetings of parliament). He should take advice before allocating liberties, marriages, lands and rents; he should consider a whole range of emotions when judging when to reward and when to distance men; he should read and speak Latin and French (and Edward indeed spoke both English and French), be able to write well, and thus be independent of clerks and scribes. A king should show mercy, and attend to the needs of poor vassals, especially old soldiers. He must wish for peace yet prepare for war, and recruit men of different stations, skilled in different ways – such as the rugged peasant who can fight on without baths and luxuries. He should visit his army and raise its morale.

The illustrations to this tract on English kingship present the king enthroned, dispensing justice and largesse, receiving the requests of people of many stations, skills and origins. Yet this was a wish, a dream, an ideal wrought from the inherited wisdoms of antiquity and inflected to emphasize the clear absences of the day: at the apex of the political process stood a leader made weak through his failure to reach accommodation with his potential advisers and supporters.

The removal of Edward II from the throne and the execution of the disgraced Despensers were not presented as parliamentary decisions, nor are they reported in the rolls of parliament. And yet parliament was the setting for the action, so that some have seen 1327 as the true birth of parliament. The parliament which Edward II had summoned for January 1327, and at which he refused to appear, was in reality his son's first parliament. The mob which had gathered to complain about misrule turned into the crowd which acclaimed the new king.

Edward II abdicated on 21 January, and three days later Edward III's peace was proclaimed. He was crowned on 1 February at Westminster Abbey at a splendid ceremony for which sumptuous garments were prepared by the King's Wardrobe, at a cost of £1,323. These marked the political community in its ranks: gold cloth for some, silk for others, and bluett for the lower ranks. Official documents moved with ease from one monarch to another, but bureaucratic continuity conveys little of the political and familial drama which was being enacted. The year 1327 also marked a new stage of parliamentary efficacy: the full set of petitions presented, the first statute arising from them. The troubles of Edward II highlighted the need for political debate and redress more than ever before.

The final act of violence in this regime change was yet to come. The king was kept throughout the winter of 1326-7 in Kenilworth Castle, in the custody of his cousin, Henry Earl of Lancaster. These were months during which Isabella consolidated her income, rewarded followers, and during which at least one attempt was made to release the king. His would-be rescuers, the Despensers from south Wales, plotted in March 1327 but the attempt failed. There were other disturbances in the south-east: in mid-March in Canterbury, in June in Rochester. Therefore in April Edward II was moved to Berkeley Castle in Gloucestershire, to the care of Thomas Berkeley and John Maltravers. Roger Mortimer marched to the north of England in July, to quell unrest, while the young king fought the Scots – who were buoyed by their recent pact with France – without much effect. The feeling of crisis and lack of purpose which enveloped the new regime led to Edward III's sense that bold action was required if he was to hold on to the throne. This took various forms: it may have led to the killing of his father at Berkeley on 21 September 1327; it definitely led to the coup against his mother.

Despite the vehement hostility with which some accounts described the later Isabella – the she-wolf of France – she was effective in her diplomatic endeavours, in her ability to create an elevated and autonomous position for herself. She bore her son, the heir, and as relations between her husband and the barons declined she came to fulfil a mediating role in 1318. But as she served the king she was also establishing her own heraldic, domestic, financial and legal domains, which ultimately developed not only into a separate life, but into an alternative to Edward's rule. Her rise to prominence began with the decline of her husband's popularity, but it gained its own momentum, ultimately leading to a total change of loyalty, and to the remaking of her life. For Isabella joined her destiny to that of Roger Mortimer Earl of March – both politically and personally – in the early 1320s. He had been Edward II's childhood friend, and had distinguished himself in tournaments as a young knight and proved himself in the challenges of Ireland. He was now caught up in Edward's family drama.

The situation was highly unusual in terms of human relations, constitutional propriety and the dispersal of authority. The young king remained strangely unblemished by the circumstances of his father's death, which was widely rumoured to have been anything but the natural death which parliament had deemed it to be. Edward II's body was eviscerated and embalmed at Berkeley, as was the custom, and was publicly viewed. There was no precedent for the burial of the body of a deposed king by his widow and his son and heir. But the burial did take place, just a few days before Christmas 1327. Edward's tomb at Gloucester Cathedral is a splendid creation in alabaster, marble and Cotswold limestone, with a magnificent canopy. After his death the deposition articles were confident in stringing together a whole series of accusations: that the king was incompetent, that he had destroyed the church and nobles and lost the dominions of Scotland, Ireland and Gascony.

Isabella's ultimate fall was ascribed by the chronicler Henry Knighton to five causes: usurpation, profligacy in use of crown revenues, links with Mortimer, the execution of her brother-in-law, Edmund of Woodstock Earl of Kent, and the shameful peace with the Scots. That she was profligate with the full treasury left by Edward II was true enough: in a few months the £61,921 in the Tower and Westminster treasuries dwindled to a mere £12,031 as a result of her reward to followers. On the day of her son's coronation – 1 February 1327 – she received a series of manors and revenues from all over England producing £20,000 in annual income. And this was not all; later, much land belonging to supporters of the dead king was also seized and reallocated.

Isabella had lived through extraordinary trials in the court to which she had come at the age of thirteen, where she also had for several years to accept her secondary position, after male favourites and pastimes. In the face of very shabby treatment – emotional, financial and ceremonial – she sought her own way. She developed an ability to resist through gesture, grand gesture: she went into self-imposed exile in 1325, wore black like a widow until she was reinstated to the dignity and familial place that were her due. She nurtured an alternative political and romantic fantasy around a talented and attractive man who terrified baronial rivals, men of lineage and wealth who had far less clout than Mortimer after 1327. A fantasy it was: she and Mortimer appeared at tournaments dressed as Arthur and Guinevere. She had a penchant for Arthurian invention which her son was to carry to new heights.

Mortimer's period of hegemony alongside Isabella was restless and troubled. While they both sought to rule after Edward II's deposition in 1327, they were thwarted by Isabella's precocious and assertive son. In his splendid residence of Ludlow Castle Mortimer prepared an apartment for Isabella's use, in an ornate wing apart from the one used by his wife. But none of this was to bear fruit. Like Gaveston, Edward's favourite, Mortimer – Isabella's partner in ambition and desire – was to die a terrible death. For he was arrested at Nottingham, and was led to a trial in Westminster, a trial at which he was accused, among many other crimes, of murdering Edward II. Although Isabella begged her son for the life of her lover, he was dragged from the Tower to Tyburn, where he was hanged from the gallows, like a thief. Isabella – the king's mother, crowned queen, daughter of a king – lived on until 1358. Visitors can still see at Castle Rising in Norfolk the remote fortress where she spent the rest of her life. Her body was buried in the Franciscan friary in London; no one seemed to suggest that she might join Edward II in death.

2

Plague and War, 1330–1377

THE BLACK DEATH AND ITS AFTERMATH

In medieval world maps – like the famous *Mappa Mundi* at Hereford Cathedral – continents are arranged around the central point – Jerusalem and, at its heart, Christ's sepulchre. The British Isles are usually to be seen close to the margin, at the edge of the universe. But the fatal linkage of the people of England, Wales, Scotland and Ireland to the fortunes of the Eurasian landmass was never more evident than in the year 1348, when the epidemic which came to be known as the Black Death reached the English shore at Melcombe Regis (now Weymouth) in Dorset in the month of June, perhaps carried by a ship which had crossed from Gascony to Bristol.

A disease which had become evident among the Mongols of the Golden Horde just a few years earlier, and which spread along the silk routes to the Lower Volga regions, the Black Sea, and was then carried into Europe by the many merchants, sailors and travellers who habitually crossed the Mediterranean. Great, rich and populous cities succumbed: Constantinople in 1347, Florence in 1348. From Dorset it was a matter of months before it reached the Highlands of Scotland and the eastern parts of Ireland. The effects of mass mortality were profound and varied: those infected usually died just days after the appearance of buboes under their armpits and in their groins, accompanied by a high fever and a vile stench. The chronicler Henry Knighton recounts that corpses lay in the streets for want of hands to gather and bury them, and people lost all: their loved ones, their neighbours, their carers, their workers. In the much longer term there were changes which only historians and hindsight can reveal.

Perhaps the simplest approach is to think of the overwhelming loss of between a third and a half of each and every community through the different social contexts in which it was experienced. Evidence from the appointment of men to clerical benefices shows in East Anglia a turnover of almost half during a period of twelve months in 1349–50, with particularly rapid change over the summer months of June to August 1349. Similarly, in the diocese of Norwich, touched by the plague in late March 1349, hundreds of vicars were instituted in these months and several heads of religious houses. So many had died and there was so much fear that the dying might die alone, without Christian rites, that the Bishop of Bath and Wells, Ralph of Shrewsbury, ordained in 1349:

The continuous pestilence of the present day . . . has left many parish churches without parson or priest . . . if they are on the point of death and cannot secure the services of a priest, then they should make confession to each other . . . if no man is present, even to a woman.

Attempts to explain so overwhelming a calamity implicated almost everyone in guilt, but especially the rich and powerful. The Archbishop of York blamed those caught up in 'the delights of prosperity', who forgot God's gift to them in the rules of Christian morality. Yet while guilt singled out the fortunate few, all were touched by the plague of 1348–9. Families could no longer fulfil their essential functions: when a manorial court wished to record legal guardians in the years 1348–50, only 28 per cent of minors had parents, compared to 60 per cent in later decades. Urban workshops missed crucially skilled members, without whom products could not be completed: even the making of a simple saddle required the coordinated work of a joiner, a lorimer and a painter. The ranks of royal officials, who travelled widely on the business of dispensing justice and collecting taxes, seem to have suffered greatly. After the initial catastrophe, mortality became more regionalized: in the second visitation of the plague, in 1361–2, King David II of Scotland moved to Aberdeenshire, to escape the plague that had already affected the Borders and southern Scottish counties. Immunity developed in some sections, creating patterns of infection in later outbreaks: that of 1361 in London killed children in the autumn, and men and women only later in the spring. None of those who had witnessed the plague could ever have forgotten it. It hit all regions, and where it became endemic it recurred. The Welsh poet Gwilym ap Sefnyn (c.1400) lamented the loss of seven sons and three daughters to the plague.

The mortality affected young and old, rich and poor: but it spread with the most devastating speed in areas of dense population and in the proximity of animals. Thus towns were badly and repeatedly affected, and nucleated villages were more prone than were the sparsely settled areas, where single hamlets surrounded by fields and meadows were the rule. Archbishop FitzRalph of Armagh wrote to the pope in 1349 with a report that two thirds of the English in Ireland had been destroyed. Since most Anglo-Irish were town-dwellers, this is not surprising; conversely, the Gaelic Irish seem to have been largely spared.

What did this mean for life in the countryside? Since some 90 per cent of the population lived in rural communities, it is this population which saw the highest absolute loss of life. A glimpse of agrarian life – cast through the artistic sensibility of the illuminator of a luxury manuscript, the Luttrell Psalter, around 1340 – depicts the countryside peopled by men and women at their characteristic chores: ploughing, breaking clods of earth, sowing, weeding, reaping, stacking up sheaves, threshing. Food is shown on its route from field, cottage yard or pen, through the gathering of fruits, slaughter of animals, and preparation by pantrymen and cooks, on to the lord's table. The countryside is represented as containing various natural resources tamed and nurtured by country people: a woman feeding her chicks, windmills and rabbit warrens, fish-traps in the mill-race. There were the labours of those who offered services, such as the smith sharpening knives, bowmen in training, a barber letting blood. The Psalter shows a manor as a differentiated and interlocking community of people with differing skills, of high and low status, active in a wide range of interdependent – though not equally rewarded – activities.

Such was the countryside before the Black Death, for, by the time it struck, the population had recovered, probably fully, from the mortality caused by the famine of 1315–22. Indeed, it seems that by the 1340s renewed pressure on resources was experienced. This is suggested by the contraction of some villages – in Buckinghamshire and Bedfordshire – where exhausted poor soils were no longer worth tilling, and were thus abandoned. It is also the underlying cause of measures aimed at increasing food production through the bringing of new land under the plough, as in 1347–8 at Petworth Park, where rabbit warrens were filled to allow peas and oats to be sown. The routines of agricultural work – on the tenancies of servile peasants or in the choice lands of seigneurial demesnes – were seriously disrupted with the arrival of the plague in the months of July and August 1348. At the death of a servile tenant the holding was transferred in the manorial court to a male heir. But in the absence of a male heir, what was to be done? Rental rolls tell the tale of tragic absences: the columns in which peasants' payments were to be noted now recorded the word *vacat*, 'it is empty'. Where much land was left unused, lords were moved to reduce the expected payment from an heir, or to waive it altogether. Order, income and the flow of payments in kind had to be re-established between the lord of a manor and his tenants, and if this meant a reduction in income, this was accepted as the price for keeping the land from reverting to wilderness. Communities were thus saved from falling into disarray, and seigneurial accounts were saved from total confusion.

The burden of commemoration of the dead, the expectations that prayers be said for the souls of those suddenly departed, fell now upon surviving individuals. An institutional framework for commemoration was considered most fitting and reliable since monasteries did not die, and confraternities lived on through their memberships, whereas family and friends might succumb to disease. These foundations came to bear the burden of prayer, and in doing so enhanced their own importance and the extent of their endowments. New types of commemorative arrangements were also created. The surviving members of the Corpus Christi fraternity of Cambridge, the religious society which united the town's leading burgesses, decided to found a new academic college in 1352, and invest in it the duty of prayer and commemoration. It transferred its properties, many of them legacies of dead members, to the college, which was in turn charged with commemorative tasks. Its clerical scholars were particularly fit to fulfil these duties in the parish church of St Benet's, which served as their chapel. The onus of commemorating and serving the dead had inspired this unique form of endowment.

WORK AND CRAFT

Apart from a small group of wealthy, landed and sometimes leisured families, the work of men and women was greatly intertwined and complementary in the households of this complex economy. Work was organized within the family, be it in the customary holding of the manorial village, or the craft workshop in the town. It was among the poorest urban labourers and the most privileged aristocratic households that male and female activities were least integrated. Among the former, both man and wife – and from an early age their offspring – worked for wages; among the latter, warfare, politics and office took men away from home regularly, and into spheres that were almost exclusively male. But for most people the household economy required high levels of co-operation and work side by side. Guild records reveal the names of members – carpenters, mercers, butchers or chandlers – but they also attest that women were involved in training apprentices, preparing raw materials and, in many crafts, occupying the role of vendor at the street-facing frontage of workshops, selling the goods produced indoors.

In the household economy a number of external rules supported the male head of household's privilege. In most instances he represented the household in secular courts, and hence entered into contracts of purchase and sale, paid tithes, delivered labour services for the tenancy and paid its dues. Furthermore, apprenticeship was a lengthy process (seven years in most crafts) of training and guidance, a contract in which the apprentice's father and the master craftsman were involved. In practice, however, women participated in training and nurturing apprentices (who began their training as young as seven), and they even completed it if their husbands died without an adult heir. Inasmuch as the craft guild was a political organization which not only administered its business but sent representatives into urban institutions, men alone were expected to partake in its activities. But women, wives of members, were accorded some benefits of social and religious support, in penury or after death. Much more interaction between men and women probably occurred informally as crafts coincided with particular quarters and neighbourhoods. In these a plethora of exchanges, debts and kinship links co-existed, necessary cooperation and craft solidarity involving women even more than men. For women, domestic work and craft work were intertwined; they also found themselves training and super-vising the work of other women, skilled or semi-skilled labourers in the workshop, or domestic servants.

On rural holdings a similar discrepancy between the legal status of women and the realities of family work prevailed. The basis of a family's existence – the tenancy – was granted to the male and his heirs, but clear expectations of benefit and usufruct were accorded to daughters and, in the eventuality, widows. As to work, women put their hands to every type of rural work. They maintained the household, participated in agricultural work as necessary, and ran a whole series of related agrarian operations such as tending to livestock, poultry, vegetable gardens and herb gardens (Plate 3). Carding, spinning and weaving took place in households which possessed the necessary tools, or in cooperation with neighbours. Much medical lore was passed on within households, and villagers rarely used the services of surgeons, let alone of physicians. Child-rearing was perceived as a far less structured set of activities than it is today, yet its priorities are familiar. Attempts were made to make houses safe for children. Special attention was invested in securing water vessels and open fires, around which a high incidence of sad accidents and deaths were recorded by coroners; ecclesiastical statutes recommended that mothers and wet-nurses avoid sleeping with babies for fear of smothering them. Children, at least up to the age of six or seven, were cared for in the household, and largely by their mothers and other female relatives.

Although a servile family was defined in law by the holding of servile land and the rendering of labour services, in fact such a family could possess properties, incomes and other economic interests quite apart from the tenancy held from its lord. The land hunger of the thirteenth century left a legacy of small parcels bought dearly but conscientiously in order to provide sons with inheritances and daughters with dowries. Serfs were active in the local land-market, in which they used savings and income from labour and exchange to provide for their young. Whereas a certain alleviation had set in following the famines of 1315–22, the trend of high land-prices continued in many regions up to the Black Death. Rural families encountered growing difficulty in providing land for their maturing sons and daughters in preparation for marriage, and so youngsters probably stayed at home longer, under patriarchal discipline and in dependence, than their forebears had done. This may partly explain the tensions underlying the high levels of violence between family members recorded in manorial court rolls. Migration to a town was an option followed by some – the more enterprising or the better skilled – and particularly in those areas like East Anglia and Kent, where a buoyant urban economy offered attractive opportunities. But wages were low and expectations similarly modest in this period of over-abundance of labour, before 1349. On Welsh estates the change was perhaps less noticeable because of the importance of the wider kin-group. Welsh tenant families never 'died out', because land passed on even to distant relatives: when Maredudd ap Madog ap Llewellyn of Dyffryn Clwyd died in 1322 without an heir, two of his second cousins stepped into his holding. So land was available from a wider range of family sources for Welsh young people than it was for English ones. One might say that English patterns of tenure and household came to resemble the Welsh ones, as pressure on resources placed greater power in the hands of older landholding men. In the years just preceding the Black Death not a single family at Kibworth Harcourt (Leicestershire) left the village or ceded its customary land.

The late medieval economy offered a wide range of sources of income and productive outlets for family labour. The village, although highly regulated by custom, also offered possibilities: there was pasture for live-stock, and in the months of low agricultural activity a variety of craft was pursued in homes. In the north, where abundance of wool was a marked economic feature, spinning and weaving absorbed much work of younger and female members of households. This in turn trained young women in a transferable craft which could also be practised in towns, in return for wages. Indeed, the fourteenth century saw a high proportion of 'spinsters', women who lived singly or in groups with similar women, and, working in the textile workshops, produced cloth of varying quality from the rougher russet to the soft woollen cloth for export.

In pursuit of greater security for the elderly the maintenance agree-ment – a form of provision for old age – developed on manors. This was a formalized exchange between a person or a couple close to retirement and a younger couple, whereby the land was handed over to the young in return for annual amounts of food and clothing, bedding and a degree of assistance. For those of higher social standing some religious houses offered a venue for such arrangements, with the benefit of a religious setting for their retirement years. Even quite modest people could benefit: in 1352 the small nunnery of Yedingham in east Yorkshire promised its dairywoman Emma Hart at her retirement a place in 'le sisterhouse'. People planned for retirement with the aim of securing a flow of food and clothing and adequate shelter – all within a familiar community.

AFTER 1348

The overall picture of the response to the Black Death and its aftermath is only discernible when we assemble a wide range of examples of the choices made by lords and peasants as they confronted a new, shifting and unpredictable reality. Inflation and demand for food still held high the prices of foodstuffs in the 1360s and 1370s, but many estate managers had already decided that the labour-intensive arable systems which typified so much of southern and central England could no longer be maintained with the decline in availability of labouring hands. A number of solutions emerged in consequence: in areas of intensive mixed farming in north-east Kent, for example, wage bills were cut by greater investment in horse-power for pulling ploughs and carting manure. In 1366 the monks of Christ Church, Canterbury, lords of the manor of Ickham in east Kent, purchased carthorses and oxen and thus reduced the number of ploughhands needed from ten to four and their plough-teams from five to two. A widely adopted change was the move from arable to pasture: the south Kent manor of Wye had 660 sheep and lambs in 1350 and 964 in 1371–2, while the manor of Ickham had some 300 sheep in 1349–51 but 499 in 1370. The Bishop of Winchester's estates had an overall number of 22,500 sheep in 1348, 30,000 by the mid-1350s and 35,000 by 1369. Cattle-herds also grew: on Norfolk demesnes the average of 5–25 cows per herd before 1350 had risen to 35–40 later in the century. With these great numbers of sheep and cows dairy production was refined in the traditional dairy centres in the south-east, but it spread, and its produce was consumed more widely, providing useful protein for the diet of working people.

Sheep-rearing required less investment of labour than did arable fields; sheep produced wool, meat and, if carefully folded on fields at night, could fertilize the remaining arable and legume fields. Areas such as the Breckland (Norfolk–Suffolk border), with poor soil and traditionally low arable yields, came to develop another profitable line, the warrening of rabbits. A modest initial investment expended on situating and enclosing warren areas and introducing the rabbits could result in high returns: meat and fur were easily marketed to London. Such moves to pasture and warrening reflected and reinforced new consumption patterns which saw a greatly increased demand for meat in the diet of workers in town and country: farm servants at Sedgeford (Norfolk) gained 2 per cent of their calories from meat in the late thirteenth century, and some 23 per cent by the 1420s.

Another notable change was the increase in the consumption of ale, probably reaching around three pints a day on average in the late fourteenth century and resulting in an important contribution to calorific intake. Demand for brewing corns also affected the landscape, in determining the type of corn sown, above all in the counties which supplied that ever-thirsty consumer, London.

Human life and relations changed following the mortality of the Black Death, and so did the environment: it was transformed both in the short and in the long term. Villages in Lincolnshire were on the verge of turning into marsh by 1375. So great had been the change in tenancies, and so confusing the emergent patterns of land-holding, that the rota of responsibilities for maintaining dykes and ditches had all but disintegrated. Rivers such as the Smallee in Norfolk became almost unnavigable through the dearth of people to clear them regularly of growth and silting. Areas previously deemed too salty for use as arable could now produce salt for the market; by the 1370s carts carrying salt were a commonplace in Lindsey (Lincolnshire) for local distribution and even for transport from Wainfleet, by sea. Changes in the landscape had unexpected and pervasive environmental effects. As the development of rural industry required and encouraged the erection of dams, timber-mills, fulling-mills and sawmills, migration of fish was blocked, and thus new species of fish became more accessible for fishermen. The annual catch from a millpond at Cryfield (Warwickshire) included bream, tench, roach, perch and pike. Indeed, the general rise in the standard and diversity of the late medieval diet generated new demand for fish and the development of inland fisheries as well as regional specialized fishing industries such as those on the south Devon coast. Tin-miners ate fish rather than meat, as it was easily available for purchase on the beach, as well as in rural fish-markets just inland from the coast. So extensive was investment in fishing that a statute of 1351 called for the dismantling of weirs and mills which impeded boat traffic on the Thames, the Severn, the Ouse and the Trent.

With greater availability of land and the dearth of settled villeins satisfied to work it, looser attachments between lords and peasants developed. Where lands had traditionally been held by villeins, outsiders (*extranei*) were now in tenure. If a single family held two or more tenancies, it might neglect buildings, ditches, gardens on those lands it did not inhabit, contributing in this way to the increase and visibility of disrepair and dislocation. The overall number of people on the land continued to decline, although the phenomenon of village desertion did not become fully evident until the 1380s: by 1381 an estate in Dyffryn Clwyd had only 47 of its previous 212 villeins, while by 1386 Kingsthorpe (Northamptonshire) had lost its entire population. Those who did

remain on the land were aware of their relative advantage and bar-
gaining position: in 1364 a manorial injunction at West Raynton (Co.
Durham) prohibited calling the tenants of East Raynton 'neifs' (*nativi*),
that is serfs, of the lord.

Even if demands from servile tenants were transformed after the
great mortality, and landlords' expectations were adjusted to the new
reality, the trend of depopulation persisted in the countryside. The
1360s and 1370s, therefore, saw a real transformation which affected
landscape, organization of labour routines and thus of family and
community relations. In England, and even more in Wales, collective
agrarian undertakings, such as joint ploughing and joint leasing of
pasture, depended on shared interests and the ability of each household
to invest time, effort and funds. The cooperation which was required
of open-field communities was clearly being eroded by the fragmentation of activities and even the abandonment of whole tracts of land to
waste. This often took the forms of contraction and ultimately desertion
of villages, traces of which can still be clearly seen at Egmere and
Pudding Norton (Norfolk). Patterns evident in the east Midlands show,
interestingly, that villages in river valleys rarely disappeared, and that
nucleated villages – settlements in which buildings were clustered
together, most common in the east and south of England – tended to
be more vulnerable in the post-plague years, especially the rather poorer
ones. In such villages households tended to be more interdependent
economically and socially, and thus more vulnerable to erosion with
the decline in cohesion of this network. On the other hand, hamlets and
more dispersed settlements were accustomed to greater self-sufficiency;
they often produced basic manufactured goods and could thus bear the
brunt of dislocation and mortality better. Furthermore, proximity to a
town sometimes hastened depopulation: the Ouse valley saw little
shrinkage in its villages, except those near towns such as Bedford,
Buckingham, Newport Pagnell, Oundle and Towcester. Status as an
administrative centre for a large estate might further enhance a community's chance of prosperous survival. In many areas this period saw
the beginning of long-term change, with a trend to depopulation that
was never halted, a fate sealed when whole villages were turned into
pasture by the late fifteenth century.

Landlords cast a sharper look and brought some radical thinking to
the question of the character of husbandry as they reassessed the assets
under their control: pasture, water, parkland, mines. This meant a

change in lifestyle for lords and tenants alike. Parkland was a lord's reserve of deer for the hunt, but it could also provide timber for construction and sale, and its underwood could be sold or leased. Parks became more closely monitored after the Black Death by a complex hierarchy of managing manorial officials: by 1385–6 the lord of Walsall Manor (Staffordshire) had his whole park enclosed to protect the wood and to fatten twenty heifers, as well as poultry and game birds. Areas of woodland which once dominated the landscape – oak, birch, ash, hazel, elm – diminished. Hedgerows continued to mark important property boundaries, while their fruits were highly valued by country people, and even more so by urban consumers. Decisions were taken in consultation with professional managers of estates, who were rewarded for success or dismissed for failure. Their status probably rose too: in 1354 Lord Berkeley was regularly joined by his reeve and household officers for meals at Raglan Castle.

The reallocation of land and other resources between lords and peasants took a variety of forms and resulted in complex life-changes, the full effect of which is hard to discern. In general, migration was more extensive: in York around 1300, 51 per cent of surnames indicating place of origin were from within 19 miles, and 7 per cent from within 19–37 miles; whereas by 1360 34 per cent were from the closer, and 35 per cent from the further points of origin. The mortality clearly affected family relations: the young tended to migrate, confident in their ability to find work, and perhaps pushed by the gloom which descended on so many contracting villages. Moreover, as land and work became more plentiful, so did opportunities for the employment of men offered by the French and Scottish wars, and training opportunities for women in the expanding textile industry. The links of dependence which had kept so many young people close to the family hearth in the days of scarcity were diminished. People were on the move, coming and going by sea and road and river, within the wide domains which the King of England ruled. There were foreign workers too, such as the Flemish men and women at work in Brancaster (Norfolk) in 1368 and known as 'Pekkers' (from Picardy), and Welsh men who worked for high wages on Midland estates in the late summer and autumn.

There was ever more land to be had within the manorial system. Increasingly we find tenants amassing large holdings: Roger de Salkeld (Cumberland), for example, held c.200 acres in 1371. By the 1370s landlords were eager to rid themselves of large tracts of arable. Where they were not turned to pasture, choice demesne lands were leased out for terms of years, and those keenest to enter into them were the greater peasant-holders who had sufficient savings to buy, stock and work the additional land. The shedding of customary duties of serfs meant that in Caldicot Manor (Gwent) the 1,000 labour days which were provided in the 1340s had dwindled to some 114 in 1362. So while average peasant holdings grew after the Black Death, the distribution of land tended to favour a stratum of large tenants, who saw their standing in their communities enhanced accordingly. New types of tenants entered into village holdings in these circumstances: on Welsh manors Welshmen now leased or bought land of English tenure from which they were previously excluded. Burgesses and priests with ready cash could buy lands which were previously customary holdings of serfs on estates. The texture of community based on neighbourhood and shared responsibility was clearly changing rapidly. Mobility affected the ability of neighbours to maintain cooperation in the many ways required by village life, down to the smallest institutions such as the communal pound for stray beasts maintained by contributions of the tenants in Glentham (Lincolnshire) or the maintenance of dykes around Wisbech (Cambridgeshire).

The 1360s and 1370s saw not only seigneurial reactions which favoured diversification of production and rationalization of estates, but a reinvigorated attention to the viability of legal and customary rights. Some lords were happy to shed some seigneurial rights in return for a regular income or a lump sum: the Bishop of Norwich accepted in 1369 12d. per annum from each tenant in Honingham (Norfolk) in place of compulsory use of his mill. The men of Brecon were obliged to pay £500 for overall exemption from tolls, and those of Denbigh village £400 in 1356. The legal profession played a crucial role in such negotiations. In areas of particularly rampant lordship, such as the Welsh Marches, compensation for decline in revenues could take spectacular form: the dues from the Brecon lordship doubled between 1340 and 1399, through the imposition of taxes on economic activity, such as the payment of £400 for the right to buy and sell land in the Tegeingl (Flintshire and Denbighshire). Lordship was asserted through close administration, and in Wales in particular it resulted in an intensified scrutiny through seigneurial land-surveys, as well as in determined exploitation of income from justice.

Serfs did not remain passive in this changing environment; they too sometimes sought and acquired good legal advice. The economic and demographic transformations which followed the Black Death contributed to the growing frequency of legal litigation and thus to the development of the professional prospects and utility of those with legal training. The array of legal frameworks and the remedies they offered was vast – ecclesiastical, borough, King's Bench, Chancery Court – as well as arbitration within families, neighbourhoods and wards and within a lord's affinity.

This fluid world where the young were on the move, where landed assets posed challenges to their owners, was shrewdly understood by contemporaries to be radical in its promise and disturbing in its effects. Those whose incomes and authority were most affected – employers and landlords – mobilized their influence in parliament, and achieved a quick royal reaction to their plight. A royal ordinance of 1349 was turned into statute by parliament in 1350: the Statute of Labourers. The statute fixed the price of labour in various sectors, and set the minimum term of contracts of employment. It became a resource that was used in localities pragmatically: it was usually ignored, but when expedient it was applied. Even the king exempted himself from its operations when his clerks sought masons for the great building works in Windsor of the 1360s. The system of labour control became increasingly integrated into the evolving system of local justice administered largely by the gentry, the very land-holders so concerned with the maintenance of a cheap and constant supply of labour. Within a generation labour legislation, although patchily enforced, became the byword for unjust oppression.

The issues of labour and wages, of poverty and merit, of vagabondage and charity – all areas of the social contract – developed into chronic preoccupations of those who employed labourers in town and in country. This anxiety elicited legislation from a third of the parliaments of the following century. It became one of the most acute political issues of the later fourteenth century, inspiring expressions repeated in all grievances, minute or spectacular. In 1356 a vicar and a hermit of Hertfordshire, Robert Gerard and Richard Fulham, were presented to court for contemptuous public talk about the statute and ordinance: they claimed that no laws should stop artisans and labourers from earning as much as they could get. When legislation was repeated in the statute of 1361 the pain for infraction was no longer a fine, but imprisonment and branding with the letter F for Falsity, although we do not know that it was enforced. Some sumptuary legislation emphasized a similar preoccupation with social hierarchy. The statute of 1363 fixed the quality of cloth appropriate for each social group: lords, knights, esquires. Although it was not enforced – the Commons even sought its reversal in the following year in support of free and more buoyant trade – these legislative acts express areas of concern and anxiety which animated political debate and attitudes in localities.

Cities attracted young labourers in particular into service in households and workshops. These were unattached youths away from home, and they came to be seen as a menace during these anxious times. In 1351 London already sensed the effect and intended to arrest 'misdoers' who had come to it since the end of the pestilence. Its efforts against migrant workers continued with a 1359 order to expel all unemployed migrants. In the growing and buoyant textile industry there was now place for many young men and women, and for servants, working for wages at a relatively young age, before marriage. It was the fear of such servants that the Statute of Treason of 1352 attempted to address, for it defined treason not only as plotting against the king's well-being, but as a series of acts against authority: servant against master, wife against husband. Coroners' records reveal very few cases of servants killing their masters, and many more injuries caused by masters to servants, but the anxieties which turned into petitions in parliament and subsequently informed statutes were those of the Lords and Commons, in a world where traditional relations of deference and dependence had been dramatically transformed.

TOWNS

The responses of towns to the pressures and the promise of these decades took administrative forms which varied by region. The towns of the north invested in maintaining and sometimes building anew protective walls, while those of East Anglia did not. The towns of Wales, especially the plantation boroughs set up by Edward I, contended with complex issues resulting from the legal and social 'dualism' – distinctions between Welsh and English – which statutes created. Irish towns faced similar problems of 'separation'. The southern English ports all feared a French invasion, and invested in and received help towards their fortification: in 1339 Edward III ordered that defences be erected in Southampton following the French raid on the port. Every town had to make a contribution to the national effort, through taxation and by raising fighting men: in 1346/7 Cambridge contributed eight men to Edward III's expedition to Calais. The funding of such ventures was one of the many tasks of the emergent group of town treasurers, under the supervision of town councils.

The men who administered towns benefited from the prestige, connections and information which such positions offered, but they could also be held responsible for failure, and they did not operate in a free field of action. Cathedral cities confronted the presence of huge cathedral households and administrations with privileges that exempted them from contributing to the city's taxation and from answering to its courts. Such exemption covered clerical personnel, their servants and their families, and a whole array of ecclesiastical institutions such as hospitals, colleges, schools, chapels and hermitages. Internal competition over influence and jurisdiction within cities moved the Bishop of Bath and Wells to build a moat and wall around his palace at Wells against militant townsmen; the wafer-thin walls marked territory and autonomy. In 1345 Coventry's incorporation marked its new freedom to elect officials and run a merchant court; the political centre of gravity was shifting from cathedral precinct into a distinct civic space. Conversely, towns were developing ceremonies and symbols of autonomy to match the heavy burdens that its officers carried. The process was encouraged and supported by the crown, which depended greatly for its income on the fluidity and buoyancy of trade. Towns were part of national political life, through their representatives in the parliamentary Commons. There were town seals, such as Winchelsea's (Sussex) combination of a ship with a tower and the royal arms, and public buildings such as guildhalls. This making of constitutions and solidification of urban institutions coincided with the invention of local traditions and myths of origin. In 1372 the prosperous town of Colchester claimed that the foundations of its Norman castle marked the site of King Cole's palace, while the inhabitants of Totnes (Devon) claimed that Brut the Trojan was their founder.

And there was London, with a population of perhaps 40,000 in the 1340s and about 20,000 by the 1370s. This was a complex city, a patchwork of some 104 neighbourhood parishes, containing over a hundred occupations, tens of guilds, hundreds of chapels, and a multitude of ethnicities, estates and languages. Although the Jews of England had been expelled in 1290, London still had its Jews, sometimes described as converts from Turkey, Spain or the Low Countries. One Jew was even moved to convert in London itself, and became John of St Mary. London was the heart of the commercial community, and inasmuch as this was becoming increasingly drawn into overseas trade and national politics, London was the stage for events that in turn affected the lives of men and women on both sides of the Channel. Any object could be bought, any service hired in mid-fourteenth-century London: sex, banking, learning, gastronomy and entertainment. News and fashion reached London easily, within a week from Paris or Bruges, and sufficiently pressing news could then reach the regions of the British Isles within days through an excellent network of rivers, roads and waterways.

EDWARD III

This country, just recovering from mortality, was also plunged into war, and some were to benefit greatly from the opportunities offered by it. The will and character of Edward III and his government made a great difference at many levels. His boyhood was marked by exile in France with his mother Isabella and later a return to England which ended in the deposition of his father and ultimately saw this teenager end his mother's rule. He had married Philippa, daughter of the Count of Hainault, in 1328, and soon after, in 1330 at the age of seventeen, was ready to rise against the rule established by his guardians: his mother and her lover Mortimer. He then painstakingly established his rule through networks of patronage which were to be cemented in the French wars from 1337 which were followed by his claim to the French crown in 1340.

Edward III's rule confronted some of the greatest challenges faced by a monarch of an empire of British and French lands: there was war with Scotland, a newly enhanced war in France, a country struck by plague, depopulation and economic uncertainty. The political system enabled the sounding of dissent and complaint through clamour for the king's attention in parliaments. Edward III was above all active in war and its finance; the politics followed. No wonder that contemporary prophetic texts saw him as a lion, where they described his father as a goat, a lover of luxury, who had been impotent at war. Edward III gave

the fighting and trading men of his country – his political community –
the taste for war and its rewards. And so even when he wished to sign
treaties for peace, as he did in the Treaty of Brétigny of 1360, and to
enjoy the fruits of his efforts, there was always a group which goaded
him towards war. Belligerent political programmes were presented as
oracular prophecies. A volume of the prophecies of St John of Bridlington was dedicated to Humphrey of Bohun, the king's lieutenant in
Calais; it pronounced that the job in France would not be complete
until the Black Prince – Edward, Prince of Wales – was King of France.

The awesome images constructed in Edward III's youth and prime –
warrior-boy, Arthurian hero like Edward I – were powerful political
tokens, which seemed to gain depth from comparison with the memory
of his father. Nowhere was this more so than in the conduct of the
Scottish wars. Here the dynastic legacy was strong: testing in the
Scottish wars marked his grandfather's and father's reigns as well as
his mother's short regency. From 1332 Edward III invested, for a while,
in efforts to re-establish English hegemony and to secure a recognition
of English overlordship; it had, after all, been the conciliatory Scottish
policy of Isabella and Mortimer that had incensed the Londoners and
pushed Edward to depose his guardians. Edward III offered support to
Edward Balliol, a claimant to the Scottish throne, encouraging him to
return from exile in France. This was a war of Bruce against Balliol,
supported by the English crown, at a moment which saw the Bruce
camp in some disarray following the deaths of Robert Bruce and his
most trusted and experienced lieutenants, the Earl of Moray and James
Douglas. Following his success in July 1333 at the battle of Halidon
Hill outside Berwick, Edward Balliol and some of the disinherited
Scottish lords landed by sea in Fife, and by 1334 accepted Edward III's
overlordship for the whole of southern Scotland, which he now held.
King David Bruce II was forced to flee to France and in 1335 Balliol's
forces reached the north of Scotland, fighting their way through Scottish
resistance by the new Earl of Moray. Yet that very year saw a reversal,
at the battle of Culblean (Deeside), where William Douglas and Andrew
Murray defeated Balliol's supporters and captured Balliol's lieutenant,
David Strathbogie.

This instability had to be settled and called for decision on Edward
III's part. He continued to pour some £25,000 a year into the short
three-month Scottish fighting season, an extravagance soon to be
stopped as his attention and every other resource was turned to another

part of Europe, against the Bruces' ally, to France. When the English armies were removed it was relatively easy for Murray to recover and recapture lands and strongholds by 1337, as had been the case in previous decades. While he did so, the young Bruce heir was safely maturing on French soil. Edward III's later campaigns to Scotland, above all his victory at Neville's Cross in 1346, where he imprisoned David II, King of the Scots (1329–71), allowed him to turn fully towards the French war. Given these challenges it was both expected and expedient that energetic border lords, whose estates were most at risk from Scottish raids, and who could raise and command forces, should be empowered to shoulder the burden of defence. The Percies, who rose to prominence as lords of Alnwick around 1309, are a good example. The Nevilles, alongside the Bishop of Durham, were charged with the tasks of defending the north and led the forces at Neville's Cross in 1346.

The Scottish wars were a burden, but they trained a whole cohort of men, bonded them to the king and to each other, and allowed tactics to be perfected which were to prove significant in the encounters on French soil. The lesson of Bannockburn (1314) was applied at Dupplin Muir (1332) and Halidon Hill (1333). Edward III now conducted battles with wings of archers fighting with longbows, either side of a group of men-at-arms. The Scottish forces led by Sir Archibald Douglas at Halidon Hill attacked uphill as a group of spearmen, but were overwhelmed by the English assault of swift archers. The combination was extremely powerful: two wings of archers – using bows weighted by over 100 pounds – shot down thousands of attackers and protected the men-at-arms in the centre. This fighting style proved highly successful in the first stages of the wars with France. Edward had also learned a great deal from the Bruces' ravages of the north of England: such raids impoverished and demoralized the affected region. The *chevauchée* – the destructive ride through the countryside, that tool of terror used so knowingly in the French wars – was developed in England's northern Marches.

A number of strands of dynastic aspiration and economic benefit came together in Edward's claim to the French throne in 1340. Although he took the ambition further than his immediate predecessors, Edward was not the author of the English claim. He was, after all, the grandson of Philip IV, King of France (d. 1314), and stood in direct lineal descent through his mother. This claim through female descent was not wholly new to the European political community: women had inherited or mediated a claim in the Iberian kingdoms and in Flanders, as well as in England itself. Edward III's direct descent through a daughter was superior, so he claimed, to a lateral descent through a man, as was the case of Philip VI. In January 1340 he styled himself King of France. Whereas his predecessors had their initials decorated at the head of royal charters, Edward had several letters presented in this way, and sometimes his whole name. The seal used by him from June 1340 styled him King of England and King of France, in a mode to be used by his successor, and he quartered the *fleur-de-lis* with the Lions of England.

In turn, French polemical writing, such as the *Treatise on the Coronation* by Jean Golein, argued that a woman cannot be anointed, hence it followed 'by the accord of all, that the kingdom of France must be held by succession of the male heir the closest of the line . . .'. Edward was simply mistaken: 'and that the king of England, Edward, who has long held that error saying that because of his mother he has a right to the kingdom of France, he is not well-informed on this fact'. Edward III was extremely well-informed of the French reality. He had long held dynastic lands, inherited by his grandfather Edward I from his own mother, Eleanor of Provence; for Gascony he had already rendered homage to Philip VI. There was the added issue of the safety of English trade with Flanders, access to which depended so much on the control of Normandy. By throwing his claim into the arena, Edward created a focal point for disgruntled vassals of the increasingly ambitious French crown, such as the Count of Flanders and the Duke of Normandy. He also created a theme for his own reign, a purpose for mobilization and cooperation, uniquely led by him.

The confrontation with France must also be linked to Edward's British vision: in recent history the King of France had supported Scottish political aspirations. Continental rulers, all of whom were linked by marriage to the French royal family, also enjoyed the thought of a dynastic rearrangement, which might cut territory away from the vast lands of the kings of France. Diplomats, lawyers, poets, chancery clerks, chroniclers and artists were engaged in the effort of making Edward III's claim to France something more than an outrage. Far from being offensive or aggressive, this claim was an assertion of justice and reparation. By the 1340s, it was a question of safety: claims were made that the King of France sought to conquer England and distribute its lands among his nobles.

Seen from the Low Countries, St Omer and Tournai, the northern-most cities of France offered obvious targets for land warfare. Already in July 1337 a small force led by Robert of Artois, containing Flemish foot-soldiers and English longbowmen, had been sent to St Omer, and Edward III himself was to lead the remaining forces to the city of Tournai. Edward and his allies had hitherto experienced relatively easy victories: this was not to be repeated. Robert of Artois burnt his way to St Omer, but was routed by the energy and the offensive tactics of the French garrison there. Forced to retreat to the English forces around Tournai, Edward III witnessed over the following months some of the frustrations of the French war, and the enormous expense which this type of enterprise inflicted on his kingdom.

While the king was learning to expect and perhaps even accept criticism from parliament, he must have reacted more sharply to the criticism of his court by someone who knew it well, such as the author of the poem *Vows of the Heron* in Anglo-Norman French. Set in 1337, and written soon after, the poem depicts the court of Edward III at a feast. Goaded by Robert of Artois, the angry exile who had caught the heron for their meal, the king vowed to go to war, as did Robert. Nobles took oaths promising prowess in the future war with France over the heron's cooked flesh. The Earl of Salisbury would not open his right eye until he had battled in France in support of his king; while his beloved, the daughter of the Earl of Derby, swore not to marry until he fulfilled his vow. Walter de Mauny would conduct a raid on the town of Godemar de Fay, burn it and return. The Earl of Derby swore to fight Louis of Flanders, and the Earl of Suffolk to fight the King of Bohemia and throw him off his horse. John of Fauquemont swore that since he was poor he would follow Edward III and spread fire in the Cambraisis, sparing no church or altar, no pregnant woman or child. The queen for her part promised that the child within her womb would not be born until his father returned from battle.

To those in the know, this was a parody: the Earl of Salisbury had already lost his eye in Scotland, and the Earl of Derby's daughter would have made him a ridiculously young bride; Walter de Mauny's attempt had been a failure, as had that of Robert of Artois on St Omer. But the representation is one of isolated vanity, of war couched in misplaced chivalry rather than in careful reflection.

Any such dissenting sentiment was countered by the first great English victory in 1340, a victory at sea, the battle of Sluys off the Flemish coast.

There the French lost their whole navy and some 20,000–40,000 men, a force amassed by Philip VI for an invasion of England. Edward commanded a row of ships – the contribution of Yarmouth and the Cinque Ports – from his flagship *Thomas*. These ships were mounted with wooden fortifications, and resembled a row of castles. Against them were 200 French ships in three close rows resembling a single flank. But they were destroyed by Edward III's manoeuvre, simply to ram into them, mount them, and fight on them man to man. It was a strange victory, sustained by an alliance created by Edward III out of a multiplicity of interests; a volatile coalition which was as brittle as it was wide-ranging. At its heart was Flanders, erstwhile fiefdom of the kings of France, whose wealth depended on turning English wool into cloth which was then used all over Europe. Edward III used vast funds to support these alliances in a decade of extraordinary extravagance and expenditure, which ended in financial embarrassment. His allies were William Count of Hainault (his father-in-law), Jan III Count of Brabant, and Jacob van Artevelde, a merchant of Ghent who had usurped the leadership traditionally offered by the counts of Flanders. The alliance suffered from tension arising between the old Brabançon noble and the upstart banker of Ghent. The victory at Sluys and its afterglow kept everyone happy for a short time, during which Edward visited his family in Ghent. The visit resulted some months later in the birth of his son in March 1341 – one of a dozen children – who came to be known as John of Gaunt.

Although the success was a famous one it was also clear that the French were not yet beaten on land, that they still had armies and allies. Siege warfare was costly and time-consuming; Tournai did not fall. King Philip VI did not engage in battle and, moreover, the dowager Countess of Hainault, Jeanne of Valois, presented peace proposals which sowed dissent within Edward's alliance, restive in the absence of the payments upon which the whole cooperative venture relied. A truce for five years was signed on 25 September 1340 at a chapel in Esplechin, and this provided a useful breathing space for all involved. Philip VI of France gained an ally in the Emperor Lewis of Bavaria and the Flemings agreed to accept Louis of Nevers as their count. In return, Philip removed his economic sanctions from the Flemish cities, and tens of villages seized by the French on the march to the north were returned to the Duke of Brabant and the Count of Hainault. All that remained was for Edward to return home in November 1340 and to vent his fury at ministers who had failed him and at nobles who had given only lukewarm support.

England's wealth was hard to collect in coin. It was assessed and scrutinized by the crown's servants, who had recommended in 1334 the move to tax quotas on each community, rural and urban. This change shifted the burden on to local assessors, who estimated the ability of members of each community to make a contribution. The new system yielded some £38,000 per collection until 1360. After 1353 another plank to the tax policy was added, as a regular export tax on wool was fixed annually by parliament. Although it no longer stated a minimal threshold for taxation as earlier subsidies had done, there is evidence that assessors used their discretion in judging who could and who could not make a contribution. Under the effect of frequent taxation, a fiscal footing for the war needs, a reassessment of priorities followed.

The new tax regime affected the economy in several ways. Large landowners did not indulge in much building, *de novo*, and cut down on maintenance: on one of the estates of the Bishop of Winchester where £458 9s. was spent in 1309–10, £356 6s. was spent in 1340–41. Investment was low, and with it demand for labour in rural areas. However, others, such as some big merchants and victuallers, stood to gain from provisioning the armies. A literature of complaint developed even before Edward III's demands reached their peak, as in the *Song against the King's Taxes* of *c.*1338:

> People suffer such ill that they can give no more;
> I do not doubt that, if they had a leader, they would rise.

Cumberland, which had been exempted from taxation following the Scottish raids of Edward II's reign, petitioned parliament for continued exemption, and was also able to manipulate the work of commissions operating in the damaged areas, to gain lower assessments. Taxation had become the major topic of local and national politics.

Taxation was not the only source of royal income in support of the wars in France. During the first years of the war Edward had been content to deal with Italian bankers and raise sums on the expectation of royal incomes. This very soon proved to be unrealistic. In 1340 Edward III had to borrow £6,500 from his trusted Italian physician, Pancio de Controne, a family adviser and favourite, who had served his father before him. This was a speedy and cheap mode of raising money, but it had to be supported by frequent taxation which weighed heavily on an impoverished countryside. As shortfalls were emerging in tax assessments in the 1330s, a novel attempt to locate sources of wealth and to assess for tax was employed in 1340–41 in the production of the 'rolls of Ninths' (Nonae). Communities throughout the realm (excluding franchises and the Welsh Marches) were asked to assess their wealth: villages were to contribute a ninth of the year's yield in grain, wool and lambs; towns to contribute according to the value of stocks of merchandise; and rural markets were assessed on grain, wool, lambs and merchant goods. The method of assessment was responding to emergent economic realities: the tax base included some tens of very rich towns and vast areas of countryside, but economic activity – manufacture and exchange – was most commonly conducted in rural markets and small towns: for a single large and prosperous Colchester, for example, there were tens of more modest towns like neighbouring Braintree. Such small towns were now caught in the net of taxation.

The crisis of 1340–41 was one of trust in the king's good judgement and in the advice which informed his decisions. Government was torn between the arenas of royal action: the councillors in Brabant with the king, and the magnates and churchmen at home around the chancellor, Archbishop Stratford. In July 1340 a loan by parliament had been agreed equivalent to 20,000 sacks of wool; but royal agents in the counties met resistance to their efforts to collect. When parliament was called for April 1341, only three parliamentary representatives from the previous assembly were present; disagreement and disaffection with their representatives was evident in borough and county meetings. Although not a central complaint, there was some mention that royal revenue ought to support crown initiatives, and not be shared around, leaving the royal coffers bare and the king diminished, dependent on his subjects' offerings. The time had come to move from loans secured by expected income from customs to direct taxes on exports and subsidies based on wealth assessed in and by communities.

Surrounded by well and carefully rewarded men, Edward III was able to make demands, some of them high-handed, for a while. When he had withheld wool from sale in 1337, magnates such as the Earl of Salisbury demurred, but remained loyal. But Edward III was a quick learner. The financially draining years of 1337–40, when he taxed England as it had never been taxed before, led to resistance in the parliament of 1340–41; after it Edward III was forced, or rather persuaded, to change his approach. He raised funds not from bankers, but from the contributions of his subjects and their production – by taxing wool exports – and from the dues paid by barons, prelates and rich merchants. This direct taxation was raised through processes of consultation which were to turn parliaments into effective political assemblies and involve the Commons in comment and advice about the war, the royal household, and strategic and military issues.

The next major campaign began in Normandy; it resulted in the ruin of Caen, and culminated in the battle of Crécy in Ponthieu of 1346 (Plate 7). Edward III drew Philip VI of France into battle after a *chevauchée* – a swift destructive ride – conducted from disembarkation and up to Caen. As Philip approached, Edward withdrew north-east to the Somme, up to a hilltop at Crécy. The French had destroyed all bridges on the Seine, and so Edward marched deeper inland than originally planned. At Poissy the bridge was rebuilt and Edward was ready for battle. He combined techniques he had observed in the Scottish wars. The force comprised three 'battles': the vanguard led by the Prince of Wales, the centre led by the king, supported by the bannerets of the royal household – and the rearguard, led by the Bishop of Durham and the Earls of Arundel, Suffolk and Huntingdon. English archers dug in here, protecting and surrounding the mounted men, all aided by obstacles such as stakes and pits. Philip's Genoese crossbowmen were without their shields because of a failure of supplies, and their bowstrings were weak and wet. As they retreated, the French ran into their own cavalry, whose men and horses were destroyed by English fire. The King of France had attempted to avoid an encounter since 1338; at Crécy he felt confident, but once he exposed his forces, he suffered defeat. After Crécy the French forces changed their tactics, gave up their horses and fought on foot as their adversaries did. This made warfare bloodier; between men wielding vicious pikes and halberds, face to face, under a shower of arrows.

Uplifted by the victory at Crécy, Edward moved on to besiege the city which represented economic well-being and military advantage – Calais. The city put up resistance, led by its bishop, in the hope that King Philip would arrive and relieve it. Although at the end of July he did, the support did not last long, and the French force retired, leaving the city, its burgesses and the many refugees from its hinterland to face the English force of some 32,000 men. The desperate leaders of Calais sent out Jean de Vienne to negotiate the handing over of the city and its wealth in return for its citizens' lives. According to the chronicler

Jehan le Bel, Edward refused to negotiate and claimed the city, which had resisted him for long tedious months, and its citizens. Geoffrey le Baker reports that after Jean de Vienne many knights and citizens of Calais, bare-headed and on foot, submitted themselves to the king, and begged for mercy for the rest. Jehan le Bel's report accorded great dignity to the citizens of Calais, and added the intercession of Queen Philippa, a mother figure reminiscent of the Virgin Mary, prime intercessor for humans. Here is a scene of capitulation and of royal strength tempered by queenly virtue. The citizens of Calais were spared, their humiliation complete. Their tale was revived in the nineteenth century as a story of French bourgeois heroism, captured so powerfully in Auguste Rodin's monument in Calais of 1895.

War offered opportunities for employment, for advancement, for glory and adventure, for vocational fulfilment, and not only to the greatest men of England – the king led an army at fourteen, his son was a hero at Crécy at sixteen – but to hundreds of knights by birth, and to thousands more, men of more modest means, who made up three quarters of his armies. No more than a tenth of the men of England took part in the wars, but this was a substantial group. Among the mounted warriors of this war, the proportion of knightly to non-knightly men was about one to ten, with a somewhat higher proportion of knights on royal expeditions. Knights were paid two shillings a day and esquires one, while foot soldiers had sixpence. Below the ranks of mounted men and skilled archers there was the valet, that factotum on whom every soldier depended. He might be the son of a servile family, who could gain training, experience and patronage which led to social advancement. Whereas knights joined by duty and vocation, modest freemen joined in regional groups in search of employment, adventure and preferment. There was never a shortage of men for the campaigns in France in the 1340s and 1350s, even if some resented the royal assessments of property by which their level of contribution was determined. The household contingents, led by the king's knights, offered leadership and example, and constituted a sixth of the army in the campaign of 1359/60.

Recruitment to the royal army allowed a son to shoulder some of his father's responsibilities and, after his schooling in regional tournaments, to make a name for himself. Famous tournaments were attended by recruiters to the contingents of kings and magnates: the Windsor jousts were attended by the Duke of Brabant in 1348 in preparation for his war against the Count of Flanders. Tournaments offered the options of fighting as if in war, or with blunted weapons. When tournaments took place during campaigns or near theatres of war they could act as a dangerous preparation for hostilities: in 1341 four English knights led by Henry of Grosmont Duke of Lancaster (d. 1361) confronted four Scottish knights at a tournament at Roxburgh in the Borders, which was fought with full arms. In a tournament at Northampton in the following year Lancaster's brother-in-law was killed and others were seriously wounded. Knightly fathers hoped to pass their armour on to their sons, as did Sir Adam of Weil in his will of 1345, leaving to his son John all armour, for both peace (tournaments) and war. The dedication page of the Luttrell Psalter, made c.1334, depicts the scene of a knight's leave-taking. This is Sir Geoffrey Luttrell bidding farewell to his wife Agnes and his daughter-in-law, Beatrice Scrope. The young woman carries the shield, marked by Luttrell heraldry, the sign of dynastic continuity. This was the armour which was later represented on his son Andrew's brass in the family's parish church of St Andrew's, at Irnham (Lincolnshire).

The work of war was tightly enveloped in myths of chivalry; the French wars encouraged the quest for fame among knights, the rise to knightly status among esquires, and the banding together of men during and especially after campaigns in a continuous invocation and reiteration of the moments of horror and glory. In some men it created the will to fight in other arenas, further afield. Henry Duke of Lancaster joined the efforts of the *reconquista* – the conquest of Muslim lands in Iberia by Christian fighters: he participated in the siege of Algeciras, and even in the seaborne attack on the city of Ceuta on the North African coast. Like Chaucer's Knight he also saw action in the north-east corner of Europe, in Estonia and Lithuania, as his grandson, Henry of Derby, Bolingbroke (later Henry IV), was to do.

Despite the ghastliness and danger of war, it could become a way of life, a quite intoxicating one. There was just enough glory and self-approbation in the wars in France to encourage those who needed it to seek justification in the culture of chivalry fostered in and around knightly families: Edward's war was aimed at defending his birthright, a just war. Yet the military orientation was not the only career path for able men. The years of the wars in France also saw the growing involvement of gentry families in administration and the judiciary. Knightly families invested in education and training which led their sons to administrative careers. Indeed, the absences which war forced upon the king, ministers and magnates, upon large sections of the armigerous class, created the need for focused thinking about provision of justice and collection of taxes in the counties. These years were also a period of experimentation and vigilance on the part of the Commons over the provision of law and order.

To be sustainable the French wars had to meet some of the expectations of the political communities of England and Wales. Rewards came in the form of war spoils, booty which flowed into the coffers and pockets of captains, and which also trickled down to lesser men. The booty had a way of making itself seen and known in the regions from which fighting men originated. Women boasted cushions, garments, hangings and jewellery which had previously adorned the persons or the chambers of French matrons. In March 1359 Robert Knolle captured Auxerre and was paid a ransom of 500,000 *moutons d'or* – the French gold coin, weighing 3.58 g – and 40,000 pearls to leave the city in peace. Successes were celebrated, and the king and his ministers insisted that news be spread far and wide. Such news – like the capture of the King of France, at Poitiers in 1356 – was announced at county courts, fairs and markets.

English lands saw no sustained occupation, no wartime brutality. This was perpetrated, indeed systematized by the men – high and low – who occupied and rode through France on *chevauchées*. During one of these infamous rides an army fed itself as it progressed, laying waste wide strips of country on either side of its route. The ride of Jean de Fauquemont through the Cambraisis in 1339 left a furrow thirty miles wide of burning and destruction in which no category of person or institution was spared – even children and pregnant women being reported as victims. When Pope Benedict XII heard of the devastation of summer 1339 he sent an official of the papal court to assess the damage. The survey resulted in the disbursement of 6,000 florins by the pope's bankers for distribution as alms in the affected areas.

The effect of such rides through the countryside is captured in the French poetry of Eustache Deschamps, and later in English, by Shakespeare. The words pronounced by the Duke of Burgundy in *Henry V* capture the earlier reality well:

> Alas, she [peace] hath from France too long been chased,
> And all her husbandry doth lie on heaps . . .
> Her vine, the merry cheerer of the heart,
> Unpruned dies.
>
> (*Henry V*, V. ii. 38–9, 41–2)

The most famous, and infamous, *chevauchée* was the ride of Edward Prince of Wales – the Black Prince – in the Garonne valley in late 1355 (Plate 6). In the company of four earls and many knights who were later rewarded and elevated by his father the king, he led a group of young warriors who wasted the French countryside. Their deeds have been immortalized in the words of Sir John Chandos's Herald:

> This noble prince of whom I speak
> Since the day he was born
> Thought of nothing but loyalty
> Openness, valour and virtue
> And he was adorned by prowess.*

When, after a ride of sixty-eight days which devastated nearly 7,000 square miles of Languedoc, they returned to Gascony in November 1355, they brought back booty which became legendary. They rested for the winter and spent the season of 1356 further north in Poitiers. Edward III had mobilized mightily his kingdom's war machine, and it was able to produce for the new season of fighting tens of ships, requisitioned from merchants and privateers by each sheriff in his county. To these were added 9,900 sheaves of arrows, 5,600 bows, hurdles and stalls to keep horses and pack animals safe during the passage – from Plymouth or Southampton or Sandwich – oats and fare for the crossing, and for the days until new provisions could be found in France. At the battle which ensued, King John II of France was taken prisoner together with several of France's greatest nobles. The effect of the devastation was deep and long-lasting. After Edward III burnt the suburbs of Paris in 1360 his fully armoured knights met and destroyed sixty Frenchmen armed with spears. In a letter of 1360 the poet Petrarch, who had favoured the English at the victory of Crécy, wrote:

They have reduced the entire kingdom of France by fire and sword to such a state that I, who had traversed it lately on business, had to force myself to believe that it was the same country I had seen before.

---

*   *Cil franc Prince dount je vous dye*
    Depuis le iour suil fuist nasquy
    Ne pensa forsque loiautee
    Ffranchise valour et bountee
    Et si fuist garniz de proesce.

These were some of France's darkest times.

News of the Black Prince's adventures travelled far. They even appeared in regional chronicles, such as that of the Grey Friars of Lynn, who also noted his return to England in the following year. On a grander scale, the English monastic chronicle, the *Eulogium historiarum*, apportioned to Edward and young Edward roles in contemporary apocalyptic prophecies. As if sensing their universal significance between 1356 and 1362, the monk recorded in great detail the Black Prince's deeds. The dynastic battles of the English assumed cosmic significance: they were interpreted as being tribulations marking the beginning of the antichrist's reign. Even Prince Edward was accordingly imagined as the future 'reforming emperor' of prophecies. The capture of King John of France was another sign that the world was in turbulence, an unstable and portentous state, full of millennial promise.

The Black Prince and his men were celebrated for another feat of military adventure in February 1367, with his departure in the company of 'good bold knights' to Spain to join his brother, John of Gaunt. There, at the battle of Nájera, they applied the tactics developed in France in support of the claimant to the Castilian throne, Pedro the Cruel. One of these good knights was Sir Richard Adderbury, who had served the Prince of Wales since 1330. He was typical of the parish gentry, men who rose through service as heads of small retinues, ultimately to be knighted. Adderbury's troop was small at first, four esquires and ten archers. The Black Prince understood the value of such men, and after the battle of Nájera Sir Richard was kept on as a retainer for life, at £40 a year, in war or peace.

The rides through the countryside and even the holding operation of garrisons gave captains great freedom of action. They impressed, seized and destroyed property, labour and lives. A simple example is the forced recruitment of labour in the port of Plavel by Thomas Dagworth, Lieutenant of Brittany in 1349, to unload a boat which carried Prince Edward's wine cargo. More damaging and brutal was the systematic capture and ransoming which developed in Normandy and Brittany. A particularly devastating form of exploitation developed through networks of protection which English captains spread over the parishes neighbouring their garrisons. The English garrison at Saint-Sauveur-le-Vicomte in the Cotentin in Normandy, left in place after the Treaty of Brétigny of 1360, was self-sufficient in income from ransoms paid regularly by 263 parishes, arrangements which the English coordinated with the French garrisons nearby. More mundane perhaps was John Fotheringay's establishment of a system of safe conducts in the portion of the Paris–Compiègne road which he controlled and which brought in vast income in the late 1350s.

Exploitation in the arena of war took the form not only of tribute, but of seizures of persons. An English squire, Jack Spore, took the ten-year-old Thenein Flamendeau captive after a raid on Saint-Julien-du-Sault, and when no one would ransom him turned him into his page. The boy had lost his freedom, and was now in service, which took him to Burgundy, Brittany and Spain before he returned to his village in 1368, knowing and known by no one. Women were supplied by local collaborators for the needs of garrisons; Robert Knolle's soldiers at Malicorne, a castle south-west of Le Mans, were supplied with girls by a local man called Guillaume Jeurbers. Periods of truce were clearly inconvenient for such activities, and so they sometimes prompted the movement of companies to other, more militarily active, areas. The companies which had ridden through Languedoc with ferocity were left idle and expectant after the Treaty of Brétigny came into force in 1360, and turned up in the 1360s and 1370s in Italy, terrorizing Lombardy, Tuscany and Apulia.

Contemporary writers were acutely aware of the horrors of war, some even placing it above the plague in the hierarchy of traumas. In the words of Thomas Brinton, Bishop of Rochester, armies go to war not with the prayers of the people, but with their curses. The wider implications of the brutalization of soldiers through the experience of conquest and occupation are hard to assess. In the companies on the move, menace and violence must have been exacerbated by the presence of hardened psychopaths, such as the forty-three murderers among the criminals pardoned for participation in the Black Prince's *chevauchée* from Calais to the Ile-de-France in 1370. What were such men like upon return to their homes and communities, men who had lived for years a brutal and violent life, who forced women into sexual slavery and took lives at will, outside the reach of the law, and directed by a camaraderie of complicity in violence? Ideals of chivalry and the realities of warfare were never further apart.

The nobility was expected to perform regularly and for long stretches at the pinnacle of military fitness: they not only led campaigns and supervised the recruitment and provisioning which preceded them, but often filled the governmental positions which followed from occupation. Most gentry families had members who had fought in the wars of Scotland or France, probably in their youth and for one or two campaigns (Plate 8). They then settled down to the work of estate management and local government. The young of such families, who trained at home and in regional tournaments, sought the opportunity for action, booty, and interaction with their peers, under the leadership of their lord or of a regional magnate. Interesting testimonies were garnered in the course of a chivalric dispute over heraldry during a relatively quiet period of the siege of Calais in 1346, a case adjudicated by the king himself. The evidence offered there reflects strong regional patterns of recruitment and training: the witnesses for Robert Morley, an East Anglian knight, remembered tournaments experienced in Bungay, Bury St Edmunds, Dartford, Dunstable and Thetford, and reflect a cohesive and loyal grouping around this famous knight, whose status was greatly enhanced by his performance in French battles. So much was he valued that, although the king was minded to favour his opponent in the heraldic dispute, he determined that Robert Morley, for his lifetime, wear the disputed device he so desired.

Such knights usually spent a limited if formative period on campaign. The lifetime of soldiery tended to be the choice of the non-knightly soldiers, men-at-arms and particularly archers, whose recruitment was also regionally specific, often from Cheshire, Lancashire and Wales. Professionalism developed in the art of war and in auxiliary occupations. Team activity characterized their work and, in the retinues of the mid-century, a continuity of training too. Thus the retinue – 160 men-at-arms and 140 mounted archers – of William de Bohun Earl of Northampton, who acted as Constable at Crécy, practised and perfected tactics from the Wear valley to the fields of France. On both the English and the French sides military surgery becomes increasingly prominent, with famous men serving in the field of battle: men such as John of Arderne and John of Gaddesden, author of *Rosa medicinae*. Arderne served on the Black Prince's campaign, where he treated the Prince's treasurer, Henry Blackburne. He composed a tract on surgery for haemorrhoids, a complaint suffered by men who rode long and hard on horseback. After periods of exertion came imposed rest for recuperation and healing: Sir Thomas Blount explained his absence from the famous adjudication of the Morley case during the siege of Calais by the need to recuperate in his tent after suffering an injury near Thérouanne.

The wars inspired distrust and prejudice towards groups hitherto tolerated and even welcomed. These were now seen as dangerous aliens: foreign monks and priests, foreign merchants, even pilgrims from the continent, who moved around the country, able to pass on information concerning the kingdom. An atmosphere of suspicion and exclusion led to acts of legislation which created procedures for arrest, expulsion or curtailment of freedoms. Innkeepers were enlisted in the service of the state, by reporting suspicious guests; bishops similarly had to report on the presence of foreign incumbents in the parishes of their dioceses. In 1362 the Burgundian physician John of Avence, whose whole career had been spent in London, decided to leave the country with his wife Mary because of the harassment they experienced. A potent mixture of anti-clerical sentiment and anti-foreigner feeling informed the treatment of non-English priests, friars and monks and was cynically exploited by the crown. In 1337 the alien priories on the Isle of Wight were seized by the crown and their monks forced to live inland and away from the sea. Edward III's Ordinance of Provisions of 1343 ruled that no papal letter or instrument which injured the king's interests could be introduced into England. In 1347 the Commons petitioned against the presentation of aliens – especially French cardinals of the papal court then residing in Avignon – to any ecclesiastical benefices. This was used to justify both the scrutiny of any person – often the protégé of a foreign prelate – admitted to an ecclesiastical living by papal appointment, and the request of a royal licence for any such appointment to stand.

Espionage was feared, as were economic warfare and the undermining of morale, and these were countered by policing and counter-espionage measures. Anxiety about spying was expressed repeatedly in parliamentary petitions. Edward III regularly used spies, ranging from retained 'explorers' and 'espies', to those rewarded occasionally for information given; thus in 1339 he sent messengers to explore the galleys in Norman ports. Esquires in the Great Company – a raiding troop of soldiers – sent news from Normandy: Roger Hilton and John de Newby earned £100 in this manner in 1370. The crown took pains to secure swift and safe crossing of the Channel in the war decades; a few days before each expedition it closed the ports to all passengers. Edward III's enemies also accepted spying as part of life in times of war; in 1359 the Dauphin pardoned men of the Burgundian town of Chitry for a double killing; the accused claimed in their defence that they had taken their victims to be spies from the English garrison.

The war was also a battle of colour and heraldics, often a struggle over the right to display the *fleur-de-lis*. When Sir John Chandos, Constable of Calais, rode to examine French positions on the eve of the battle of Poitiers (1356), he encountered the Marshal of France similarly occupied, wearing the same *fleur-de-lis*. The war of symbols affected strategy: Edward III besieged Reims in 1359 with the hope of being crowned in its cathedral, the traditional venue for the coronation of the kings of France. Dynastic awareness and ambition grew on both sides of the dynastic dispute: the title of *dauphin* was created by Charles V for his son born in 1368, the future Charles VI; just as the Black Prince had been granted a new principality, that of Gascony and Aquitaine, to join the Principality of Wales, which he had held since 1343 (Plate 2). The long contest between England and France was fought on several fronts: diplomatic, economic, military, symbolic.

EDWARD III'S PATRONAGE

Having come into his youthful inheritance through the blood of a *coup*, Edward III knew more than most the value of loyalty and friendship. In the first decades of his rule he sought both to neutralize potential enemies and to compensate and empower the men who had supported him in 1330. This could range from the minute business of maintaining the womenfolk of political opponents, such as Margaret le Despenser and her nurse, at Watton in Yorkshire since 1329, to the systematic offering of title and lands to the men who bonded with him on campaigns in Scotland and later in France.

During his minority Edward had wielded little political or patronage power. Mortimer appointed and dismissed royal officials – seven custodians of the Privy Seal and five treasurers of England in three years – and plundered the coffers in Westminster. Edward's control was aided initially by the surrender of lands by Isabella in December 1330 (in exchange for an annual income of £3,000), and of Mortimer's lands in the Marches. Although the king wisely kept most of his mother's lands intact, Mortimer's were widely distributed: William Montague received, as part of a £1,000 per annum land grant, the lordships of Denbigh, the cantreds (the Welsh equivalent of counties) of Rhos, Rhufoniog and Carmarthen, and the commote (a sub-division of a cantred) of Dinmael, as well as some of Isabella's lands in Hampshire, Berkshire and Kent. Royal favourites benefited in this redistribution:

Robert Ufford received in 1331 Gravesend (Kent) and Burgh (Norfolk) of Isabella's lands. The confiscated lands of French subjects in England were similarly brought into the pool of patronage: £100 worth of land was granted to Hugh de Audeley in 1337, land previously held by Robert de Stuteville in Eckington (Derbyshire).

The Principality of Wales was especially useful for the reward of loyal men. Its many offices, such as the Justiciarship of North Wales, went to royal favourites like Roger Mortimer of Chirk, Earl of March, grandson of the disgraced Roger Mortimer, Edward II's enemy. Edward III was careful about handling hereditary titles, but he boosted some old titles with panache, especially by creating dukes – Henry Duke of Lancaster, for example, in 1351. Only a few new earls were created: Thomas Dagworth, who died young in an ambush in Brittany in 1350, and in the 1350s some of the companions of the Black Prince, Reginald Cobham for example. There were several bannerets among his new men, some rewarded with that rank for acts of bravery in battle in the king's presence, like John Copeland, elevated for having captured King John at Poitiers. But even as he rewarded his loyal supporters, Edward was wary of granting them too firm and enduring a power-base, or of diminishing royal power in the process of reward. It was easier to stop the payment of an annuity than to recover a manor from a vassal who had fallen out of favour. When men were favoured by Edward they rose through the ranks of gentility and chivalry. Yet this was done in stages, not with the abandon and passion which had robbed Edward II of so much power and respect.

Many of the larger grants to his favourites were made for life alone: of 93 land grants only 41 were in fee, and 52 for a term or for life. Some received payment from the Exchequer for a number of years before a suitable manor became free, 'in expectation'. One of the most favoured was William de Clinton, who received 1,000 marks in land upon becoming the Earl of Huntingdon: 500 marks were produced by the manor of Kirton (Lincolnshire) and the rest was to flow from manors held for life by Queen Isabella and the Duchess of Pembroke. Until they reverted to him, the new earl was to receive 500 marks from the annual fees paid to the crown by the counties of Cambridgeshire, Huntingdonshire, Kent, the towns of Winchelsea, Rye and Sandwich and the manor of Higham (Sussex). Hugh de Audeley received in March 1337, upon his elevation to the earldom of Gloucester, £100 per annum, and in September received the manors of Kirkby-in-Ashfield (Nottinghamshire) and Eckington (Derbyshire), which produced £90, the remaining £10 being paid by the Exchequer until another source of income was found. As a reward for long service, Reginald de Cobham was granted an annuity in June 1337 worth 100 marks until lands became available. In March 1337 he had received the manor of Chippenham (Wiltshire) and the farm of Great Yarmouth (Norfolk), valued together at £119. The payments of alien (French) religious houses to secure their lands in England, such as 500 marks paid in 1340 by the Abbey of Fécamp, could similarly be made into an annuity for a royal favourite such as Thomas Bradeston. The collection of some of the incomes from the source – a port, a county's farm – was fraught with expense, effort and uncertainty.

Through his clerks of Chancery and Exchequer Edward cleverly controlled these grants, and the Exchequer became more of a clearing-house for payments between the crown and its servants than an accounting house for royal servants. Such clerical household staff benefited in turn from the many ecclesiastical livings which were in the king's gift. He gave his men opportunities to excel, marry well and improve their positions greatly, but not at the expense of royal wealth or with any ambiguity around loyalty. Edward managed his regalian rights over minors and unmarried aristocratic women without male relatives, and handed these rights to his favoured men. Here was another way of rewarding men with income and even with the prospect of an advantageous marriage: so in 1349, when the three-year-old son of William Welle, an heir to manors in Essex, Suffolk and Cambridgeshire, became the king's ward, his wardship was handed to Guy Brian. Seventy-five grants of land in wardship were made to the king's favourites: William Clinton, Richard Beauchamp, William Bohun, Guy Brian and others. To some it was a pleasing gift, but to those of lesser expectations it was an important step up the social ladder, especially when it resulted in a good marriage.

Edward managed men well, and some of his charisma clearly inspired his son Edward the Black Prince, who never attained the throne, but passed into legend as a chivalric icon. Edward III also came to terms with the memory of his troubled father, by granting gifts in 1343 to his tomb at Gloucester Cathedral, where an intermittent cult was in evidence.

PARLIAMENT AND ROYAL GOVERNMENT

Parliament came to play a growing role through the process of deliberation on taxation, the life-blood of royal military endeavours. Although it was an institution dependent on royal summons, a balance of consultation and persuasion developed under Edward III, which created an increasingly confident and activist Commons. Parliaments of Edward III's reign acquired procedures for action and an increasingly political character. The amount of business transacted in them grew and its composition was diversified; its petitions are fully recorded from 1327 onwards. It continued to combine three essential functions: firstly, it was the court of highest appeal, the court of peers and of state trials; secondly, it dealt with petitions presented by individuals and communities; thirdly, it was the forum for the deliberation of royal demands for taxation.

Inasmuch as the king summoned the members of its constituent parts – peers, Commons, and the clergy – to attend him at parliament at a place and time of his choosing, he defined a parliamentary knighthood separate from the other great landholders, the Lords, who still invigilate over legislation. Parliaments thus comprised those magnates obliged to offer counsel; secular and spiritual great lords; as well as representatives of the Commons – of knights and some towns. Summoned to present their petitions and to assent to taxation, the Commons developed skills and political acumen in tying taxation to other requests and needs which arose from the landed and mercantile communities. They were also an excellent source of information on the provinces, and regularly reported on sensitive issues such as the mood in the Welsh Marches or the Borders. By the 1340s there was habitual 'intercommuning' – joint discussion and consultation – between the Lords and the Commons, usually through the presence of a number of Lords in the Commons' debates on taxation. This could also work the other way; in 1348 members of the Commons were invited to join the Lords in discussion of recent trailbastons – ordinances or commissions against violent criminals – appointed especially during periods when kings were distracted by military affairs.

From 1340 the clergy were summoned to Convocation separately, and no longer sent their representatives to the Commons. Bishops continued to form a large section of the peerage: in 1341 Edward III had summoned 51 prelates, 8 earls and 45 barons, whereas in 1377 he summoned 46 prelates, 13 earls and 47 barons. Those summoned could not always attend parliament: episcopal registers from the north of England abound in letters apologizing for absence during seasons of Scottish raids. Bishop John Kirkby of Carlisle wrote in February 1337 that he could not appear since all the churches in his diocese were being attacked by the 'Scottish enemies', a reference to Andrew Murray's initiative in regaining the Scottish counties in 1336 and 1337. In the crisis of 1341, John of Stratford, Archbishop of Canterbury, incurred the king's wrath. He warned in a letter that bad counsel had been the unmaking of Edward's own father, had marked the beginning of Edward's own reign, and threatened to lose him the hearts of his people and his rightful authority (*emprise*). According to one chronicler, he said:

And, sire, let it displease you not, you may remember it in your own time; for by the evil counsel which our lord your father . . . made seize, against the law of his land . . . and what happened to him for that cause, you, sire, do know.

Thus a moral and political critique developed in parliament, a language of cajoling and persuasion. Unpredictable, parliament was often a dangerous occasion, but without it royal enterprises on a large scale could not be achieved.

As parliaments were summoned more frequently and came to play a significant role in a wide range of governmental and economic decisions, a professional group emerged: parliamentary representatives who were re-elected, or successively elected, by two or three (usually adjacent) counties. The fortunes of war and royal need affected the composition of parliament: in 1340, a demanding war year, Edward III's writs of summons requested that belted knights only be returned to parliament. Such men, veterans of the wars in Scotland and France, were indeed prominent in his early parliaments. Richard Mounchessy (d. 1342), elected to parliament for Hertfordshire eleven times between 1320 and 1336, had seen action in Scotland and France and was singled out for expert consultancies. In 1341 he was asked to determine responsibility in the loss of a tariff ship in Sluys, and to advise on measures against pillaging of royal ships. Sir Stephen Bassingbourne (d. 1350) of Astwick (Hertfordshire), who sat in seven parliaments between 1335 and 1348 and served in Gascony, was used in 1339 to raise the array of arms, and as keeper of the peace in between his periods as representative in parliament. Members representing towns often possessed mercantile and legal expertise, which incorporated complex loyalties. John Parles was a lawyer of Colchester (Essex), active in the royal courts and as representative in at least eleven parliaments. The combination of military experience with knowledge of local government and of the system of justice recommended such men as reliable representatives. Their petitions expressed the sentiment of a county's middling land-holders, but they could also offer a useful critique of royal and noble proposals.

A more legislative tone came to inform the business of parliaments in Edward III's later years. Royal officials and ministers busied themselves in preparation for parliament, and summons had to be sent out at least forty days in advance. Here the involvement of justices in the wording of legislation is increasingly notable, as it is in the drafting of responses to petitions. This involvement carried over to the aftermath of legislation: justices were confronted in the courts with questions about the interpretation of laws which 'they had made'. There were growing areas of the law that king and Commons interpreted differently, and over which the king and his judges might differ. In 1355 the judges of King's Bench, Common Pleas, Barons of the Exchequer and the serjeants-at-law all insisted before the king that no change could be made to statute, except with the agreement of parliament. A growing role was played in the Commons by non-armigerous gentry. These were men whose prominence resulted from their service to the crown, from their manifold roles as brokers of patronage, arbiters and experts in law and procedure.

Where the opening speech in parliament in the early fourteenth century tended to be given by a chief justice, from 1362 this was offered by the chancellor. Gaining in gravity of tone, the speech presented draft legislation and general statements of intent. Thus the institution that had mediated the deposition of the king in 1327 was developing interestingly into an indispensable and complex assembly, fairly sensitive to the array of political wishes and complaints harboured by the landed people of England, and by some in the Principality of Wales. Even as the political tenor of its deliberations was enhanced, parliament did not cease to be a venue for the airing of private grievances in petitions by individuals, by corporations, arising from conflicts between individuals, between corporations, between an individual and a corporation, and involving men, women, religious houses and towns. Hundreds of such petitions were brought to each parliament, creating a plethora of discussions, arbitrations, and in a few cases leading to the creation of statute law. Whereas the Lordship of Ireland possessed its own parliament in Dublin, Irish policy was still the business of the English parliament, as were Irish finances, operated through the Dublin Exchequer, but scrutinized at Westminster. The resulting information was copied and distributed. At his first parliament the king acceded to the Commons' request to circulate the resulting statutes far and wide. Upon return from the York parliament of 1332 the representative for Leicester reported his news to the town's burgesses, his tongue loosened by their wine. Similarly, King's Lynn (Norfolk) and Bridport (Dorset) incorporated parliamentary reports into their archives. Parliamentary business reflected local interests, and with its growing importance in the political life of the realm it could provide precedent for future political action.

The politics of England – and to some extent that of Wales and Ireland too – achieved a clamorous and public realization in parliament. Many of the petitions which reached it expressed discontent with the elaborate system of devolved government performed through local institutions of the shire. There almost any free man could come in touch with justices and coroners, bailiffs and foresters. The system of justice in the counties was a combination of the procedures initiated by local men appointed as justices of the peace and by *ad hoc* royal commissions appointed to hear and determine (*oyer et terminer*) cases. Central appointment of commissioners was a tradition bequeathed by Edward II, who used the method in order to deal with severe disorder, which was often related to periods of political instability during his reign. Thus in February 1332 an ex-junior justice of King's Bench, Sir Richard Willoughby, was sent to arrest and punish members of the Folville gang who had plagued Leicestershire with abductions, robberies and murders. The 1330s saw some experimentation with the appointment of local justices of the peace under the supervision of magnate commissions of keepers of the counties in 1332 and keepers of the peace in 1336, and the establishment of a trailbaston in 1338. But magnates still retained 'friendly' justices, who then provided their men with pardons for heinous lawlessness. Petitions to parliament continued to urge powers of keeping the peace being granted to those who were local in origin and able to act fast and with relatively autonomous powers, just as they sought to have local men, rather than outsiders, elected as sheriffs.

Under Edward III the challenge to order became acute during decades which saw a large number of magnates and knights – the natural providers of deterrence and judgement, though often also the most unruly – away at war, just as the king and ministers were frequently absent. Hence the creation of trailbastons – the special commissions appointed to deal with specific outbreaks of criminality and disorder in a region – which characterized the first three decades of Edward III's reign. Such national and county trailbastons were sometimes interrupted, as in 1336, when officials turned to deal with preparations for war. The knights who served in local courts were also crucial to the effort of assessment and recruitment in the shires. The men who offered themselves as natural peacekeepers were the very figures who possessed the knowledge of local resources and the networks for mobilization of men and materials during concerted preparation for war. With the growth in the confidence of the Commons in parliament in the 1340s came the pressure there for provision of justice and peace in the counties, voiced strongly in 1341 and in 1346. This argument gained strength since to the habitual business of the courts were now added cases of deserting archers, war profiteers and, from 1350, the enforcement of the Statute of Labourers. From 1351 king and council appointed justices of the peace, who ultimately were also to hear labour cases. Parallel to this development was the Commons' pressure to ensure that sheriffs were local men. Above this local provision, assizes of royal justices still itinerated and the King's Bench did its business, but the land-holders in the shires were able to determine a considerable amount of local legal business, thus augmenting their own influence and creating a dense array of reciprocities.

By mid-century there were three royal writing offices which produced thousands of documents each year: Chancery, which was the chancellor's office (including Exchequer payments and disbursement and liaison with sheriffs), Privy Seal (representing the king's and council's authority) and Signet (private instruments related to the king's household, sometimes called Wardrobe). A growth of business by bill is in evidence, as a form of communication with justices, by which the king's will and his duty to provide justice were expedited. Although landed people seem to have been involved continuously in litigation, what is most striking about England and the Englishries – areas of Wales in which people of English descent settled and lived by English law – is just how secure titles were. Through marriages of heiresses the landed class incorporated professional men, soldiers and lawyers into gentry and noble networks. Alongside the operations of common law in local courts and King's Bench, a Chancery court was also developing, providing yet another remedy for those who could not find equity within the forms of evidence and procedure recognized by common law. The chancellor conducted his court as a court of conscience, which usually met at Westminster Hall, representing the king's role as giver of justice notwithstanding legal convention. Chancery grew as it responded to petitions from most counties of England, though not Wales, in remedy of debt, in settling of complex enfeoffments and breaches of promise.

THE CLERGY AND ITS USES

Growth in royal administration required a constant flow of adequately trained and suitably motivated personnel. Already Edward II had displayed awareness of the need to provide training and channels of recruitment. Men of the court, such as the queen's chaplain Robert of Eglesfield, followed that example, with the foundation of Queen's College at Oxford in 1341. In the following decades college foundation became quite a fashion, with the initiatives of a variety of patrons: rich widows such as Elizabeth de Clare, who founded Clare Hall at Cambridge in 1326, or Marie de St Pol Countess of Pembroke, who founded Valence Mary Hall, Cambridge (later Pembroke College) in 1347, with guidance from Edmund Gonville, Bishop of Norwich; or activist bishops such as William Bateman, Bishop of Norwich, papal judge and royal ambassador, who emphasized training in canon and Roman law, at Gonville Hall in 1348 and Trinity Hall in 1350. As opportunities allowed, Bishop Bateman confirmed the appropriation of parishes in his diocese and their livings to these new institutions: Foulden, Wilton and Mutford to Gonville Hall, Saxthorpe to Pembroke Hall in 1354, and to his own foundation a string of churches among which were Briston, Kimberley, Brinningham, Wood Dalling, Cowlinge and Stalham. Universities increasingly attracted monks to higher study, and religious orders maintained halls for the use of their members in Cambridge and Oxford. In this they were led by papal policy, which required that Benedictine monasteries support 5 per cent of their members in university study. Some monks must have felt out of place in the bustling towns: Uthred of Boldon, monk of Durham, received his doctorate in theology at Oxford, but lamented its 'excessive intellectualism' at the expense of spiritual progress.

Much of the talent which went into making Edward III's court and administration was managed by highly educated men, royal servants, in priestly orders. On the one hand, England had a strong, confident crown which insisted on an English tradition by which the prelates were important magnates in the land, and according to which issues of taxation of the clergy, provision for ecclesiastical courts and patronage were settled between the king and his bishops. But England was also precocious in managing the usual tasks of ecclesiastical administration. Pronouncements of the ecumenical councils overseen by popes, new collections of canon law, newly created liturgical feasts and practices, all reached England quickly and were absorbed effectively through the working of an ecclesiastical administration which linked prelates to parish priests and thus to parishioners in town and country. Church courts in England, Wales and the Lordship of Ireland were similarly developed, well-staffed and active in the business of marriage litigation, probate of wills, detection of religious error, defamation and blasphemy.

Prelates advised kings and served as chancellors more frequently than did laymen. They were trusted diplomats whose lack of overwhelming dynastic ambition, as well as their education, recommended them for royal service. For more modest men work was cut out in the parishes, where the complexities of life demanded definition and remedies within the boundaries of liturgy, sacraments and instruction. Bishops were involved in administration, diplomacy and even medicine. This versatility was always fraught with tension and the subject of criticism, even danger. When Archbishop Stratford was blamed for the inadequacy of government in 1341 Edward is said to have declared that men holding high office 'if convicted of corruption could be tortured, hung and beheaded'. This was quite unlike the case of priests.

Clerics of all orders were immune from such accountability, since they could not be tried by the courts of common law. Even more complicated was the fate of those who held high office through papal patronage: the Dominican Thomas de Lisle, Bishop of Ely, had begun his career in royal diplomatic service, but he was taken up by Pope Clement VI, who appointed him to the see of Ely in 1345. There he became embroiled in a dispute over property in Huntingdonshire with Blanche, widow of Thomas Lord Wake of Liddell, and mobilized with impunity a gang of thugs who perpetrated arson and murder in furtherance of his claim. Here is an extreme case, which none the less demonstrates the disorder in lives of local communities and modest folk which followed from the realities of overlapping jurisdictions and clerical immunity from secular prosecution.

In their absence on royal or papal business bishops relied upon professional administrators, men trained in canon and civil law who managed the wide range of business covered by canon law and episcopal authority. These men provided the legal underpinning for the actions and choices of laity and clergy alike: when the rector of Fledborough (Nottinghamshire) wished to go on pilgrimage to Santiago de Compostela in 1334, he had to apply for permission to leave his parish. When in 1331 Agnes and Geoffrey Luttrell, scions to prosperous knightly families, chose to inform the bishop that they were relatives in the third degree – that is, second cousins – it was his official who had to formulate the stipulation that their marriage be recognized despite the impediment. In 1330 he had been called to order the enforcement of the payment of alimony by William del Clay of Markham to Beatrice, daughter of John the Spencer of Upton, for the children he had with her – £5 a year.

Ecclesiastical law intervened at important moments of kinship and social relations. It also had a disciplinary edge, seeking out trouble through episcopal visitations or through the information networks of rural deans, who presided over deanery courts, into which the jurisdiction of a large province like York was divided. At the archiepiscopal manor of Thorp in 1330 Thomas of St Albans, rector of Misterton and holder of a prebend from Durham Cathedral, abjured his mistress Alice Misterton, with whom he lived in the village, promising never to know her again on pain of losing his livings. Similar accommodation had to be made with the vagaries of monastic lives: in 1329 brother Roger de Mar was allowed to rejoin Shelford Abbey (Nottinghamshire), from which he had absconded, reversing the excommunication which had been imposed on him. Episcopal courts were thus a service which not only the high but also the very modest approached either as supplicants or witnesses, and could leave as vindicated victims or as chastised wrongdoers.

The church enabled and circulated a formidable array of teaching, preaching and supervision, devices by which it sought to inform, inspire and correct the lives of parishioners for the profit of their souls and the enhancement of peace and even justice. There was bound to be a chasm between the pronouncements of theologians and canon lawyers, on the one hand, and the perceptions and formulations appropriate for transmission in parishes, on the other. Parishes differed greatly in size, in wealth, and in the degree of sophistication of their priests and congregations. Bishops aspired to provide simple and useful, above all correct and accessible teaching material to assist the work of priests and to make teaching uniform. Take, for example, the initiative of Archbishop Thoresby of York, who around 1357 created a catechism in English for the laity, one which was marked with Latin rubrics for the use of priests. Here was a booklet which adhered to the accepted framework of belief which all Christians had to know – the Lord's Prayer (*pater noster*) and the Creed – and which described the moral operations of the five senses, the Ten Commandments, the seven sacraments and the works of mercy. Archbishop Thoresby's catechism was in turn transmitted to the diocesan clergy after its approval at the annual synod. Henceforward parishioners in Yorkshire were taught from it, through its combination of doctrinal pronouncement, explanation and mnemonic ditties, which remained with people long after they left the church.

Greater depth was provided by Latin texts which aimed to fortify the priest's own understanding. Only a minority of parish priests acquired specialized university education, but many had a basic Latin education, which could be gained in the grammar schools of most towns. It was for them that a work such as William of Pagula's *Oculus sacerdotis* (*The Priest's Eye*) was written, with simple summaries of weighty theological and canonical discussions. Such works were not condescending but practical, and although a very expensive manuscript when complete, sections of *The Priest's Eye* were often excerpted, copied out in parts, a digest of useful material at a more modest cost. Priests' wills habitually listed works such as *The Priest's Eye* among books bequeathed to colleagues or relatives, other men of the cloth.

Formative social relations and central events of the life-cycle were experienced, attested and remembered in the parish. Marriage was not always celebrated in church, but rules of Christian marriage crystallized by the late twelfth century. They became widely known, and were used knowingly by men and women. The ideal was marriage celebrated before witnesses at the church door, but the binding element was the exchange of vows. The exchange of words and a token between consenting people of canonical age was a simple act, all too easily committed.

It is, therefore, not surprising that so many cases ended up in the courts. Seeking to make good her marriage to John of Bristol, Agnes Huntington arranged for a former worker in the household, Margaret Foxholes, with whom she had shared a bed, to bear witness to the exchange of promises of marriage in 1339. People were aware of what made a marriage, and also of how it might be dissolved. In 1342 Alice, widow of Walter of Kirkbride, was claimed by Sir Thomas Lengleys as his wife, but she sued for divorce in the Bishop of Carlisle's court, on account of cruelty, seeking to be separated from him. Higher up the social scale, Katherine, daughter of Sir Ralph Paynell, approached the church court of Lincoln with the complaint that her husband Nicholas Cantilupe had used force and abducted her. In the background was her claim that he was impotent (she could not find his genitals), a claim he denied. This led him to abduct Katherine and her servants to Greasley Castle in Nottinghamshire, using force to extract an oath that he was indeed sexually potent. This dramatic case between informed and privileged individuals is one among hundreds brought to the courts every year. The Bishop of Rochester's court heard seventy-five cases in eleven court sessions in 1363–4: forty-eight on fornication, seventeen on adultery, and one on brutality. Since marriage could be transacted even without public solemnization, many cases dealt with clandestine unions: about 80 per cent of marriage cases heard by the Bishop of Ely's court between 1374 and 1382 dealt with such unions.

Ecclesiastical courts also dealt with actions deemed to be breaches of charity, especially defamation and harmful magic. In 1346 in the diocese of Lincoln the parish priest of Friesthorpe sued John Joliff for claiming that many of the priest's patients died following medical treatment at his hands. In 1363 Philip Russel of the village of East Greenwich was presented to the church court of Rochester for working magic on his sheep; he hung around their necks a little purse containing a frog, to cure their scabies. For this he was caned three times in the market-place and was enjoined to perform penance. A deanery court in Lincolnshire mentioned a woman suspected of magic who was tried in each of its sessions of 1338 and 1340. The dividing line between local cures and magic was a thin one, but only the few who blatantly crossed it attracted heavy-handed attention by the courts.

Priests' responsibilities were many and wide-ranging when undertaken with commitment: theirs was the care of the chancel, an area of the church increasingly adorned with stained glass and wall-paintings, like the enchanting arrangement in glass of *c*.1320–40, still to be seen in the parish church of Eaton Bishop (Herefordshire) (Plate 4), or the impressive cycle of paintings depicting the Life of Christ and the Assumption of the Virgin (the parish's patron saint) in Chalgrove (Oxfordshire) of *c*.1350. In absence or neglect not only did pastoral care suffer, but material provision did so too. In 1341 the executors of the rector of Adisham (Kent) were required to compensate the parish for the deceased's neglect of the chancel. In the same year the vicar of Rainham (Kent) was accused of using the juice of berries rather than wine at communion.

The ability to engage with such cases and to provide reassuring and authoritative guidance depended on the presence in parishes of suitably trained and convincing priests. All this provision was of no effect when the crucial link between bishop and parishioner – the parish priest – was absent or ineffectual. Bishops attempted to enforce canonical requirements for suitable replacement of priests when they were absent on pilgrimage or on university study. This was never an easy task, and the reality of pluralism was rife. Master Roger Ottery explained his pluralism in 1366: he held six livings, of which five were sinecures, and he claimed that a diligent man could serve his parish while holding other responsibilities. As a graduate in law, he served the Bishop of Hereford, and was suitably rewarded. There was real competition for skilled educated clerks like him. In 1342 the parishioners of St Mary, Carlisle, complained directly to the Chapter at York, over the Bishop of Carlisle's head, that for many years they had had no parish priest, and were served by an unsatisfactory locum. Desiring to have a 'perpetual and vigilant minister', they appealed for help. In defence the Bishop of Carlisle complained that he had much other pressing business; indeed he and his predecessors had been deeply involved in managing a ravaged diocese during the period of the Scottish raids. Parishioners desired a stable and predictable parochial provision for Sunday preaching, baptism, confession, penance and comfort to the sick and dying. They often complained, and sought justice by turning to bishops' courts and exalted patrons.

People appreciated the provision of parochial services, and were quick to recognize the limitations of priests unsuitable in manner, education or life-style. They may have wondered whether the man they knew to be deficient as a neighbour could fulfil the promise of the sacrament at the altar, and turn bread and wine into Christ's flesh and blood. Could his rough hands and faltering Latin transmit the grace which erases the traces of original sin from a newborn babe and makes it into a member of the Christian body? Such thoughts need not have led to a fundamental crisis of faith. In England there were as yet no widespread alternative theologies and churches, but rather a practical scepticism about the clergy, about the role of good works, a vein of doubt which surfaced frequently, and especially in moments of crisis. The church worked long and hard to explain and allay such doubts in works such as the accessible *Lay Folks' Catechism* or the *Lay Folks' Mass Book*, in strings of exemplary and accessible tales which were inserted into sermons, and in the constant efforts to make the spectacle of liturgy reinforce the truths which underpinned it. This was a continuous struggle on the part of the church, which also explains why new feasts, such as the feast of Corpus Christi, were promoted so warmly. Promulgated on the continent in 1317, by the mid-fourteenth century this celebration of the eucharist was a ubiquitous spectacle of summer open-air festivity which exemplified orthodoxy and encouraged participation.

The desire for a trained clergy entailed long periods when they were absent and, as importantly, required a deflection of funds from use in the parish to support in a university town. The administrative machine of Norwich diocese was clearly hard at work devising ways of spreading personnel and resources: modest religious houses were allowed to divert income from parishes in their patronage to their own daily use. Creative solutions were authorized: the family chantry at Thompson (Norfolk), founded by Sir Thomas Shardelowe and his brother in 1350, was allowed to serve the parish's needs. In big cities the problem was an abundance of overlapping claims for the attention of believers. In 1328 the Archbishop of York arbitrated between the Carmelite friars of the city and the rector of St Crux church, with a resolution that required the friars to remove an attractive statue of the Virgin and cease holding public services, since these drew parishioners away from St Crux parish, to the detriment of the priest and the parish's income.

The parish church was the centre of community life, and the venue for personal and collective worship. The pinnacle of the ritual year was reached, following Lent, in Holy Week and Easter communion. There was a proliferation of activities in age groups, in fraternities, around special altars and their saints, which allowed further devotions and social interactions to take place. Beyond the parish, people went on pilgrimage, both clerics and lay people, and pilgrimage as far as the Holy Land was not unknown. Rome was an especially desirable destination during the jubilee year of 1350, for which special indulgences were granted. For most people pilgrimage was a local affair, to celebrate and benefit from local shrines and memorials to holiness. Around St Edmund's chapel at Sailholme, Wainfleet St Mary (Lincolnshire), a number of miracles were recorded, involving deliverance from the dangers of seafaring. A group of sailors off the sea at Skegness appealed to St Edmund when their craft was caught up in a storm: when they were saved they offered a wax ship as a votive sign of their thanks. People treasured souvenirs of their journeys, and there flourished an industry of pilgrim badges to be worn pinned to cloaks or hats, of which hundreds have survived.* The most numerous surviving badges are from the shrines of Our Lady at Walsingham and Thomas Becket in Canterbury. Although most experiences of the holy were sought in local places and through familiar artefacts, occasionally the styles of other regions impinged dramatically on the mundane: in 1349 a group of 120 flagellants – penitents who scourged their bodies with whips, and spread their message through public display and itineration – arrived in London from Zeeland and Holland, an unusually enthusiastic and macabre scene.

People recognized and rewarded holiness around them: they supported those who undertook particularly demanding religious lifestyles. The king granted a modest budget to the hermit Geoffrey de Bolton in 1328, and charged him with filling in the pits in a road near Doncaster. Here were combined hard work for the common good, and God's work 'out of charity'. Although for most people adherence to the routine of the parish sufficed, they made use of the spiritual athletes among them, seeking example and wisdom. The fourteenth-century Welsh anchorite of Llanddewi-Brefi composed a summary of theological and pastoral writings for his patron Gruffydd ap Llewellyn ap Phylip ap Trahaearn of Cantref Mawr (Carmarthenshire). People worshipped saints, but also detected holiness in those closer to them: in 1334 Bishop Kirkby of Carlisle allowed the Abbot of Shapey, near Appleby (Cumbria) to exhume the body of Isabel, wife of William Langlays of Appleby, from her tomb, and to have it buried in a 'more suitable place' because of her honourable life and conduct, suitable for the veneration which the bishop wished to promote. More modestly, within the con-

---

* The Museum of London has an excellent collection of badges on display.

fines of a home, in the state of widowhood which granted women relative autonomy over body and resources, daily life could be made into virtuous endeavour. Some women chose to intensify their attendance at church, pray at home and move to a vegetarian diet. The use of sacred materials and prayers became a habit which led to a certain capacity for spiritual self-help.

THE KINGDOM'S PARTS

The power to pronounce messages and display images was increasingly appreciated by the crown, just as the gentry recognized the importance of patronage and display within the churches on their estates. The Scottish and then the French wars presented the crown with challenges of communication and persuasion. Kings had to keep their subjects, and especially the ranks of the Commons, who were increasingly empowered in parliament, informed about successes, warned about setbacks, and in touch with the necessity that forced the king to fight in France for his own dynastic rights and, increasingly, for the safety of his realm. From the 1330s writs brought royal communications, first to the shires and then to the parishes, where they could reach everyone. The news of the lifting of the siege of Berwick (1333), of the victories of Sluys (1340), Crécy (1346) and Poitiers (1356) and the exotic news of the victory won by John of Gaunt in the Castilian dynastic wars, the battle of Nájera (1367), was announced in parishes.

The challenges of this extended realm were many and varied. The military effort which the crown chose to concentrate in France also had implications for arrangements for security in other parts of the realm. In the Irish Lordship the earlier part of the century had seen attempts to use levies of fighting men – or scutage, a payment in lieu – to support the seasonal, small-scale yet continuous display of might which the government had to perform. Between 1326 and 1360 some £200 was raised per annum from scutage, a not inconsiderable sum in the Irish arena. Contributions were spread more widely on the basis of a schedule of arms related to wealth: in 1333 the inhabitants of county Dublin were assessed for arms although warfare took place in distant border zones. Once the French front was opened, the crown attempted to minimize expenditure on Ireland and to make its rule as self-financing as possible: funding the Lordship's retinues came to reflect the complex social and political relations which bound the Anglo-Irish aristocracy and its Gaelic-Irish counterpart.

The English parliament envisaged Ireland as an extension of the kingdom, sharing a single set of laws, but with some administrative peculiarities, like those which characterized the Gascon and Welsh Marches. Yet while English Ireland was governed by English rule, protection and aspiration, it was clearly populated by two people: the English 'liege' and the Irish, separate by race, language and culture. The Gaelic Irish were perceived as savage, and were the subject of fantasies long held by English communities when encountering societies of pastoralists – as was the case with the Welsh – with different kinship structures, language and values. The Statutes of Kilkenny were presented by the Irish parliament of 1366, which was presided over by the Duke of Clarence, Edward III's son. It legislated distinctions between the ethnic groups: like more modern racial systems it aimed to keep groups apart through prohibition of marriage and sexual contacts. Henceforward only the English – born in England or in Ireland – were considered the king's subjects. This group was distinguished by its attire, and the laws which regulated its land tenure, work and trade. Here was an attempt to nurture those who did not 'go native' by privileging adherence to a notional set of English moral and social characteristics. Like all such systems the statutes created personal tragedies, were hard to enforce, indeed were risible in their attempts to contain very fluid social relations. Contemporary observers, such as John Clyne in the Kilkenny annals, noted that the English in Ireland spoke a different idiom of English. None the less, the law did create categories: of title to land, of access to royal patronage and of urban self-government.

Retinues in Ireland, like those raised in England, tended to be made of men-at-arms (on horseback), hobelars (light cavalry) and infantry. Sometimes general assessments were used to raise arms, like that of 1333 on the burgesses of Dublin; at other times service was commuted into payment, a custom well established by mid-century, and the income was used to pay soldiers. In 1352 the town supplied 160 troops for six months; in 1358 county Kilkenny paid for 262 men. In Irish retinues the hobelar element tended to be much larger, fitted to rougher terrain and to the challenges of cattle rustling. Whereas an Irish tradition of foot-archers was well established, Irish retinues came to be influenced by technological development in the English army with the introduction, after 1337, of the longbow. The justiciar's retinue came to depend on the companies which followed his Anglo-Irish magnates, and these could draw from near and far within existing affinities. Companies of foot-soldiers, known as *kerns* – familiar from *Macbeth* as 'skipping kerns' or 'wretched kerns' – hired for low wages by contract, accompanied Gaelic and Anglo-Irish lords alike. The Gaelic element in the justiciars' retinues of the mid-century could number around half or more. Contacts with the Gaelic-Irish were created through the mediation of the Anglo-Irish aristocracy. The Butler Earls of Ormond (with lands spanning south Leinster and east Munster) could mobilize a large number of Anglo-Irish gentry as well as raise *kerns* from Kilkenny and Tipperary; in the 1350s the O'Kennedys of Ormond first appear as recipients of pay during royal expeditions, clearly through the mediation of their Ormond protector.

New arrivals to Ireland were often shocked to witness the degree of involvement of Gaelic-Irish troops in the crown's military efforts to secure its rule. Far from remaining separate, Gaelic Irish and English Irish developed complex institutions, characteristic of border zones: customs which regulated ransoming, parleys and negotiation were at the core of cohabitation in Ireland. Government sought to define clearly demarcated areas of peace or war, but on the ground men like Maurice son of Thomas, future Earl of Desmond (d. 1356), regularly negotiated with Irish leaders. Even the justiciars were implicated in rituals aimed at defusing incipient violence: when Donal son of Art MacMurdharha claimed the title of King of Leinster he was imprisoned in Dublin Castle, but by 1335 the same man was fighting with Edward III in Scotland, and for his hegemony among his clan Art's successor was recognized as a 'MacMurrough' chief.

The histories, myths and memories of Gaelic Ireland became part of the cultural world of the Anglo-Irish aristocracy. They patronized bards, Gaelic poets who employed native metre and themes, in eulogies and panegyrics. To their Anglo-Irish patrons such poets could ascribe courage, strength, love of country and generosity. In the lament for Richard de Burgh, the 'Red Earl of Ulster' (d. 1326), the anonymous bard mourned the fact that he had not died with his lord. Gaelic musicians were offered patronage: in 1329 John Bingham, Lord of Louth, employed the tympanist Maolruanaidh MacCeabhaill. In both Ireland and Wales men wrote with enthusiasm of the king's exploits: as did John Clyn of Kilkenny in his annals about the deeds of Edward in Scotland and France, or Iolo Goch in his eulogy for Edward III.

The reality of common warfare, interdependence and mutual authorization which these complex affinities could breed was clearly matched by personal and symbolic relations which newcomers from England found incomprehensible, indeed reprehensible. In 1357 Edward III confessed in his ordinances for Ireland that in the past he had failed to provide appropriate defences and justice. He acknowledged that careless neglect had characterized the early years of his reign, when some men were sent to Ireland more to grasp than to remedy. Theirs was a separate identity but they were loyal to the crown. A political class that was Anglo-Irish evolved; an ethos of the Irish Bench was also emerging, many of its members having been trained in law in England. Such men reminded Edward III of his duties to Ireland in messages sent by the great council at Kilkenny in 1360, describing the parlous state of the king's lands and lieges there. In response, Edward III sent his son Clarence to Ireland in the following year. This expensive campaign marked a new high level of expenditure which lasted for the rest of his reign, of some £91,000, with only a small part paid by the Irish Exchequer.

The Anglo-Irish developed a strong sense of their links to the polity and exhibited wounded pride when the kings showed less interest and exertion than they deemed appropriate. The Anglo-Irish magnates held little land outside Ireland, and were closely bonded by kinship and mutual exertions and almost constant warfare. Such group identity never developed to the same extent among Marcher lords, who had lands and business and patrimonial lands outside Wales. Yet there was a greater integration of Welshmen into the activities of the crown. A sizeable part of royal contingents in the wars, about half of the infantry of England between 1280 and 1350, was recruited in Wales. The Welsh counties were exempt from parliamentary taxation, and although they were hard pressed by the demands of the administration in the Principality and the demands of the Marcher lords, many Welshmen saw in the wars an opportunity. Far from the counties bordering on the Channel, away from war taxation, enjoying the benefits of employment and rewards of war, an involved and enthusiastic attitude to Edward's wars developed in some circles in Wales. Welsh captains could make a name and a fortune, as did Sir Gruffydd Llwyd (d. 1335) and Llewellyn ap Madog (d. 1343). Inasmuch as royal presence was so much rarer, and never in the form of direct rule, the patronage which bonded men like Llewellyn Gruffydd to Edward III was rarely exercised in Ireland.

Magnates played that role instead in Ireland, with intricate affinities, and even marriage alliances with native Irish families.

EDWARD III AND CHIVALRY

In the midst of the hectic activities of their courts kings were lonely figures. The young Edward III attempted to break through to those who had supported him and whose support he would always need. He cherished his nobles: restoring some who were sullied by the events of 1330, and creating new ones among his favourites. When, in the enthusiasm of the successful war years, he created the most exclusive club of chivalry and loyalty to the crown – the Order of the Garter – he aimed to balance new valour with old title. Granted its statutes in 1348 and probably already in place on the eve of the battle of Crécy in 1346, the new brotherhood included his closest advisers: it exalted among its twenty-six members knightly status and chivalric accomplishment. Dedicated to God, the Virgin, St George and Edward the Confessor, the Order met annually on St George's feast-day at Windsor Castle for a three-day assembly. The chapel there was rebuilt as the Order's own chapel, and St George's Day 1349 was celebrated there; the members' cloaks blended with the altar-hangings with their matching garter theme. The Garter was not a royal retaining badge; its rhetoric transcended royal politics and parties, even as it strengthened loyalty to the monarch as chivalrous warlord. It mobilized noble interest in the war, and loyalty to the king who provided the occasion for valour to shine and profit to grow.

The French war is all-important in the early conception of the brotherhood: its Garter of gold and blue displayed France's colours, and its first members were the band of knights who supported the king in his wars. Edward III ensured that princes were initiated early into the prestigious club: his three sons, John of Gaunt, Lionel of Clarence and Edmund of Langley, were elected in 1360 at the ages of twenty-two, twenty and eighteen respectively (the Black Prince was a foundation member); his sons-in-law were similarly elected in 1365 and 1369, as were his grandchildren, Richard and Henry, in 1377. Peers could expect admission some five years after inheriting their peerage. But service and valour equally won men admission in the spirit of the Order's inception: Richard of Pembridge, a knight of the king's household and then of the

Chamber, in 1369, as well as retainers of the Black Prince's household such as Simon Burley and Nicholas Sarnesfield. A few women were granted livery on St George's Day in a muted sibling institution dedicated to that saint.

A careful balance between noble families, royal officials, favourites and members of the royal family characterizes the composition of Edward's brotherhood of the Garter. It provides a useful code for Edward's politics more generally. Royal prerogative was wide and unassailable; the king took great interest in his family – he may even be seen as a 'family man' – arranging very good marriages for his numerous progeny: Lionel to the heiress of the Earl of Ulster; John of Gaunt to Blanche, co-heiress of Henry of Grosmont Duke of Lancaster; Thomas of Woodstock to Eleanor, co-heiress of the Earl of Northampton, Hereford and Essex.

Such focused dynastic aspiration was tempered by the advice of the greatest nobles and the promotion and support of a group of royal servants. Royal servants and nobles benefited from the opportunities of revenue offered by warrior kings – Edward III and later Henry V. William Bohun, Earl of Hereford and Lieutenant in Brittany, had crossed over with an expedition in 1342, later to fight with the king during the sack of the lordship of Rohan. In 1345 he led a royal contingent in the Duchy and soon made Thomas Dagworth his deputy, charging him on 28 January 1346 with command of 14 knights, 65 esquires, 120 archers and more. At La Roche Derrien in June, Dagworth was to deal a terrible blow to the French: he took Charles of Blois, Duke of Brittany captive, for which King Edward rewarded him handsomely. Without servants like Dagworth, the younger son of a modest Suffolk family, an erstwhile official of Humphrey Earl of Hereford in some of his Marcher lordships, a nobleman such as William could not prosper in administration of estates, still less in war. William thought so well of his lieutenant that he gave him his own sister, Eleanor, a widow, in marriage. With her came in 1344 the estates of one of the greatest Anglo-Irish families, the Butlers, Earls of Ormond.

The fellowship of the Garter was further reinforced by the Arthurian imagery of the round table revived and explored by Edward and his court. At the Dunstable Tournament of 1334, led by John of Eltham, the king's son Edward dressed as 'Lionel', cousin of Lancelot. A veritable Round Table was re-created at Pentecost 1344 at Windsor Castle, and presided over by the king and queen in furred red gowns, who led a procession of earls, barons and knights to the castle chapel. There they heard a mass and swore on relics to follow the king and queen in creating a Round Table anew, as Arthur had once done.

The court was an arena of complex exchanges of information, favours, gifts and advice. An intimate language of symbol and ritual encouraged relationships, and clear boundaries between the acceptable and the unmentionable were known and observed. Although Edward III's chancery was producing more letters than ever before, the dimensions of play and entertainment were not diminished in consequence. His court was adorned by minstrels, players and acrobats, servants to whom the king showed singular attention and loyalty. He was also surrounded by bookish people: his mother Isabella, his wife, and Henry of Lancaster, an interesting devotional writer. The courts of England and France, already linked by marriage and blood, were brought even closer with the arrival of a French court with the captive French King John, and new hybrid forms of etiquette and ceremony evolved. Three queens welcomed King John on his arrival in England in 1357 – Queen Philippa, the Queen of Scotland (Edward's sister Joan, d. 1362), and Isabella, the king's mother. A royal progress from Bristol to London saw the entry of the captive king into the City, where he was lodged at the Savoy Palace. It was claimed that he had never seen anything like the celebrations of St George's Day at Windsor, and Queen Philippa's surviving accounts show just how sumptuous these events were.

Brilliant French writers and musicians captured in their creations the excitement of Edward's active years. Jehan le Bel had fought with Edward in the Scottish campaigns and recorded the king's early years. Edward was the epitome of chivalry and prowess rather than an executive ruler of vast lands. The most prominent chronicler was Jean Froissart (d. c.1410), who was part of Queen Philippa's entourage in the 1360s. Froissart developed an extraordinary mastery of English political mentality, which he deployed in his *Chroniques*, into which he incorporated Jehan's earlier work. He also wrote love poetry, and his presence in court, together with the infusion of French literature during the years of King John's captivity, created a familiarity with French writing which contributed much to the poetry of Chaucer in the following generation.

The court was colourful and exciting on occasions when entertainment rather than strife and anxiety prevailed. Courtiers and guests were cheered by figures like Queen Philippa's fool. He was dressed in a costume made of striped Ypres cloth, decorated with a lamb's coat, and a hood of budge fur (lambskin worn inside out). Care was given to the recruitment of staff such as the minstrel Walter Hert, hired by the queen straight out of 'minstrelsy school' in London in 1358; a piper was hired for Easter celebrations, and an acrobat was brought in for entertainment on Whitsun of that year. Men in court were becoming more like such minstrels in their own dress: around mid-century the Italian and French fashions which favoured narrow and tight clothes and rich varieties of colour – especially for young men – were introduced into the English court. The men of the court of the captive King John of France used an exclusive style of marbled colouring of cloth, a livery of sorts for the knights and valets of his chamber. Queen Philippa favoured embroidered silks for her body and on the walls of her chamber: in 1348 her evening attire was an ensemble in blue velvet with gold borders – the colours of the Virgin Mary – and her day attire was red, embroidered with figures and pearls.

During the years in England, at court, the king was somewhat insulated by those close and trusted favourites around him, although he was probably well advised by active and informed sons. He was surrounded by trusty guards (*vigiles*) – such as Ralph le Geyte, William and John Hardyng – who also provided entertainment, as well as by trumpeters who announced his presence as he moved throughout his palace – his favourite was Windsor, though he spent more time at Westminster – and park. Kings sought out advisers and confidants who could comfort and support: one such was the physician Peter of Florence, who earned £40 a year serving both the king and the queen. The holistic understanding of health in this period, which was particularly well expounded in English writings, encouraged this type of dependence: bodily regimen was seen not only as necessary for physical well-being, but for moral fortitude and good judgement. It was a crucial aspect of kingly demeanour and life-style that the king's body be beautiful, free of pain, a fitting home for a great spirit.

Kings and princes offered their subjects occasions for identification with a land and a language, as a people, as an 'imagined community', but they were also extraordinarily uprooted persons, who might share their table, as well as their bedchamber, with men and women quite different in age, ethnicity and language. Perhaps that is why they spent so many resources and so much effort on building homes for themselves, sumptuous and restful places. English kings were great builders, chief among them Edward III. Under him Windsor Castle became a splendid dynastic centre, the hub of an international court of one of the longest-ruling kings of Europe, and home for the chivalric ethos epitomized in the Order of the Garter. Edward was to die in his palace at Sheen, a home which would be deliberately destroyed seventeen years later by his grandson Richard, in a grand gesture of mourning at the death of Anne of Bohemia.

Few English kings could boast the scale of artistic and artisanal patronage of continental courts. But they were stylish organizers of tournaments, to which they drew talented participants from all over Europe. The greatest achievements in building and art were attached to dynastic magnificence: the continued beautification of Windsor Castle, with the adornment of St George's Chapel there, until the last of its painting was completed in 1362. The style favoured here was not English but European, the fine gilt, ornate and expressive style of painting developed by Trecento Tuscan artists.

EPILOGUE

The intensive drive and excitement of Edward III's first decades had altered drastically by the 1360s. The court of the ageing king was demoralized and lacking in inspiration. The turning point may have been the death of his dashing queen and partner in rule, Philippa, in August 1369. The mourning and burial rituals lasted for months and ended in a procession from Windsor to Westminster with stops at five churches on the way, to her burial in a tomb which she had commissioned and designed, a queen among her relatives, with heraldry that stressed her own great lineage. The tomb was all the more powerful for being not flattering but distinctively realistic. This was a remarkable queen, of whose times her court chronicler Froissart wrote: 'Since the time of the Queen Guinevere, who was wife of King Arthur and Queen of England . . . there was no queen so good or so honourable.' This is flattery indeed, but cast in an idiom and imagery which Edward and Philippa had knowingly inhabited and fostered.

The king was seen in public less frequently, his court was less in evidence, as he spent his days on his favourite estates with a small entourage and infrequent itineration. The treaties of Brétigny (May

1360) and Calais (October 1360) meant that a process of disengagement was possible, from campaigns and from their political and financial costs. Having secured his claim to Aquitaine he kept a watchful eye from the strategic garrison of Saint-Sauveur-le-Vicomte in Normandy. He could thus assign Aquitaine to his son, his future heir, and expect the fruits of peace. His son's son, who was to become Richard II, was born in Bordeaux in 1367, attended there by the kings of Spain, Navarre and Portugal. During these years John of Gaunt became embroiled in the dynastic wars of Castile, in which English and French troops and interests met in battle, and out of which he came with a wife and a claim to the throne of Castile. The companies, left idle during a period of peace, continued to fight and ravage territories in southern France and Italy. When Edward reclaimed the title of King of France in 1369, he marked it as being the fortieth anniversary of his accession. He did so with a great sense of achievement, and with little desire to go further.

Edward's hopes for his family were dashed. The Black Prince fell ill in 1371, and died in 1376, a death which coincided with the resumption of war. He was buried in Canterbury, not in the undercroft chapel as his will had requested, but above, in the chapel of the Holy Trinity. The space was decorated with his livery sign of feather and scroll, and the Flemish motto which still serves the Prince of Wales, 'Ich dene' – 'I serve'. Outliving a son must always be a depressing and crushing experience. John of Gaunt tried but never succeeded in replacing Prince Edward as his father's heir, though he did remain a prime military and political actor.

In his last years the king disengaged from politics and warfare. At court others filled the vacuum created by his absence. The household officers, William Lord Latimer the Chamberlain, John Lord Neville the Steward, together with the financier Richard Lyons, linked to the king's erstwhile mistress Alice Perrers, came to dominate the court. Favours to friends, such as Garter companionship, were awarded to knights associated with the court group: Richard Pembridge, John Lord Neville, and Alan Buxhill.

When in 1375 the last outpost in Normandy was relinquished, this epitomized the mismanagement and lack of leadership which had long worried parliament. Those in charge were brought to account by the parliament of 1376. It was opened on 29 April by Chancellor John Knyvet, who addressed the question of a subsidy and was answered by the Commons' Speaker Peter de la Mare. In his words an articulate analysis of the country's troubles was presented: too many interests and factions were undermining the general and common good. This was a critical engagement with the crown, not as an institution, but in the particular state of flawed helmsmanship. The king was being exploited and defrauded by those he had favoured: the staple merchants of Calais across the Channel, and Alice Perrers closer to home.

This best documented of medieval parliaments, the Good Parliament of 1376, reveals how widespread was the malaise. William Langland's poem *Piers Plowman*, in its version from the 1370s, echoes literally and metaphorically a desire for justice which kings and officials were little able to answer. The Good Parliament made a number of important constitutional innovations, like the creation of the continual council, mainly for fear of the influence on the young future king of his uncle John of Gaunt. A whole generation was passing, men who had mobilized a country's resources – in soldiers, energy and wealth – to the project of military exertion. Their exploits were just glorious enough to help quell the frustrations and abuse which recent years had inspired. Yet Edward's years left useful institutions for debate and expression of grievances, a peace of sorts, and a set of expectations. For at his jubilee parliament of 1376 Edward III presented Richard, his grandson, as his heir. Like the infant Christ he was brought to parliament, where he was adored and given gifts. The parliamentary sermon likened the gathering to that of Christ's Presentation at the Temple.

Edward died at Sheen in June 1377 of a stroke, an imposing figure even at his death, if we are to judge by the wooden funerary effigy carried at his last state ceremony. Even today the authenticity is striking: as in the dog hairs which made up his eyebrows, the flakes of dry glue which had once attached a wig to the wooden head, and the threads of red velvet from his gown. The reign which had seen some of the greatest calamities of European medieval experience, both natural and man-made, was busy and transforming. The political system which he headed mobilized the energies and involved many of the approximately 2.8 million subjects of the king in England and Wales, in the Borders of Scotland and English Ireland, in Calais and Gascony and parts of north-west France. He reigned long and hard, yet, unlike his father before him and his grandson after him, he died, in his bed, in peace.

3

An Empty Land and its King, 1377–1399

THE LAW

The Black Death and its aftermath left communities marked by bereavement, yet surrounded by the challenges of opportunities created by death. Kingship, lordship, administration, and above all family, strove to benefit from possibilities and to alleviate pain. People sought the remedy of law, the durability of records, in efforts to enshrine and make safe so much that was new: tenancies, contracts of domestic service, arrangements for retirement, enclosure of fields for pasture, membership in fraternities. Law was a common facet, and many understood and participated in its multiple occasions and rituals. It offered a framework from which new lives could be made; and it was authorized by the person of the king.

Awareness of the law pervaded all aspects of life and affected all classes of society: no one was too far from a legal nexus or beyond it, even if many could subvert its processes or despair of its workings. Although some evidence was admissible – a bloody knife, torn clothes, stolen goods – the legal process depended largely on the reputation of an accused presented to court by a jury of men from the locality within which the crime occurred. Reputation was secured by friends, or, in legal terms, 'on oath helpers'. Thus it seemed easier for a rich man to be true – to be surrounded by supporters – than a poor woman. The law was not only a process but a labelling system: it defined servility or freedom, a distinction from which flowed a multitude of consequences to do with rights to land, the status of offspring, suitability for clerical office, or participation in the public life reserved to free persons.

The law recognized men and women as agents with differing capacities. In the Welsh Marches, in Ireland and in the northern Borders, ethnic affiliation determined people's rights to hold land, the pool of marriageable partners, and liability to pay certain dues, such as the *ambor* marriage fee in the Welsh lordships. In Ireland common law was used by the Anglo-Irish, in parallel to Gaelic law by Gaelic-Irish, with its emphasis on resolution between kin groups. Many more people participated in public legal processes than is true of western democracies today, and although a long-term professionalization of legal skills was at work during our period, it was still possible for lay people to state their own cases in royal courts and to plead and give evidence in ecclesiastical ones.

The law was far from being a coherent code, but rather was fragmented into many jurisdictions and inflected by a series of cases which demonstrated its possible applicability. In manorial courts local custom of the manor was retained in the memory of jurors under the scrutiny of the lord's stewards, and custom could vary greatly as to what might seem very basic questions such as the age of majority and the forms of inheritance. Enfranchised towns were granted the freedom to act on a wide range of business related to the operations of their markets – control of the quality of goods, punishment for minor violent acts – in borough or leet courts. Criminal cases remained the business of the royal courts, as was the increasing business of statute law, with the growing body of parliamentary statutes enacted from the mid-fourteenth century. People were to be judged by other men of their region, their *visine*. A writ to the sheriff directed him to empanel some twenty-four men on a certain date, of whom twelve were to be sworn. Yet this apparently straightforward system was dogged by the failure of men to appear as summoned. Those most likely to serve were men of middling rank: free tenants who in turn often served as church-wardens, or townsmen of a high tax assessment. Trials were often postponed repeatedly for lack of twelve jurors; they could be adjourned also for a shortage of the right type of jurors, as in the case presented to the King's Bench of a Gloucestershireman suspected of theft, until the time that a Gloucester jury could be empanelled.

Ecclesiastical courts controlled marriage litigation, probate of wills, defamation, judicial action against clerics and those suspected of heresy. Their business coincided frequently with cases related to inheritance brought to royal courts. A dual system was at work regarding inheritance of property, through civil action on land, and ecclesiastical action on moveables. Since issues of inheritance often hinged on decisions over the legality of a marriage and the legitimacy of its offspring, the jurisdictions frequently overlapped. Certain ecclesiastical institutions – like the Durham Palatinate – constituted separate jurisdictions, and some religious institutions held peculiar jurisdictions carved out of the bishop's or archbishop's normal remit, such as that of the Dean and Chapter of York over parishes in York, the East, West and North Ridings, and Nottinghamshire. Cathedrals had their precinct privileges and immunities; jurisdiction produced influence, patronage and income.

People were adept at using and moving between the broad avenues offered by this complex network of law and courts. Yet much legal business was transacted *outside* courts, through arbitration, conciliation and the offices of trusted and respected local individuals, saving the litigants time and money, and avoiding the adversarial drift which court action created. Peasants sought arbiters among their neighbours, say in complaints about debts; for knights the circle of the magnate in whose sphere they dwelt offered that service. The mutual deterrence and responsibility achieved by the system of mutual oaths to keep the peace – the ancient 'frankpledge' system – was widely accepted, and was not challenged even by the activists of the Peasants' Revolt, who criticized so many other aspects of prevailing legal practice.

So an extra-curial world of law coincided with the services of the manorial, baronial, royal, urban and ecclesiastical courts. Among other forums for adjudication and the settlement of disagreements were the internal courts of guilds, whose statutes regularly required that arbitration between members – most frequently members of the same craft – be sought within the guild before turning outside it, on the pain of high fines. The preoccupation with settling within the guild must be related to a fear that secrets, often industrial ones, might leak out of the trade group. In London, judicial business took place simultaneously in the sheriff's court, the Hustings court (the mayor's court), in the ward assemblies (*wardmotes*) and in guilds, and that was just for civil and secular business.

The overlapping of authorities and the influence of powerful men in their localities also produced famous examples of miscarriage of justice, or the failure of attempts to enforce it. The complaint of Thomas Brinton, Bishop of Rochester, in a sermon of the 1370s, conveys more than the generic lament of a moralizer: according to this informed commentator, England's laws were many, yet their application was null. Excuses seemed always to be found to mitigate guilt, with claims such as 'He is a youngster', or 'If indicted his shame would stain us all.'

Those in the best position to make forceful mitigating claims were members of influential gentry families, or those protected by magnates. In consequence, opined the bishop, homicides and notorious thieves went unpunished. The poet John Gower similarly expressed the idea, around 1381, that mankind was coming to an end 'since there is no justice in their laws', a complaint echoed in a petition to the Scottish parliament in 1399 about 'misgovernance of the realm and the default of the keeping of the common law'. The test of legal probity even touched the king, the fountainhead of law. By the end of his reign, Richard II was seen as lacking in commitment to common law, and as practising wilful and sectional legal favour.

It was not only influence that could distort or retard the legal process; sometimes the personnel involved were at fault. Officials such as coroners, charged with the investigation of sudden or unnatural death at the request of the sheriff, were not paid for their services. They were thus required to prove good financial standing before they could take office. So it is not surprising that recurrent accusations of corruption became attached to them. Occurrences such as the case at Salisbury in 1384 where six serving coroners were fined for extortion were common.

By the second half of Richard II's reign the chancellor offered some alternative services as judge: he dealt with bills of complaint which he could remedy and adjudicate on in vast areas left uncovered or hampered by common law procedure. Where common law was notoriously lacking in suppleness, such as in cases of debt and promise – in the realm of conscience – Chancery court provided a relatively cheap and accessible service. It even became a forum for the discussion of issues of heraldry and honour, as in the case of John Lord Lovel against Thomas Lord Morley over the design 'over argent and lion rampant sable crowned and armed'. In time, Chancery also provided training for clerical apprentices, a training so valued that by 1389 Chancery ordinances attempted to prevent infiltration of its Inns by ambitious law students keener on the law than on clerical status. As the legal profession grew, its reputation declined: in 1381 rebels burnt books and committed murder in the Inns of Court.

However varied the styles and judicial orientations of the various jurisdictions, the king's person, personality and persona were expected to guarantee the operational integrity of law and justice in his lands.

THE KING'S MINORITY

Richard II ascended the throne at the age of ten in 1377, and began his rule under a 'continual council' – a council of magnates and administrators charged with rule during the years of his minority. At his first parliament the accumulated discontent with his grandfather's last years led to the restatement, through petitions, of fifteen of the ordinances presented earlier in the century to Richard's great-grandfather, Edward II. At the next parliament, at Gloucester in October 1378, the Speaker of the Commons and the Steward of the Household debated the uses made of the tax awarded the king on his accession. The Commons claimed that while the kingdom's wealth was flowing to recipients favoured by Edward III and the Black Prince, there was little left to be used by the king. The Commons also requested reports on the actions of the king's counsellors. The young king's first years were repeatedly affected by a lack of trust in his counsellors. Another important player distrusted by the Commons was John of Gaunt Duke of Lancaster, the uncle who had never ruled, but whose interests ranged very widely over parts of England, Wales, Ireland, Aquitaine, Normandy and Castile.

Parliamentary taxes from 1377 took the form of a poll-tax, paid at the rate of one groat (4d.) per head by all men and women over fourteen, and in 1381 1s. for each person over fifteen, with a graduated provision for a 4d. contribution by poorer taxpayers, and several shillings by richer ones. In Richard's third parliament, of April 1379, open dissent against the poll-tax was strongly voiced. Yet the taxation of these years, 1377–81, matched very closely the military expenditure required in Gascony and for defence of the sea.

In these years the king was challenged by his most important responsibility, as protector of the realm. The ports of southern England and their hinterlands were under attack from France and later from Flanders too. One can sympathize with the poetic exclamation, 'Woe to the land in which a boy is king' ('*Vae terre ubi puer rex est*'), expressed in the 1370s by William Langland, the author of the poem *Piers Plowman*. Conversely, another poet, John Gower, saw in the king's youth proof of his blamelessness. Here was a boy who had grown up hearing glowing praise of his father, the Black Prince, but who now as a young adult sought his way without that trusted father at his side. There was something of charm and promise about the young king: on Twelfth

Night 1378 he held a performance of the traditional scene of the Adoration of the Magi, which his father had staged in January 1367 in Bordeaux, on the occasion of Richard's own birth. Untried and pure, one thing was certain: the young king was bound to mature, and political sense as well as tradition dictated that the young king be given a chance to prove his mettle.

The lands of Richard II were many and varied, and several dilemmas touching their rule faced him and his advisers. The French wars had resulted in an expansion of French lands under the rule of the kings of England: alongside Gascony there was Normandy, and there was expectation of further conquests, with the myriad sources of income that prisoners and protection afforded. Yet the French counter-attack did not only touch these foreign territories and populations. In the years of Richard's adolescence there were sacks of Rye (1376), Plymouth, Dartmouth and Exeter (1377), Winchelsea (1380) as well as a Scottish raid on Beaumaris (Anglesey) in 1381. Magnates and gentry considered investment in fortification of their domains: in 1381 and 1383 John Lord Cobham fortified his castle in Kent, in 1385 Edward Dallingbridge acquired a licence to turn his manor house into a castle, at Bodiam in the same county. The 1380s saw diplomatic experimentation with new alliances against France, such as that with Wenceslas Duke of Brabant, and it took the Franco–Flemish alliance of the late 1380s to direct the young king towards peace. Richard's apprenticeship was wide-ranging in its content and swift in its pace.

Some of the most testing moments of Richard's reign occurred over a few days in June 1381 which saw what has come to be known as the Peasants' Revolt. Since this was neither led by peasants nor unfolded as a revolt, it is probably better to use the French term *émeute* – a tumultuous sequence – than words suggestive of a sustained threat to social and political order. The events of June 1381 were a series of occasions for action created and seized by those not represented in parliament. These were expressions of political opinion in the broadest sense, comment on an administration and its policies, through partially ritualized violent action. The majority of 'rebels' were Londoners, and as Londoners they were savvy, acquainted with a variety of political jargons and modes of public behaviour. London life was, after all, based on association: in guilds, neighbourhood fraternities, apprentice companies. One person's fellowship was another's coven; and so even regular gatherings of apprentices for drink – admittedly rowdy occasions – seemed, to town governors, dangerous political meetings. The possible affinities between associational groups – those of London, and those marching on London – terrified London worthies. As the Westminster chronicler put it, they feared that London commoners might join in with the serfs.

Events in and around London and Westminster were bound to carry the utmost resonance. Already, on 11 June 1381, before the tumult reached London, a royal serjeant-at-arms had rushed to the Scottish border to alert John of Gaunt with the news. Gaunt was conducting a ceremony meant to ensure peace, known as the March Day. He moved south to his castle of Pontefract, but also sent commands for the garrisoning of his Welsh castles against possible rebellion. Regional unrest was never a limited affair to men of state; the borderlands were particularly sensitive to lapses in royal concentration. But even as he took these actions, he remained in the north to settle a personal feud with Scottish and northern magnates. The interests of the realm were here mediated through personal and dynastic considerations.

THE 'PEASANTS' REVOLT'

Before we see the marchers in action, what were the conditions which affected the people who came from the provinces to protest? In the countryside opportunities abounded, beyond the routines and limited rewards of small arable cultivation: in fishing and handicrafts, in extraction of mineral resources, which were increasingly explored by landlords and which created openings for labourers. Even those primarily cultivating land were engaged in hectic activities of exchange and leasing in order to make their holdings more profitable and their cultivation of them less hampered by customary obligations. Hence, between 1370 and 1420 there was a sustained rise in the purchasing power of wage-earners. Servile status seemed to curtail opportunity and limit freedom of movement and action; the court through whose workings it was enforced became the focus of political discontent. Even after the death of their leader Wat Tyler and the disintegration of the movement he had led, Essex men sought the abolition of manorial courts.

Domestic service became an attractive work opportunity, especially for women willing to learn the skills and prepared to live away from home and save money towards marriage. Tax returns reveal just how widespread service was: 20 per cent of Rutland households had one or two servants, whereas a third of urban households contained servants. The poll-tax returns of 1377 allow us to glimpse the distribution of servants in the paying population: in Worcester, Carlisle, Dartmouth and Northampton, servants account for 19 per cent, 17 per cent, 20 per cent and 30 per cent respectively. Most servants were women, especially in those areas where the textile industry was the predominant one, such as Yorkshire and Essex. Sons and daughters no longer adhered so closely to home, since opportunities for work and land-holding had improved; they married later, and so family size declined. In a rural community like Kibworth Harcourt (Leicestershire) it fell from 4.84 on average in the late thirteenth century to 3.72 in 1379, and so servants now provided some of the services which family members had done before. The emergence of service also meant that a significant social reality emerged in late medieval England, one which saw an abundance of young women in towns and of young men in the country. In Hull there were nine men to every ten women in 1377; whereas in the rural hinterland, the opposite prevailed. The mobility and opportunity of a society abundant in resources, and one in which industry offered work for young men and women alike, further enhanced the experience of singlehood, of isolation from family, and of villages full of older folk, without the young people who might care for them in old age.

The sense of looming disorder and volatility predated 1381. Men moving about the countryside, often in search of profitable work, epitomized the threat to employers' well-being. In 1377–9 Gilbert Rougge, a labourer of Sturmer (Essex), was thus deemed 'a rebel' against the law-enforcers since he was 'unwilling to swear or justify himself'.

The law was at the heart of the fantasies of those who marched on London in June 1381, in events that are remembered as the 'Peasants' Revolt'. The political events which unfolded in the second and third week of June were enacted by two groups – from Essex and from Kent – and were enabled by Londoners. This was not a movement of peasants alone – several bailiffs marched too – but it did reflect worries, complaints and grievances experienced in rural England, on manors, in small towns, and by people not represented fully by the Commons in parliament. Grievances were attached to the traditional arrangements of serfdom which constrained people's movement and work, but it also objected to the state of national politics, which had brought a heavy and repeated tax burden to poorer folk, in a period of anxiety about invasions from France. The 'true commons', as the marchers called themselves, sought the king's intervention. They asserted themselves as an alternative citizenry, by taking an oath to defend King Richard. Professing no interest but the king's own, they imagined and proposed a world without manorial lords, and without the gentry justices by whose hands the 'peace' was kept and the Statute of Labourers was enforced. *True* law was invoked, rather than the system of prevailing custom, supported by lawyers and epitomized by their Inns of Court – Gray's, Temple, Middle – which were sacked during the rising, and by prisons, such as the Marshalsea, which was stormed. The problem was not the country's laws, but those charged with applying and safeguarding them. This was a deep vein of feeling, a sentiment akin to that expressed by the 'King's poor liege men of Shropshire' in the 1370s, who claimed that by statute sheriffs were now being appointed for a year's service, in a county where that office had frequently been held for life.

On 6 June a group of men of Kent approached Rochester Castle with the request that prisoners held there be released. On the next day they marched to Maidstone, where their leader – Wat Tyler – seems to have emerged. He then led them to Canterbury where the venerable cathedral and its monks were terrorized with the threat that soon their head, the Archbishop of Canterbury, Chancellor of the Realm, would be executed (and he was, on 14 June). By 10 June a group was at work in Essex. London became the obvious next stage for the buoyant, and so far unstoppable, crowds of hundreds. The men of Kent were also encouraged by an eccentric preacher, the lapsed priest John Ball, who reproached the clergy for its greed and worldliness, a common trope in reformist preaching, favoured by unlicensed itinerant preachers. The Essex group settled north of the Thames and that of Kent on the south bank; both groups wished to see the king, who was only thirteen years old. The king was aware of the events, not least through the message conveyed to him by his man in Rochester, the constable Sir John Newton, who was sent by Tyler with a message of their intent. On 12 June the king, surrounded by some of the less unpopular magnates, sailed down the Thames on a barge to meet Wat Tyler, but the extent, sound and energy of the reception, flanked on either bank by the armed groups, led him to turn round and take safety in the Tower, where the chancellor, the treasurer, magnates and members of the royal family had also sought safety.

Young Richard never seems to have been afraid, understanding how central he was to the fantasies of transformation and betterment woven by the marchers. On 14 June he agreed to meet the Essex group at Mile End, and left the Tower with the mayor of London and an armed retinue. It is hard to reconstruct the exact demands made, but the people of Essex and Hertfordshire were happy to depart with the promise of charters of liberation from serfdom, and pardons for their recent actions over the past week. But Wat Tyler and the men of Kent were not satisfied: they freed prisoners from the Marshalsea prison and entered the Tower to kill Sudbury and Hales – chancellor and treasurer – and other royal servants. That night also saw great violence in the streets of London, and there was counter-violence the next day. At the meeting Wat Tyler acted in a familiar fashion; he only half-bent his knee and took the king's hand, shook it and said 'Brother, be of good comfort.' Tyler may have made further demands, but by now the slightest provocation, Tyler's drawing of a dagger, provoked the armed reaction which the mayor of London and his men sought to inflict. The king intervened and, according to a chronicler who stayed with him, led the remainder of Tyler's men out of the city (Plate 9). All they could do was flee – away from the armed force which the Londoners had prepared over the preceding week.

Despite the venom poured upon the marchers by most chroniclers, a pattern arises from their actions in London: the repeated attempt to create a 'community' of decent working folk, loyal to their king, against treacherous advisers, such as the chancellor, Archbishop Sudbury, or John of Gaunt, the king's uncle, whose Savoy Palace was sacked and burnt. The chronicler Walsingham noted with derision their rhetorical stance:

For at that time they . . . considered that no name was more honourable than that of community, nor, according to their stupid estimation, were there to be any lords in the future, but only the King and Commons.

Favouring the labourer, the rural worker, and claiming the king as their master, the political ideas which animated some of the marchers suggested that the country's misery might well have been caused by ambitious magnates, and by the hundreds of officials and members of the gentry who applied the king's law. Poets appreciated this affinity between labourer and king. Iolo Goch (1320–98) praised the labourer, stating that 'there is no life, no world, without him', and the same could be said of the king's political role.

The marchers presented themselves as the 'true commons', opposed to the Commons, who legislated evil and enforced it on their lands. Their actions seem deliberate and discriminating: they chose for destruction not the Kent estates of the archbishop, but the archiepiscopal headquarters at Lambeth, near the centre of political events, where records were kept. They piled up high court rolls and muniments and memoranda, documents which were the vehicles of oppression and the bearers of old, often coercive custom. They attacked but did not loot the treasures of John of Gaunt's Savoy Palace.

They were bound by oath, and some even wore liveries. The march was also an occasion coloured by playfulness, by the pleasure of unmaking symbolic edifices, in turning a world 'upside down'. Some accounts describe the sacking of the chambers of the Tower of London, while King Richard was on his way to Mile End, and the attack on the bed of Joan of Kent, the king's mother. She was not hurt or violated, but truly terrified, as her bed was sacked and the rampagers asked her for kisses. Similarly, chroniclers described with horror the lowliest of peasants pulling the beards of knights, or hacking away at the effigy of the absent John of Gaunt, whom they mockingly called 'King of Castile', for his dynastic ambitions in Spain.

The collective march for justice built up a momentum of self-justification, which touched communities intent to right their wrongs: at Bury St Edmunds (Suffolk) the Benedictine abbey was attacked, as was St Albans Abbey in Hertfordshire; in Cambridge, the university with its special court and court records was the focus for violence.

Procession and pleasure, self-assertion and bravado could not alone produce the desired transformation. Only the king could do so: true lord, fount of justice. The *Anonimalle* chronicler reports that the rebels greeted the king at Mile End: 'Welcome our Lord King Richard, if it pleases you, and we will not have any other king over you.' The unknown quantity at the heart of the events was the young king's reaction to the challenge thrown at him, cloaked in the rhetoric of millenarian expectation and of utopian justice. The meeting between the king and his 'true commons' took place on Corpus Christi, the feast which celebrated the eucharist, a habitual, outdoor summer celebration often processional in form.

After its dispersal the movement of marchers met concerted judicial responses: aldermen in London were charged with naming those members of their wards who had participated, though most were granted pardons. Some 150 persons were tried for trespass and damage to property where specific cases could be made, while John of Gaunt attempted to identify the hundreds who had attacked his home. Yet the very men who were expected to set the record straight, five aldermen, were themselves accused of collaboration with the men of Kent. Moments of political uncertainty enacted in public, rather than in council chambers and palace halls, saw the meeting of a multitude of interests and temperaments. It also brought widows into the public domain, women whose autonomy and status earned, for a while, a political voice. The marchers of 1381 saw just such a convergence of the utopian, the opportunistic, the exhilarating and the reckless.

Although efforts were made to reassert control and deterrence in London, the men and the issues that interacted in the early summer of 1381 did not, of course, go away. There was insurrectionary talk and planning in Norfolk as late as the late summer of 1382, aimed, according to Thomas of Walsingham, at the capture and killing of the Bishop of Norwich and other local magnates. There is mention of the use of the fair of Horsham St Faith's (Norfolk) as a recruiting ground, and of a plan to occupy the Abbey of St Benet Hulme, a danger which clearly worried the monk-chronicler. The instigators were caught and beheaded, and the record of the properties seized shows the men to have been of quite modest means – from villages around Norwich, and led by a single more prosperous man, William Spicer, who was worth 40s. in goods and chattels at his execution. The drama of the thwarted insurrection in Norfolk in 1382 is further deepened when we note that the man who headed the judicial effort and the trial of the suspects had been a humiliated victim of the Norfolk chapter of the 1381 rising. Unrest continued in other areas too. In March 1383 five 'insurrectors' were named for treason for having tried to kill the sheriff of Devon, and several cases presented as treason ended up in acquittal. A new level of suspicion, fear and resentment had been injected into the localities – the villages and market towns of England – in the aftermath of 1381.

The events of 1381 showed that London was not only a symbol of the country's well-being and good rule, but was itself a cauldron of competing associations and groupings. Just as landed men and their followers were clustering into affinities, so association marked the experiences of work, power and leisure in the capital. This constituted the tenor of political life, and also produced a high level of visible political expression. Politics took place not only in council chambers and guildhalls, but in the streets, where enemies were publicly ridiculed or defamed. John of Gaunt was the subject of campaigns of denigration, like that of 1377, when rumours were spread claiming that he was no prince, but the bastard issue of a liaison between his mother and a Flemish butcher of Ghent. Magnates were involved in the politics of the capital, which often provided the stage for the meeting of nationally significant factions. Parliament met in Gloucester in September 1378 because the summer had seen violent attacks by Londoners, led by John Maynard, on the Earl of Buckingham's household. A petition to the king and council at the Merciless Parliament of 1388 accused Alexander Neville, Archbishop of York, of posting bills against his enemies even during the sessions of parliament. The walls of Westminster Palace, like those of St Paul's, were favourite surfaces for posting political comments. Although the king had managed to defuse the crowds of 1381, there was a great sense of unease and volatility around the centres of power. Social and economic forces had for decades been creating both capacity and expectation among workers, artisans and tenants, producing greater mobility and less dependence on traditional bonds of authority. The language of these groups was English, rather than French or Latin, and their arenas for action were the guild, the parish, the local court. They were often on the road, as soldiers or small traders, or as labourers in search of a good contract of employment.

RICHARD II'S RULE

The king was not erratic. He favoured the royal uncles, creating Edmund of Langley Duke of York, and Thomas of Woodstock Duke of Gloucester, while John of Gaunt Duke of Lancaster required no further honour. The king was maturing fast as a political actor. He also became a married man, through a union with the daughter of the Holy Roman Emperor, Anne of Bohemia, in 1382. His home was his palace, and London his playground. As he matured the king was expected to develop, with the advice of his council and parliament, a long-term strategy on finance and war, as well as a system for promoting talented people and rewarding loyal and useful men born with status and expectations. He was planning his first military campaign, put to parliament in 1382 with a request for taxation. But before long he was drawn into another adventure, a crusade, no less.

In fourteenth-century double-speak the Bishop of Norwich's campaign to Flanders came to be known as a crusade. With the revolt of Ghent against the Count of Flanders in 1383, and punitive action by Count Louis de Malle against the import of English wool into the Flemish cloth-making cities, England's trade stood to suffer dramatically. Bishop Henry Despenser, who had suppressed the uprising in Norfolk in 1381, came up with another idea of violent action little fitting a bishop: an expedition to the Low Countries with papal sanction. As papal representative in England and Wales, he succeeded in obtaining papal approval and crusading status for the campaign, with all the spiritual and financial support which crusades enjoyed. The aim was to offer succour to the Flemish rebels, and thus to unseat the Count, on whom a Flemish alliance with France depended. And so in April 1383, at a cross-taking ceremony in London, recruitment began for the army which Despenser was to lead in May 1383 from Sandwich. The army crossed the Channel, soon taking Gravelines and Bourbourg, and then continued further north-east up the Flemish coast. At the siege of Ypres the progress ended, as the force was ill-equipped and suffered disease. With the approach of a French relief force, the bishop called a truce, and withdrew to Calais. Although the young king had not led the expedition, this was undoubtedly a frivolous use of men and funds. If he were to impress and reassure, he would have to do better by leading a successful campaign.

These were years of fear of invasion, when France appeared intent on energetic action, and the Scots added to the anxiety in the north. John of Gaunt invaded Scotland in 1384, and destroyed Haddington (East Lothian). This in turn brought retaliation led by the Earl of Carrick, a rival to King Robert II, which prompted a stronger response. This time the army was led by Richard II, who campaigned in Scotland in 1385 with 4,500 men-at-arms, his sole act of military leadership, and succeeded in reassuring the north. But there were other worries: in October 1386 parliament expressed its discontent with the preparations for defence against a French invasion, and its distrust of the advisers who surrounded the king. Parliament did not refuse to raise taxes, but it demanded closer scrutiny of the uses of funds and the planning of war.

The parliament of 1386 came to be known as the Wonderful Parliament, and it impeached and punished Michael de la Pole Earl of Suffolk, the king's chancellor since 1383. Leading the assault was a group of magnates, known as the Appellants – the Duke of Gloucester (the king's uncle) and the Earls of Arundel and Warwick, with the support of London. There was great fear of a French invasion from Sluys; all those involved in planning and financing sea defences were under public scrutiny: chancellor, treasurer, keeper of the Privy Seal – de la Pole, Segrave and Skirlaw – for neglecting sea defences in the years before 1386. Those in charge of defences, the communities of the south-east of England, acted. There was a rush of activity in Kent, Sussex, Hampshire, the Isle of Sheppey and Portsmouth. At the same time the Scottish border was also watched, for fear of an opportunistic attack. Armed boats were sent on reconnaissance in Sluys and its vicinity. All this was supported by local finance, at the same time as parliamentary finance supported ship-building, the efforts in Castile (1385), and in Scotland (1385), and the relief of Ghent and Calais.

The confrontation did not end with the complaints and trials in parliament; a period of recruitment of armed followers ensued, with the expectation that discontent might also take extra-parliamentary form. During the summer, at Nottingham and Shrewsbury, Richard II inquired into the legal underpinning of the complaints against his rule. At the same time he directed Robert de Vere Earl of Oxford, whom he had made Duke of Ireland and whose elevation was one of the bones of contention with the Appellants, to raise a royal force. De Vere led a royal contingent of some 4,250 men from Cheshire to London, with the aim of asserting the king's authority and protecting his household. The Appellants, recently joined by Henry of Derby and Thomas Mowbray Duke of Norfolk – engaged and defeated the royal force with their own 4,000–5,000 men on 20 December 1387 at Radcot Bridge in Oxfordshire. Here was civil war after half a century of relative domestic peace.

In what followed Richard was as good as deposed for some three days, during which no credible alternative emerged to his rule. The Appellants continued to London; they also provided a menacing presence during the parliament which followed – the Cambridge Merciless Parliament of 1388. State trials for treason were held against de Vere and John Beauchamp, Steward of the King's Household, which resulted in their execution. The king was drawn into factional politics; thus he was reduced to behaving like another magnate, not as an unassailable king. After the execution of his followers Richard was a fatally wounded figure. He was forced to keep the Appellants on his council, but at the same time aimed for a rapprochement with his uncle, John of Gaunt, an alternative power broker. Richard also recruited men who would be loyal to him, such as John Waltham, Bishop of Salisbury, who in turn recruited northern clerks into royal service. The king claimed his majority, in 1389, at the age of twenty-two, at a solemn mass. This was a mark of reconciliation and consolidation; men offered their oaths of allegiance and kisses of peace. Yet the traumatic events of 1386-8 had created a bloody memory, one which was to be fatally re-enacted a decade later.

The Cambridge Parliament of 1388, which was such a low point for royal prestige, also resulted in twenty-five acts of legislation aimed at containing disorder and enforcing a social peace. Movement and association were deemed dangerous: the Vagrancy Act criminalized movement of able-bodied persons without licence and the abandonment of contracts of service. Moreover, craftsmen, servants and apprentices who were out of work were now obliged to provide agricultural labour during harvest. Such legislation was only patchily enforced, but it bears witness to a mood of discontent and distrust among landlords and employers towards those they might employ or to whom they might grant land in tenure. A nostalgia for greater social fixity and a clearer demarcation of status and estate is evident even in minor acts of legislation, such as the ordinance passed in 1389 at Havering manor court (Essex) against keeping of greyhounds for hunting by anyone with land that yielded less than 40s. per annum. In his poem *Confessio Amantis* of 1390 the poet John Gower used the story of Icarus and Phaeton to express distaste for those who soar above or plunge below their prescribed social boundaries:

> In high estate it is a vice
> To go too low, and in service
> It grieves for to go too high.

The same parliament initiated a countrywide survey of sworn groups and voluntary associations, bodies which were indeed dangerous and potentially disloyal. Every association in the land which owned property and was bound by oath was obliged to report by February 1389 on its aims and capabilities. The resulting returns to Chancery make interesting reading: sets of statutes and the histories of some 500 social and religious clubs, most from the east of England: Norfolk, Suffolk,

Cambridgeshire, Lincolnshire and London. The country was shown to be supporting hundreds of local groups for worship and mutual help, in which the language of community and brotherhood was used to form bonds of cooperation. Despite parliamentary rhetoric these were not traitorous bodies; the challenge to royal authority came from a much narrower group, which sought scrutiny of foreign affairs and the domestic processes by which the necessary finance for them was procured.

FOOD — URBAN AND RURAL

Richard II's London was a ravenous eater. Food – its production and preparation – posed special problems for town-dwellers. In the later fourteenth century diets became more diversified: England and parts of Wales developed a commercial and agrarian regime, which remained susceptible to harvest failures, but in which few people, even the poor, actually starved. Most regions produced enough grain for local needs. Even large cities – like London or, further afield, Ghent – consumed grain grown over considerable, yet neighbouring hinterlands. Grain was stored for its many uses. The barn at Bredon (Worcestershire), on a 300-acre estate of the Bishop of Worcester, was built from the bishop's own timber and contained an apartment for the reeve with a fireplace and toilet. Sheaves were kept dry, sorted by grain type, and threshing took place on the barn floor under the vigilant eye of the fathers and sons of the Fryg family such as John (d. 1385) and Richard (d. 1401), who also maintained a lofty dovecote beneath its roof. The corn was sold to the corn-factors of Tewkesbury; its chaff and straw was used for manure and thatching. As the century unfolded, demand for high-quality white wheat bread remained high, affecting sowing patterns, which reeves such as the Frygs were obliged to evaluate and plan.

Feeding the towns and maintaining standards of hygiene became and remained the responsibility of town authorities. Food producers were singled out for special attention in urban by-laws which aimed to control prices and quality: in 1350 London limited the price of baking a capon or a rabbit in pastry to a penny. In 1378 the capital's authorities ordained a tariff for foods habitually prepared by its cooks, including roasts and pasties of fish, fowl and game. Two years later, anxiety about putrid and malodorous meats cooked in pastry cases led to controls on the work of the pastry-cooks of London. In 1381-2 a

London ordinance directed sellers of food and drink to market portions worth a farthing (a quarter of a penny) – portions which even the poorest labourer could afford. The city's cooks, flan-makers and bakers were responding to a wide range of demand and price: the patrons for this 'fast food' were not only travellers and single people, but often the urban poor, who could not afford the substantial cost of maintaining a kitchen with its utensils, supplies and glowing hearth. Even quite substantial households used the services of bakers for their pies and flans, as ovens were rarely possessed by small or even medium-sized households. The kitchen of the London vinter Richard Lyons boasted in 1376 pots and pans, cauldrons and kettles, and a variety of serving utensils; but even this prosperous urban household bought in its bread and ale. William Langland's poem *Piers Plowman* offers a lively image of town life with the cries of street vendors: 'Hot pies, hot! Good piglet and geese, go dine, go!'

Those who had access to fresh produce from their estates tried to consume it even when they were residing elsewhere, or were on the road. Prelates, royal officials and nobles travelled with foodstuffs, or had provisions brought from their estates to temporary residences. Oxford colleges, similarly, consumed bread baked from the wheat grown on their estates, and consequently bought less food in the Oxford market than the town's merchants would have desired. Merton College's mathematical scholars – known as the Oxford 'calculators' – applied their interest in probability and equilibrium to the working of the markets, as they managed the college's agrarian produce and purchased necessary foodstuffs and domestic goods. The accounts of the hospital of St John the Evangelist in Cambridge record the purchase of spices and cheese but never of grain, which was brought to it from its estates. Great aristocratic households consumed the specialized provisions of London cooks, of the makers of sauces, flans, wafers and pasties, but required few purchases in bulk of grain for bread and ale, or of meat and fowl, for these arrived cured and salted from their estates. Spices were desired by all who could afford them for the preservation and flavouring of food. Fourteenth-century cookery books abound in instructions for the use of pepper, cinnamon, cloves and ginger. When Edmund Mortimer Earl of March set off to Scotland on a diplomatic mission in 1378, he stocked up in London with large quantities of saffron, ginger and pepper. With these his cook prepared meals from foodstuffs bought on the route to the north: at Royston,

Huntingdon, Stamford, Grantham, Newark, Doncaster, Darlington, Durham and Newcastle.

The urban poor used their wages for the purchase of food, and towns attempted to regulate price and quality, particularly at the lower end of the market. Many single people were in domestic service, being fed and clothed by their employers. But towns were full of poor working people, who had to provide for themselves and sometimes for dependants. Poor women appear as recipients of testamentary gifts, as tenants of modest rooms, as persons too poor to pay taxes, and depended on cheap food, bought daily and meagrely. Such food was readily available in towns: Southwark alone had six cooks and four pie-makers in 1381. Smaller towns held weekly markets at which many of the goods known to modest Londoners could be purchased.

But what of rural folk of the poorer kind? About half of the rural population of Suffolk villages were wage-labourers; they too required provisions that were cheap and reliable. Their diet was much more vegetable-based than that of urban workers. The poet William Langland describes the lean winter diet as including bread, cheese, curds and vegetable pottage. Peasants ate root vegetables, onions and leeks, and probably more fruit than their lords and richer neighbours. Harvest and early autumn brought some variation, with better bread and some meat from freshly slaughtered pigs. And some food was free: in gardens, on hedges, and at the edges of parks. What they ate reflected their tenancies and their work pattern: Peter Aldred of Sizewell (Suffolk) was a master fisherman, who earned much by the sea but also held land and reared animals; his family's table reflected all his pursuits.

Even more than cooks' pantries and pie-houses, taverns proliferated in the towns and provided a growing part of the nourishment of poor and rich alike. Ale was drunk by all, although the rich also drank wine, usually imported from Gascony or Anjou. Ale was brewed from barley, or a mixture of barley and oats in the south-east. The decades after the Black Death saw a rise in the consumption of ale, reflecting the improvements in wages. This thick and nutritious drink – nothing like most modern ales – supplied a ready source of energy for poorer working people. A 1345 London ordinance aimed at protecting the city's water described it as 'the drink of the poor', but by 1381–2 the city aimed to regulate the price of ale 'in order to assist the poor'. Adults drank some three pints of ale a day on average, in a period which saw, not surprisingly, a growth of home-brewing for household consumption and modest sales. In Maidstone in Kent around 1386 a third of households were engaged in brewing, usually under the supervision and through the labour of women. Besides its beneficial effect as provider of nutritional plenty, greater alcohol consumption also affected – in public and at home – the tenor of sociability, and it undoubtedly led to accidents and violence at work, at home and at play.

Food was closely linked with notions of justice and order. Mayors used the shaming and degrading pillory in meting out punishment to those who defrauded the poor by overpricing or by the sale of deficient food. Long-standing royal legislation, such as the Assize of Ale and the Assize of Bread, was embellished and extended by the provisions of individual towns and communities. London's *White Book* (*Liber albus*) stipulated that if bread were found to be defective – in price, grain or weight – its baker was to be drawn through the city on a hurdle after the first offence, put in the pillory after a recurrence, and lose his right to bake altogether after a third offence. Cornhill – where a pillory stood – became a focus for the expression of public disapproval. Offenders were led to the pillory in painful and degrading processions, carnivalesque parades through the streets leading to it. Brewsters, bakers, butchers and cooks were punished in such pillories and pinning stools. William Langland's *Piers Plowman* explains why: 'For they poison the people secretly and often.'

London's needs affected the life-choices of families and communities in the counties surrounding it: Surrey, Sussex, Essex, Middlesex, Buckinghamshire, Hertfordshire, Kent. Estates in these counties moved from the predominance of wheat in the corn basket to a larger share of barley and dredge (a mixture of barley and oats). The interaction between different types of consumption was complex: the rise in the demand for ale, for example, required more fuel to support the brewing process. Regional specializations developed as reeves of estates decided, and continued to assess, whether greater profits were to be had from tending their woods – the price of a pack of faggots rose from 1d. *c.*1300 to 2s. 5d. *c.*1400 – or extending their arable. The decisions of reeves in Henley (Oxfordshire) or in Faversham (Kent) about the management of wood on the estates in their charge were increasingly affected by the need to provide London with faggots – grown, cut and packed – for use in the kitchens and workshops of the city. The woods of south-east England were tended in cycles of eleven years to produce both the fuel which the city needed to stoke its fires, furnaces and breweries, and the timber needed for its continuing efforts of construction, reconstruction, partitioning of houses, workshops, churches and wharves. Stocks of wood unloaded at Woodwharf, Castle Baynard Ward, were soon distributed by an army of woodmongers. City officials intervened during periods of shortage and seized stocks in wharf storehouses.

LONDON GOVERNMENT AND POLITICAL CULTURE

Mayors stood at the head of an urban bureaucracy which invigilated over the teeming city of London, over wards which contained noble households, religious houses, noisy workshops, interspersed with havens of verdant pleasance, herb gardens and orchards. These men were 'between the king and the commune to keep the laws', as the Cornhill poet William Langland put it. In these words he captured some of the essence of their roles: to ensure some measure of justice, through fair competition, decent pricing, and safety for the weak. Without idealizing these shrewd and ambitious men of affairs one can none the less note the city's need for persons at the helm, even while citizens still regulated large areas of their lives in small groups: in guilds for work and production, in parishes for sociability and religious progress, and in life of family, kin and affinity. City officials aimed to leave office considerably richer and better connected than they were upon entry, but they were also able to promote some aims which fitted prevalent notions of good urban rule.

London – with its size and variety – offered especially attractive opportunities for progress and growth in professions, crafts and politics. In his *Testament of Love* of *c.* 1384 Thomas Usk presented himself as a 'scrivener' – a writer – and as a Londoner, a resident of Newgate. To be a writer was to possess a specialized skill: the craft's prominence was recognized by the grant of guild status in 1373. As a writer Thomas Usk probably plied his trade around St Paul's, copying documents and books and composing legal texts. Men like him, articulate and urbane if not rich and well connected, were drawn into the followings of political faction. In 1388 Usk met his death by execution, as punishment for defecting from the faction led by John Northampton, representing the craft guilds, to what became the 'wrong side', led by Nicholas Brembre. Brembre was a grocer, who had served as mayor four times and as alderman twelve, following a career as a customs collector. He represented the great merchants and support for King Richard during the events of 1381 with colleagues such as William Walworth, fishmonger, and John Philpot, another grocer, who were all involved in running the Calais staple and in tax collection. As testimony to the prominence of neighbourhood and kin in political affairs, Thomas Usk's head was displayed at Newgate for his friends and neighbours to see.

In the 1380s and 1390s London mayors and aldermen were embroiled in politics more than ever before: in 1381 London had stood by the young king. The independence and importance of London's governing group, its expectations of office, were not easily relinquished and were defended with violence if necessary. Such sentiments led to the murder of a Genoese merchant, Janus Imperial, in London in 1379. Following parliament's confirmation of special trade privileges for Italian merchants in the autumn of 1378, Imperial was in London to supervise the loading of his ship's cargo. He was accosted, trodden on and then murdered just outside his house in St Nicholas Acon Lane. The trial records show that the henchmen were servants of the leading merchants of London, all of whom were involved in the export of wool. London shippers had dominated the trade and its profits, even to the exclusion of their own provincial compatriots; they were intent on sabotaging any attempt at enhancing competition from abroad. An appeal stated clearly that the accused believed that 'Janus Imperial would destroy and ruin all wool merchants in London and elsewhere' if he were to complete the negotiations. The Genoese opened London not only to their own countrymen, but to Florentines who used Genoese transport. This was too dangerous a development for London's leading merchants to accept; so Janus Imperial was killed.

This case captures several important aspects of London life: the strength of its merchant patriciate; the benefits which had accrued to merchants from commercial policies during the French wars when trade and taxation were so intimately linked; and the power of older men to recruit and move young men to violence. The Londoners who saved the king in 1381 – many of whom were knighted for their efforts – were a uniquely powerful group of grocers, fishmongers and mercers, with the power sometimes to determine policies at court and in parliaments, to affect the state of the kingdom in meaningful ways.

Foreign traders brought fine cloths, ivory, rare pets; the Datini company specialized in spice and grocery goods from the east: saffron, ginger, cinnamon, cloves, nutmeg, mace, pepper and dyes. They also brought Mediterranean goods: almonds, tin, soap (a mixture of soap-plant ashes and oil), and rice. A Genoese *tarita*, wrecked off the Brittany coast in 1386 and plundered by Dartmouth men, contained dates, alum and parts for crossbows. Households, and not only the kitchens of the lavish gentry and magnates, came to depend on a regular stream of eastern spices and southern foods; food was laced with their flavours during the festivities of midwinter.

In return all foreign merchants took away wool. Some were so well acquainted with the Cotswolds wool-towns that they coined Italianate names for them – *Borriforte* for Burford, *Norleccio* for Northleach – while others did regular and lucrative business with abbeys or with gentry middlemen. But these purveyors of good things were resented by local traders. Lombards were accused in parliament of introducing not only usury but also sodomy into England. Foreigners were at times as vulnerable as they seemed dangerous. In the week of political unrest in June 1381, after setting Archbishop Sudbury's head on the gate of London Bridge, activists turned to the parish of St Martin's in Vinery, dragged out thirty-five Flemings and slit their throats. Around 150 other Flemings were robbed. Morbid humour was had by Chaucer in *The Nuns' Priest's Tale* where the confusion of domestic animals caught up in the massacre is imagined:

> So were they scared by barking of the dogs
> And shouting men and women all did make,
> They all ran so they thought their hearts would break.
> They yelled as very fiends do down in Hell;
> The ducks they cried as at the butcher fell;
> The frightened geese flew up above the trees;
> Out of the hive there came the swarm of bees;
> So terrible was the noise, ah ben'cite!
> Certainly old Jack Straw and his army
> Never raised shouting half so loud and shrill
> When they were chasing Flemings for to kill,
> As on that day was raised upon the fox.

Here is opportunistic violence and simmering distrust and envy, which made life unsafe and unpleasant for its trading minorities, only a hundred years after the mass expulsion of the Jews.

Although London patricians resisted change, change was everywhere: in politics, in religion and in the tenor of family life. Prosperous aldermanic families suffered from the demographic realities of the age, like everyone else, and this meant that few parents had more than a single son to inherit and succeed them, and often not even one. Such families were also attracted to the opportunities available in the country, just as sons of gentry families were entering the law and finding their place in the capital, and even abroad. These merchants were also aware of the constraints upon their world, and its dependence on greater people.

London was a cosmopolitan city: in it the king could engage and benefit from the services of men such as the Florentine Mannini, Richard II's jeweller, and of other financiers for diplomatic activity. International events affected their trade greatly, such as the alliance struck between John of Gaunt and Portugal in 1386. Since the 1360s only single traders had been given privileges in Portugal, but henceforward opportunities were greater: in the fifteen months between September 1390 and December 1391 twenty English ships sailed from Bristol to Portugal carrying arms, wheat and horses, and returning laden with wines, figs, raisins and salt. With the advent of French control of west Flanders by 1386 the French used Flemish ships to threaten invasion and disrupt English trade. Such vicissitudes worried merchants such as Chaucer's own:

> He would the sea were held at any cost
> Across from Middleburgh to Orwell town.

For the wool staple had moved from Calais to Middleburgh in Zeeland in the years 1384–9.

Despite the elevation of some such men to knighthood, despite their riches and involvement in high politics, the great London merchants inhabited an ambiguous position in relation to magnates and the king. Chaucer's *Tale of Melibee* sets the arguments of chivalric honour against those of urban and urbane 'prudence'. Chaucer translated from French sections of a tract on peace, originally presented to Richard II, a vision of peace which is politic and subtle, not blandly and naively eirenic. The *Tale of Melibee* argues for the staying of vengeance and the working at concord. It is a parable about Richard II: his detractors saw him as effeminate, lacking in bellicose instincts; yet the making of peace was harder and more dangerous than any campaign.

In a city like London, and in parliament, mercantile and landed leaders mixed and cooperated, sought and maintained a fragile peace which was far better than its absence. Yet some cultural spheres enshrined the differences between merchants and gentry, counting-table and sword. An event such as the Smithfield Tournament of October 1390 benefited some great merchants through the demand it generated for rich cloth, supplied to the court by the clothier John Hend. The mayor, the financier William Ventour, was invited to view the proceedings from the royal stalls. But such men fitted uncomfortably into the world of prowess and display exhibited on the field. Unlike the equivalent urban festivities of the Low Countries, which many Londoners witnessed as passing merchants or as soldiers, this was an aristocratic celebration, the preserve of grandees such as the king's brother John of Holland, or the Count of Hainault. Neither magnate nor soldier, the merchant did not aspire to the glory and the easy authority which magnates and knights commanded. Such display was nowhere more evident than in the ostentation of Richard's later years: his entries into London rivalled those of any Renaissance prince.

RELIGIOUS LIFE

Richard's court revelled in the art and poetry and music which only a cosmopolitan outlook could nurture. In all sections of society people experienced a local version of the Europe-wide Christian culture with its sacraments, offered by clergy and supervised by bishops, who were often themselves figures of European dignity and importance. Ecclesiastical politics became even more complicated as the Papal Schism – a dispute over the identity of the pope which broke out in 1378 with the election of Urban VI to the Roman see – divided Europe along lines of allegiance to one or other (and even a third) pope. English bishops continued to provide English versions of Christian books for pastoral instruction, often of continental origin. Frequently these were confessional handbooks, such as the summary of penitential practice by Raymond of Peñaforte, which was translated into English and into Welsh before 1400; or collections of sermons for feast-days in the vernacular such as that composed by John Mirk, Augustinian canon of Lilleshall Abbey (Shropshire), *Mirk's Festial*, part of which was translated into Welsh. Texts circulated for instruction, but for most people reading was not necessary or common for religious practice.

Efforts were continuously invested in the provision of workbooks for the clergy: every church was expected to have a missal, a lectionary (with readings for the mass), an antiphonary (with music for the beginning of the mass), a psalter, a book of sequences (special prayers), and an ordinal (with the order of services). Bishops attempted not only to supply the clergy with the necessary working tools, but also to create a uniformity of correct practice within a diocese. As can be expected, many parishes were ill-provided, stripped of basic adornment and supplies. When the Bishop of Hereford visited the churches of his diocese in 1397 he found that the rector of Ollingwick had removed the church door, churchyard lamps, and a large breviary (service-book), which he read to his servant in the privacy of his home.

Around the basic tenets of faith and practice there developed a wide range of activities such as private prayer (the rich could pray with the aid of highly adorned books), pilgrimage to the shrines of saints, processions around parish boundaries, and religious drama. People from all parts wended their ways on pilgrimages. Some ventured far afield: the poet Gruffydd Gryg (c.1360–1410) has left a description of a pilgrimage to Santiago de Compostela. In Wales and Cornwall strong traditions were attached to holy wells, and to the chapels built around them, as in Ffynnon Gybi (Caernarfonshire) or Ffynnon Seiriol (Anglesey) and St Mawes (Cornwall), where healing was sought and frequently found. These adventures were not obligatory; they were arduous, but they could also be enjoyable and invigorating forms of religious participation. The laity could also elicit the aid of various types of religious: monks guarded saints' relics and their legends, friars composed plays, bishops led processions, hermits chided and pronounced prophecies, and visionaries composed prayers. Biblical reading and reflection on the text of scripture played a limited role in the experience of most Christians, while stories about saints and cautionary *exempla* were a staple. Scripture offered the verses around which preachers composed their sermons, and furnished some of the English words which actors in religious drama declaimed, but the Bible was rarely encountered directly by lay people. It was read by few, and even those who could read it were encouraged to encounter it through the guiding and corrective mediation of preacher or priest.

The priest was the central pivot of sacramental life, and the onerous task of representing and mediating doctrine, morals, enthusiasm and ritual, with which he was charged, was all but impossible to fulfil adequately. He was meant to live among his parishioners in most cases, managing the land or rents from which he derived his income, and operating over a wide range of some extremely private and other highly public activities. There was a literature to guide him, and church-wardens supported the fabric of his church, but the demands of celibacy and the knowledge and understanding of the purpose and contents of priestly office proved very demanding for many.

The church's own internal scrutiny, through visitations conducted by bishops and their officials, was often prompted by the complaints of parishioners. Shortage of personnel meant that some men were appointed to jobs they could not fill adequately, on the condition that they improve. So John Laurencz was appointed as clerk to the parish of Great Wishford (Wiltshire), and swore that he would leave at the end of the summer to attend the schools and return when he felt competent. William Colet was examined and found lacking; he was ordered to attend grammar school and acquire the ability to understand scripture and offices within a year. The quality of personal life was often denounced by parishioners who offered details of uncanonical conduct by their priests. In many cases priests cohabited with women, often with a family, a domestic unit in all but law. In 1394 Isabel Seman confessed to having been the partner of William Smyth, vicar of Chobham (Surrey), and the mother of his children, the youngest of which was in her arms while she made her confession. In the life of John Swell of White Waltham (Berkshire) several weaknesses were found: he secretly kept a woman called Joan who had come with him from his previous living, a woman said to be another man's wife, making this a case of adultery. He was also remiss in providing extreme unction, was given to drinking and could not sing, read or understand the services. Here were more deficiencies than a few months at a school could remedy. Swell denied having had intercourse with Joan, and swore to do penance and correct his life, in a different parish.

We witness in such records accusations, some real, some malicious, some exaggerated. Some of the resentment harboured towards priests was expressed in the shocking events at Wye in 1382: a group of men seized a priest and mutilated his face with a sign of the cross produced by ashes and sulphur. The centrality of parish priests was tested and matched by the vulnerability of their personal authority. The dilemmas of celibacy and clerical abuse clearly challenged priests and communities in ways which Catholic bishops still confront today.

Every man and woman, child and adult, belonged to a parish. Urban or rural, in bustling streets or on a country lane, the parish church claimed a person's loyalty from the moment of birth. It was here that children were baptized, marriages were solemnized, and funerals unfolded, with burial in the adjacent churchyard. Parishioners were expected, at the very least, to make confession and take communion at Easter. But a wide range of other services was offered in those parish churches where an adequate priestly presence was to be found. These ranged from exhortations by Sunday and feast-day sermons to celebration of Easter Week and participation in the drama of the Christmas season. There was teaching for boys, the comfort of visitation to the sick and dying, the offering of death-bed communion and extreme unction, and, when necessary, even the committing to writing of a parishioner's last will and testament.

The parish was not only an ecclesiastical administrative unit in which people were expected to perform their duties, to which they paid tithes and where they dutifully appeared for annual communion. In it, work and kinship, age and gender were regularly expressed in conflict and celebrated in joy. Those who entered a church in breaks from work – seldom in summer, more frequently in winter – were reminded by the rood, by wall-paintings, by elaborately carved fonts like the ones East Anglian villages boasted, of their duties and failings. The Christ of Sundays displayed the wounds inflicted on him by those who toiled on his day; the works of mercy beckoned, and even in the poorest church a chancel cross brought to mind the very rudiments of the Christian story. Parish churches offered space for a wide range of social and familial celebrations: church-ales at which money was raised for the support of newlyweds as they set up their new home, marriage celebrations, dramatic performances of biblical tales. The safe and relatively protected space of the parish church was sometimes used as a place of safekeeping for documents or treasure, a meeting place for the transaction of business, even as a market on rainy days. Men and women could express their interest through small contributions made to the parish – holy bread, embroidered vestments, works of art, offerings to the altar, testamentary gifts of plate or cash or cloth – each as he or she could make or afford to buy.

The chancel, the church's east end and the site of the altar and its precious ornaments, was the responsibility of the rector, while maintenance of the main section of the church, its nave – with its long and wide areas of wall, windows and ceiling – in which the parishioners huddled as they stood during services, was the responsibility of the parishioners. Sometime in the thirteenth century the office of church-warden emerged, and pairs of such officers, usually prominent and always men, undertook the task of collecting funds and managing them in support of the parish church's fabric, furniture and plate. The accounts rendered by churchwardens were drawn up annually for scrutiny, and display a wide range of activities: distribution of alms from the parish box and weekly collections, fundraising for special purchases (a canopy or a chalice), and even moneylending from parish capital. The accounts for 1394 of the church of St Margaret's, York, record small expenses, such as payments for the mending of surplices and altar linen (probably by female parishioners), for the purchase of parchment, of a clapper, of bell-strings and a trunk. The restoration of the fabric was always a serious undertaking, and the efforts it involved could enhance prestige and solidarity between those who underwrote the project. In Ripon (North Yorkshire) a fraternity was founded in the 1370s for the maintenance of a then ruined chapel, said to be of St Winifred.

Churchwardens were leading local men, who were sometimes called to subsidize the parish when it ran into deficit. They demonstrate the many ways in which the parish and the social unit of village or neighbourhood, as well as the judicial and productive unit of the manor, overlapped. The parish sometimes coincided with the urban ward, and often fully with the manorial village, and it sometimes included a number of hamlets. In the parish were displayed not only Christian symbols and artefacts, but, increasingly in these decades, marks of seigneurial presence or patrician involvement. Crests and armour were displayed on walls, as above the north doorway of Castle Acre church in Norfolk, or on shields in spandrels such as those of the de Warennes, Earls of Surrey, and of the Fitzallans, Earls of Arundel. Gifts from local families came in the form of chalices, hangings or vestments, and brasses marked the passing of prominent parish members. The brass of the Admiral, Thomas Lord Bergavenny (d. 1417), and his wife Mary (d. 1392) was probably made in London in the year of her death. It is situated in the north aisle of the church of Wotton-under-Edge (Gloucestershire), where it displays in modest but effective fashion their estate and pursuits: she is a lady in distinguished though restrained dress, he a warrior, with a mermaid collar invoking his maritime pursuits, and a lion and a dog at his feet. Family pews and chantries similarly marked off spaces within the parish church, creating a clear sense of hierarchy within it, as these were invariably placed as close as possible to the chancel-end, the church's liturgical focus. Entering a church was not so much stepping into another world, but rather entering into a space which depicted and reinforced some of the social and political realities which were encountered outside it. In the parish church, royal proclamations were made, banns of marriage announced, and news of campaigns, treaties and coronations was disseminated. Humiliation and punishment were also practised there, as the excommunicate were named, adulterers shamed and penitents were viewed in their hairshirts and torn garments.

In the plenitude of its social and religious functions, the parish was a meeting-point for rich and poor, the powerful and their dependants. The parish was increasingly the favoured venue for collection, distribution and perpetual provision for the poor. One manner of provision was the allocation of annual incomes to be used in the form of distributions at the discretion of the parish priest. In his will of 1396 Robert Holme of York left 100 marks for the heads of poor families in parishes where he had bought raw wool. This was an act of restitution as well as an act of charity. Parish loyalty mattered greatly to those who gave – not only as a way of perpetuating their names in exchange for future prayers, but also as a vestige of family and lineage in a local setting. Similar understanding of the centrality of parish relief was to be displayed in the sixteenth century in the Poor Law legislation of Queen Elizabeth.

Embedded in the spheres of power and social relations, the parish offered the instruction and support which was meant to keep people away from sin, and to integrate them as good members of a Christian community. Priests aimed at promoting some basic Christian beliefs, the very minimum of structured knowledge that could provide a basis for a discerning Christian life. This knowledge, conveyed by parents and reinforced by priestly attention before confirmation between the ages of ten and twelve, was bolstered by exposure to explicit visual representations. Wall-paintings, statues and stained-glass windows adorned churches to the extent that their members and their benefactors could provide.

People could attend and even join many liturgical enactments such as viewing a procession with the eucharist to the sick, or the elevation of the host at mass. People attended funerals and – especially women – watched over Christ's sepulchre, carved out of stone, like that at Eastbourne (Sussex), from Good Friday to Easter morning. All these performances reinforced the tenets of the Christian story with its promise of salvation. Late medieval imagery concentrated much attention on Christ's suffering on the cross, and cross-related imagery abounded, from the rood cross that hung above the crossing in front of the chancel, to the cross which was habitually embroidered on the priest's vestments, such as the splendid chasuble still to be seen in Skenfrith church in Gwent, with scenes from the Virgin Mary's life. Parish provision was thus varied and occasions for voluntary participation were many, especially in the summer months when much of the liturgy was enacted out of doors. Rural parishes occasionally pooled their resources for the support of a group of players who performed biblical plays, while the sophisticated communities of towns could mount grand cyclical plays with many scenes and sumptuous props and costumes, planned over months, and involving wide participation of a large part of the male citizenry.

INHERITANCE

Dynasty linked past and present and offered a focus for identity and aspiration. If the parish offered the channels towards salvation to all, then dynasty offered additional security, by contributing to spiritual well-being. Most commemorative arrangements were set up and maintained by families. The rich could depend on the services offered by chaplains whose whole purpose was commemoration of the dead in family chapels and chantries placed within parish churches, or in cathedrals for the socially exalted. Thousands of chantry priests were paid modest sums – in 1378 a maximum stipend was set at seven marks a year, three in cash and four in food – as wages for incessant intercession for the dead relatives of their employers. Links with previous generations were similarly cemented by the inheritance of objects for daily use, for adornment, for pleasure: clothes, hangings, jewellery, keepsakes, prayerbooks; people invested value and retained memories through them. The great minster at Tewkesbury was the recipient of a bequest made in his will of 1375 by Edward Despenser, Lord of Glamorgan and Morgannwg: a suit of vestments, two chalices and a ewer given to him by the King of France, which he wished to have used for the containment of the consecrated host on Corpus Christi day. The rich were far more able to commemorate previous generations as their lives abounded in objects of value and beauty. Tangible objects, enduring stone structures that could be held by a family for centuries, crests and emblems, documents and muniments, all these cemented a sense of dynastic loyalty and privilege.

Through actions within the locality and beyond it, family members were expected to promote dynastic honour and refrain from bringing shame and damage upon it. An all-important occasion when dynastic considerations were intense was, of course, marriage. The church's view of Christian marriage required free entry into the relationship, a morally significant act of free will which merited recognition as a sacrament. But in most social milieus marriage was arranged, and it was the prerogative of patriarchs, the result of careful dynastic assessment and planning. The fact that ecclesiastical courts in England and Wales abounded with cases of marriage breakdown, broken promises and unconsummated marriages, demonstrates the degree to which the church's legal system – canon law – provided avenues for rearrangement of marital situations. Margaret, wife of Robert Handerby, brought her case for spousal cruelty to the ecclesiastical court of York, and although the court attempted a reconciliation it also ordered that, were violence to recur, legal separation would follow. A steady stream of English and Welsh petitioners sent representatives to the papal court in search of such life-changing separation or annulment. Young people clearly often defied parental choice, and prevalent demographic conditions favoured periods of work outside the home, before marriage. Young people seized opportunities to work and train away from family and home, and thus developed greater autonomy in the period leading up to marriage. Richard Carter and Joan ate Enges were domestic servants in a York neighbourhood; when they exchanged vows in 1370 it was before their employers, not their families. But in the landed and wealthy classes less volatility was demonstrated, and in royal marriages there was the least of all. Here, marriage and procreation were affairs of state.

WYCLIF AND 'LOLLARDY'

From the 1380s and throughout the remaining medieval decades, the church in England and Wales faced sustained challenges from groups which came to be known as Wycliffites, followers of John Wyclif, and later from those who were labelled 'Lollards'. What began as a set of theological discussions at the University of Oxford in the 1370s was soon considered to be an onslaught upon the relations of church and state, and a critique of most practices of religious life as known to parishioners. Inasmuch as religion and notions of order – familial, political and communal – were intertwined, this threat was a matter of urgency to every man of power: to every father, every priest, every bishop, to the king.

A subtle interaction existed between religious ideas and ideas about politics and the social order. Whereas the great upheavals experienced by many in the decades following the Black Death may have made some people more independent and relatively sceptical about the fixity of hierarchies and order, it is also clear that for others an adherence to traditional religion, to the system which made sense of suffering and loss and which offered a comprehensive world-view and personal morality, was also attractive. Thus we have seen, in the decades which coincided with the late years of Edward III and with the reign of Richard II, the flourishing of what some have called 'traditional religion' – in the work of religious fraternities, foundations of chantries and establishment of masses for the dead.

At the same time a trend was at work which may be called 'radical orthodoxy' rather than heresy. This was religious experimentation by members of several distinct social groups: gentry, lower clergy, university scholars, culturally eclectic courtiers, independent and informed merchants. They were attracted by the belief that individuals might forge a personal morality based on a close reading of scripture and outside the promise and mediation of sacraments through the hands of the clergy. Just as the Commons were inveighing against corrupt royal officials and ministers, so the servants of God – clergy and episcopacy, friars and theologians – became the subjects of criticism, dissatisfaction and public lampooning.

Like so many other positions we have already encountered, seemingly deeply contradictory, yet residing cheek by jowl, this diversity in religious styles reflects some regional differences between the lands ruled by the kings of England. It was diversity anchored in regionality – in the agrarian and climatic regimes which differentiate people's work, diet, appearance; in history – with some regions being conquered lands, exploited by a dominant group of land- and privilege-holders; in geography – as regions which were seafaring or connected by riverine systems displayed more mobility and eclecticism. Diversity and hybridity need not surprise us, for they confirm and explain the expressions of dissent and the burgeoning of ideas in the later decades of the century.

A wide range of attitudes brought into question aspects of the conventional Christian life upheld by 'traditional religion'. These attitudes were considered and expressed first by scholars in the University of Oxford, and then more widely by their sympathizers, preachers who travelled the country supported by communities which welcomed their message, and harboured them, protected them and committed their words to writing. First among them was the north Yorkshireman John Wyclif (c.1335/8–1384). By the 1360s he was a Fellow of Balliol College, where many northerners came to study. There he stayed to teach and write. In 1372 he was awarded a doctorate in theology, and he went on to lecture on Oxford's arts course. Teaching Aristotle's *Physics* was an occasion to reflect on God's competence, on the degree of divine intervention in the world, issues which touched on fundamental questions of Christian ethics. Wyclif cherished above all the sense of God's underlying commitment to the world through his unseen yet formative laws for it. Appearances were surfaces that revealed little of these underlying truths – scripture alone was a sure guide to them. The invisible church was rarely reflected in the visible actions and objects of the practice of liturgy and church law; this was mightily proven by the miserable state of church politics, plagued by papal schism and dispute. Inspired by the political world of the late years of Edward III, this philosopher-theologian wrote tracts on political theory, just as he served in the 1370s as a diplomat in royal service, as part of John of Gaunt's circle. Wyclif was not a scholar shut away in an ivory tower but an intellectual who brought rigour to bear upon the realities of his day, such as the relative authorities of church and king, the uses and abuses of church wealth. He found particularly harmful – both morally and politically – the involvement of prelates in government, for this necessarily made them agents of oppression. He asked with rhetorical flourish: 'What is an archbishop doing as the King's chancellor, an office which is the most secular in the kingdom?' The clergy's advantages set it apart from its flock; when the country was groaning under taxation, were not the clergy exempt from the poll-tax of 1381?

In 1377 Wyclif was denounced by Pope Gregory XI for his views on the eucharist and the endowment of the church, views which were the subject of many heated disputations in Oxford. When he was arrested by the Chancellor of Oxford University, Wyclif's release was secured by John of Gaunt, his patron. The crown was slow to respond to Wyclif's challenge, but when English prelates finally caught up and began examining his books, Wyclif retired to his parish of Lutterworth in Leicestershire, where he died in peace in 1384, having seen his works condemned at the Blackfriars Council in London in 1382. In a sermon preached in the summer of that year, Bishop Brinton of Rochester represented Wyclif's views as an attack on the sacraments – especially on the all-important remedies of baptism, confession and eucharist – by a 'pseudo-prophet'. After Wyclif's death the task of cleansing Oxford of the Wycliffite disease became an obsession, a concern of the Bishop of Lincoln, to whose diocese Oxford belonged. Cambridge gained from Oxford's notoriety; throughout the fifteenth century it became the university of choice for much royal and episcopal patronage.

Wycliffism was a relatively limited movement of scholars, yet its international links and the spread of the Wycliffite Bible – the Bible in English – made it much more meaningful. The chronicler Henry Knighton coined the pun in his appalled report on the Bible's effect: 'Master John Wyclif translated the gospel into the English – not angelic – language . . . the pearled gospel is spread and trampled by pigs.' Indeed, over 250 manuscripts of the translation still survive, such as the famous 'Cider Bible' on display in Hereford Cathedral Library, in which references to wine were substituted by the word for the local tipple, cider. The prodigious literary production of a small group of scholars and preachers spawned the fantasy of a much wider movement of dissent and reform – to which the label 'Lollardy' was attached.

'Lollardy' was the term used to describe a multitude of views about the sacraments, on the cult of saints and relics, and on pilgrimages, disavowal of the power of images, criticism of religious drama and the vivid preaching of friars, rejection of purgatory and of the efficacy of prayers for the dead. The understanding at the basis of all these positions was opposition to trivialization of faith, to religion experienced through external signs, mediated by material procedure, to instruction in Christian belief through 'curiosities and novelties' rather than through exposition of the Bible. It saw in many practices inventions of priests who wished to extort payments from the laity, rich and poor. Some Lollard writings targeted the interpenetration of church and state institutions: a clause of the *Twelve Conclusions*, a Lollard manifesto of *c*.1394, judged the cooperation of 'prelate and justice in temporal cause, curate and officer in worldly service' to be contrary to God's rule. Wyclif believed that had Christ come to visit fourteenth-century Europe, he would have been persecuted and burned. Some Lollard teaching had a disturbing apocalyptic edge; the *Opus arduum* (*Hard work*) even saw the year 1390 as an apocalyptic sign, with chaos in the rule of antichrist (the pope). Walter Brut, a layman educated in Latin, who wrote an account of his imprisonment and trial in the diocese of Hereford, believed that the pope was the true antichrist, 'contrary to the laws and doctrines of Christ'.

At its most elaborate, dissent offered a total alternative to Christianity as lived in late-fourteenth-century parishes. It promoted instead a spirituality based on scriptural texts, a piety which saw no reward for external signs of faith, and cherished an emphasis on belief and spirit rather than on materiality. It was austere, and could appear egalitarian; it supported the offering of the Bible in the vernacular, and inspired the creation of groups of women and men for reading and discussion in homes and workshops. Through preaching and exposition such groups aimed to teach, but also to animate that third of all men, and an unknowable but substantial number of women; so, as the chronicler Knighton put it, 'for the laity and those women who could read'. We often learn about so-called Lollard preachers from the sources of examination and persecution: in 1382 the Bishop of Lincoln issued a mandate against the hermit William Swinderby, who dwelt in a chapel near Leicester and claimed the authority to preach against church doctrine. Swinderby may have learned his views at the Abbey of St Mary, Leicester, which he had recently visited, a centre for dissenting opinions and patronage in the Midlands. Bishops were charged with licensing preaching and supervising its contents; anyone who arrogated to himself the right to teach without licence, or in defiance of recommended styles and topics of preaching, posed a challenge to episcopal authority, upon which the whole structure of the church depended.

The positions which were identified as 'Lollard' expressed a desire for simplicity and accessibility of worship which was cherished by people who were never related to Wycliffism. See, for example, the cry for God's love unmediated by preachers in the words of the poet Dafydd ap Gwilym (*c.*1320–80) directed at a friar:

> God is not so cruel friend
> As old dotards would pretend . . .
> Pleasure grown from poet's song
> For sick and whole, old and young.
> We have equal warrant each,
> I to write verse, you to preach.

Some men in clerical orders, and some who judged themselves to be suitable teachers, traversed the dioceses of southern England offering alternative teaching and worship. Such must have been William Ramesbury who was investigated by the Bishop of Salisbury in 1389. This man defied all categories of ecclesiastical propriety: he was a 'virtual layman' who preached and feigned holiness. He claimed to have been tonsured, by a Thomas Fishburn, and thus to have entered into clerical orders. He donned a russet tunic and mantle, and celebrated a type of mass. His mass retained the crucial elements of elevation of the host, prayers for the dead, and blessing of bread for distribution among members of the congregation. He celebrated in this manner for four years throughout the diocese, from Sherston near Malmesbury to Warminster, to his native Ramesbury.

Was his a mock mass or a 'Lollard mass'? William had congregations, and an amount of local support that allowed him to survive for so long unbeneficed and undetected. He clearly retained central aspects of Christian ritual celebration. He was a powerful preacher and teacher, who talked and exhorted people everywhere: in churchyards, taverns, while travelling. Judging by the erroneous opinions listed by the investigating bishop, and which William then chose to renounce, he held a recognizable and coherent set of convictions: against ecclesiastical hierarchy, against clerical celibacy and against the worship of images. The claim that he advocated sexual intercourse with nuns should be seen as a stock accusation aimed at further embellishing his challenging and transgressive image.

Men such as William were numerous. Some were placed more advantageously as beneficed clergy, who could use their own pulpits for the exposition of reformist views, as did John Coryngham in Diddington, near Huntingdon, up to the spring of 1384. In some cases, and in the early years of Wycliffism, preachers were invited by a mayor to bring illumination to a town, as was William Swinderby, who was the guest of Leicester in 1382; in 1392 Northampton probably initiated a similar invitation to a dissenting preacher. What congregations got was a plain sermon – one which adhered doggedly to scriptural text – which did not deploy the age-old and familiar tales, *exempla*, and other diversionary tactics which provided comic relief in the midst of traditional sermons. Even on feast-days, some preachers would prefer to adhere to a relevant scriptural text rather than use the legends embedded in hagiographical writing. For this some were labelled 'Lollards'.

The tens of surviving sermons branded or self-identified as 'Lollard' are testimony to preaching which provided food for thought, and which must have impressed with the fervour, commitment and starkness of its message. The *Prologue* to the Wycliffite Bible, produced in the late 1390s, is a tract on the value and manner of reading scripture. Though simple in tone, and provided in English, here is a distillation of classical rhetoric and Christian exegesis, based primarily on the writings of Augustine: the Bible should be read literally, in its original word, by people of little learning, but not so literally as to denude it of its figurative, poetic qualities. Such new vernacular works and the preachers who spread them and their message did not fit into existing liturgical niches, nor did they require priestly guidance. Rather, they were meant to initiate discussion and reflection. Some preachers even left copies of their sermons with congregations for further rumination at a later time. Although they were presented as novel and disruptive to the Christian tradition, some 'Lollard' preachers were university-trained, and were minded to seek links between their views and those of earlier reformers. An interesting juxtaposition is the appetite in England for the reformist and prophetic texts associated with the twelfth-century Rhenish visionary Hildegard of Bingen, who is probably better known nowadays for her musical compositions. In turn, by the 1390s, even orthodox writers, such as the author of the *Pore Caitif* (*Poor Captive*), used 'Lollard' commentaries on the gospels and drew from biblical translations in the compilation of their teaching materials.

Views deemed 'Lollard' went to the heart of clerical privilege in mediating the sacraments to believers, and since only men could become priests, this was also an attack on male privilege. During his examination for heresy of October 1391 Walter Brut was said to have claimed that women had the power and authority to preach, to make the sacrament of the eucharist, that they had the power of the keys, to bind and to loosen, invested in St Peter and thereafter in the clergy for all time. The same ideas were expressed in the *Twelve Conclusions*, a set of principles nailed to Westminster Hall in the winter of 1394, during the king's absence in Ireland, by men who presented themselves as 'poor men, treasurers of Christ and his Apostles'. The first and second conclusions attacked the papacy in Rome, the third claimed that clerical celibacy led to incontinence and sodomy, the fourth that 'the feigned miracle of the sacrament of bread induces all men but a few to idolatry'. The Dominican polemicist Roger Dymmock, who replied to the *Twelve Conclusions*, accused the instigators, whom he took to be clerics, of ingratitude towards a church that had educated and nurtured them, and of bringing dangerous harm to simple folk who were misled by their errors.

The church's administrative machine, led by the bishops, many of whom were leading royal servants, was entrusted with the task of correcting such error and controlling preaching. It set out to identify and correct such preachers, but the task proved to be a difficult one. This is made clear even from a single career: that of William Swinderby. In 1382 Bishop Buckingham of Lincoln moved against a hermit from the Leicester area, who claimed to have been ordained. The latter upped and moved to Herefordshire, where he was apprehended almost a decade later by Bishop Trefenant, who found him to be 'but simply lettred'. While it is easy to think of a Puritan preaching in whitewashed churches from which much ornament had been dismantled, it is difficult to imagine a 'Lollard' preaching from a typical late medieval pulpit, such as that in Castle Acre church in Norfolk, as it was by 1400. The pulpit was adorned with figures of the Latin fathers of the church – Augustine, Gregory, Jerome and Ambrose – and next to it stood the screen, of which only the bottom survives in a colourful display of traditional saints' legends: Philip, James, Matthias, Jude, John, James, Peter, Andrew, Bartholomew, Thomas, Simon and Matthew. The call for reform was an assault on the aesthetic of worship, accumulated in churches by communities over centuries.

VERNACULAR LITERATURES AND CULTURES

While English came to be associated with mistaken, even treasonous, religious inclinations, its powers were also being tested by aspirant writers – professional, such as Thomas Usk, or leisured men of letters, such as John Clanvowe. In his *Testament of Love* Usk opined that clerks should write in Latin, Frenchmen in French, which comes naturally to them, and 'let us show our fantasies in such words that we learned from our mother's tongue'. Such reflections on the robustness of English as a tool for learned and poetical writing are in themselves a sign of the commitment and excitement which using it engendered. In his *Treatise on the Astrolabe* Geoffrey Chaucer (d. 1400) wondered whether 'light English' quite suited scientific writing. He was soon to move on to the most sophisticated writing about human affection, community, government and justice. Inspired by Italian and French poetry (which he had heard as well as read), he made English – hitherto the language of the home and locality, of women and children and peasants – into the language of kings and magnates.

Chaucer also wrote the elegy *The Book of the Duchess* around 1369, in memory of Blanche Duchess of Lancaster, first wife of John of Gaunt. Female traditions of great richness and broad reference were available, and influenced the aesthetic of such highly programmatic royal works as the Wilton Diptych and the images painted in Westminster Abbey, as well as images made as offerings, such as the stained-glass window at Beverley Minster which featured the royal pair. Anne of Bohemia adopted the emblem of the white hart, which had been reintroduced by Philippa of Hainault in the 1340s. Dominicans loomed large in Anne's court, as they did around most female royals on the continent. Even the queen had few female servants: there were no more than twenty women around her, and she a queen famed for her patronage and lavish hospitality. Yet the cultural resources of this female group were considerable. Queen Anne read Latin, German and Czech, and may have commissioned Geoffrey Chaucer's *Legend of Good Women*. A cult developed around her following her early death in 1394 at the age of twenty-eight, a cult promoted by her husband, and enlivened by her sumptuous funeral (two months in the planning), and her elegant death effigy, which still survives, in the Museum of Westminster Abbey. Yet for all her impact, the active and creative elements of the Ricardian court, the core audience for Chaucer's poetry, for ceremonies of diplomatic display or the discussion of Wycliffite ideas, belonged to a male sphere of sociability. These were groups which readily and knowingly discussed war, art, commerce, poetry and love. Chaucer's English and his literature form part of this world; its first audiences were restricted, almost private, chiefly male.

The chronicler Thomas Walsingham claimed that the *Twelve Conclusions* had been publicized with the aid of knights of King Richard's chamber, and that when he returned from Ireland the king chastised these errant, privileged men of his close acquaintance. The royal household was almost wholly male: when it was criticized, barbs were directed not at indulgence in sexual licence – as was the case during Richard's great-grandfather's reign – but at expenditure and patronage. Few women attended the court; a celibacy of service was encouraged, or at least an appearance thereof.

Yet a rhetoric of inclusion in a new-born language came to be attached to Chaucer's poetry even in his lifetime, and became even stronger in the following decades (Plate 10). In his *Troy Book* of *c.*1412–20 John Lydgate, monk of Bury St Edmunds and court poet, described Chaucer as the one who magnified English, and 'adorned it with his eloquence', 'adorn' and 'eloquence' both being words which Chaucer had coined. Lydgate also opined that *The House of Fame* was as good as Dante's poetry. French penetrated English parlance through Chaucer's inventive leadership. The French poet Eustache Deschamps, whose self-portrayal as a victim of war found poetical form in a play on his name, *brulé des champs* – burnt of fields (referring to the destruction of his ancestral lands in Champagne) – described Chaucer as '*grant translateur*', transmitter and conveyer of literary worth.

The mythical status earned by Chaucer's English poetry diverts attention from the powerful vernacular poetry in Old and Middle English and in Welsh. English Marcher lords developed a great liking for the sounds and the generic diversity of Welsh poetry; for the Welsh *cywyddau*, a eulogy which fitted well with lordly self-perception, and for the elegy, or ode (*awdl*). Such was Ieuan Llwyd ab Ieuan's elegy for his wife Angharad:

> A fitting pain, a shower of tears wets me,
> My cheek is sallow and withered by languishing grief;
>
> . . .
>
> Sad work for the sight, the long enforced weeping;
> Woeful work of longing, the memory of Angharad.

So advanced was Welsh poetry that it spawned a critical tradition of treatises on the bardic art. Not only did the Welsh gentry crave it, but so did English lords of Wales, their stewards and officials. Welsh poetry shared with Chaucer's a love of alliteration and an inclusion of daily patterns of speech. It often displayed, like Chaucer's, a frisky anti-clerical sentiment and a worldly-wise stance towards authority, while at the same time participating in traditional forms of worship and deference within the social and political order. Irish bardic poetry was the subject of repeated legislative bans by bishops in the fourteenth century, yet clearly those who could perform the art were rewarded with food and hospitality, and their works were appreciated by Anglo-Irish lords.

There was also the variety of English dialects, regional languages with traditional genres, sounds and poetics. While Chaucer built upon London English, Langland worked through the dialect of the south-west, the author of *Gawain and the Green Knight* was from the west Midlands, the devotional text *Cursor mundi* was northern, and the penitential guide *Ayenbite of Inwyt* was Kentish. In 1382 John of Trevisa wrote from the West Country about northerners:

The language of the Northumbrians, especially at York, is so sharp, piercing, grinding and misshapen that we southern men can scarcely understand it. I believe that is because they are near strange men and aliens that speak strangely, and also because the Kings of England always live far from that country.

Trevisa ought to have known that London too was full of 'aliens', as were Bristol and Norwich. But the final remark is insightful: in these and the following decades English was shaped and endowed with dignity and force by the example of the court, the language of royal proclamation, the habits of Chancery and law-courts. By the fifteenth century it was *the* language of politics.

The burgeoning of English, the rise of its utility and prestige, is notable in wide areas of practice and experience. Not only does the literature of amusement and leisure display this trend, but so does that of work and vocation. In the latter a distinctive style of mixing English with Latin terms is evident, like the functional bilingualism demonstrated by the barber-surgeon of London, Thomas Plouden (d. 1413). A medical compilation was translated for his use, which combined university texts with practical directions. English was becoming not only the language of oral practice, as between surgeon and patient, but that in which the surgeon read and learned his craft. This was not a total replacement, but a merging of languages, into a bilingualism for a wide range of the literate population. In an English astronomical text Latin was frequently used when a word did not come to mind; the inscription on an amulet turned from English to Latin for the words of prayer. Collections of English medical recipes contained Latin names of ailments in the margin, to facilitate consultation of Latin texts. Another sphere of professional practice, that of Chancery, was also producing an English particular to its practices. In this last quarter of the century English, French and Latin coexisted and enriched linguistic resources, with English in the ascendant in spheres of professional work, religious instruction and private reading and amusement.

So rich was poetical production during Richard II's reign that the term Ricardian Poetry has been coined to include Chaucer and the *Pearl* poet, as well as John Gower and William Langland. Poetry had a public and political set of preoccupations: morality, poverty, social change and disruption. Its characters were stock figures of satire, but also identifiable within contemporary life: the Man of Law, the Squire, the pious Prioress, the Plowman. French was the language of reading and writing for lay men and women, but the uses of English were growing: in devotional writings and increasingly in poetry. English was also becoming a vehicle for the learned discourse of the law-courts: the oldest surviving private legal document is in English, a petition of the Mercers of London to parliament in 1386; the oldest will in English was enrolled at the London court a year later.

War had brought England and France together over almost a century; Richard's second marriage was planned to bring them even closer – war and kinship are links almost equally intimate and revealing. French poets were in the service of John of Gaunt and the Earls of Derby and Pembroke. The Savoyard Oton de Graunson transmitted French poetry that influenced Chaucer, just as music and the entertainment of diplomats at court did; John of Gaunt's own chapel boasted the finest French music. Where the court of Edward III delighted in French romance and in Arthurian imagery – not least with the creation of the Order of the Garter – in Richard's court such games would have seemed puerile. In its place Chaucer and the Ricardian poets were experimenting with European poetry expressive of complex social interactions and moral dilemmas, a poetry of the now and the future, not of the bygone past; it was worldly and pedagogic, all-embracing and cautionary.

RICHARD II: THE MATURE KING

It is a curious paradox about Richard II that he possessed so marked a capacity towards imaginative thought, and yet judged so inaccurately those enduring, more predictable, aspects of kingly rule, his relations with the peers of the realm. As a young man, as yet unsullied by extended rule, he had been the recipient of the political aspirations and requests of those who marched to London in June 1381. But only a few years later, by 1386, he was seen as a promoter of factional interests and destroyer of fabrics of loyalty and cooperation. He did not shine militarily, nor did he attend to the exercise of power in the council chamber. His court was the seat of poets, in it diplomacy was vibrant.

Richard's aspirations were laudable, and he sought example in the right places: he impaled his arms with those of Edward the Confessor, and turned to trusted administrators in affairs of state. In an act of dynastic piety and self-presentation in 1390 he sent to the papal Chancery material to be used in the process of canonization of Edward II, his great-grandfather, another ruler troubled by his magnates. He believed that gestures of generosity and images of great beauty might turn foe into friend and scepticism to loyalty. When his conflict with London over the city's financial and legal privileges was settled, this was celebrated in a pageant of concord of 1392: the city's capitulation was visualized in processional form from Great Conduit to Little Conduit in Cheapside, and ultimately to Temple Bar. The king and queen offered themselves as actors in scenes of offering and worship: the capital became a celestial city with young men and women descending from overhanging towers with offerings of gold plate to the royal pair. A plethora of religious images pervaded the event, undercutting for a while other political interpretations: the king was bridegroom and the city his bride, in a celestial Jerusalem where John the Baptist was shown preaching and a final, humbling, scene of the Crucifixion was staged.

No single adjective can capture the diversity of political moods and cultural forms experienced in England and Calais, Wales, and the parts of Ireland ruled by Richard II. The collapse of trust between the young king and his most natural advisers, in the events of 1386–8, pushed Richard into the arms of his uncle, John of Gaunt. The Duke of Lancaster became in 1390 also Duke of Aquitaine for life, and he supported the king's policy of peace with France, which his arch-foes the Percies in the north-east opposed. Yorkshire was a region of constant disorder and insurrection, not least by men in Lancastrian service who disrupted the life of towns and the rhythm of courts. In 1392 300 armed men entered Doncaster and stopped the collection of tolls from tenants of the Duchies of Lancaster and York. Men of the Lancastrian affinity seemed to be immune from punishment. Rather than encouraging people to appeal to royal justice, this realization created disaffection towards the king, who was seen as ineffectual and partisan. As is often the case when the balance of power is unsettled, men like the Beckwiths in the West Riding took matters into their own hands.

In court another set of concerns was being explored and represented. The early 1390s saw intensive efforts at securing peace. Philippe de Mezières, French diplomat, soldier and pilgrim, wrote a letter on peace which begged Richard to join a coalition of peace which would free the hands of England and France to lead a Crusade to the Holy Land. This royal French tutor and adviser composed *Le songe du vieil pèlerin* (*The Dream of the Old Pilgrim*), an allegorical account of a journey taken by Queen Truth and her sisters Justice, Mercy and Peace. Each country is described and then offered words of advice for reform: in England the 'white boar' Richard, son of the 'black boar' of Crécy and Poitiers, has lost his lands (in France), in France there was mayhem and disorder. All this misery would come to an end once the kingdoms turned towards the ideals of peaceful government. Here is a vision of peace, of sovereignty and virtue, worthy of its Aristotelian antecedents and of the Christian morality which nurtured it.

All the elements of the universal Christian vision came together in rich fruition in the Wilton Diptych (Plate 11), a representation of Christian kingship: Edward the Confessor, St Edmund king and martyr and Richard, under the tutelage of John the Baptist, appear on the left panel. Facing it is the prime mediator of grace (a model of what a good queen could be), the Virgin Mary with the Child Christ, surrounded by a heavenly court of angels. Here was a European vision captured in courtly gothic – with dexterity in portrayal of detail, respect for royal dignity, delicate and insightful portraiture, and attention to lineages of right and rule. Richard entertained a European vision; the Diptych belonged to a political moment – sometime between 1395 and 1399 – when Anglo-French rapprochement suggested new horizons of crusading virtue. This vision was promoted in 1396 through the double rituals of a peace accord for thirty years and Richard's marriage to Isabella of France. In the Wilton Diptych he faces the Virgin Mary in hope of regeneration, dynastic continuity and peace. But this vision failed to ignite his partners in rule – the magnates of England. When this became clear to him, he had no other vision to replace the one spurned, and so his majestic and responsible rule turned sour, reclusive, tyrannical and withdrawn. In the last years of his reign Richard II alienated even those magnates who were tied to him closely by blood and affinity.

MAGNATES

English magnates were a group of extremely powerful men – there were six earls with annual incomes greater than £5,000 and eight with incomes over £3,000 – who enjoyed the expectation of leadership in peace and in war. These men were meant to provide kings with counsel and to ensure that the regions of their greatest influence dwelt in peace. To them were related women who inhabited positions of great influence, as wives, heiresses and dowagers. As we have seen, marriage was a carefully calculated and ordained undertaking, particularly first marriages. When magnates married, kings and kin could express opinions and bring strong pressure to bear, but great men conducted domestic lives which suited their sentiments and prospects: John of Gaunt, for example, made his mistress his third wife.

The magnates' world was regulated by the seasons of the year: times for war, for parliament, for public communal pursuits, for conviviality. Throughout the fourteenth century and in parallel with the growth of the frequency, duration and importance of parliament, they developed substantial urban residences. Whereas they had always played a role in trade, the generations which benefited from war-spoils, and who sought to diversify their economic activities in the period following the Black Death, became deeply interested in commerce, speculation and finance.

The English magnates are best understood not as a class but as a political grouping which was formed and reformed around rival claims to leadership and smouldering enmities. Thus even when they had relative success as a group of Appellant Lords in 1386–8, offering an alternative vision of rulership with considerable effect, the competition between the Earls of Derby (the king's cousin) and Gloucester (the king's uncle) ultimately tore the group and its programme apart. Derby and Gloucester were part of a vast family created by the many sons of Edward III. The political aspirations and blocks wielded by such men were enormous, and these marked Richard with the traumas of 1386–8, for the rest of his reign.

Because they wielded extraordinary power in the regions, and were looked to as providers of justice and protectors of peace, magnates also created dependent relationships that reflected and implemented this power. The vast estates of an earl, lying in different parts of the kingdom, its isles and domains, had to be administered, maintained, protected by arms and defended in law. Large groups of men of humbler status, usually but not always of knightly rank (of which there were some 1,100 families at the time), were marked by association with magnates. Justice, estate administration, lines of defence, all depended on this group of magnatic servants, members of what we call the gentry, men who were stakeholders in magnates' interests, and who had some experience at law, war and the management of people. These men had their own complex dynastic connections, privileges and aspirations, all of which could be bolstered through links to a magnate, at once forbidding and reassuring. This is not to say that men of the knightly class or who aspired to it were subservient to and embraced wholly by magnatic association. They clearly formed a group with important horizontal links of mutuality, sociability and kinship. But particular distinction could be had through association with a magnate. The toll which this system then exacted was clear in periods of magnatic strife, as lesser men were drawn, necessarily, into disputes between magnates, each with his respective local following. Above all, there was the problematic and distorting political situation created when the king behaved as a magnate, and developed strong affinities in the many regions where he held substantial land.

Although London played a growing part in the lives of magnates and the parliamentary gentry, home was the country – family seats enjoyed and used in a seasonal rhythm. The 3,000 or so free landed families of England ranged vastly in status and connections. Like the magnates to whom they turned for example and protection, they had estates scattered over considerable distances. Marriage brought land and reward, as did the taking up of advantageous leases; travel and supervision and the fostering of local connections in several localities could keep a gentleman and his servants very busy. All these posed difficult decisions of policy and politics as they weighed commitment and advantage, loyalty and expectation against each other.

As visitors and hosts, magnates jousted and displayed their status and prowess. At the Smithfield Tournament of October 1390, a reciprocal match to one played in Paris, the English team played a foreign one, the former wearing the king's emblem of the white hart with a crown and golden chain, the sign of the king's affinity. The king led the company to the field, twenty English knights led by ladies with golden chains; the knights proceeded to disport themselves in *joustes à plaisance*, meant to entertain and to cause no serious harm, through a series of engagements with blunted lances. John Holland (the king's brother), Hugh Despenser, Thomas Mowbray (a reconciled Appellant, now Lord Marshal), Sir Lewis Clifford, John Devereux and Sir William Beauchamp all took part. Three days of jousting were celebrated in leisurely fashion at a banquet offered by John of Gaunt.

The nobility also took part in an international world of politics, dynasty, art and religion. Not only had the French wars brought them into frequent contact with France, the Low Countries and parts of the empire, but other ambitious campaigns followed. Such were the ill-fated Flemish crusade led by Bishop Despenser in 1383 and the crusade to Spain led by John of Gaunt (for this dynastic campaign was blessed as a crusade, with fifty honorary chaplains appointed to serve those going on it). The crusade into Prussia in summer 1390 saw the Earl of Derby and a household entourage of around 150 depart from Boston (Lincolnshire) to Danzig. They rode through Brandenburg to Vilna under the leadership of the Teutonic Knights, and the earl returned for another tour in 1392. The crusade to Nicopolis of 1391 similarly broadened horizons and bonded English magnates with continental peers. The poet John Gower, member of a Kentish gentry family, described such a knight in his *Confessio Amantis*:

> So that by land and also by ship
> He must travel for honour
> And make many hasty rides
> Sometimes in Prussia, sometimes in Rhodes,
> And sometimes in Tartary.

He was not unlike Chaucer's Knight of the Prologue to the *Canterbury Tales*:

In Latvia he fought as well as Russia,
No Christian man so oft of his degree.
In far Granada's siege also was he
Of Algeciras and of Belmarie.

Distinguished knights such as Sir John Clanvowe and his close friend, Sir William Neville, members of King Richard's household, even met their end on such crusades. The Westminster chronicler claimed that after Clanvowe's death of disease during the crusade to Nicopolis, Neville refused to eat, and died a few days later. They were buried in the Dominican church of Galata – a Genoese colony in Byzantium – and the stone placed on their joint tomb displays their helmets facing each other (as if in a kiss), and their arms impaled, as the arms of spouses were on such monuments. Here was a very deep friendship, not unlike a union solemnized three decades later by two English knights in the church of St Martin in Harfleur: John Winter and Nicholas Molyneux swore solemnly to be '*frères d'armes*', brothers in arms. It is hard to appreciate the full scope of these past relationships, but they must have been enhanced by the intense bonding of camaraderie, away from conventional expectations and support.

Some knights and their families lived in very fine houses, combining combat training and leadership in war with local government in peace and the pursuits of country life, to which risk and profit were added by participation in business and investment in trade. Their books reveal interests which ranged from law to books of advice on religion and on warfare. One of the most popular books in this genre was the *Arbre des batailles* (*The Tree of Battles*). This work was dedicated by the monk Honoré Bouvet around 1386 to King Charles VI of France, and became a popular text for gentlemen who read in French, from king to squire. This moralizing work lamented the state of violence and discord which tore Christianity apart. War could be ennobling, even holy, as were those fought by Judas Maccabeus, but nowadays it seemed merely to cause misery to women and children. Some, like Sir John Clanvowe, penned their own reflections on the challenges of a virtuous active life. Here are words from an experienced soldier and courtier, through the life of Christ from birth to passion. Since life in the flesh is frail, trust must be placed in that which is not. Thomas Woodstock Duke of Gloucester used writing to capture the lessons of war, bitterly won, in his *Ordinance and Form of Fighting*. Magnates like him were attracted to extravagant contemplative writing by mystics such as Richard Rolle (d. 1349). While their lives drew them into strife and discord, they were fortified, comforted – led into some solace – by reading texts and contemplating images in which the body, trained and trusted in this world, was a mere 'wretched and sinful' thing.

Besides the soldiers there were the lawyers. Sometimes sons of knights, usually sons of more modest landed folk, they recognized the reward and rank which royal service could bring, since the key to royal administrative service was the common law. They could become sheriffs, coroners, justices of the peace, and be appointed to the many ad hoc commissions detailed to investigate and supervise local government – on subjects ranging from the state of sea walls to the maintenance of ditches. Challenging careers were also offered by magnates' households.

The magnates aimed at creating chains of dependence and interaction with such professional, experienced and reliable men. These underwent a modification in periods of political instability and insecurity. The war years had seen the expansion of the peerage to include not only old families such as the Bohuns, Beauchamps and Fitzallans, but also the ennobled warriors Mowbray, Scrope and Holland. When magnates felt threatened, often by the aspirations of the king, they attempted to arm themselves with followers renowned not so much for administrative and legal acumen, but rather for muscle and their power to intimidate – their aggression. The expected patronage and interdependence between magnates and their men was transformed into the phenomenon of 'maintaining', the proactive creation of followings, of men who comported themselves, often wearing hats or badges of a particular hue, as if to say 'I am the Earl of Surrey's man', or 'the Duke of Norfolk's'. That this phenomenon was intimidating and that it caused a deterioration in the quality of life in the regions is evident from the recurrent complaints to parliament about it: petitions for the restriction of 'maintaining' were presented by the Commons in 1384, 1388 and 1399. These aimed to restrict to the king alone the right to distribute badges among followers. Henry of Derby had famously snatched the collar off the neck of one of his men in 1393 in order to hand it to the poet John Gower. A year later, Richard Earl of Arundel complained to parliament that the collar of S-shaped links (see Plate 15), associated with the retainers of John of Gaunt, was now being used as royal livery; the king retorted that it was merely a sign of love.

DEPOSITION AND USURPATION

The twenty-two years of Richard's reign saw a great deal that was lively and good in economic life, religious creativity, and cultural exchange. They broadened the horizons of men and women, but ended in spectacularly unsettling actions, first by the king and then by his magnates. The king's sense of his realm had shrunk to areas in which he could move comfortably, and in which he would be hailed with enthusiasm and undivided loyalty – areas like Wales and Cheshire. Elsewhere leadership fell more clearly and routinely, unfettered by royal intervention, into the hands of men who would be kings. In the absence of the constant reminder of the limits to their powers, through regular parliaments and the rituals of face-to-face engagement in a court, fantasies of transformation were harboured by some magnates. They were occasioned by the understandable grievance of a magnate, Henry of Derby, who was banished from the kingdom in April 1398, to seek exile in France, and then was denied his Lancastrian inheritance when John of Gaunt died in February 1399. Such designs were also imagined by families of great regional prominence – such as the Percies – who could determine the flow of national politics. An absent king – not exiled or banished or waiting to make his claim – could hardly rally enthusiasm for the defence of his title and prestige in the land. The king was acting like a magnate, and made magnates believe they might be kings.

Yet before his withdrawal Richard achieved considerable success in generating income for the crown, through the negotiation and administration of indirect tax on the major imports of wine and general merchandise. Throughout the 1380s and 1390s, crown income was impressively diversified in customs and dues, and administration was scrutinized closely and in innovative fashion. Where Edward III had only occasionally requested and applied tonnage and poundage, Richard managed, from around 1386, to convince parliament repeatedly that this form of tax be granted, and, after the Truce of Leulingham (Pas-de-Calais) which halted warfare between 1389 and 1392, granted even in times of peace. The resulting revenue, now an expected part of crown income rather than an intermittent grant, rose from some 3 per cent in the 1350s to 8.75 per cent of the value of wine and luxury goods which the consumers of southern England purchased in the late fourteenth century. Income also flowed from exports of cloth, even by those favoured tradesmen, the Hansards – the members of the Hanseatic League of mercantile cities. Much of the stability of the 1390s might be explained by this fiscal and political success.

Yet even this flow of income, and the efficiency and purpose which it demonstrates, could not deflect the sense of unease which related to its recipient, its profligate spender. Richard II's receipts, buoyed by his period of relative confidence from the late 1380s and by the lower levels of military expenditure required during years of peace (although expenditure continued, not least on the diplomatic efforts which maintained peace), increasingly attracted criticism of a public and defiant kind. He did not counter this by gestures of largesse, such as his grandfather had grandly and wisely made. The occasion of the reversion of Queen Isabella's dowry to the crown after her death – a protracted accounting and legal affair – benefited the royal treasury, but alleviated none of the burden imposed by the royal household on public finances. The combination of politics of regional patronage and the recurrent investment of resources in Ireland was to unmake the achievements of Richard's administrative policy. The 1390s produced income which was borne indirectly, and thus burdened mainly those who could afford to pay for expensive foreign goods; yet the rhetoric of profligacy and haughty disdain for the welfare of his subjects was none the less made to stick to the king.

The peace which was renewed in 1389, and endured until Henry V chose to break it in 1415, allowed a great deal of prosperity and rebuilding to take place in England and Wales. But its political significance was rather mixed. In the north, especially Cheshire, where so many families had seen men in constant employment in the royal armies for three generations, rumours circulated in late 1398 that the king intended to relinquish his French title. Under Sir Thomas Talbot, 20,000 men gathered for a great public protest meeting. The West Riding saw the ravages of unrule in the form of gangs of lawless men, such as the Beckwiths, to whom the king's response was hesitant. But where the king was interested he invested intelligent effort – as in Ireland, where he boosted the standing army, and campaigned to calm violence in Leinster (Plate 19). Here Richard was able to transcend the habitual stereotypes of the Irish, which even his court writer Froissart penned following the 1394–5 expedition: that the Irish inhabit forests, ride without stirrups or saddles, and are cruel captors without a sense of chivalry. Just as he did in the French arena, Richard was able to think the unthinkable, and this set him apart from many in the political community of which he was the head. No single adjective quite captures these last years of the century. Richard's experiments with peace and with regional rule were disquietingly unfamiliar.

A dramatic, yet not isolated example of the sentiments which Richard inspired by the late 1390s is the petition put forward by Thomas Haxey in January 1397. This petition to parliament criticized the court and royal administration and resulted in its bearer's trial for treason, but also in his pardon. Haxey, whose family came from the Isle of Exholme in north-east Lincolnshire, was one of the many northerners who held high office in Richard II's administration, men from south Yorkshire and north Lincolnshire. These men combined ecclesiastical careers and administrative capacity, and even as they served their king, they attended to the requirements of friends and relations within a closely knit regional brotherhood. Haxey's advance had been facilitated by Bishop (later Archbishop) Thomas Arundel, who had presented him to his first living in 1384. Work at court also underpinned a career in moneylending and legal surety work. Men like Haxey were ready for any purpose in which knowledge of the ways of government could be usefully deployed. Thus Haxey was sent in 1385 with one of the king's serjeants-at-arms to Cornwall to deal with business relating to 'some royal fish, called *whalles* or *graspeys*'. Two years later, he was in the West Country again, attending to the recovery of the wreck of a Genoese vessel and its cargo. Rising in the ranks, he was by 1387 keeper of the rolls, the records of royal expenditure.

Whose grievances was Haxey expressing in his four-clause petition? His were complaints about administration: about inadequate provision for sheriffs and escheaters; that the Scottish March was exposed, causing great suffering; that liveries still proliferated despite statute provision; that the royal household's costs should be reduced. The king answered in person, point by point, but he was enraged when addressing the last point. It was tantamount to treason, he claimed, to question royal conduct. So the petitioner was tried and condemned to death. Arundel and several bishops lobbied for his pardon, which Richard granted, responding to the request of 'bishops and multitudes of ladies', an ironic dig, as these were the two groups that had epitomized the court's disorder and extravagance in the original petition.

What can the Haxey affair reflect of the mood within the higher echelons of political society? It teaches us a little. Haxey rose from a group of professional administrators, educated men, a closely knit group of clerics who expected to end their careers with wealth, status, rewards to their family and friends and a bishopric. The king's actions in the 1390s may have placed some of their expectations in doubt. He used patronage to bolster a circle loyal and able, but which seemed to close down some pre-existing avenues for preferment. Between 1375 and 1400 only one Welshman was promoted to a Welsh bishopric; these sees went to royal favourites such as Alexander Bache, the royal confessor, invested as Bishop of St Asaph in 1390, or Tideman of Winchecombe, the royal physician, at Llandaff in 1394. This logic further worked itself through the lower ecclesiastical orders in prebends and livings in cathedrals and collegiate churches. After a protracted struggle with the papacy over the patronage of St Anthony's Hospital, London, John Macclesfield, a clerk of the Privy Seal and royal secretary, was appointed as its master.

The king had several ways of marking favourites and rewarding dependants, for he was a keen granter of title and privilege. The by now 'old-fashioned' Order of the Garter included young noblemen, sons of magnates, royal intimates, and knights of his Chamber such as Simon Burley, elected in 1381, or Thomas Lord Despenser, the son of the Black Prince's companion in arms, in 1388. Long records of service to the crown were rewarded. Richard also used the Garter to favour relatives, and especially women – sisters, mother, aunts, sisters-in-law – honouring thirty-six women in all (who didn't count towards the quota). The oldest surviving Garter stall is from these years: that of Ralph Lord Basset of Drayton, still to be seen in St George's Chapel, Windsor. Titles could be created when favour demanded, and never more so than in 1397 when Richard turned Percy, Despenser and Surrey into Earls, and Huntingdon into a Duke. But he also found new ways to build his faction and mark his friends: he turned Cheshire into a Principality and its men were drawn closely to him. Foreign scions of friendly nobles were also raised, like Albrecht of Bavaria in 1397 with his son William of Ostrevant, who was married to Margaret of Burgundy, and was thus Count of Holland and Hainault.

Chastised by parliament and made to feel extremely uncomfortable in London, Richard created in his last years an alternative kingdom from the provinces he loved, some of which his father had cherished before him. Loved in Cheshire, feared in the Irish counties, followed by Welsh archers, Richard II withdrew from the business of Westminster rule. He made Cheshire and the Principality of Wales, including Flint-shire and the Arundel lands, seized by the king in 1397, his special realm. This building of an affinity around him resulted, not surprisingly, in complaint and resentment at all levels. When a Cheshire knight, John Haukeston, was pardoned for having murdered William de Laken in the king's presence this was no longer a case of administrative corruption, but a blemish on the royal person itself.

The king withdrew into places which he associated with safety, and he failed to create bridges to those who most resented his rule, but who might have been guided or enticed to support him. The Westminster portrait – a large painted image of the king – was created in these years, a unique image of magnificence, placed in the Abbey choir. This icon of the king as devotional focus was new and disturbing; it was the custom in Prague and even in France, but had not been so in England. This gesture was known by only a few, but important, political actors. It combined with the incontrovertible evidence of the king's curious action against a peer and a cousin, Henry of Derby. The less he appeared to understand the concerns of the magnates, the easier it was for that peer – and his supporters in England – to make a case for opposition, even if initially not for deposition. Henry of Derby managed to mobilize the strong regional magnate, Henry Percy Earl of Northumberland, in support of his dynastic claim to the Lancaster lands. In the face of this cohesive regional block the royal affinity was too distant and too dispersed to act swiftly and decisively.

This was a period of apparent peace, during which alternative habits of solidarity had to be composed to keep a group of powerful men and their dependants harnessed. The political process served not only to remind subjects of their loyalty, but to remind kings of the very purpose of their privilege, that they headed a subtle system of enormous power and of onerous responsibility. When Henry of Derby, Richard's cousin, the disinherited son of John of Gaunt, returned from exile and landed in Ravenspur in July 1399 he found not only the terrain prepared by his supporters, the Percies, but also support in Lancastrian territories. Edmund Duke of York (d. 1402) was guardian during the king's absence in Ireland in 1399, and when he heard in late June that the king's enemies were assembling in Calais ready for crossing he directed sheriffs to prepare, and sent word to Ireland. Richard heard of the challenge a few days later, but left the country only on 24 July, by which time Lancastrians in the south (especially Sussex) were organizing and Henry had begun his march from Ravenspur. The Duke of York attempted to shore up London and control the sale of arms to Derby's forces, but by early August Henry was making his way through the king's favoured lands of Cheshire and into Wales. By the time Henry reached Conway Castle to meet Richard II, recently returned from Ireland, he had traversed a large part of the kingdom, north-east to south-west, practically unopposed. The meeting was meant as submission and reconciliation following the restoration of Henry's hereditary title, but ended as an abdication (Plate 12), and Richard II was made to come to London. Henry's appetite was whetted for more: Richard faced a trial in parliament in late September – a trial which could never be by his peers – deposition and banishment followed. And a coronation, on 13 October 1399.

The legal and political minds in parliament created a case against the king, of mismanagement and failure to fulfil his sacred kingly oath. It was not unlike the complaint voiced by the Appellants against the king's servants, eleven years earlier. The language of deposition suggested that the king was a boy who had never grown up, a man lacking in manliness, a ruler who lacked respect for nobility and historic duty. There were rumours that Richard intended to sell Calais, that he was negotiating secretly with the French. He fell out with the Commons, whose mood was described in 1399 by the French prince, the Duc du Berry, as 'wanting nothing but war'. Faced with an alternative – a magnate among magnates – the accusations of perversity carried the day, and became political truism: the king had perverted his office. Yet who was to judge him? This quandary was expressed neatly in Shakespeare's words spoken by the spiritual lord, the Bishop of Carlisle, in *Richard II*:

> What subject can give sentence on his king?
> And who sits here that is not Richard's subject?
> (*Richard II*, IV. i. 112–13)

For the second time in that century the polity's head was removed; the rest is chaos and ambition – a claimant in search of inheritance soon became a usurper king.

Richard's downfall was not the result of widespread disaffection, but of the convergence of strongly held sentiments and interests with swift action in the king's absence. Most of the evidence of his unpopularity is in chronicles written after the deposition, often using the parliamentary records as source material. Parliament was the site of national political conversation, and it had been faced with the facts of a king handing over his crown, and a magnate taking it from him.

The parliamentary chastisement of the king turned into affirmation of the many ways in which Henry of Derby could, should and would rule in Richard's place (Plate 13). The king was banished to prison in Pontefract Castle, and ultimately died there aged thirty-two, of hunger, it was claimed. Richard II received no state burial, no lying beside his beloved first wife at Westminster. These events were so unsettling that before his body had disintegrated in the ground, rumours of his survival were about everywhere. The expectation of Richard's imminent return became the stuff of nightmares for Henry, now Henry IV, and his Lancastrian progeny and friends, for decades to come.

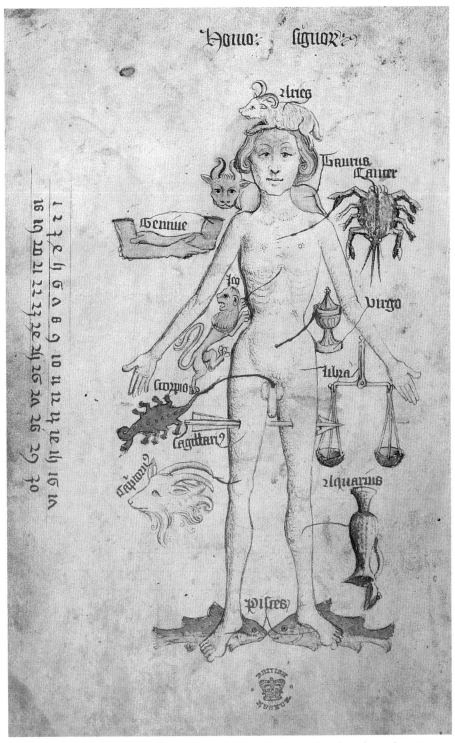

1. Drawing of a body with instructions for bloodletting, related to the zodiac signs, from the Guild Book of the Barber-Surgeons of York, *c.* 1486.

2. An illustrated initial E, depicting Edward III enthroned, handing over the Duchy of Aquitaine to his son, Prince Edward, who is fully armed and kneeling in a gesture of homage.

3. A woman throwing corn to a hen and chicks, and holding a spindle. Domestic spinning and weaving were usually the work of women, as was tending to poultry and the farmyard. The image adorns the Luttrell Psalter, made before the mid 1340s.

4. This stained glass panel depicts the Virgin Mary holding Christ in her left arm and a flowering branch in her right hand. It is part of the sumptuous east window of Eaton Bishop parish church, Herefordshire, made around 1320.

5. Much rebuilt in the nineteenth century, Bamburgh Castle still exemplifies powerfully the strength of late medieval fortifications and the control a well-situated castle offered. In its Norman keep Piers Gaveston was held prisoner. It first succumbed to siege only in 1464, when it was badly damaged by cannon-fire.

6. A gilt bronze tomb effigy of the Black Prince, made soon after 1376, showing him in full armour and with a lion at his head. It is located in the Trinity Chapel, south of St Thomas Becket's Shrine in Canterbury Cathedral.

7. The Battle of Crécy (1346) is depicted in this illumination from a manuscript of the *Grandes Chroniques de France*, c. 1415. Much attention has been paid by the artist to the bulk of the bodies of war horses.

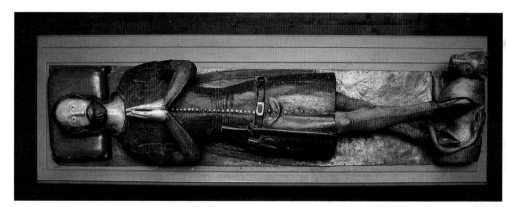

8. Wooden effigy carved out of a single block of oak, probably of Walter de Helyon, who lived and held land in Much Marcle, Herefordshire, in the 1350s. He is wearing close-fitting clothes, with a belt and a short sword, the image of a landholding gentleman. Now in the nave of Much Marcle church.

9. The execution of Wat Tyler in June 1381 by a sword wielded by Mayor Walworth of London, and in the presence of king Richard II, is depicted in a manuscript of Jean Froissart's *Chroniques de France et d'Angleterre, c.* 1460–80.

10. Chaucer reads to a crowd of exalted men and women in a rocky and wooded outdoor location, in the frontispiece to the manuscript of *Troilus and Criseyde* (c. 1415–25). This fanciful scene shows how greatly Chaucer was honoured soon after his death.

11. The Wilton Diptych was created for Richard II some time after 1394. In it the King is presented on his knees, with the martyred King Edmund, Edward the Confessor and St John the Baptist; he gazes across at the Virgin Mary and Child Christ, surrounded by angels. Here is one of the most accomplished European representations of the sacred dimensions of kingship.

12. Richard II receives Henry Percy Earl of Northumberland, at Conway Castle, in 1399; this is the beginning of the end of Richard's rule. From *Histoire du Roy d'Angleterre Richard II*.

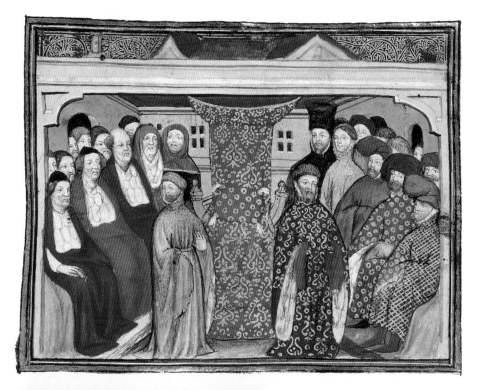

Top

13. Henry of Derby claims the throne (shown to be empty) in Parliament (1399) in the presence of assembled lords spiritual and temporal. From *Histoire du Roy d'Angleterre Richard II.*

Left

14. Tomb effigies of Henry IV and his second wife, Queen Joan of Navarre, in Canterbury Cathedral; the effigies bear personal traits, and were commissioned by Joan herself.

15. Tomb effigy of Thomas Duke of Clarence, son of Henry IV, who died in battle in France in 1421. Thomas is in full armour and sports a Lancastrian collar with the 'SS' emblem of the Lancastrians. St Michael's Chapel, Canterbury Cathedral.

16. Henry Prince of Wales (the future Henry V), receives a work of guidance from the kneeling author Thomas Hoccleve, clerk of the Privy Seal.

17. The Battle of Agincourt (1415) is depicted at an advanced stage in this illustration from the St Albans Chronicle: the English bowmen dominate the field, and many slain French knights have fallen to the ground. Note the trumpeters, crucial for communication and the rallying of forces in battle.

18. John Duke of Bedford, brother of Henry IV, kneels in a chapel in front of St George, dressed for battle and wearing a saint's halo. The image is an illustration to the Bedford Book of Hours, commissioned by the Duke of Bedford and made *c.* 1423.

19. Thomas Mac William Burke (d. 1405), an Anglo-Irish knight, with sword and shield, and his dog. Dublin, Trinity College.

20. Henry VI offers the sword of the Constable of France to John Talbot Earl of Shrewsbury. This image comes from the book of prayers, tracts and romances which the Earl and his wife offered Henry VI and Margaret of Anjou as a marriage gift in 1445.

21. This misericord – a ledge attached to a choir seat to ease long periods of standing – depicts two men playing a board game, probably backgammon. Misericord carvings often depict scenes of daily life, with humorous and parodic images. Now in Manchester Cathedral, carved *c.* 1500.

22. The West façade of King's College Chapel, Cambridge. The building of the chapel began at the foundation of the college by Henry VI in 1446, and was completed only under Henry VIII. Every king in the period contributed to its construction and decoration.

23. This decorated roll from the 1470s contains diagrams and portions of text which depict and discuss the genealogy of Edward IV and his claim to the throne. Edward is finally represented just off-centre right.

24. The illustration to the entry 'clandestine betrothal', in the *Omne bonum*, an encyclopaedia of the 1360s–70s composed by the friar John Le Palmer. Note the friar joining the man's right to the woman's left hand.

25. Edward IV holds a sword and a shield, seated on a boat, on this obverse of the rose-noble, the gold coin which he had minted in 1465. Edward IV took great interest in trade and fiscal policy.

26. The painting of the Last Judgement – the Doom – that is now mounted on the north wall of Wenhaston (Suffolk) parish church, of the 1480s, was originally placed above the chancel arch, for all parishioners to see during the services. It depicts in vivid fashion and warm colours the sufferings of those destined to Hell, while those few who enter Heaven pass through a narrow gateway.

4

Usurpation and the Challenges to Order, 1399–1422

A new century, a new dynasty, a new king. However unwise or vain Richard II was, however much his acts facilitated the ascendancy of his cousin Henry of Derby, the usurpation was not an act of necessity or corrective justice. And it was to breed its nemesis. Under Henry IV's rule there developed not only the greatest constraints on royal action, in the shape of a mighty council and scrutinizing parliament, but, conversely, also the most concerted efforts to build loyalty and instil conformity into the lives of subjects. Henry IV worked hand in hand with church leaders to create procedures which tested loyalty to the crown through scrutiny of religious choices. A Lancastrian political will emerged, quick to fear dissent – against its right, against creed – and to reward conformity, in England and Wales and the Borders which were bubbling with opinions and factions. The usurper was rightly alert to the many possibilities which endangered him; usurpers are open to usurpation, and this became the keynote of Henry IV's reign. He was supported, however, by the unparalleled resources of the Duchy of Lancaster, amassed by his father John of Gaunt, and extended through adventures in Britain and abroad.

These were years full of spying, informing, persecution and menace. These were times in which people were receptive to conspiracies and conspiracy theories. The first months, while Richard was still alive, saw a number of attempts to unseat the new king and restore the old. In January 1400 an attempt was made on the royal family during the celebrations of Twelfth Night, and later in January Richard's half-brother, the Earl of Huntingdon, attempted a rising from Devon. There is a great deal of episodic evidence about dissenting talk, and some local mobilization around charismatic preachers or knights. In 1402 Roger Frisby, a Franciscan of Leicester, was arrested for inspiring a vigil in Oxford in expectation of Richard's return. As ever, England's discontents found refuge in Scotland; an erstwhile member of Richard's household issued charters signed with the royal signet until his capture in Scotland in 1404, and an official Richard double was guest of the Scottish court until 1419.

Some strange occurrences followed the traumas of 1399: during the winter of 1400 the deposed king was still alive, a reality which the country's rulers – king and council – found highly inconvenient. By St Valentine's Day 1400 it was rumoured that the erstwhile king had starved himself; and from Pontefract Castle, his prison, the body was transported south, for a requiem mass, and towards the expected burial alongside his first wife Anne of Bohemia, in Westminster Abbey. But these last dignities were not accorded to Richard. Not surprisingly, Henry IV decided against a state funeral and his predecessor's body was interred in a respectable but insignificant tomb, at the Dominican house at King's Langley (Hertfordshire).

This quiet and private burial bred a commotion of rumours and imaginings, which were to follow the Lancastrian kings until Henry V provided Richard II with a burial fitting a king. In a syndrome not unfamiliar in times of rumour, the dead can be made alive through the strength of yearning for their presence, facilitated by the bizarre circumstances of their deaths. Richard haunted the living, as did the lively ghosts whose stories circulated in books – such as those copied out by a monk of Byland Abbey in Yorkshire c.1400 – and were told as cautionary tales to relatives who failed to fulfil promises, or whose hands were stained by misdeeds towards the departed. Such were Richard's kin – the Lancastrian cousin and his progeny – and so were by association the guilty parties who let it happen, modest and exalted folk alike. So Richard haunted the land, a revenant, a remnant, the living dead – delighting his supporters and terrorizing his enemies. He watched on as a mighty magnate became king. How would a magnate rule as king? How would his affinity, spread as it was in Lancastrian lands all over the kingdom, become a court, with its heart in Westminster?

Lancastrian rule only partially succeeded in shaking off the weight of its turbulent origins. Some contemporaries even claimed that the impeccably sacred oil of St Thomas Becket, which was used at the new king's coronation, caused an infestation of lice in the royal head of hair. Henry IV was too much implicated in the trauma of regicide to be able to heal; so he aimed to maintain rule in the face of rebellion, and built cautiously his relations with magnates and parliament. At the same time, a literature of discontent was being composed in France, filling libraries – including Charles VI's collection – with diatribes against the man who spurned sacred succession through bloodline, and unseated a king. A genre of genealogical chronicle came into being, texts punctuated by diagrams of bloodlines, often bound with polemical commentaries denigrating English claims to French territories. The momentous event of 1399 – the first effective invasion of England since 1066 – generated discomfort and confusion and distaste; and Henry IV was utterly aware that this was so.

Yet the usurper's son – the future Henry V – enjoyed an uncontested succession, and was able to work reconciliation with greater confidence, with imagination and flair. He was to heal through the exultancy of success. He never spared those who rebelled, but he beckoned to his side those who were still suffering under displeasure earned by their fathers. Henry V managed men well, in peace and in battle, and attempted to settle the many accounts his usurping father had left open: he completed Henry IV's penance for the execution of Archbishop Scrope and offered his dead uncle, Richard II, a proper state burial. In doing so he was prudent and virtuous but also clever, burying political hatchets which still had the power to inflict pain.

The legitimation of the new dynasty was the work of those closest to Henry IV, and of those who sought to play a part in the political and cultural activities of the day. John Gower's philosophical poem *Confessio Amantis*, originally dedicated to Richard II, was rededicated to Henry IV. Contingency and necessity led to the mobilization of talent. Around Henry IV congregated able and ambitious lawyers, soldier-magnates and churchmen, adept at governance, provisioning, war and public propaganda. All spoke the language of 'common profit' presented as the king's aim at Henry's first parliament. Gower's words aimed to distinguish Richard's and Henry's moral qualities:

> R. hated the nobles and plundered their estates;
> H. cherished them and restored their heirs to their homes.
> The vindictive R. laid waste his kingdom and stood over everyone;
> H. mitigated fear and brought back brotherly love.

So intertwined were father and son in their exploits, so linked in a common aim, that England and Wales in the early fifteenth century will be studied here in a single chapter, on the rule of Henry father and Henry son.

OWAIN GLYN DŴR

In September 1400 a former legal trainee at Westminster, who was also a seasoned soldier, declared himself the Prince of Wales – Owain Glyn Dŵr, Lord of Glyndyfrdwy in Denbighshire. Through his establishment of a decade of rule in Wales a momentous chapter of Welsh history and memory was created. Owain Glyn Dŵr, whose hopes were to be dashed with the fall of Aberystwyth and Harlech castles in 1409, ruled for a while as a king: he called and held parliaments, his arms were emblazoned with those of Gwynedd, he entered treaties with the French, negotiated with the papacy on reform of the Welsh church, planned the foundation of Welsh universities, and wedded his daughter to a great English magnate, Edmund Earl of March. His mythical dimension benefited from the fact that he was never caught, and thus never suffered a humiliating traitor's death. Through the eyes of the contemporary poet Howel Davi, Glyn Dŵr's residence at Sycharth (Denbighshire) appears to have been a place of splendid hospitality as befitted a ruler: a moated manor house with nine halls, pristine white-washed walls and fine windows, situated among orchards, rabbit warrens, vineyards, fishponds and a mill. This was a self-sufficient paradise. The poet Iolo Goch (d. 1398) expected pleasure and reward for his poems at this court, which was comparable to Westminster:

> Coupling secures the rooftree,
> Each rafter safely coupled in,
> Like Patrick's belfry, fruit of France,
> Or the fine-linked cloister of Westminster . . .
> There'll be no lack of gifts,
> No fault, no famine, no shame,
> Nor thirst ever in Sycharth.

Prophecies were composed around Glyn Dŵr: he was an Arthur returning to defeat the Saxons. Irish and Scots were invoked in this venture as brother Celts. Such prophecies were disseminated widely in oral renderings and copied into chronicles. They envisaged a reordering of England's relations with her neighbours, through the destabilization of England's ruler, Henry IV, represented as a mole. It is not surprising, therefore, that in 1402 the London parliament decided to outlaw Welsh minstrels and diviners, the Welsh spin-doctors of the day.

The momentous events in Wales – which have since lived on in legend, monument and collective memory – may also be seen as symptoms of wider political realities. Henry IV and his son Henry were on campaign in Scotland, which they had invaded that August 1400, when they received the news from Wales. Yet Glyn Dŵr's challenge was not solely a Welsh affair. It came to encompass the heightened ambition and action of magnates: the Percies in Northumberland, and later the Scropes in Yorkshire. The Welsh proclamation of separateness was simply the most successful and dramatic event in a decade of constitutional instability and political disorder. And the roots of such disarray were deeply embedded in the events of 1399–1400. As Glyn Dŵr tried out his new title – Prince of Wales – a committee of bishops and lawyers was still busy at Westminster, poring over records and muniments, seeking legal grounding for the usurpation they had recently witnessed. The tumult was of a particular type: it involved the questioning of dynastic legitimacy but also of the geographical and territorial integrity of the lands ruled by the English kings from Westminster.

Henry IV's son – Prince Henry – was made Prince of Wales in October 1399, and he soon had to fight in Wales and the Marches for this inheritance. While father and son achieved a decisive defeat of a Scottish force at Humbleton Hill in September 1402, they realized that large armies would not overcome the Welsh. The years 1402–5 saw successes for the Welsh under Glyn Dŵr: an attack on Ruthin led to the imprisonment of Lord Grey, though Henry IV's counter-attack forced Welsh allies to return to royal service at Bryn Glas. In 1402 Edmund Mortimer was caught during an attack on southern Welsh strong points at Usk, Caerleon, Newport and Cardiff. While Henry IV ransomed Lord Grey, he left Mortimer captive. This fomented bitterness in the great Marcher lord that soon led to a new type of alliance, pregnant with threat. Catherine Mortimer married Glyn Dŵr, and linked through blood the English and Welsh royal families. Henry IV soon responded in 1403 to the emergent coalition of Welsh and northern forces. In April the Prince of Wales was made Lieutenant in Wales, with command of castles, with barons and bannerets in support, twenty knights, 500 men-at-arms and 2,500 archers.

But attention was diverted for a while from the agenda set by Glyn Dŵr alone to the challenge from the most important northern magnates, the Percies. Henry Percy had welcomed Henry Earl of Derby in 1399, and paved the way for the reclamation of the Lancastrian inheritance.

Before too long, Derby had become king. It is probably true that although the Percies supported a fellow magnate they never had deposition, followed by a Lancastrian usurpation, in mind. The first three years of Henry IV's rule had allowed Percy frustration, expressed through a language of legitimism, to grow strong. So in July 1403 Henry Percy Duke of Northumberland marched south with his son Hotspur and some 14,000 men. The king and his son with some 6,000 men met them at Shrewsbury. Prince Henry cleverly surrounded the northern force and won the day. Although wounded when an arrow struck his head, he was saved thanks to swift action by his personal surgeon John Bradmore. At the battle, which the *London Chronicle* lamented as being 'between Englishmen and Englishmen', Percy's annihilation was completed with the death of Hotspur in battle, and the executions which followed at Worcester. In the rush of fear and suspicion which followed the rebellion, even Italian merchants were accused of having played a role in the Percy plot, leading to violence against foreign traders in London.

Despite the collapse of the Percy forces, more local and less directly confrontational attacks were mounted by Glyn Dŵr, actions akin to guerrilla warfare. But this was not all, for the aftermath of Shrewsbury saw the Welsh cause promoted by another strategy, one which involved the French. In May 1404 a treaty was signed between Glyn Dŵr and Charles VI; the French supported the Welsh claim and promised military aid. Indeed, attacks from the sea were launched in the autumn of 1406, at Kidwelly (Carmarthenshire), the Lancastrian lordship gained by the Welsh, and at Caernarfon, the capital of the principality of North Wales. At the same time a diplomatic effort in European courts was under way, seeking support for the Welsh cause. Armed resistance was still active, with Aberystwyth holding out for months against a siege in 1407–8.

For about a decade Wales and the Marches were a battleground; the fine manors of the Welsh gentry were raided and burnt. Steps had to be taken to defend residences, though the statutes of 1401–2 forbade the fortification of Welsh homes. Either side of the conflict destruction was felt: the manor house at Woolaston (Gloucestershire) had its thatch replaced by the more durable roof of Pengnant stone, following a raid. Others like Weobley Castle (Herefordshire) and Penhow near Chepstow (Monmouthshire) maintained defensive features which still exist. All this warfare exacted a heavy economic and human price: the Vale of

Glamorgan was devastated; in the Lordship of Ogmore alone, accounts show that half of peasant tenements were destroyed. In response, the Westminster parliament passed statutes which limited the participation of Welsh persons in the privileges and responsibilities of administration: the statute of 1401 prohibited tenure of land in England or in plantation boroughs in Wales by Welsh people, and that of 1402 aimed to stop trade outside Welsh market towns. Political separation was also attempted in the prohibition of the use of Welshmen as counsellors to English lords. Henry V's first parliament (1413) dealt with the aftermath of the conflict; it debarred the Welsh from bringing court cases in respect of injuries suffered during the rebellion.

Anxiety about rebellion and insubordination resulted in a clamp-down in Wales through a series of military and judicial acts, but attention was also directed at another March, the northern Borders. Royal commissions identified traitors who were punished for acts of *lèse-majesté*: an inquisition of 1411 resulted in the execution of a man who had handed over Roxburgh Castle to the Scots in 1408, just as it led to the accusation of Robert Kendall for delivering Jedburgh Castle in 1409. Although the Borders had always seen much economic and social contact and mobility, wardens of the north believed they could tell which men came to England on legitimate business, and which did not. In such an atmosphere of suspicion, even dining with a Scot could lead to indictment for treason.

RULE AND RESISTANCE

In his sermon at Henry IV's first parliament, on 7 October 1399, Thomas Arundel, Archbishop of Canterbury, opened with the words: 'Behold the man . . . this same shall rule over my people' (1 Samuel 9.17). After being 'ruled and governed by children and the counsel of widows', a man and his virile son were now in charge. Arundel praised God for providing such 'a wise and discreet man to govern the kingdom'. The new king was to rule in justice, in close observance of the law, and would maintain each person in his proper status, all through good advice and wise counsel. He would reverse those grievances, which a hostile poem such as *Richard the Redeless* attributed to Richard: that he had broken his own crown by treating grooms and nobles alike. Henry IV, by contrast, was presented as circumspect and manly. Indeed, his responses to the political and military challenges of the decade were swift and determined, as much as the weather and the terrain of Wales and the Marches allowed. Even when Henry IV failed in health and was all but captive at Westminster, dynastic power was maintained through the charisma of his son, a figure of enduring fascination. Although father and son by no means agreed on several important policies – above all regarding the future of the French wars – Lancastrian loyalists and wage-paid armies were mustered in North Wales, where, fierce and capable, the English Prince of Wales acted as the military arm of the crown.

While the events in Wales offered an alternative to the vision of unified dominions under an English dynasty, the north also challenged this Lancastrian aspiration. The later years of Henry IV's reign saw a regionalization of royal power. While it was expected that regions should possess their own character, style, customs and affinities, royal justice and Christian practice were meant to be more uniformly spread. Richard II's last years saw a fragmentation of the country into royal and, by association, non-royal zones. The rule of large tracts of France for most of the fourteenth century similarly cast a new type of relation-ship between different regions, creating in its wake the phenomenon of highly autonomous warlords. The later years of Richard II, and then the brutality of his removal, put every aspiration uniting these regions to a severe test. Each of the rebellions of the early years of Henry IV was a regional initiative, an opportunistic play for aggrandizement during a period of political uncertainty. These were attempts to rethink the map of England and the relations between the components of the British sphere. Root-and-branch change seemed possible and appropri-ate since the breach of dynasty and the violence of deposition offered an occasion for rewriting the rules of the political game.

The first few years of Henry IV's reign were so punctuated with threats that a hasty mobilization of existing ecclesiastical resources for the hunting down of renegades and insubordinates is hardly surprising. As we have seen, the Epiphany Plot of January 1400 was planned by the Earl of Huntingdon (Richard's half-brother) and the Earl of Kent (Richard's nephew), as well as by the Earl of Salisbury and Thomas Lord Despenser, who aimed to seize and murder the royal family during the Epiphany celebrations at Windsor. It was a shock but it also brought into royal hands a vast amount of confiscated land, which was held for some years and then returned to widows and heirs in the pursuit of political allegiances. Henry IV was keen to receive submission and offer pardon on this occasion. That same winter a pair, including Robert Marner, erstwhile confessor to Richard II, were accused of plotting against Henry IV with occult acts of magic. And, as we have seen, only two years later, in 1403, a northern uprising brought Henry Percy, his son and some 14,000 men to Shrewsbury to confront the king and the Prince of Wales. At the same time minor local, though defiant, acts expressed still-divided loyalties. Maud Ufford Countess of Oxford attempted to whip up resistance in Essex while king and prince were busy in Wales: she distributed Richard's white hart as a badge of dissent. Time and again East Anglia appears in judicial sources as the breeding-ground of rumour and political restlessness, though it saw little violence or punitive action.

Yet Henry IV had learned some of the lessons of brewing rancour and long-nurtured revenge, which had poisoned the politics of Richard II. So he reacted vigorously to what he took as another rebellion in the north in 1405, a gathering of Yorkshire gentry around Archbishop Scrope of York at Shipton Moor. Here the prelate preached and Thomas Mowbray, the Earl Marshal, addressed the gathering, calling for political activism to voice discontent with heavy and repeated exactions. To Henry IV, still occupied in Wales, the news sounded too much like another northern rebellion, and the archbishop and marshal were executed.

Once the perceived threat from the north was dealt with, the most immediate dangers to the Lancastrian regime had been dissolved. But political hegemony did not destroy memories. These lingered and offered material from which future dreams could be woven and in which sentiments of resentment were nurtured. The cult of Archbishop Scrope, rebel and martyr, drew a loyal following of northern men and women who remembered his shrine in their wills, sought his prayers and promoted his cult through gifts and devotional objects for a century to come. This new martyr was incorporated into the literature of complaint and unease, which was expressed in moralizing texts. The act of usurpation was a blood-letting which continued to unsettle, as the author of the *Dives et pauper* (*Rich and poor*) c.1400 observed:

For the more martyrs the more murder the more manslaughter and the more shedding of innocents' blood . . . [the] English nation has now made many martyrs; they spare neither their own king, nor their bishops, no dignity, no order, no estate, no degree.

Conspiracy did not arise only from the political formations of magnates, about a hundred leading political actors. It affected more widely the behaviour of rural and urban subjects and official attitudes to them. For the crown came to identify loyalty or treason not only in political acts in parliament, or on the battlefield, but in the wide range of beliefs and practices which made up the religious life. Henry IV's regime was particularly eager to counter the industry of prophecy and rumour which claimed that Richard II was alive, and with a little help might be able to return. In the summer of 1402 a group of friars – from Leicester, Nuneaton and Nottingham – were executed for preaching that Richard was alive. These preachers were using well-known traditions of English prophecy to create comment and guidance for new, turbulent times. In December 1403 the Abbot of St John's, Colchester (Essex), was accused of preaching a prophecy, and of providing instructions to guide a French army to Northampton, where it would meet the 'risen' Richard.

The anti-authoritarian tone of prophecies was taken seriously, and parliament legislated against their dissemination in 1402 and 1406. In its mood of suspicion the political class aimed to dispose of those who were predicting apocalyptic gloom by featuring contemporary Englishmen within Christian millenarian narratives. But the apocalyptic tone was to be found not only among heretical writers; reformers cleverly used traditional materials in their call for reform of the church. A dissenting sermon used a perfectly orthodox Dominican commentary on the Apocalypse when it dangerously predicted disendowment at the hands of princes, when 'secular princes take these temporalities again into their hands and reduce the clergy to heavenly living'.

PARLIAMENT AND POLITICAL ORDER

A political settlement was desired by most. Nothing was more useful than the fact of dynastic continuity. Henry settled the succession on his son in 1406, and further wished to entail it on the male line for ever. In that year a new mode of political cooperation evolved at Westminster. Criticism and discontent from the Commons was not too threatening, since it was offered through well-regulated procedures. Parliament's speakers – Sir Arnold Savage in 1401 and 1404, and Sir John Tiptoft in 1406 – were royal servants of long standing, but they did not couch the demands of the Commons in parliament in veiled allusions. It was decided in 1406 that a panel of six men of the Commons would henceforward audit the crown's balance-sheets. This Long Parliament also attempted to make parliamentary elections more transparent. For a while parliament successfully contained underlying tensions and the potential for violence. Protection was offered to parliamentary representatives and their households: when Richard Chedder's servant was attacked in 1404 by John Savage's man, the Commons called this treason, and the culprit paid a fine as well as damages. Henry IV was careful to make requests of parliament only when all other resources had dried up. Over his reign he spent £113,000, of which he received £76,000 from parliament. The rest was raised from crown lands, income from justice and the highly sophisticated system of customs and duties. Rare additional demands were occasionally added, such as tonnage and poundage in 1403.

Henry IV did not find parliament too hostile a place, for it was full of men long of the king's affinity: there were some forty recipients of annuities from his hand, among them no less than seven who had served Richard II in the previous decade. Henry did not seek to reward men by offering a place in a colourful court; his was notoriously dull, and was run on a shoestring. Rather he struck unostentatious deals of mutual trust, trust which was repeatedly tested in Wales and its Marches, in the north, and later, in Henry V's years, on the battlefields of France. Men, great and small, were linked to the king: Henry offered denizenship – secure residence for aliens – to loyal men, such as the Breton Peter Busseby, who did homage in 1405 and lived the next forty years as a Lancastrian in Derby; or to the many foreign merchants, even Jews who converted for the purpose, who settled peacefully and industriously. Far more exalted was the king's cousin, the Duke of York, who translated a French tract on hunting, and was retained as Henry IV's master of hounds in Somerset and Dorset in 1408, a position which allowed him to create a paid retinue of houndsmen and grooms.

Trust and loyalty, friendship and bonding, were the hallmarks of participation in the Lancastrian court. Although some subjects still thought it wise to use the grandiloquent formulae of Richard's reign when addressing the Lancastrian, as did the men of Dunwich (Suffolk) in a petition to 'vostre roiall magestee', the atmosphere of Henry IV's court was quite muted, and its constituent parts were finely balanced. Lancastrian retainers, already prominent within the vast lands of the Duchy of Lancaster, were now even more prominent within their localities. This is evident in parliamentary representation: Suffolk was represented in Henry's parliament three times by Sir John Strange, a Lancastrian retainer and controller of the royal household from 1406; twice by Sir Andrew Botiller, who was linked to the most eminent Lancastrian of East Anglia, Sir Thomas Erpingham, through his wife; and once by Ralph Ramsay, who had been retained by Henry even before his accession. Henry managed his closest men well and intimately. He arranged for a comfortable place at St Albans Abbey when his shield-bearer, John Crosby, retired. Such men were linked to Henry by the bonds of the Lancaster and Derby affinities, tested at the invasion of England in 1399 and the *coup d'état*, and forged in the consolidation of a new political order. The space for such promotion was created by exclusion of others. Some men who had been promoted by Richard II, his standard-bearer Simon Felbrigg for example, were excluded even from traditional tasks such as membership on commissions in their locality after 1399.

Friendship meant a great deal, and was a real political resource. Henry was lucky in being able to build upon his father's – John of Gaunt's – loyal supporters. He used Richard II's favourite institution to reward those who would support and aid his regime: the Order of the Garter. The drama of usurpation and accession had produced six empty stalls in the Fellowship of the Garter as a result of the execution of protagonists of the rising of January 1400. These were filled with men of Plantagenet affiliation whose loyalty the king had earned, as well as by long-standing Lancastrian supporters: John Montague Earl of Salisbury, Thomas Holland Duke of Surrey, Thomas Lord Despenser Earl of Gloucester, John Holland Duke of Exeter, John Lord Bourchier and Sir William Arundel. Henry's choices were made with great care, continuing the policy of promoting the kin of executed rebel magnates in return for loyalty, as was the case in 1404 with the promotion of Edmund Duke of Holland. After the Percies' revolt another nine places were vacated, and these were filled in the following years with a more diverse array of noblemen: the Duke of York, the Earl of Warwick, Wilhelm Duke of Guelders. A similar rapprochement was probably attempted by the admission of Henry Lord Scrope to the Order in 1410. As the king's confidence grew, he promoted talented men of middling social rank, such as Gilbert Lord Talbot, a man central to the defeat of the Welsh at Welshpool in 1408, or Hugh Lord Burnell, an intimate of the Prince of Wales.

When Henry IV met the German envoy Arndt von Dassel in 1407 at Gloucester, he reminisced about his youth as a 'crusader' in Prussia. His time abroad had been a period of glamour, adventure and immersion in the variety and pomp of continental courts. One of his first foreign state visitors was Manuel II Palaeologus, the Byzantine emperor, who had set out to meet Richard II, and then spent Christmas 1400 at Eltham, trying to awaken an interest in a salvage crusade in aid of the Christians of the east. But Henry's royal years were not attuned to foreign ventures. They were plagued by rebellion and conspiracy, constrained by limited funds, and so his court emerged by default as more English, less British or European. It was always overshadowed by the anxiety that attaches so strongly to usurpers.

King and prince, father and son, fell out in 1412 over a variety of issues, diplomatic and personal: above all, Henry IV suspected his son of opposing the abandonment of the Burgundian alliance in France, the king being mysteriously in favour of the flimsy association with the Armagnac faction in the French civil war. Henry IV had reacted harshly to his son's criticism by dismissing him and his party from the royal council. He appointed his other son, Thomas Duke of Clarence, as leader of an army, which landed at Vaast-la-Hogue, aiming to counter piracy and possess Normandy. The chronicler of St Albans preserves a letter attributed to Prince Henry, in which the son protested his loyalty and denied any intention to rebel, promising his utmost support in protecting the English 'inheritance' in France. But the rift was a serious blow to the failing king. Informed insiders, such as Thomas Hoccleve, appreciated the nature of this tension at court. His *Regiment of Princes*, a poem of 1411, was a work of petition and advice, based on an Italian tract which was adapted to the English political reality (Plate 16). It celebrates the Prince as the epitome of knightly valour, robust action, traditional piety. This is cast in stark opposition to the old king's practice, which had laid England to 'waste and destruction'. The prince was encouraged to listen to parliament, to be open to his subjects, to reflect on the always imminent danger of loss of royal authority, the fountainhead of governance. A king's rule of law was not only an act of justice, but the soundest foundation for the security of the realm:

> While law is kept in land
> a prince in his estate may secure stand.

'LOLLARDY' AND RELIGIOUS DEBATE

A most unusual, strong and sustained friendship developed between Henry IV and the Archbishop of Canterbury, Thomas Arundel. Veterans of Richard II's years, both men understood the political vagaries of exile and banishment, and the danger of confrontation with royal power. This produced in Henry IV's years a famous working relationship. Religious heterodoxy and political inconstancy were bound up by them in the suggestions of a single label – Lollardy. As we have seen, the beliefs associated with it ranged widely and blended seamlessly into the ideas and practices of folk who were never suspected of heresy. It may be more useful to think of 'Lollard' as a label attached to people who failed a number of tests of social acceptability through sexual incontinence, clerical wandering, an outspoken manner in criticism of the clergy, suspicious puritanical yearnings, attachment to vernacular books, or distaste for ostentatious religious expression. A generation after the death of Wyclif, 'Lollardy' had become a category in law. It allowed neighbour to inform on neighbour, and it put into motion a legal procedure. As to people's beliefs, these remained a mixture of widely varying attitudes to the power of images, to the efficacy of indifferent priests, or to the role of personal initiative in religious improvement. People who seemed particularly eager to read and discuss religious issues may well have earned the label 'Lollard', as did women who argued vehemently about points of scripture or belief, people who were attached to English religious writings, or who were less than deferential to their local priests.

As challenging as the political field was, even more intellectually and logistically frustrating to the crown were its attempts to bring uniformity to the thousands of parishes in which hundreds of preachers defied the authority of the church and, by doing so, that of the state. England was perceived as a polity under attack from malign Ricardians and misleading preachers who spread religious error together with political conspiracy. To counteract this dual threat, two institutions forged an alliance never before seen in England, although it was known on the continent: the marriage of church and state, aggressive in its pursuit of religious and political orthodoxy through the use of law.

A thousand years earlier, in the newly converted Roman empire, Christianity had become the state's religion, and was headed by an emperor in whose person church and state coalesced. But this had never been the case in western Europe, least of all in the British Isles. Ecclesiastical courts dealt with blasphemy, even very occasionally with heresy, but the state did not seek out heterodoxy, and major heresies – Cathars, Waldensians – had never touched England, Wales, Scotland or Ireland. Yet Henry IV's kingdom turned into a suspicious, persecuting, punitive state. In 1401, following clerical petitions and the pleading of three royal commissioners, hastily drafted and somewhat melodramatic in tone, the statute 'On Burning Heretics' (*De heretico comburendo*), or more correctly 'Against Lollards', provided a procedure by which royal justice became actively involved in seeking out and punishing heretics. This was a difficult parliament for Henry, one in which the return of Richard II's officials was requested in order to ensure better government, a year which saw rebellion and unrest. The legislation turned men and women identified as persisting in 'Lollard' views into traitors.

The writ resulting from the statute was a directive for implementation by sheriffs, for the burning of those deemed lapsed heretics by an ecclesiastical court, courts run by bishops and their staff. It was established English practice that royal writs be issued in promotion of ecclesiastical objectives as requested by bishops: by the mid-thirteenth century writs had been created for the capture of an apostate, a religious person fleeing enclosure, and for the arrest of an excommunicated person. In both cases the writ directed a sheriff to use royal resources and personnel to achieve the end. So it was to be with the writ for the burning of heretics.

Sedition and religious incontinence were perceived as mutually reinforcing: Gilbert, once canon of Malton Priory (Yorkshire), was acting as parish priest in Wales when he was denounced by his erstwhile abbot as having left during Scrope's uprising, possibly to support Glyn Dŵr. Dissenting habits could be quite subtly immersed in the rhythms of life and death: Sir John Cheynne, a Lollard knight, asked to be buried clothed in russet, a cloth of sound quality in an unostentatious grey. 'Lollards' could range from the crusty eccentric to the cheekily insubordinate.

Although Wyclif's writings had been condemned for their reformist criticism of the relations of church and state, engagement with church reform was intense in these decades. Two major ecumenical councils were assembled – the Council of Pisa of 1409, and of Constance in 1415

– and leading European scholars, including robust English delegations of bishops and theologians, engaged with issues that Wyclif had raised a generation or more earlier. Less reformist and more polemical were the ideas promoted robustly and triumphantly in the tens of tracts copied in regional centres of book production. Yet an interest in reading these texts, and even in using the Bible in English – a desire practised by many privileged readers – did not necessarily lead to detection or persecution. To be hauled in front of an archdeacon's visitation or to a bishop's court was a misfortune which befell few. It was usually the lot of people who, during periods of episcopal activism, were openly and persistently insubordinate, unwilling to blend into the social fabric, or into appropriate forms of subjecthood.

In the years which followed the deposition of Richard II, perceived malcontents and ranters posed the type of threat which crown and church equally resented and feared, and were willing to attack with mutual zeal. The actions of an archbishop of Canterbury who was also chancellor of the realm took place under the approving eye of the monarch, and created a machinery of persecution which suggested a new pact between both powers. In 1410 Henry Prince of Wales sanctioned by his presence a public trial of a craftsman, William Badby, suspected of recurrent and persistent heresy. This was William's second trial, and it was staged as a trial of state, at St Paul's Cathedral, under the archbishops of Canterbury and York and with an audience of the highest and mightiest bishops and nobles. Badby refused to recant, despite Archbishop Arundel's attempts to persuade him. The Prince of Wales offered the last chance to save his life, but William rejected it and was transported to Smithfield for execution. The Prince had aligned himself here with the powers of proactive orthodoxy, an unsparing alliance of church and state created by his father. The burning of Badby was clearly a strong message in a country whose ills had all come to be seen as products of the 'Lollard' poison: a few years later a sermon warned that it was the 'serpentine venom of the abominable Lollardy' which had caused such a weakening in the country that the 'slightest wind from Wales' could blow it down.

In the work of religious correction authorities confronted the problem posed by borders and definitions. The range of religious sensibilities was wide, and the rigours of religious perfection were achieved through a whole array of opportunities offered by conventional religion. Those who had money and properties to spare could order their priorities in their wills, entrusted to reliable executors. Joan Peyl (1382–1412) spent most of her adult life, from the age of seventeen, as the widow of a London mercer. She helped found Irthlingborough College (Northamptonshire) in memory of her husband and for the good of his soul. Like her contemporary, Margery Kempe of Bishop's Lynn (Norfolk) (c.1373–1438), she went on pilgrimages and was a habitual guest at the house of Minoresses in East London, but she also conducted the daily business of a lay person highly engaged in prayer and charity while living among these women religious. William of Erlakar, of Winfleet (Lincolnshire), prepared his will in 1415 in meticulous detail: while taking care of the needs of his widow and unmarried daughters he left sums to his parish church, to the orders of friars in Boston (Lincolnshire), for the foundation of regular prayer in his memory within his parish church, to nuns in two local nunneries, for the fabric of local chapels and churches, to the poor of his parish, and some money as well as a squirrel fur garment to warm the limbs of Philip, 'the hermit of Boston'. A book of instruction to the lay parishioner of c.1400 sought to curb some forms of enthusiasm, such as the dangerous and unseemly practice by some of climbing up to the rood-loft to pray as close as possible to the hanging crucifix.

Knowing and careful participation in the wide variety of religious efforts – through prayer, charity, hermitical life – signified not simple compliance, but informed discernment. Such practice around prayer, charity and parochial adherence was very different from the affective devotion by which Margery Kempe lived, and in which she claimed to have been directed by Christ himself: 'I have often times, daughter, told you that thinking, weeping and high contemplation is the best life on earth.' Margery was accused of Lollardy; yet she claimed that Christ came to comfort her, calling her a 'pillar' of the church. Margery had borne fourteen children, she was a wife living in chastity and then a widow, she was a bereaved mother, and she was an inveterate seeker of religious experience. She inspired some admiration while she lived as a respectable matron and pious pilgrim. Through her travels and quests, and through the reaction of bishops and archbishops – Repyngdon of Lincoln, Peverel of Worcester, Bouvel of York, Arundel and Chichele of Canterbury – a variety of devotional activities is revealed. She was inspired by conventional devotional texts such as Nicholas Love's *Mirror of the Blessed Life of Christ*, which she had heard, and which she claimed to have 're-written' with her tears. Despite the disapproval of the many churchmen she encountered, she led an interesting, adventurous and famous life. Her femininity added scandal to her notoriety, but she was tolerated, even admired, in England and abroad. More tragic was the situation of John Claydon, a skinner of London, burnt in 1415 for nothing more adventurous than possession of English books, among them the recently composed dissenting tract *The Lantern of Light*, written on fine parchment and well bound in red leather.

The machinery of persecution – operated by bishops in their dioceses – penetrated each parish, not only as a threat, but as an opportunity. For through the denunciation of suspects and the reporting of abuse, reputations for probity and good-standing could be developed. The politics of the parish/village were often centred on the operations of churchwardens, always men, and usually substantial tenants. The collective entity of parish/village offered a field for administrative action, leadership, and the exercise of influence. In the hands of churchwardens were moneys from collections, such as those habitually made after the Robin Hood play, church-ales and other revels. From these funds they were meant to maintain the church's fabric. Yet even around these local events a politics of interest and difference could develop: in 1415 the people of the hamlet of Horsley (Somerset) refused to make their contribution to the Bridgwater parish collection, arguing that they maintained their own chapel and need not support any other. Parishes also benefited from occasional gifts, which immediately elevated the donor family into a higher sphere of worth: these were gifts like the window of St Christopher in the London parish church of St Andrew Baynard Castle, or the splendid wall-painting of the life of Christ, which decorated the Fishermen's Chapel at St Brelade's, Jersey, from 1425.

Everywhere images were endowed with power, and some especially so, like that of St Christopher in Woodeaton (Oxfordshire), for which the inscription read:

> Whoever sees this image
> Will not die a bad death on that day.

The Charter of Christ, a devotional image accompanied by verse, emerged in this period and later became widespread in Ireland too. Christ's body was likened to a document written on parchment, in legal idiom, recording a bargain between humanity and Christ – faith for salvation. Every aspect of Christ's body was likened to the charter: it was written in blood:

> On my face the ink pours down
> when the thorns sink into me.

It was sealed with Christ's five wounds:

> O, my red blood, it rains down
> Five seals were set thereon.

Finally the Charter was witnessed:

> And the witnesses more than one
> Mark, Luke, Matthew and John
> And namely my mother sweet
> Who for me bloody tears did weep.

This is the sort of religious display which dissenters found so distasteful. *Pierce the Ploughman's Crede*, one of the earliest imitations of the poem *Piers Plowman*, tells of a man who sought instruction in the Creed before Easter. Looking at a parish church he wrily comments on the abundance of shining windows with thick script and heraldic shields, with marks of merchants. The church had become a multitude of signs pertaining to status and wealth; no longer a good place to learn one's Creed. The narrator later describes friars' churches as full of 'pennants and pummels and points of shields' which distract from the mass and draw away from devotion. Exactly such a convergence of worldly and religious imagery is evident in the north doorway of Castle Acre parish church in Norfolk: shields hang in spandrels, commemorating the de Warennes family of the Earl of Surrey, and the Fitzallans, Earls of Arundel. Inside, the rood-screen of c.1400 displays a whole series of saints, while the sides of the pulpit fittingly represent the fathers of the church. The visual sense stimulated by heraldry absorbed the messages of dynastic grandeur, and rendered saints familiar. It was this very similarity which dissenting writers found so inappropriate.

All people dwelt in parishes and religion was lived within a nexus of interwoven familial, tenurial and administrative activities. A quite different order – of magnitude, of self-awareness – was maintained by the routines and actions of large religious corporate bodies: cathedrals, monasteries, nunneries, collegiate churches. For these endowed bodies were wholly devoted to the maintenance of excellence and splendour in liturgical action, and served as beacons of intellectual, artistic and spiritual achievement in the pursuit of religious perfection. Enthusiasm for the monastic life waxed and waned; around 1350 there were approximately 1,480 nuns in England and Wales, and 2,360 around the year 1422 – within a stable number of religious houses (some 144 nunneries) and in a period of population decline. As corporations which never died, religious houses could seem more durable even than the crown. Untroubled by dynastic strife, they maintained traditions and a sense of lineage as strong as any aristocratic family. The historian of St Albans was only too aware, as he penned his annual entries, that he could finger leaves written by brethren past, going back some 300 years. Monasteries impinged little on the daily experience of most people. But they concerned aristocratic and royal patrons, as well as those who benefited from around 8 per cent of monastic income which was disbursed in relief – in almonries, through subsidized rents, and by distributions at funerals and commemorations. Monastic houses were chosen for the grand commemoration of the dead: their rituals could enrich and glamorize special occasions of state, as well as reinforce family worth.

A single artefact demonstrates the extraordinary mobilization of talent and wealth within rich religious houses. The Sherborne Missal is a liturgical book produced sometime between 1400 and 1407 for the Benedictine Abbey in Dorset. It contains 347 parchment leaves, and is unique in being of English production. The Dominican friar John Siferwas was seconded by his convent in Salisbury to take on the job of truly sumptuous decoration of the manuscript, the text of which was copied by a monk of Sherborne, John Whas. The work of copying was tedious, and the words issuing from his lips on John Whas's self-portrait spelt 'it is hard toil'. This was work of discipline and penance – the *opus dei* – God's work. The illumination is exquisite, offering a comprehensive liturgical guide to the calendar year, but also a compendium of images of religious and royal personalities of the Lancastrian dynasty. The monastery was rich and confident enough in about 1425 to invite the master-mason of Winchester Cathedral to build a vault for its choir, the like of which had rarely been seen: it was a fan vault predating those of Eton and of King's College, Cambridge. Political loyalty and religious provision co-existed in this niche of social and cultural privilege. Monasteries and cathedrals also received sumptuous books from patrons, such as, for example, the Lovel Lectionary, *c.* 1408, made by the same friar-illuminator John Siferwas at the request of John Lord Lovel of Titmarsh, for Salisbury Cathedral. An illuminated page in the Lectionary depicts the solemn act of exchange: a man in a black habit, the maker of the book, places it in the hands of his richly dressed lay patron.

Cathedrals were similar centres of religious artistic production, but unlike most monasteries they were situated in cities, and there they employed craftsmen, were visited by pilgrims, and participated in the urban land-market. Cathedrals enjoyed a special status of judicial autonomy within their precincts – spaces which still retain a unique appearance and atmosphere in today's York or Norwich – and lives were affected by their imposing presence and economic might. Cathedrals maintained almonries which disbursed charity, and developed schools in which sons of the urban elite could gain an education. The two were combined – charity and schooling – in the almonry school of Winchester Cathedral. Here a further experiment was developed c.1402: a bequest of £12 a year to the cathedral, made by a lord and lady of a modest Hampshire estate, John and Alice Talmache, supported musical scholarships for almonry schoolboys. The cathedral priory hired a musician previously engaged at Westminster Abbey, the organist and composer John Tyes, to train four boys and conduct the combined sounds of boys, monks and organ in the daily office of the Virgin, sung in the cathedral. Tyes was an enterprising musician, and the city of Winchester granted him citizenship around 1418. Since citizens were expected to serve their cities, Tyes had to pay £3 for an exemption from public office, due to the onerous nature of his musical duties. Inspired by the great composers of the royal chapel – John Pyamour (d. 1431), John Dunstable (d. 1453) and Leonel Power (d. 1445) – schools such as Winchester nurtured the roots of the English choral tradition, which was transformed and augmented at the Reformation.

The Sherborne Missal and the music of the Lady Chapel of Winchester both demonstrate the high level of skill and workmanship – of a friar and a layman, respectively – which was available in cathedral cities. A sophisticated system of reward, organization and quality control, of licensing and policing had developed in these urban centres, to produce such variety. Furthermore, the beneficiaries were a small section of the urban population, the rest of which laboured as unskilled and daily workers. The demarcation of professional expertise was pronounced and highly guarded. The work of fifteenth-century builders who toiled in the many rebuilt churches of London was organized and supervised – men such as Walter Walston in St John Walbrook in 1421, or the carpenter William Serle, who installed a rood-loft in St Mary at Hill in 1427. Builders frequently operated as contractors, in a way reminiscent of modern arrangements. They hired the expert craftsmen, who executed specialist plastering, plumbing and carpentry under the scrutiny of churchwardens who carefully monitored the use of the parish's funds.

In the cities books circulated widely. Rich persons and rich religious houses owned sumptuous volumes, but far humbler folk owned books too. These were not all books for leisure reading, the pastime of noble and gentry folk, but the workbooks of surgeons, merchants and clerics. A whole literature had developed over the previous century to strengthen the hand of the priest: summaries of pastoral theology, guides for sermons, lists of vices and virtues, liturgical books. And these, clearly, were circulated, shared and copied. The will of John Hovyngham (d. 1417), Archdeacon of Durham, instructed his executors to return borrowed books to the Cistercian Abbey of Byland (Yorkshire), to a London rector, and a missal borrowed from a chaplain. Here the recommendations of John Mirk in his *Instructions to Parish Priests* are reflected in practice: that those who possessed books should share them with colleagues, perhaps for a period of copying by a scribe. Some of the most accessible handbooks for the clergy and for lay people were distillations and digests of highly academic and technical books of sacramental theology, and penitential tracts such as the *Memoriale Credencium* written *c*.1400 by an author from south Gloucestershire. The circulation of books was considered highly beneficial for the instruction of the clergy and, through them, for millions of illiterate and less literate parishioners.

Henry IV's decade saw the most unambiguous formulation about the power of books, above all their power to mislead and pervert. In the Constitutions of Thomas Arundel, Archbishop of Canterbury, of 1407 and 1409, a certain class of book was deemed illegal, for example any translation of scripture into English, and theological discussion in the vernacular. Archbishop Arundel decreed in the seventh Constitution of 1409 that, under pain of excommunication,

no one should henceforward translate any text of holy scripture into the English tongue or any other by his own authority, be it by means of books, pamphlets or tracts, nor should anyone read such book, pamphlet or tract composed since the time of the said Wyclif, or to be written in the future, in part or in whole, in public or in private,

Despite this attack on unauthorized vernacular religious writings, more than 250 copies of the Wycliffite Bible survive. The Constitutions also singled out other forms of communication and instruction by which people might gain access to contaminating and harmful teaching: schoolteachers were warned against instruction on the sacraments, preachers against discussing the eucharist and other sacraments in their sermons, and a close gaze was to be cast on Oxford – the university which had bred Wyclif and his followers – through monthly inquiries into the orthodoxy of discussions and writing there. The next Archbishop of Canterbury, Henry Chichele, was to extend the remit of the Constitutions by setting up, in 1416, a procedure in canon law for regular examinations, at least twice a year in every deanery, to identify 'those believing in errors or heresies, owners of suspicious books in the English tongue'.

In this manner not only lay readers but, more importantly, misleading preachers were to be identified and apprehended. For despite the Constitutions, heterodox preaching was still taking place, often as a complement to parish preaching, even from parish pulpits. William Taylor used his friend Thomas Drayton's pulpit in Holy Trinity church, Bristol, to spread his dissenting views. Even more shocking was a report made by the anti-heretical polemicist Thomas Netter, that a certain woman, a well-known disciple of Wyclif, taught in London in 1410 that Mary did not remain a virgin after Christ's birth, and that the Bible nowhere supports such a view.

Books could harm, and the act of translation into English was a subtle and dangerous one, through which divine word could be perverted, and writing could become a vehicle for dissimulation. This was the prime offence of dissenters, 'Lollards', according to their detractors. Indeed there is a knowing playfulness in the use by dissenting writers of well-established orthodox genres: they produced versions of the Creed, of *Piers Plowman*, of traditional tracts on Vices and Virtues. In these familiar forms, and peppered with necessary biblical citation, such books could seem safe and edifying. And since the world of textual production was so multi-layered, genres so accessible, and because 'Lollards' based themselves on an unimpeachably true source – scripture – that no working definition could be offered for determining good from bad text. Only a total ban could ensure total safety. And just as the Constitutions constrained lay people's reading, it tied the hands of priests; their meagre collections of books could now easily damn them.

Priests had to be vigilant in these years, since dissent had heightened the scrutiny of priestly living. Parishes were full of activist parishioners; they are made visible in the lively and detailed testimonies brought against priests and clerks in episcopal visitations. The visitation of John Chandler, Dean of Salisbury, in 1405, heard that in the parish of Farringdon (Devon) the vicar neither preached nor instructed, failed to provide parish chaplains, left St Alban's chapel to ruin, celebrated the daily hours away from the church while out on business, and that he frequented taverns, and committed 'adultery and incest' with his parishioner Emma Webbs. In Wantage (Berkshire) it was claimed that the parish chaplain, William Hardyng, served at the altar despite being married, carelessly used the parish silver (some of which he broke), refused to accompany the vicar to visitation of the sick, took vestments home for the use of his family, and sometimes slept with his brood in the church on top of the same vestments. In the face of this scrutiny of priestly living it is not surprising to find that Arundel's third Constitution of 1409 required that preaching be directed to the sins of the laity, and that the misconduct of priests be addressed only in Latin sermons read or heard by priests alone.

The mood of persecution and heightened official attention to religious expression created an underground of anxious people, particularly scholars and priests. As late as 1412 the vicar of Bere Regis (Salisbury diocese) had to clear his name, subject as he was to suspicion for having been a Fellow of Exeter College in the 1380s together with a known follower of Wyclif. Rumours developed even wilder fantasies; for not only were Lollard preachers perverse clerks, women preachers perverted the natural order even further. Thomas Hoccleve's poem *Remonstrance against Oldcastle* of 1415 derided the recent distortion of reading practices. To a knight with heavy scriptural reading habits, he recommended more suitable reading in romance or on the art of war:

> Beware, Oldcastle, for Christ's sake,
> Climb no more so high in holy writ
> Read the stories of *Lancelot of the Lake*
> or Vegetius' *Of the art of chivalry*,
> *The siege of Troy* or *Thebes*.

Even worse was women's reading:

> Even some women, though their wit is thin,
> Make arguments in holy scripture.
> Lewd old women, sit down and spin,
> And cackle about something else
> Because your mind is all too weak
> for disputation on it [scripture].

Vilification of the 'Lollard' sphere poured into visual imagery: an early fifteenth-century illustrated *Piers Plowman* contains a figure entitled 'lunatic lollard': a barefooted man, naked, scruffy and perhaps without the power to reason. An imagined minority had been created: erring priests, misguided knights, misplaced women – and against them were poised agencies of state, the energies of prelates and the vigilant eye of neighbours, as well as the imagination of the caricaturist.

The issues associated with Wycliffite critique were not only related to devotional practice, access to books, and the use of the vernacular, although these became the most widespread markers of alternative religious taste. There were issues pertaining to the governance of the realm, and disposition of wealth within it. For the Commons came to appreciate some of the points which Wyclif had developed in his political theology: the question of relations between church and property, priesthood and wealth, stewardship and social obligation. Even as ecclesiastical jurisdiction sought out and tried suspected dissenters, some of the criticism of clerical privilege was being aired in parliament. By ancient custom and historical development the income of about 40 per cent of the parish churches of England was assigned to religious houses. These houses were meant to apportion some of the income from each such parish's tithes for the support of a resident vicar, whose task it was to provide the parishioners' spiritual and sacramental needs and to maintain the church's fabric. When such provision failed, parishes were ill-served: well-endowed religious houses were seen to profit at the expense of humble parishioners. The very administration of temporal goods by clergy was seen as corrupting – as argued carefully by Wyclif – and the deflection of parish incomes from the poor and needy to institutional coffers seemed equally to be corrupt.

In the first decade of the century a series of petitions to parliament raised these issues with a contemporary inflection, culminating with the 'Disendowment Bill' of 1410. This bill linked charity and secular control of funds with a proposal for the foundation of 100 almshouses for the poor, administered by secular authorities out of ecclesiastical incomes. It also linked worldly status and charitable duty on a sliding scale from earls down to squires. This vein of political and social reform continued in parliamentary petitions: in 1414 proposals were made for reform of hospitals, whose headships were frequently held as sinecures, and which no longer fulfilled the functions laid down by their founders. Here was a serious critique of ecclesiastical administration of relief; not a doctrinal challenge but lay concern with the ecclesiastical order, in terms often similar to Wycliffite complaints. Supporters among the parliamentary Commons were the gentry and merchants, into whose hands stewardship of the new institutions, within local communities – if they were to be created – would fall. This is what did indeed happen a century later with the Dissolution of the Monasteries.

A strange type of truth is contained in the defensive accusations made by crown and church: there was a notable group of people of means and training, of standing and power – to whom the tradition of religious exploration offered by the vernacular world of theology was a precious privilege and a badge of autonomy. Moreover, such traditions were strong in certain regions and within certain social circles. The Midlands saw men such as William Burleigh, who in 1407–8 was visited by Bohemian scholars, who corrected their versions of Wyclif's Latin writings against the reliable texts in his library. A manuscript produced c.1400 in the north-east Midlands contained sermons for Whitsun based on gospel commentaries including one by Wyclif, with sections of pure orthodoxy and others which might have been deemed heretical – certainly after 1407.

'Lollardy' was not a coherent identifiable group, but the label provided occasions for the display of royal purpose, of the power of activist bishops, and of probity and responsibility on the part of denouncing neighbours. Royal servants were involved in the support of famous 'Lollard' preachers, yet were rarely taken to be traitorous. An event in January 1414, which has come to be known grandly as the Oldcastle Rebellion, shows just how much political capital could be generated even from a small act of defiance. Oldcastle was son of a knightly family of Herefordshire. He had served in all of Henry IV's campaigns: in Scotland in 1400, in south Wales from 1401 (where he held several castles in succession). He was a special companion of Prince Henry and from 1404 played his part in parliament, later acting as sheriff, and soon made a good marriage. This union in 1408 may have brought him into contact with a household that disregarded strictures against banned books. In 1413 Oldcastle's views were examined, as were those of several other knights, and the evidence was put to the king. Henry V allowed for indictments to be served against Oldcastle and men of his retinue. Oldcastle ignored these and sought safety in his castle at Cooling (Kent). The summons was repeated and he was ultimately taken to the Tower, whence he was led to St Paul's to face Archbishop Arundel. At the examination he was asked about his attitude to the Cross. Oldcastle answered that his own body was like a cross, a quip often found in the records of examinations of suspects of heresy. He was excommunicated, and Henry V allowed forty days' respite in which he could save his life by recanting. Oldcastle managed to escape, no mean feat, and with some supporters rode to St Giles's Field outside London on 9 January 1414. Hearing that a royal force was approaching they escaped, but Oldcastle was taken at Welshpool (Powys), and was brought back to the Tower, where he was drawn and then burnt as a heretic. Several men in royal service had supported Oldcastle's acts, and enjoyed the pardons which Henry V chose to offer those who would become orthodox and loyal: Thomas Haseley of Hertfordshire was even knighted in 1445, despite his awkward, short-lived period as counsellor to Sir John Oldcastle. By crushing Oldcastle and acting generously towards his supporters, Henry displayed both orthodoxy and power in the early months of his reign.

RURAL LIFE

For peasants this was still a period of opportunity, as the trend of leasing out prime agricultural land still continued. In these decades the long process of leasing out of choice demesne lands was reaching its completion. Management of estates had become a difficult and risky affair in an economy characterized by a falling supply of labour for agrarian work and declining efficiency. The repeated visitations of plague constantly changed the balance between humans, livestock, pests and the built environment, which was increasingly in a state of decay. The job of estate manager was hard to fulfil successfully. In Hinderclay (Suffolk) fourteen managers were in post between 1379 and 1406, of which only one – a very successful one – lasted in the post for ten years. Such men had to take hard decisions: on manors in East Anglia sheep-breeding was centralized in order to reduce cost, but this resulted in greater inbreeding with raised susceptibility to disease in the flocks. At Wisbech (Cambridgeshire), in a desire to cut costs while wool prices were low, maintenance of sheep-cotes was neglected, and so sheep grazed on marshland, where they often developed rot, and even drowned. A constant and subtle assessment of cost and the benefits of investment occupied the minds of manor officials, and determined the conditions of work for agricultural labourers.

Some secular lords chose a different direction altogether – that of labour-intensive and scrutinizing enforcement of traditional manorial rights: men such as the Lords Grey of Ruthin in their Bedfordshire estates, who saw their manorial incomes rise steadily throughout the fifteenth century. The fact that agricultural land was now available through the simple device of a lease created opportunities for expansion in villages, and occasions for migration to neighbouring manors. Yet even as leases proliferated, claims to land through inheritance were cherished and remained the major mode of transmission of land, even from the distance of generations, and even to kin who had long left the community. In 1404 Thomas Adams succeeded to half of a half-yardland, once Roger Ketel's in Illey (Warwickshire), after the death of his niece; it was to pass to his younger brother were he to die. But in 1420 a blood relative of Roger Ketel came to claim it, and the jurors preferred this claim, an indisputable though hitherto unrealized link of blood and expectation which predated Thomas Adams's. Customary land, held through inheritance, incurred only a low customary rent, while new leases, even of better land, deterred modest folk by the higher rents demanded for them.

Supervision of village cooperation belonged to rural communities. The documents created by them in these decades reflect the processes. In Harleston (Norfolk) c.1410 the north-east and south fields were sown to produce a full year's need in wheat, barley, beans and peas, while leaving one field fallow. At the same time a jury of nine, which included several villagers, supervised the feeding of stock in meadows and pasture. For his part, the lord promised to enclose his own demesne land and thus create a clear demarcation between lord and tenants, and between their beasts, for the straying of beasts on to sown land was a cause of serious financial damage, and the creation of seething enmities. In Wymeswold in Leicestershire around 1425 three lords agreed with the villagers on the course of sowing in 'white corn field', 'peas corn field' and the fallow. Agrarian work and village charity were linked, for the fines on animals straying and disturbing the lord's crops were to be apportioned at the rate of a penny per foot of field damaged, and rendered to the parish church. Similar care was reflected in village by-laws concerning gleaning, where it was emphasized that only those who could not work for their own support were allowed to glean in the fields after harvest.

Every aspect of rural life, every chance to use or sell resources, continued to be closely scrutinized, and decisions were local in nature. Those in charge sought to confront trends in prices and demand, read through a plethora of available signs and rumours. This was true for decisions taken at the level of sowing routines on a Norfolk manor, just as it applied to the sophisticated actions of London merchants in their livery companies. An examination of the choices made by stewards of estates is illuminating: at Felbrigg (Norfolk) between 1400 and 1408 a sowing rhythm was developed which saw fallow, wheat and then barley. The prime crops for bread and drink were allowed to enjoy the best chances of plentiful growth after the soil had been allowed to rest fallow. At Hinderclay (Suffolk), similarly, a nourishing course of legumes preceded the planting of barley for bread and drink. On some estates of Peterborough Abbey (Bedfordshire) barley was also preponderant, a response to the demand for drink. The routines and patterns were specific to each village, even within the estate of a single lord, and reflected custom, local needs and an interpretation of what the environment, the market and the local lord's table required. But everywhere tenants and lords, represented by their stewards, were confronting shrinking profitability, and thus regularly took decisions to contract their agrarian cultivation, since tenant farmers were always scarce.

Those who stayed on the land negotiated rents and were occasionally even given a helping hand by their landlord: in 1412 and 1413 Ramsey Abbey provided new tenants in Kings Ripton and Abbots Ripton (Huntingdonshire) with four bushels of wheat and three quarts each of barley and peas, to be used in the first sowing, reflecting the proportions of crops to be sown. According to the agreement between the abbey and John White and his wife, who leased six acres of demesne land, the tenants were to sow an acre of wheat, two acres with barley and one acre with peas. In the mixed agrarian economy of the Sussex Weald beans of various types appear more prominently. They provided food-payments to agrarian workers (together with some cash and oats), and were used to feed pigs, some for market and others for landlords' household consumption. Thus on Claverham and Chalvington, estates of the Sackville family in Sussex, in 1413–14, 106 acres were sown, a quarter of which were beans, while by the 1420s, more than half the acres were beans; some twenty locally reared and fattened pigs, fed on these beans, were consumed by the household at Blackhurst every year.

Arable was contracting everywhere. Demand for corn bread was giving way to meat and dairy products, in a population that showed no signs of growth. Attention was directed by stewards not only to pro-vision of seed for sowing, but to resources for maintaining buildings and dwellings. At Podington (Bedfordshire) the tenants received portions of timber or underwood from the landlord's park for construction and repair of farm buildings. In 1413 Richard Tommes was even paid to do the maintenance work, in addition to receiving the wood used. In south Bedfordshire, Peterborough Abbey leased out its whole estate to tenants, together with barns, stables and cowsheds. Similarly, most of the estates of the cathedral priory of St Swithin's, Winchester, in the chalk downs, were leased out by the 1420s. The leasing out of land involved a large institutional lord such as St Swithin's in a complex array of relations with local people. In 1400 John Mascal, who farmed the demesne estate at Stockton, was also the father of a monk of St Swithin's, Ralph. This relationship may have helped John to gain his freedom through the process of manumission (a ritual of liberation from serfdom conducted at the lord's will), in 1417, and to gain the privilege of retirement as a corrodian, a guest of the community, whose upkeep was charged to the Stockton estate which he had cultivated during his working years. The freeing of John Mascal at this time marks the fruition of a long-term process, roughly between 1380 and 1420, by which personal serfdom declined and almost disappeared. Yet free persons could hold 'unfree' tenures which existed under a long-standing set of customs that required work and services over and beyond the payment of rent.

Out of the abundance of land and the fragmentation of estates interesting and complex holdings were being created. In this extremely busy land-market greater landlords were divesting themselves of land, and so estates could occasionally be bought whole: Lord Edmund Grey was able to buy Ampthill Castle in Bedfordshire. More often peasants were exchanging and rationalizing holdings. Some rose to the state of yeoman, or developed even more substantial and ambitious positions on the local social ladder. This was as evident in early fifteenth-century Bedfordshire, as it was in Wales throughout the century. As estates changed shape and ownership, the landscape was transformed. A fifteenth-century survey of the Arundel lands in Cornwall noted that names of fields were forgotten as erstwhile arable was turned into grazing land for feeding cattle.

The size and shape of village houses reflected the social gradation of agrarian pursuits: the growing number of shepherds tending the increasingly numerous flocks of England and Wales spent several months a year in a wheeled hut which moved with them and their sheep. Those more settled lived in simple dwellings, with stone foundations and constructed with wattle and daub in the east Midlands. In south Bedfordshire, for example, the average number of hearths in a household was 1.5, but in the better-off villages, and among better-off families, there were two or even three rooms with hearths. Tenants fulfilled their families' needs in a variety of ways. Game and fish were bartered with neighbours, they brewed their own beer, and used local rural markets for other purchases. These markets were numerous in England and Wales and easily accessible for most people.

A hierarchy of consumption patterns mirrored the social hierarchy. The poor bought locally, and in small quantities, while the better-off ventured to small towns and provincial centres. Magnates bought from cities, even from London, where wares and goods from the whole of the known world were available. A rising knightly family such as that of Sir Hugh Luttrell of Dunster (Somerset) purchased most of its goods in the accounting year 1405–6 in provincial towns around its home: fish from Porlock and Minehead (6 and 1½ miles away), lime and horseshoes from Watchet (5 miles). It ventured furthest for purchases of wine, from Taunton (17 miles away), and spices, wax and pewter goods from Bridgwater (19 miles away). The servants of the great household of Richard Mitford, Bishop of Salisbury, similarly satisfied most of his needs in provincial towns, although wax and paper, major items of expenditure for a busy bishop's household, were bought in London (75 miles away). Services of pedlars and sellers of wares, as well as of physicians and surgeons, were to be had even in the smallest hamlet, for a price.

Gentry households lived well if they made the best of their produce, bought wisely and did not over-extend in the purchase of land, in building, or have the misfortune of owing a ransom for a family member captured in France. The widow Alice de Bryene ran her Suffolk household in 1418–19 generously: it consumed 46 head of cattle, 44 pigs, 57 sheep, a lot of poultry, 3 pheasants, 13 partridges and 3 herons, as well as 102 rabbits and 5 cygnets; in addition there was cod and haddock but only rarely pike and sturgeon. Almost half of her household expenses were on food, as she fed not only kin and guests, but also those who helped her maintain the manor and her widely spread estate of some 3,000 acres in Essex, Suffolk and the West Country. These ranged from carpenters to bailiffs, auditors and trustees to squires; all were fed at her table and were often given a bed for the night after travel from distant parts of her domain. In monastic institutions portions distributed to monks seem large, and were probably shared with family members who lived nearby. In aristocratic households the lavish provision of meat, bread and wines led to calorific intakes so gargantuan that we must assume that much of the food bought, cooked and served was offered as much for conspicuous display as for the satisfaction of appetites. In households such as the Duke of Buckingham's at Goodrest, in Wedgenock Park (Warwickshire), colours made of spices and herbs added to the food's untouchability – food for the eyes, not all for the belly.

The links between town and country worked in several interesting ways. For while artisans flourished in towns, protected by guild status, they were also linked to villages and smaller towns for the hire of labourers and the purchase of raw materials. In the hope of creating greater visibility and amenability to control, towns increasingly required that all burgesses join a craft guild, as did Norwich in 1415 and Coventry in 1421. The guilds monitored training and exercised quality control in a contracting market: the goldsmiths of London, for example, fined members for the use of faulty weights. In 1403 the goldsmith John Welford was fined for offering inadequate workmanship when he mounted a silver horn; Robert Howes was chastised for sharing the craft secret of melting silver with 'aliens'. Falling profits also created an incentive towards diversification in skills and practice. The mason Hugh Grantham of York (d. 1410), who undertook contracts for church repairs, was also a trader in cattle and sheep, corn and barley, and supplied bakers and brewers. At his death he was owed £85 for grain alone, and £9 for cloth.

Initiative and diversification, movement and new types of association typified the process of adaptation to the changing economic environment. The growth in movement is reflected in the place of hostelling and victualling among the most flourishing urban occupations: York was probably able to provide 1,300 beds a night for visitors – pilgrims, traders, royal officials – and increasingly hostellers entered into the ranks of respectable townsmen who merited the status of citizen. English inns had the reputation of being warm and welcoming: foreign visitors commented that (amazing as it might seem to us) hostesses greeted guests with kisses.

THE LAW

As legal attachment to land and to person was slowly but surely becoming less fixed and predictable, people could imagine situations for themselves in terms previously unthinkable. New types of legal provision and training helped spread legal formats and conventions to a wider array of activities and thus to new groups of people. Chancery English developed in these decades – supported, no doubt, by the frequent use of English in political and military reports by Henry V and his household – a standardized language for administrative use, to which those emerging from mercantile backgrounds could adapt with ease. Contemporaries were aware of this choice, and appreciated its impact:

Our mother tongue . . . has in modern days begun to be honourably enlarged and adorned, for that our most excellent lord, King Henry V, has in his letters . . . more willingly chosen to declare the secrets of his will, and for the better understanding of his people . . . procured the common idiom to be commended by the exercise of writing.

The law, which was rooted in activities experienced and conducted in English – loans, promises, partnerships – received comfortable hearing in the Chancery court. New concepts of justice were developing there in these decades: whereas common law worked well in disputes over land, it required a documentary trail for claims, and thus was less fitted to activities in which no parchment trail was ever created, such as contracts sealed by the handshakes and promises of merchants.

The court of Chancery attempted to offer remedies to those left out of the provisions of common law, and in seeking its inspiration and principles it borrowed from jurisprudence which reflected on conscience and natural law – Roman law and canon (ecclesiastical) law. Roman law, known throughout Europe as the *ius commune*, the law shared by the countries of Europe, was useful in all ecclesiastical courts as its jurisprudential underpinning, as well as in courts of admiralty, equity and diplomacy. Training in Roman law opened opportunities for work at Chancery, where the amount of legal business was rocketing. Although the foundations were laid in Richard II's reign by some acute royal servants, Henry V was a frequent user of his Chancery when he sought to provide justice in unusual cases. Sometime between 1415 and 1422 Richard II's *Ordinances of the Lord King's Chancery* were revived, and some fifty-four cases were heard in an average year, at its seat in Westminster Hall. By the end of Henry V's reign, and during that of his son, Chancery provided an arena for the discussion of 'equity', the application of principles of justice, rather than of due procedure as in common law. Its main users in these decades were knights, esquires, priests, clerks and merchants, as it made good cases relating to promises and oaths, and took decisions on disputed land-holding. This department, which was run strictly through nepotism and patronage – of mainly Yorkshire clerks, few of whom were university graduates – offered what seemed a superior type of justice for those whose grievances fell outside the clearly defined remit of common law and assize courts.

Legal careers could be fostered in the Exchequer too; Nicholas Dixon's brass in Cheshunt church (Hertfordshire) bears witness to an impressive rise: from entry as a young clerk of the Exchequer in 1402, to the grade of senior clerk in 1413, to the responsibility of clerk of the Great Pipe Roll in the following year, on to deputy treasurer in the Exchequer in 1421, and then to the prestige and influence of a Baron of the Exchequer in 1423. Royal servants were required to travel a lot, to follow kings around the country, to make financial provision during the royal court's absences abroad (none under Henry IV, several under Henry V). It was a life of service, but one with tangible personal rewards.

Through training at Inns of Court men of modest means could gain valued expertise. Group identity was developing among lawmen, not least with the institutionalization of training and apprenticeship, and the creation of their collective bodies – the Inns of Court – which were social as much as professional. By this period lawyers trained in the courts, but were also taught the law by judges during 'learning vacations' when the courts were in recess. This system paralleled the tutorial teaching which was developing in Cambridge and Oxford colleges, whereby senior members of the college taught the juniors. Like the academic colleges, the Inns of Court combined learning and fun. In Furnivall's Inn, an Inn of Court, activities ranged from legal training to festive Christmas meals eaten together, to joint entertainment at performances by actors and mimes.

The law recruited widely and was used widely too. Even small towns and village communities required such services. In the London Court of Hustings in these years a growing number of cases were brought by widows to recover their dower, the women being represented by attorneys who perhaps even specialized in such business. Lower down the scale and in a rural setting, skilful legal play was apparent as people exploited the spaces and opportunities created between canon law, manorial custom and the procedures of common law. Statute law grew in prominence and precedence over common law; even Pope Martin V acknowledged its rise when he complained that it detracted from the traditional primacy of canon law in all that concerned ecclesiastical matters and persons. The accumulated body of legislation in the form of statutes from parliamentary petitions and debates was formidable. Since the mid-fourteenth century a wide range of issues had been deemed fit for parliamentary discussion and royal legislation: wages, poverty and begging, heresy, consumption patterns and dress code, prices of foodstuffs (bread, ale), and the circulation and quality of coinage.

This proliferation of legal avenues and styles, and their growing accessibility even to small communities, is evident from the dispute which animated the neighbourhood of Dunwich (Suffolk) in the early decades of the fifteenth century. The borough of Dunwich (with 62 burgesses in 1411 and 153 taxpayers in 1413) retained two lawyers during the 1410s, two members of gentry families, one a justice of the peace, at the cost of 20s. per annum in retainers. Even this small fishing port needed legal protection, for it enjoyed the privileged status of a port, with the right to collect tolls from ships entering its harbour. When in 1403 the lord of neighbouring Blythburgh, Sir Robert Swillington, claimed Kingsholme marshes between Walberswick and Dunwich and thus offered an alternative haven to that of Dunwich, a mighty battle began. Dunwich officials were attacked and in turn Dunwich burgesses were bound over to keep the peace. The struggle was settled in 1408 when Swillington managed to produce a royal charter of 1229 which confirmed the status of Blythburgh's harbour jurisdiction, a charter which was confirmed by Henry IV.

Canon law was another legal avenue towards a distinguished career in the British Isles and abroad, and it too found its recruits among the sons of men of lower social status, but of some financial comfort. The great canon lawyer William Lyndwood was born in Lincolnshire to a wool merchant in about 1375. He began a conventional career in the church with a string of benefices, the income from which supported him in the pursuit of his studies, and by 1403 he had gained a Cambridge bachelor's degree, followed by a doctorate in 1407. He served as the king's clerk, and then entered the service of the Bishop of Ely; he later served the Archbishop of Canterbury, Henry Chichele, all the time accumulating livings. He reached the highest administrative position in the church of England, as Chancellor to the See of Canterbury, and ended his life as Bishop of St David's (1442–6). Men like him were much in demand. Most of his work involved scrutiny of canon law and its adaptation to new needs: this often meant involvement in the examination of suspected heretics and rebels.

TOWNS AND TOWN LIFE

The gentle swell in the size of middling towns bears witness to the economic reality of competition and opportunity, as does, in a more dramatic fashion, the growth of London in this period. London attracted the sons and daughters of farmers from far afield, especially from East Anglia and the Midlands. At the same time the arrival of workers, and their departure, preoccupied both corporations and oligarchic councils. In the 1420s rent yields were in decline, making planning of urban taxation difficult, but also producing opportunities for development by the far-sighted and deep-pocketed.

Migration is often associated with improvement and opportunity. In towns employers continued to seek young people to train and employ. According to the Commons in 1406, landless peasants were swelling the ranks of apprentices in London, sending children younger than the statutory age of twelve years. Londoners sought exemption from this age-restriction in 1426; it had been legislated after the Black Death, to stop the drain of agricultural labourers. But what of the communities left by migrants, left by their young, strong and ambitious? Those who remained reorganized their lives, wedged between customary routines and new forms of tenancy and social relations. While the production of food for market was not so profitable, rural communities still needed food, towns had to be fed, and landlords' households required a wide range of cereals, fish, meat and fruit for their tables.

The relationship between town and hinterland could be one of continuity and gradation, but even middling boroughs could entertain rather complex international contacts. By the early fifteenth century Colchester marketed its middle-range cloth, which was simple and modest but of good quality and wearing properties – the russet. It was produced in grey and brown and fitted the needs not of the poorest, but of those of modest means, or those who wished to present themselves as modest and humble. It was the cloth of choice of beneficed clergy, students, members of religious orders and layfolk committed to the religious life, for its colour was thought to signify 'simpleness'. By offering a modest but good-quality cloth – a quality guaranteed by the operation of the Colchester standard – the town gained renown and an attractive commodity for export. It was bought by merchants for sale in Prussia (where it was much desired by the Knights of the Hospitaller Order) and in Aragon (to which it was brought by factors of the Datini firm of Prato). It even reached Damascus in 1416 through the service of Venetian traders. Colchester merchants could sell their russet cloth in exchange for 369 tuns of wine at Bordeaux (some £1,800 in value) as they did in 1397–8, trade which has also left records in the custom accounts of 1410–11 and 1413–14. A foreign ship docked at the Hythe, Colchester's harbour, every twelve days on average, taking away cloth, as well as hides and butter and cheese. But Colchester merchants also brought their cloth to London for sale to Tuscan and Venetian merchants. If one wonders where Essex men and women bought their own cloth, they seem to have done so from smaller cloth towns like Braintree, some only a few miles from their doorsteps. While the peak in cloth exports of 1401–2 was not to be sustained, Colchester had a product and continued to see relative prosperity. This is deduced through demand for burgess status in the town, a burgeoning market in food and drink for its workers and visitors, and a soaring number of fines for illegal brewing in this decade – a sign of the industry's buoyancy.

Such trade flourished in times of security but was tested when regular traffic across the Channel was disturbed. From 1403, uncertainty disrupted the trade with Bordeaux, as the Anglo-Hanseatic treaty of 1392, which supported it, was not renewed at the end of its ten years' duration. Piracy was a problem for most spheres of trade, and local men exploited perceived gaps in policing and punishment. In May 1404 two ships carrying northern goods for a company trading from Hamburg were taken by force off the Suffolk coast. The ships' merchandise (beer, copper, ham and tar) was distributed among the pirates – men from Earl Soham and Wickham Market.

Towns such as Colchester were sensitive to breaches in the defence of the realm through diplomacy and war. Suffolk towns suffered a 27 per cent fall in their takings in market tolls between 1400 and 1430 and this was accompanied by dilapidation of buildings and public facilities. The great traders in wool had not only regional connections but international ambitions and commitments. By 1421, the isolation felt earlier in the century gave way to an enterprising organization. Shares in ships which traded in wool could be bought from the holding company of Merchant Adventurers. They met in Antwerp, a centre from which the safety of their canvas-covered, tightly packed wool was monitored and the terms of its sale negotiated. When a merchant died, his wool-sack was as important a sign of identity and pride as a knight's sword: a brass in the church of the Cotswolds town of North Leach has a wool-pack at the feet of a local wool merchant c.1400.

Towns offered kings opportunities for raising income on special occasions. Parliament examined every privilege and custom attached to the royal person, in an exercise of administrative application impressive by any standard. So when his daughter Philippa was about to marry Eric, King of Sweden, Norway and Denmark, Henry IV revived a feudal aid, an old royal exaction, not a parliamentary contribution. Royal hospitality was planned and used so as to minimize the expenses of a court which in any case travelled very little beyond the call of military campaigns. Tallages were imposed on boroughs, and charters were renewed actively and willingly, for a charge. Those who lent money to the crown were allowed to export without duty and to benefit from tax exemptions. Henry V, though sound in financial planning, was on occasion brazen in his deeds. When he needed to raise funds he even pawned the quintessential symbols of kingly dignity – swords, coronets – in the knowledge that few communities would auction them when the day of payment had passed and they were not redeemed. Coronets were offered to the boroughs of Norwich and Lynn in 1415 as security for a loan; in 1417–18 the townsmen pleaded to the Exchequer for repayment, and in 1420 the formidable jewels were even brought to London as evidence, but with no result. Expense, time and political connection were deployed in the handling of the royal surety, and only in 1429 did the townsmen see some satisfaction with the repayment of 40 per cent of the loan. Nor did church property escape the royal gaze and grasp: the Leicester Parliament of 1414 produced a statute on foreign priories, which confiscated almost all properties belonging to foreign religious houses and added their ecclesiastical livings to the circle of royal patronage.

In assessing the effect of war finances on simple folk who did not hold commissions and who did not stand to benefit from the provisioning of armies, one might think of the levies exacted from cities in this period. Henry V imposed a levy each year, and on occasion two. In 1415 and 1417 Norwich lent £1,000, as did York. And about a third of this sum was raised by a common levy on the city, which was collected from all townspeople. The relationship between king and towns was complex and many-sided. Under Henry IV during years of such financing, Norwich was able to petition for and acquire recognition as a legal corporation, in 1404. Londoners were fascinated by the presence and demands of the Lancastrian kings. Several companies recorded in their muniments the great events of the court: the Brewers' Book includes a minute description of Henry IV's death and burial, and the *Chronicles of London* devoted a great deal of descriptive power to ceremonies of state.

The rather insular court of Henry IV used London as its back-yard: one Midsummer Eve sometime after midnight, the king's sons Thomas and John were walking its streets, and were entangled in a street affray. The city, now home to a growing number of ruling parliamentary and courtly households, offered frameworks for inclusion and networking. Henry IV recuperated from illness in the summer of 1409 at the house of the Knights Hospitaller in Clerkenwell, and was offered hospitality by the Priory of St Bartholomew. Members of his household came to know the neighbouring parish, St Botolph's, well. Some courtiers and their wives became members of the fraternity of Holy Trinity and Saints Fabian and Sebastian in that parish – Lord Willoughby and his wife Johanna, Lord William de Roos and his wife Mary and two esquires,

Sir William Farringdon, Constable of Bordeaux, and other royal officials and a number of heads of religious houses. There they rubbed shoulders with London merchants, lawyers and prosperous artisans, men committed to their city, who might for purposes of health, diversion or investment buy up land in the country, but who, on the whole, still chose to be buried and remembered in their London parish church. A typical foundation for commemoration was the chantry created by John Weston, a London merchant, in 1407. It provided that after the death of his wife Joanna his property should pass to the church of St Mary at Hill, its rectors and churchwardens, who were to pay £4 a year to a priest whose task was the singing of mass at St John the Baptist's altar in memory of John, his wife and their predecessors. The civic leader Dick Whittington, four times mayor of London, was buried in 1423 in St Michael Paternoster beside his wife Alice and near the almshouse for thirteen poor which he founded, a chantry in which prayers for his soul were offered.

HENRY V

The 'crooked ways' by which Henry IV had come to the crown did not mar his son's succession. Like his father, Henry V was vigorous in youth and possessed a strong sense of right and purpose. The shaky dozen years of Henry IV were an extraordinary achievement in confronting and dismantling plans and campaigns mounted against his usurping self and his family. There could have been little doubt that Henry V, already renowned for military achievement, and bonded with the military cadre of England and Wales, was to be king. But Henry IV's legacy was brittle, and Henry V displayed some irritability in his first years. He allowed his father's widow (his own stepmother), Joan of Navarre, who commissioned Henry IV's magnificent alabaster tomb at Canterbury Cathedral (Plate 14), to be accused of witchcraft, and to be confined in castles between 1419 and 1422, her dowry confiscated. The 1414 uprising by a group of disgruntled knights around the old retainer John Oldcastle, with a rhetoric of reform associated with heresy, was not a welcome start to his reign; but he dealt with it cleverly. Oldcastle's companions were pardoned in a staged act of pacification. Henry V proceeded with his business abroad only after the principle was established – as put by Hoccleve in his *Remonstrance against*

Oldcastle – to 'let holy church meddle with doctrine/of Christ's laws and of his belief'. The Leicester Parliament of 1414 repeated the commitment to cooperation between church and state over issues of heresy, and as Thomas Arundel handed over the chancellorship of the realm to the king's uncle, Henry Beaufort, a continuation of surveillance was assured.

In planning his policies and taking counsel, Henry V kept the group around him small, some ten earls, of whom Arundel and Mortimer were the greatest. In 1413 his household included 10 knights, 23 esquires of the chamber, 35 other household esquires, 31 yeomen of the chamber and 27 clerks, all under the supervision of Sir Thomas Erpingham. Shakespeare imagined in lively manner the intimacy between the king and those who had known him, commanders at his side, or who were led by him in the battles of the first decade of Lancastrian rule. In Pistol's words in *Henry V*:

> The King's a bawcock, and a heart of gold,
> A lad of life, an imp of fame;
> Of parents good, of fist most valiant.
> I kiss his dirty shoe, and from heartstring,
> I love the lovely bully.
>
> (*Henry V*, IV. i. 45–9)

Henry V came to the business of rulership well prepared. He had effectively ruled in 1410–11 during his father's illness, though he had to keep his counsel in 1412 when he was marginalized during the rapprochement of Henry IV with his son Clarence over their anti-Burgundian policy. The campaign to France in 1412–13 had quite negative results. It was a campaign of brutal destruction, especially in the Cotentin region of Normandy, and much was said by shapers of French opinion about the loss and spoliation of churches along Clarence's route. All this seemed to have strengthened French resolve against Clarence and the Armagnac faction, and ultimately produced the sort of sympathies which were to coalesce into the great French army which took to the field at Agincourt in 1415.

Henry was particularly aware of his responsibilities as Prince of Wales, and knew from personal experience how badly Wales had been scarred by the warfare of the previous decade. After his coronation he sent a commission, headed by the Earl of Arundel, to North Wales, to seek out corruption among royal officials; he had already taken steps to restock and replenish estates in Carmarthenshire and Merioneth. Wales was not just his inheritance, it was a crucial source of trained fighting men and support for his emergent cause. At Tretower Court (Powys) – a still impressive fortified manor house – the archers, so decisive to the victory at Agincourt, were mustered. His links to Wales and the nurture of his closest officials were enhanced, as Henry turned to moulding a new national enterprise.

Even among his group of privileged kin and brothers in arms, so close to the king's person, the bitter fruit of resentment could easily grow. Henry V was secure, no longer fearing the challenge of the faction attached to his brother Thomas Duke of Clarence, whom Henry IV had preferred. But other discontents bred worrying disloyalty. Edmund Earl of March felt a grievous harm had been done to him in the imposition of 10,000 marks for the right to marry Anne, sister of Humphrey Earl of Stafford. Richard Earl of Cambridge, who had served Henry IV on several occasions, both against Glyn Dŵr and on European embassies, was disaffected. He had been granted no tangible reward from royal father or son, and lived with his family as a guest in his brother's Coningsby Castle. It was from such sentiments that the Southampton Plot – uncovered on the eve of the king's embarkation for France in summer 1415 – was made, planned by Richard Earl of Cambridge, the Duke of Northumberland and the Earl of March. It was ill-judged, the result of frustration with the young king's coolness, a sentiment which might have been borne more lightly had dynastic fantasies – which blossomed for a while in the years 1405–9 – not clouded their judgement.

To follow his French ambitions Henry needed behind him a realm in which justice and order appeared to be secured. The contours of justice and peace were complex and were the product of an interaction between the royal court, the lawyers, and the responsible conduct of local juries, justices and the powerful men who were able to influence their operation. Henry inspired an activist justice system, which resulted in many trials but very few convictions. Although many people were killed in armed confrontations, few people were found guilty of murder, and executed for it. In a roll of cases heard by the justice John Cokayn, which covered Derbyshire, Leicestershire, Lincolnshire, Northamptonshire, Nottinghamshire, Rutland and Warwickshire, few were found guilty of murder, although murder accusations outnumbered those of homicide. Self-defence was the only acceptable ground for killing another with impunity, and the fear of being killed by an attacker was enough to justify a killing. The care with which cases were reconstructed is impressive, and when no claim for self-defence could be made, the accused could be found a murderer even without evidence of malicious foresight or planning. Justices were assisted by the professional opinion of coroners, local officials who came to the scene early on and heard fresh evidence close to the place and time of the crime.

The prince needed a wife, and marriage to a French princess had repeatedly been considered a useful move towards pacification of the two kingdoms. In 1411 Thomas Hoccleve believed that 'by matrimony peace and unity be had'. The Duke of Bedford was in charge of the diplomatic endeavour, and dispatched an embassy in 1414. A note from the French court on the possible marriage of young Henry and Katherine of Valois, daughter of Charles VI, reveals the resistance which was felt by those who sought not settlement, but confrontation, and to whom Henry son of Henry was merely the heir to a usurper. Would the King of France allow his daughter to marry the son of a traitor? Such considerations were, however, put aside by the extraordinary events of 1415, in the aftermath of which marriage was settled and added closure as well as glamour to Henry's return to England as a victor, in November of that year.

The Oldcastle flurry behind him, it soon became clear that France was to be the reign's defining issue. France, which his father had never been able to confront, the home in exile of Henry IV as Earl of Derby, was to make the name and the fortune of his son. Henry V completed a number of his father's projects. Where Henry IV had promised to found religious houses, Henry V delivered – in the foundation of the magnificent Brigittine house at Syon. Here diplomacy and religion converged. Henry Lord FitzHugh had returned from a mission to Denmark in 1406 regarding Philippa's dowry, inspired by this new religious order, founded by Birgitta of Sweden and supported by the Danish royal family. Henry V was thus familiar with its ethos and came to be considered the founder of the Brigittines in England; he was also interested in the austere and scholarly Carthusian order, and supported their house at Sheen.

Henry V offered the magnates new purpose and rewards. Where Henry IV had left the death of Richard II an oozing wound in the body politic, Henry V had him properly buried. Where Henry IV nurtured the bond between church and monarchy, Henry V mobilized piety in the service of war and conquest. Where Henry IV had attempted to tie men to loyalty and evade political confrontation, Henry V created a caste of warriors at a permanent state of service to the Lancastrian state. In doing so he was supported by his brother John Duke of Bedford, whom he later appointed as regent in France. This talented administrator applied himself to the tasks of war, but also appreciated the well-being generated by abundance and good rule. He commissioned a book of physiognomy which unravelled the secrets of character and health. His religious books were many and impressive: an image in his Book of Hours of *c*.1417 depicts the joining of hands of King David and his wife Michal, daughter of King Saul, by a priest. In this rare biblical scene one perhaps glimpses an allusion to the recent marriage of Henry to another princess, Katherine of Valois. This pretty book was to become a favourite of John of Bedford's nephew, the young Henry VI.

The king's making was a long apprenticeship, from his youth in the battles against Glyn Dŵr in Wales and his study with the royal clerk and court poet Thomas Hoccleve. He appreciated good music, prayer and poetry, above all for their pragmatic ability to signify and make power felt. Under him, in the 1420s the Chapel Royal comprised a dean, thirty-two chaplains and clerks, and sixteen boys; he may even have composed a setting for a Gloria, attributed to 'Roy Henry'. Henry had been raised in an English court, with few occasions to travel abroad and meet other types of ruler and rule. In his years of training he formed friendships of great durability and duration. Even as Prince of Wales he had some of his closest friends made Knights of the Garter: William Harrington, John Blunt, John Grey, Louis Robbessart. The brothers Robbessart, knights of Hainault, were granted letters of denizenship, and remained close to the king's person. Henry V rewarded families who served the crown, fathers and sons, such as William Lord Willoughby and Hugh Lord Stafford, who became Companion Knights of the Garter in 1416 and 1418. Several gestures exemplify the importance of friendship and the exaltation of camaraderie in arms. In 1415, before the siege of Harfleur, Henry V wept as he closed the eyes of his friend Stephen Courtenay, Bishop of Norwich.

Against the background of civil war in France Henry V identified a favourable time for action. Charles VI, King of France, was deemed so unfit to rule that Louis of Orléans was appointed regent in his place. The Burgundian Duke, John the Fearless, probably had Louis murdered in 1411, and created an opportunity seized by Henry IV for an expedition in support of his claim. In 1414 parliament agreed expenses for an expedition, and poets celebrated the confrontation to come. By October 1415 the system of retaining was producing a formidable army. Men gathered around the captains according to links of affinity, blood and region. Sir Robert Plumpton, of Plumpton Hall (Yorkshire), for example, was retained for life by the king at 20 marks per annum and wages of an esquire and two valets. On the second tour, of 1418, Sir Robert and his neighbour Sir Halnath Maleverer joined Lord FitzHugh in Southampton: 20 marks were paid to Plumpton, who was to command eight archers at 40s. each per annum. He died outside the walls of Meaux in 1421.

AGINCOURT

Few battles have been described so often, in so many media, and to such effect. From the sunny vista created by Laurence Olivier, to the dark tones of Kenneth Branagh, Agincourt has been hailed as an epoch-making battle, in which Englishness was forged, tested and vindicated. It is seen as the triumph of the longbow technology, as the triumph of the few against the many, David against Goliath, of a rugged and well-led English and Welsh force against a luxurious, ineffectual French one. The explanatory power of meteorology, archaeology, geology and mineralogy, as well as the enthusiasm of men eager to relive battles – a strangely vibrant hobby – have been applied to understanding how it really was.

Henry V crossed the channel on 11 August from Portsmouth, where forces had been assembling since the spring, some 10,000 strong. The army was likened to the Israelites, sure of the rightness of their cause, a guided cohort. It was a tight-knit army, made of regional groupings led by local gentry in companies of fifty. The captains were Lancastrian loyalists, and the overall commander was a highly experienced king and his able brothers. Henry's army landed and pitched camp west of Harfleur in Normandy, and began a siege a few days later. This lasted five weeks, a siege decided by the terrible dysentery which decimated Henry's armies as well as the besieged. The town opened its gates on 22 September, after 2,000 of Henry's men had died, and another 2,000 or so were sent home, unfit for battle.

Henry V rejected advice and decided to continue his march north-wards towards Calais, the English stronghold in northern France, in search of a decisive battle. Marching towards the Somme at a rapid pace, he hoped to cross at Blanchetaque, where he found a garrison blocking the way. He drew his army further inland, unable to turn back, since a force led by Marshal Boucicaut was on his heels, slipping in the mud and engaging in skirmishes the rear sections of his army. The crossing led to Agincourt, where a large French army was massed. Henry had his men – many ill and hungry – settle and prepare over the night of 23/24 October, subsisting on berries, expecting the worst, pressed to fight an army almost three times larger. Above all one must remember that it rained very hard and long in the north-west corner of France in October 1415.

The now famous formation which Henry V adopted was an imaginat-ive plan, which made use of the woods on either side of the plain of battle (Plate 17). He set up a group of 900 men-at-arms at the centre, supported by archers – 2,500 on each side – who defended their positions with sharp stakes. The French had hoped to attack the archers head-on, but found themselves flailing in the mud, and with little space for flanking manoeuvres because of the surrounding vegetation. Examin-ation of the remains on the battlefield show that the French soldiers were well-armed, and most died not of wounds inflicted by the torrent of arrows, but of suffocation, as they slid into the mud and were crushed to death. The arrows were probably far more effective in terrorizing and irritating the French soldiers' horses. As the French attack was thus halted, it was time for carnage. With anything that came to hand the French were cut down. Fearing another French onslaught Henry commanded that the French prisoners be killed, an act which Shake-speare inventively attempted to justify. The discrepancy in the relative loss of life is huge: some 500 among the English and 7,000 among the French, including hundreds of gentlemen or 'sires'. There were great prizes among the captives, including Charles Duke of Orléans, who spent the next twenty-five years in England, joining his brother, Jean d'Angoulême, who had been handed over as a hostage at the age of twelve in 1412.

The poetry and prose which poured forth after Agincourt was exult-ant; it picked up the rumours and experiences remembered by veterans of the battle. Thomas Elmham recounted the hunger of Henry's army, but also Henry's genius in motivating his men: he wore his crown in battle. Some men claimed they had seen St George fighting on their side. The ballad *The Battle of Agincourt*, written soon after the event, paid special attention to Henry's physical courage and to the dead and wounded, both English and French:

> Our lord the king he fought right well
> Sharply on him his spear he spent . . .
> The Duke of Gloucester also that time
> Manfully, with his company,
> Wounds he wrought there wondrously wide.
> . . . Huntington and Oxford both
> Were wondrously fierce all in that fight . . .
> Of French folk in that affray
> Three Dukes were dead, with doleful dent,
> And five Earls, this cannot be denied.

A triumphal entry to London for the victors was planned by the king's half-brother, the Chancellor Henry Beaufort, as an entry into a city basking in the king's justice. The procession on 23 November 1415 marched from Tower Bridge to St Paul's with several themes and scenes on the way, which referred to female lineage. Maidens, pure and virginal, welcomed the king at Eleanor's Cross in Cheapside, with poetry attributed to John Lydgate, which invokes that fertile moment of the Nativity:

> Virgins glided out of the castle,
> For joy of him they were dancing . . .
> They knelt down all at that time
> 'Nowell', 'Nowell' they all sang.

Henry was greatly aware of his place in history and the support which religious imagery could offer.

Religion and politics were deftly intertwined by Henry V. When his uncle Henry Beaufort, Bishop of Winchester and Chancellor of England, addressed parliament in 1416 after the victory at Agincourt, he conjured the miraculous nature of the victory. In a letter which he may have written to his nephew, he likened his successes to that of the Maccabees, Saul, David, Solomon and Alexander the Great. Divine intervention was invoked by the royal biographer, who had been present at the battle, and who wrote only a few months later:

Just as a dispute between those having a superior on earth is resolved in earthly judgement, so one between those having no superior under heaven is made plain by a heavenly arbitrament carried out by the sword.

Henry V mobilized clerics in support of his claims; they wove his ambitions into the fabric of divine plans. His chaplain, Thomas Elmham (d. *c*.1420), who wrote a verse account of Henry's campaign, opined that the French were so obdurate that no amount of negotiation could soften them.

Henry's charisma inspired reflection on the craft of state, an interest which was to develop in the less stable times of his son, both in England and in France. John Lydgate, monk of Bury St Edmunds – the closest thing to a Lancastrian poet-laureate – brought ancient history to bear on Henry's achievements in France, in his *Siege of Thebes*. A sermon of the period developed the metaphor of a Ship of State: the forecastle was the clergy; the body of the ship, the commonalty; and the hindcastle, the baronage and king. The craft was weakened by the decline of virtue, hence the necessity for a saviour king – celestial warrior, the column which supports the edifice, the temple of the kingdom. Never, proclaimed the preacher, had so few 'passed so tearful a battle with palms of victory' as did that 'hardy group of Agincourt'. Henry's success was part of a divine plan, secured by his virtue.

Henry V's biography, *Gesta Henrici Quinti* (*The Deeds of Henry V*), probably by Thomas Elmham, was well informed about Henry's first years, which he witnessed, and sought further detail from contemporary records. The resulting picture is of immense energy in pursuing several interlocking strategies at once: pursuit of war in France, building of alliances with Emperor Sigismund, persecution of heresy, encouraging the punishment of criminals, raising of finance through negotiation with parliament. But there were tensions around several of these projects: by 1416 parliament was anxious about future demands for finance. Further afield, the astrologer Jean de Rubeis offered several charts to John the Fearless Duke of Burgundy in which Henry's death within three years was predicted.

The success of the two expeditions to France, 1415 and 1417, was turned into policy by the Treaty of Troyes of 1420. The treaty marked a new political, military and domestic order, and was facilitated by a crisis in France, following the murder of John Duke of Burgundy in 1419. The new order was inaugurated by a royal marriage and recognition of a vast occupied domain in Normandy. Lancastrian Normandy was for the next two decades to be dotted with garrisons, organized for war, and in some places for settlement too. Some 200,000 men were to see service in this territory, a large proportion of the able-bodied free men of England, Scotland, Wales, Brittany and Gascony. Administering Lancastrian Normandy was to be the task of princes of the royal blood with the assistance of the greatest magnates. Indeed, Thomas Duke of Clarence, the king's brother, died in battle at Baugé in 1421 (Plate 15).

Sea-power was always an important component of English military capability, but under Henry V the number of vessels and the frequency of use were at their highest. The navy was part oared barges and part sailing ships. The victories of 1416 and 1417 were victories at sea, with battle-ships, sailed not oared; by 1417 Henry V owned over thirty ships. Together with regular patrols, and the bases at Harfleur and Honfleur, Henry V had established an unparalleled supremacy in the Channel, which many in England and Gascony appreciated. The demand for ships created a great deal of work for shipwrights, carpenters and masons in the ports of England: tens of men worked over two years on the *Grace Dieu*, Henry V's fourth great royal ship, which cost just over £289, and was launched with a blessing by the Bishop of Bangor in July 1418. Its construction required 2,735 oaks, 14 ash trees, 1,145 beeches and 12 elms, from the royal New Forest and from neighbouring monastic forests. It saw service as a patrolship in the Channel under the Earl of Devon. The military policy brought demand and jobs and, as even the making of this one ship shows, depended on joined-up thinking and action by departments of state and cooperation between royal administration and private enterprise.

The Treaty of Troyes raised several anxieties in parliament: a creeping subordination of the English part to the French part of the emergent dual polity was feared. There were calls for the restatement of Edward III's statute of 1340, by which England could never be subject to France. In the same vein, parliament insisted that the dual monarchy be managed as two financial centres: that the French territories bear the cost of their defence and administration. A system of garrisoning continued the traditions developed in Aquitaine: of career soldiers on long periods of years of service. In the course of such service they created a whole variety of relations – through property-owning, learning the language, marriage to local women, local administration – which was to mark them as a distinctive generation, a cohort of men.

The evidence about the nature of revenge and spoliation on the campaigns is mixed, and hard to assess. Henry V allowed the attack on the monks of Holy Trinity in Rouen in July 1418, but by the following January their properties were restored to them. War and sieges were expensive and messy, and Henry V tried to persuade towns to surrender to him where possible. Building on his reputation in battle, after his first victories he attempted to cajole defenders into yielding, by promising mercy if they did and the threat of cruel displeasure if they did not: where a city gave in, this led other smaller towns to follow. Henry V attempted to pacify by intruding as little as possible upon local patterns of life. Castles, walls and towers once inhabited by French garrisons were now to house the garrisons of the King of England. Sometimes other spaces were requisitioned, the outbuildings of the Abbey of St Ouen, for example. But billeting was used only sporadically, and wages were meant to provide for soldiers' needs. Yet a population of unattached men, away from family and community, able and armed, occupied with guard duty and little else in the way of regular training and work, was bound to be a disruptive, violent and threatening presence. One unlucky soldier confessed that, on an errand to buy food, he was tempted by a chicken running in the yard of a neighbouring farmer, and tried to shoot it dead. Tragically, his arrow hit the farmer's wife in the neck and thus he became a killer.

The king promoted an image of impeccable and enthusiastic orthodoxy: a translation into French of the *Meditations on the Life of Christ* was made for him by the Norman cleric Jean Galopes, who claimed to have 're-written' it 'with tears'. No text was more orthodox; this was the work recommended in Archbishop Arundel's Constitutions of 1409 as the sole theological work which could be rendered into the vernacular without misleading its readers. Such reading may have inspired Henry to commission the monk John Lydgate to compose a *Life of Our Lady*, which was completed around 1421, not long after Henry was recognized as the future King of France in the Treaty of Troyes. The Christian sense of mission infused the views of his servants. News from the ecumenical church council at Constance of 1415 included the rumours of prophecies that a Christian victory over the Turks was imminent. Although in many ways a very English king, Henry V toyed with a grander, almost imperial vision. Some of this ambition was expressed in the hope that Henry Beaufort, his uncle, might become pope. His contemporary biographers modelled his triumphal entries on imperial ritual, and devoted much space to descriptions of Emperor Sigismund's visit in 1416.

But as any Lancastrian knew only too well, enemies could come from within as well as from without. While Henry was away from the British Isles – for three years, between 1418 and 1421 – no amount of display, poetry and chant could mask the discontent with the political priorities his rule had so powerfully imposed. In 1421 Robert Waterton Lord of Methley in the West Riding, steward of the northern lands of the Duchy of Lancaster, wrote a response to Henry V's request to recruit men to military service for wages. The roll records the excuses given by those approached – old age, sickness – and on occasion his own doubts about their veracity. Several men even denied being 'gentlemen' so as to avoid the recruiter's approach; some argued that they had already seen service, or that a close family member was fighting in France or Scotland at that time. After questioning almost 100 men, Waterton succeeded in recruiting five. The king's council had to assess this emergent reality, evident in other parts of the country too, like Norfolk, and judged that England had reached its full capacity to raise men and generate interest in the war in France.

Vigilant, and aware that the most dangerous moment in a monarch's life is the moment of succession, Henry wrote into his will detailed instructions that French prisoners be kept in custody until his own son had grown and inherited the dual monarchy. He understood that his achievements would have to be defended by war and conquest, against those who were not charmed by his vision of a dual Lancastrian empire, and who remained loyal to French lineal succession and to a dauphin as the future Charles VII.

5

'For the world was that time so strange', 1422–1461

THE MINORITY OF HENRY VI

It is hard to think of decades more turbulent, times in which anxiety and suffering affected so many sections of society, than the later decades of Henry VI's reign. The causes were not so much the accession of an infant king in 1422, nor the impossibility of living up to the charisma of Henry V, who died so young of dysentery in the Bois de Vincennes in August 1422, leaving little bitterness or disappointment behind him. Rather, the erosion of links of trust and responsibility between crown and subjects, combined with devastating economic hardship, meant that by 1450 individuals and communities, in towns and in villages, were rendered restless, weakening the civic responsibility felt by political and military leaders.

There were times of some comfort and confidence following the death of Henry V: trade benefited in the aftermath of conquest and settlement in France, routines of garrison life were established, and there was relative peace. The birth of Henry V's son had been an occasion for joy in dynastic continuity of a family recent in its ascent. Celebration reached throughout Henry V's domain, even in the lands he had secured by conquest: in January 1422 fireworks displays and wine were offered by the captain of the garrison of Mantes for the pleasure of soldiers and townsfolk.

The royal uncles, John Duke of Bedford and Humphrey Duke of Gloucester, and great-uncle Henry Beaufort, Bishop of Winchester, ruled the country, formally and informally, for their young nephew. As Regent of France, Bedford governed the territories in France (Normandy, Gascony and the Channel Islands), maintained a substantial household and commanded the military establishment (Plate 18). A bodyguard of 100 men-at-arms and 300 archers accompanied him on his movements between Paris, where he maintained a palace (on the site of today's Musée de Cluny), and Rouen in Normandy. He became one of the greatest European patrons of art, music, poetry and works of gold and silver. In England, the Duke of Gloucester was Protector, and under his supervision a minority council handled domestic affairs with care for political equipoise. Or at least this had been Henry V's desire, when he composed his will and its codicils: a succession without strife. The king was a baby, but he had an impeccable pedigree. His could be a reign even greater than his father's short-lived one.

At Henry VI's English coronation of 1429 at Winchester, when he was aged eight, the Garter Fellowship held a cloth of state over the head of the young king, during an acclamation which invoked the spectacles of Edwardian monarchy. After the coronation of Charles VII in Reims in 1429, famously orchestrated by Joan of Arc, Henry was forced to claim his French throne, too. He entered Paris on 2 December 1431, and was crowned there a fortnight later, in fulfilment of the terms of the Treaty of Troyes of 1420. After a lavish entry ceremony which saw members of the Parisian guilds and clergy hail him as a sacred being, on 16 December the young king processed from the Royal Palace to Notre Dame Cathedral on foot, and in its choir he was crowned.

This was a very English ceremony, officiated by an English archbishop, accompanied by English musicians, all adorned with the *fleur-de-lis*. The king's right to the French throne was displayed at the command of his uncle, Bedford; the ten-year-old's genealogical table was made public, charting his right to the dual monarchy. Images were accompanied by French verses penned by the Duke's notary, Laurence Colet. Richard Neville Earl of Warwick requested that the poet John Lydgate translate these verses under the heading, 'The title and pedigree of Henry VI'. In these Henry VI is shown to be the descendant of the sainted Louis IX, King of France:

> On the other part behold and you may see
> How this Harry in the eighth degree
> Is to Saint Louis son and very heir.

The genealogy was copied and recopied throughout Henry VI's reign and has survived in a variety of sizes, shapes and formats.

The young king was surrounded by powerful kinsfolk whose experience stabilized rule, but whose ambitions could cause the deepest division. During his minority many of the sympathies of his father's generation were maintained. He used the grant of membership of the Order of the Garter to reward men for service in France: John Lord Talbot (1424), Thomas Lord Scales (1425), Sir John Fastolf (1426), Sir John Radcliffe (1429), John Fitzallan Earl of Arundel (1432) and John Lord Grey of Ruthin (1436). This was a roll-call of service to the Lancastrians in battle. Under his uncles' tutelage, Henry VI was expected to emerge with all the virtues of a ruler. Kingship's good qualities were encapsulated in the words of the poet Thomas Hoccleve, which echo those of Walter Milmete before him: a good king took counsel, listened to young and old, the great and the humble, but reserved his judgement, to be reached in the light of universal consideration and attention to the common weal.

John Lydgate warned against division within the political elite in his *The Serpent of Division* of 1422–3, a prose treatise based on the Roman history of Julius Caesar and the Civil War. This was offered to his patron, Humphrey Duke of Gloucester, Protector of the Realm, 'to consider the irrecuperable harms of division'. The Roman elite 'among themselves stood in such controversy that they doubted to which party they should incline'. So the republic suffered, and was ultimately dissolved. The disputes over jurisdiction and influence which erupted in 1425 between the royal uncles Gloucester and Beaufort were contemporary examples of such disruptions.

The kingdom possessed several strong institutions and components of a stable political culture. In 1422 a little short of half the representatives at parliament had fought with Henry V in France, and their loyalty had a personal resonance. Well into the 1430s Henry V hovered over his son in spirit, as his brothers and trusted appointees still worked at the implementation of his will. Henry, Cardinal Beaufort, was charged with the erection of a commemorative chapel, a chantry in Westminster Abbey where the dead king's helmet, shield and saddle were to hang. All Souls College in Oxford was founded by Henry Chichele, Archbishop of Canterbury, a monument to dead warriors and kingly piety. It offered unceasing prayer for the king and the archbishop, for Henry V and all those who had been lost in the wars in France. Built under the warrior king's less heroic son, the college still boasts the limestone statues of the mitred Chichele and Henry VI in his royal robes.

Inherited charisma favoured the young king, but so did the kingdom's institutions. Parliament was one such robust arena. Even after the experiences of deposition and dynastic change under Henry IV, it depended very intimately on royal presence to put its increasingly complex procedures into motion. Thus little Henry was bounced on his mother's knee at the parliament of 1423, summoned in his name. Here was an infant king with a minority council that ruled for him, in his presence. There were serious issues to decide: the diplomatic and military effort in France, the legacy of enormous outstanding loans – from the Calais Staple, from towns, from Italian bankers – amassed by his adventurous father, and some even by his grandfather. The infant had yet to grow into the full realization of his inheritance. Henry V had insisted in his will that none of the prestigious French captives – Charles d'Orléans, Jean d'Angoulême – be released before Henry came of age and into his dual inheritance. Even after the end of the council's tutelage in 1436–7 its members continued to serve the king as a close group of advisers. In many ways he never came into his own, except in his building projects. This made the expression of political criticism easy: 'the king's reason was indistinguishable from that of his counsellors' was a trope used in the political crises of the 1440s and 1450s.

During the reign of Henry VI's father and grandfather religious conformity had been established as a central political objective. Procedures were in operation for extirpating behaviour that was too publicly disruptive, even though the privacy of hearth and heart allowed people to maintain a wide range of ideas and aspirations in religious life. There seemed to be no chink in the armour of the dynasty and the polity: the talent which had been drawn into government in the extensive fields of church and state activities was confidently working through problems of law and order, economic regulation and religious probity.

Men such as Henry Chichele, Archbishop of Canterbury, part of Henry V's competent government, were to serve his son – as chancellor, in diplomacy, and by promoting the projects closest to the king's heart with utter loyalty. Chichele was a noted advocate of religious orthodoxy; he devised a uniform list for interrogation of suspected heretics, which was disseminated in 1428 for use in every diocese of the land. It was said that he travelled the long roads, often on horseback, to any place where religious orthodoxy required decisive defence. Chancellors of the realm were often such archbishops of high calibre, men of broad political vision, who by Henry VI's reign were usually lawyers in training rather than theologians. The Chancery saw continuity of personnel and processed a great deal of business. It comprised a close-knit professional group, admitting few new ideas and skills from universities. In 1448 Richard Weston joined as the sole trained lawyer, and remained such until his death in 1465. Clearly the qualities favoured in Chancery were loyalty, hard work and administrative acumen. The king may have been young but governance was not lax – for a generation or so.

The 1430s were Henry VI's apprenticeship, during which time he enjoyed the relative indulgence accorded to youth. In November 1429 the protectorate of Humphrey Duke of Gloucester ended, though Gloucester recovered his power in 1432, while John Duke of Bedford led the government in 1433–4. During the king's boyhood some dramatic choices faced the men who governed the interests in France. The most dramatic was the challenge presented by the rallying of French will under the extraordinary inspiration of a young woman: Joan of Arc (1412–29). Above all, Joan encouraged the legitimist claims of the French prince – the dauphin – whose right had been sacrificed in the search for peace after Agincourt. She encouraged him to be crowned at Reims, and to lead under her tutelage an aggressive French campaign against the English. Joan's life is the stuff of which legends are made, although it left little mark in contemporary English sources, until her spectacular death. After a series of dismal defeats (Cravant in 1423 and Verneuil in 1424), the French forces, led by the 'maid', were galvanized into success. They defeated the English by raising the siege at Orléans in 1428, and drove them out of the Loire valley in the following summer. The Armagnac branch, which supported the Bourbon crown, called her *'pucelle de dieu'* (God's maiden), but the English and their allies called her a witch.

The capture of the maiden Joan by the English and Burgundians and her trial as a wanton witch had little sustained effect on the politics of the English war. But it forced the French military and political class out of a sense of inevitable defeat, and came at a time when new military technology, above all gunpowder artillery, could change the rhythm of war based on the capture and holding of walled towns. The fate of Joan of Arc also demonstrates forcefully the perilous position inhabited by women who exhibited their religion in public ways and entered into public spaces, without the support of male kin. Dressed as a soldier, Joan was to her enemies like so many of the later witches: vulnerable to the powerful double accusation of sexual incontinence and religious heresy.

In 1435 the king made his own personality felt, as he assumed his full title. By 1436 decisions in council were headed 'The King with the advice of council'. There was much for him to learn, to discuss and decide in both domestic and French affairs. England was losing ground in France and clear factions had developed around his uncles, each representing a different approach. Following the dismal policy negotiations at Arras in 1436, which severed the Anglo-Burgundian alliance, Henry VI began his personal rule. The diplomatic premise upon which English conduct had relied for over a decade, as far back as the Treaty of Troyes, was a separation between Burgundy and France, supported by an agreement between England, Burgundy and Brittany of 1423. This political order was now over.

In a report to Henry VI and the council offered by Bedford's lieutenant John Fastolf in 1435, a hawkish and pessimistic picture of the future was put forth. With the collapse of the terms of Troyes, England could expect Franco–Burgundian cooperation against which it would have to fight in all arenas. Economic warfare was foreseen as a shift from the purchase of English wool by Flemish towns to an economic alliance with Genoa and Venice. In reality, little of this came to pass, since the Duke of Burgundy was soon absorbed in confronting large-scale unrest in his own territories and cities. None the less, from 1436 the Burgundian court and other European princes addressed the Lancastrian king as 'Roy d'Angleterre', without mention of France. The reversal of the policy which had linked England and Burgundy seemed complete.

The consequences for military policy at home were clear. In the spring of 1436 widespread mobilization of men and arms was under way under the commissions of array in England and Wales. Above all, Calais had to be protected, for it was the main outpost of English military might and a key to commercial well-being. The task fell to Humphrey Duke of Gloucester as Captain of Calais. His task turned out to be an easy one, since the siege had been abandoned by the French before he arrived to relieve the city. Yet the rush of enthusiasm and pride in the outcome, which so many English chronicles, poems and reports expressed, made this into a propaganda coup for Henry VI and his court.

The court entertained differing visions for the future. In the face of the doom and gloom of autumn 1435, there was the good news of excellent stewardship in France, and the raising of the siege of Calais of 1436. A Latin tract written in the late 1430s for Henry VI's edification recommended that he seek peace, though not at the price of honour.

He was to act as befitted his crown, with the support of the elements of the polity represented by its jewels: *jasper* – the loyal lords and magnates; *carbuncle* – the bishops and prelates who toiled against heresy; *sapphire* – the parish priests and monks who served the people; *onyx* – the commons of the kingdom, communities of concord and harmony. The learned author playfully uses imagery from popular prophecies, which formed a vital part of the political culture. The poet John Audelay, an Augustinian from the Shropshire house of Haughmond, predicted around 1426 that Henry would be the man to free the Holy Cross, by ridding England and France of war and redirecting their efforts towards crusades. Such texts were written by learned men but circulated widely among politically minded lay people. In reality, the king was not a political leader, but a young man liberal with favours: he often turned lifetime gifts to perpetual grants, a habit for which the council rebuked him in 1438. The late 1430s were probably his best years; he participated in a wide range of royal activities, helping to create an image of a boy maturing into a king.

WOMEN OF THE COURT: MARGARET OF ANJOU AND ELEANOR COBHAM

It is a truth widely acknowledged that a mature king also needs a queen. Like all royal marriages this was an opportunity to make an important political and diplomatic deal, with benefits to both sides. The choice of royal partner could promote or retard the cause of peace, and thus was bound to divide the royal counsellors. Here widespread expectation and speculation centred on the hope that the king would emerge as supreme governor and regain power from the Earl of Suffolk, who effectively controlled the court in the early 1440s. Royal marriages were diplomatic challenges. Philippe de Mezières, a well-connected French soldier and diplomat, saw them as obstacles to peace and even the cause of dynastic wars and confusion. Yet the council deemed it right, and an embassy was sent by it to examine possible brides. Margaret of Anjou was a princess, daughter of the gallant and pious René II of Anjou. Her father was to become King of Naples, but she brought no land or dynastic claim. She was an unexpected choice as partner for the King of England, who required dynastic assurance of a different calibre. Fourteen at her betrothal by proxy in May 1444, fifteen at her marriage in the following year, Margaret received as her dower much land of the Duchy of Lancaster. A retinue was led by a loyal Lancastrian servant, Sir Thomas Harrington of Brierley, with four gentlemen and twelve yeomen, to bring her to England, inaugurating ceremonies which cost over £5,500 and culminated in the marriage in April 1445. Pageants were staged in London for Margaret's entry: from Southwark, through Cornhill, Cheapside and on to St Michael's in Querne, St Paul's Gate. This was a hopeful, innovative, lively combination of image, biblical verse and poetry.

A sumptuous book, a lavishly decorated compilation of poetry and treatises, was offered to Margaret and Henry by John Talbot Earl of Shrewsbury, as a wedding-gift (Plate 20). Like the royal couple it was the product of an Anglo-French match: a workshop in Canterbury provided the texts, and one in Rouen copied the texts and appropriately illustrated them. The frontispiece depicts a garbed and crowned couple sitting in state and graciously receiving the gift from their loyal courtier. Indeed, Talbot and his wife had accompanied the young bride from France to England that spring, and they probably came to know her well. The book is a combination of useful and edifying texts, entertaining romances and heroic narratives, and it ends with the statutes of the Order of the Garter. A particular compliment to female wisdom was the choice of the French poet Christine de Pizan's *Fais d'armes*, a work on the arts of war, while a venerable text originally offered to Charles VI, *The Tree of Battles*, was an excursus on the immorality of warfare. The king and queen were to be diverted and informed; war was never far from their reality. English and French fates were closely intertwined.

Like all women in public life, and this still holds true, Margaret of Anjou had a loud camp of detractors. By 1447 she was playing an important role in Anglo–French diplomacy, and soon complaints were sounded about her involvement in the talks preceding the cession to France of her father's domains of Maine and Anjou. In England the royal couple was keen to excite as much sympathy as possible. In 1447–8 they spent only some seventy nights in London; most of their time they travelled the country, as far as Glastonbury in the west and Durham in the north. Here was an attempt to project control and dignity, especially after the scandals at court, such as that which led to the death of Humphrey Duke of Gloucester in mysterious circumstances while awaiting trial in 1448. The French chronicler Jacques du Clercq was horrified by the fall of a man once so revered:

They made him die an inhuman death . . . they struck his back quarters, where human nature purges itself, with a cow's horn, through which they inserted a red-hot iron bar the length of his body.

Into the void left by a less than potent king stepped the blossoming figure of Margaret. She soon discovered her husband to be self-indulgently pious, not without dignity, but totally incompetent in politics. When Henry collapsed in 1453, as a result of an unexplained illness, she claimed the right to act as regent, confronting Richard Duke of York, who had been named Protector. When Henry rallied somewhat she was there to stand by him, with a son and heir, who had been late to arrive, in 1453, but was all the more treasured for the wait. When Richard of York relinquished the Protectorate following Henry's return to health, Margaret took over the reins, now protecting king, son and herself.

Margaret of Anjou's entry into domestic politics cannot be dissociated from her husband's collapse. Encouraged by a group of court officials in the 1450s, Margaret developed into a remarkable ruler, as her husband began to fade. When neither alchemy nor medicine nor prayer seemed to invigorate the king, she became queen in earnest, a figure whom many came to hate and fear, a woman of some learning and good sense, energy and emerging charisma. A Londoner, John Blocking, wrote of her in 1456: 'a great and strong active woman, who spares no efforts in pursuing her affairs'. In religious matters she was conventional and far less interested than many other contemporary women in new devotional styles: a roll of hymns associated with Margaret of Anjou contains only hymns to the Virgin Mary.

Margaret has been identified with factions – creating them and exploiting them – at a time which saw the political fabric torn asunder. She has been accused of promoting favourites and developing a court circle, as so many royal women have been before and after her. The courts of king and queen were close, but distinct, entities, with separate administrations, budgets and records. Her household grew, and although her rooms boasted comfortable bay windows and intimate galleries rather than the more formal royal design, her dwellings increasingly resembled courts, with all the circumstance and personnel of a great aristocratic household, and more. Margaret laboured to arrange marriages for members of her household to leading courtiers: Joanna Cherneys, her lady-in-waiting, born in Anjou, married Thomas Sharnebourne, squire of the queen's household, in 1449. The queen had counsellors and nurtured apprentices-at-law on to judgeships, as she did Robert Danby, who became Chief Justice in 1461.

When men are shamed and degraded, women associated with them – mothers, wives, daughters – are often also denounced. Women were seen not only as purveyors of bad influence, but as suggestible, vulnerable to the spell of another's personality. When the Protector, Humphrey Duke of Gloucester, was discredited in 1441 by a faction led by Henry Beaufort, he stood fast in council, and succeeded in defending himself. But when his wife, Lady Eleanor Cobham, was accused in July of that year of witchcraft, he could do little to help her. Eleanor Cobham was said to have conspired in treacherous divination aimed at causing the king's death, with the hope of securing the throne for her husband. She was accused of enlisting two learned clerks and a notorious witch, Margery Jourdemayne of Eye (Middlesex), and of together enacting magical incantations against the king. The Duchess fled to sanctuary at Westminster, but she was made to stand trial and was found guilty by the council. While her conspirators were executed, she underwent humiliating penance: she travelled through London from Tower Bridge to Cornhill, over three days, sometimes barefoot with taper in hand, sometimes by water.

Eleanor probably got involved with a woman known for her occult knowledge in the hope of bearing a child with Gloucester. The men she consulted were a learned medic and an astronomer, university graduates both (Plate 1). Margery, the 'witch of Eye', served the noble lady that heady mixture of medicine and magic which so many people believed could cure disease and ward off misfortune. She was a figure well known at court, who a decade earlier had been arrested for sorcery. Eleanor had been a lady-in-waiting to Gloucester's first wife, Jacqueline of Hainault, and may have already used Margery's services then. But the heavy spin of 1441 turned the casting of her horoscope into a major act of treason; it was claimed that the horoscope was aimed at hastening the king's death. Her household clerk and her physician, Bolingbroke and Southwell, were accused of predicting the king's illness, thus affecting the king's power in the land. So anxious was the king to counter doubts about his health that he immediately requested that an analytic horoscope be cast for him by two leading scholars: John Somerset, his private physician and Chancellor of the Exchequer, and John Langton, Chancellor of the University of Cambridge. As for Eleanor's clerks, they were tried and suffered horrific deaths. Bolingbroke was first humiliated at St Paul's Cross, with a paper crown on his head, then tried before the king's council, and when found guilty was dragged to the gallows, hanged, drawn and quartered; his head was displayed on London Bridge and his quarters sent as deterrent offerings to Oxford, Cambridge, and possibly York and Bristol. Margery was burnt as an unrepentant witch.

The types of knowledge and practices which led to Eleanor's trial and public penance and to the death of her associates were widely known and used. Magical knowledge was systematically collected and disseminated, like the wonderful manuscript of the *Ars notoria*, an encyclopaedia of magical knowledge ascribed to King Solomon, large in size and beautifully laid out on the page. Magic-workers used less sumptuous pocket-books which contained recipes and curses, and invocations to ward off all sorts of evil and attract benign forces too. This knowledge could be used as self-help books are today, or by people who were recognized as experts, as Bolingbroke and Southwell and Margery seemed to be. Both canon and common law aimed at countering magic, sermons and pastoral handbooks denounced the use of it, but it was clearly everywhere, available and desired by people of all social situations.

Magic was never far from the official operations of saints' relics and liturgical blessings. If Eleanor had originally hired Margery to use her magic and make Duke Humphrey love her, and later, to help her bear him an heir, such desires were shared by people everywhere – and still are. A decorous yet puzzling ceremony took place annually in Bury St Edmunds: monks led a white bull, adorned with garlands, in a procession along the precinct boundaries. Women who sought to conceive stroked the bull's flanks, and then made an offering at St Edmund's shrine and prayed for a pregnancy. This was the place and these were the relics which Henry VI sought out for his own spiritual refreshment – his visits to Bury were probably the happiest times of his troubled life.

Women's inspiration was abundant within political circles high and low. Henry V had invoked a mystic, St Bridget of Sweden, and her prophecies in support of his reign and campaigns, and celebrated the triumph at Agincourt with Marian imagery. Richard Beauchamp Earl of Warwick maintained a special relationship with the anchoress Emma Rawghton of All Hallows church, North Street, York, who received visions and prophecies about his political fortunes. Religious rigour offered women of means an occupation and orientation in solitary widowhood. While men of stature and muscle were expected to act in the world, they could relax in the sphere of female piety, and occasionally draw inspiration and hope from it. What might seem an odd combination of extraordinary worldliness and sentimental piety is a creative contradiction characteristic of this world. The milieu of piety, and especially of female piety, was reassuring, seemingly unsullied and seemingly unworldly, a place from which powerful and troubled men could regain solace before facing the world again.

HENRY VI'S RELIGION AND LEARNING

Far more traditional was Henry VI's own religious taste. He probably felt happiest during times spent in colleges and monasteries; he spent Christmas and Easter 1433–4 in Bury St Edmunds, one of England's finest monasteries. There he resided in the abbot's grand lodgings, which were rebuilt for his visit – a monastic palace not unlike the royal apartments at Poblet (Catalonia); he even held parliament there. At Bury Henry was entertained by plays such as *Wisdom*, a moral allegory which reflected on human frailty and the hope for improvement. He read contemplative texts, often of continental origin, which guided towards the 'mixed life', that of devotion and contemplation in the midst of worldly affairs. His stay at Bury inspired the composition by John Lydgate, the monk-poet of Bury St Edmunds, of a hagiographical account of St Edmund, the abbey's patron saint, and St Fremund (d. 866), a Saxon hermit killed by the Danes. The book, now in the British Library, took about a decade to complete. Near the beginning, above the first verse, 'The noble story to put in remembrance', is an image of a presentation ceremony, with a very young Henry VI surrounded by monks and courtiers, among them the author, book in hand. Yet all this religious immersion may have served more as a distraction than a training for one who was expected to move among men of action and to act in the ugly, violent and soul-destroying business of war and dynastic strife. The choice to involve himself in the sphere of contemplative religion was no alternative to the vigorous life of politics and court. It might inspire a king, but could never substitute for the execution of his responsibilities.

Yet Henry's interest in moral education did result in some spectacular initiatives executed by able men in his court. He stayed at Winchester College in 1441, and there formed the idea of founding his own school, Eton College, a task entrusted to the hands of the reliable William Waynflete – formerly Headmaster of Winchester College – whom he directed to the see of Winchester after the death of Cardinal Beaufort in 1447. King's College in Cambridge was founded as a sibling institution to Eton, to which the boys of Eton destined for the royal chapel were to progress. Officially founded on the king's birthday on 6 December 1441, it was built upon the area of the parish of St John Zachary and adjacent academic halls. In 1445 it was named the College of the Virgin Mary and St Nicholas, and was modelled after the example of Wykeham's New College in Oxford. Under a rector twelve fellows were to pursue the Arts course and maintain the commemoration of benefactors in a magnificent chapel worthy of the royal founder. The chapel progressed little in Henry's lifetime, but it received some support from every king over the next century. It was ultimately completed and decorated with the glass and wooden furnishings commissioned by Henry VIII (Plate 22). These are still in use, providing the backdrop to the music of the most famous choir in the world. King's was a royal institution, and an institution of orthodoxy. It was founded in Cambridge, the intellectually 'safe' university, which, unlike Oxford, had not been tainted by heresy. The Fellows of King's College were obliged to take an oath, against the 'damned errors, or heresies, of John Wyclif and Reginald Pecock, or any other heretic'.

These activities, which combined education, religion and a certain amount of administrative capacity, created the milieu in which Henry VI felt most comfortable and safe. It is not surprising, therefore, that in future years he chose from among Eton men his chaplains and confidants, those who were to see him through very hard times. Clerical scholars were Henry VI's alternative court and, like all courtiers, they were promoted to bishoprics and offices of state. John Carpenter, Bishop of Worcester, assisted in the foundation of Eton; Henry's chaplain Henry Sever was the college's first provost. While dealing with his foundation the young king was alert, engaged and interested, eagerly awaiting important items of correspondence related to the project. He got his way, and in this sphere inspired respect and loyalty, even in years when his presence and effect in council, diplomacy and parliament were lacklustre. He inspired loyalty in men such as John Blacman, Fellow of Eton, who was his chaplain and later went into exile with him in the 1460s and survived to become Henry VI's hagiographer. Blacman's writings express a world-weary spirituality, which fitted the king's later years.

BOOKS

A sophisticated world of letters and writing was available in England, and in it met poetry, politics, propaganda and the display of taste and wealth. In Henry V's day poetry was invoked in the service of state and dynasty, and several of the projects which he began saw their fruition during his son's reign. The royal uncles were great collectors of books and artefacts, patrons of artists and poets and musicians. They exchanged cultural commodities in the furtherance of diplomacy, dynasty and personal glamour. Books aimed towards self-help were popular in these years of political turbulence and contested claims to power: physiognomy tracts were not only part of classical heritage, they were manuals which guided their readers to judge the character of future retainers, counsellors, spouses, friends. Such collectors were fond of history, too, and from the fashionably reworked history of antiquity sought to learn lessons of conduct and speech which might tip the balance in their favour, to distil past experience into argument and advice about tyranny, conspiracy, loyalty and fortitude. And as their bodies frequently suffered in battle and imprisonment, during long and uncomfortable periods of travel, they collected books on bodily comportment, diet and exercise and rewarded the men who could help them implement useful regimes of training and improvement.

Gloucester's chancellor, Thomas Beckington, later Bishop of Bath and Wells, was sent by his master to Italy to acquire books which might guide education in the humanist curriculum and ultimately make it available for public service. These were exciting times in the world of pedagogy and learning; the ethical debates of scholars in Tuscan schools spread widely, and were soon available, interacting with local cultures in all European regions. Various educational institutions were affected by the idea of combining learning, virtue and eloquence, all in the service of *utilitas*, the greater good. Beckington introduced these insights into his own diocese; the choir school of Wells Cathedral professed in 1460 to direct the training of its choirboys towards manners, instruction and utility.

Humphrey Duke of Gloucester used all his contacts to promote the project of book collection and acquisition of humanist knowledge. A book now in the Bodleian Library in Oxford carries his own autograph: 'Cest livre est A moy humfrey duc de gloucester'; he had bought it from the executors of Nicholas Bildeston, once Dean of Salisbury (d. 1441). He had similarly bought books from the executors of Thomas Polton, Bishop of Worcester (d. 1433), a man of extensive European experience, an English representative at church councils and a royal diplomat. Like his brother John Duke of Bedford, who was host in England to the leading Florentine humanist Poggio Bracciolini between 1419 and 1422, Humphrey Duke of Gloucester became a patron of men of letters. He had two Italian secretaries in succession – Tito Livio Frulovisi and Antonio Beccaria – and by the 1430s humanistic texts were dedicated and presented to him as a recognized and appreciated patron.

Advice on comportment and behaviour was garnered not solely from conduct literature written by clerics, but from the experience and reflection of political and civic actors. William of Worcester, for example, was secretary to Sir John Fastolf, and with him served with the Duke of Bedford in Normandy between 1422 and 1435. He composed the Book of Noblesse for his ducal patron. In it contemporary politics mingled with translations from Cicero on the all-important subjects of friendship and old age. Worcester's book of conduct was adapted for Henry VI's use, and then for that of his adversary Edward IV. Magnates sought tutors for their sons from among university scholars familiar with the new learning: Lord Tiptoft chose Master John Hurley of University College, Oxford, to teach his son (the future Earl of Worcester) and offered him his first benefice. Hurley in turn travelled with the young man on his study tour to Padua and later on pilgrimage to Jerusalem. In the service of great men, those of lesser status could none the less travel, go on pilgrimage, visit great homes and be involved in momentous business.

Similar to Worcester's Book of Noblesse and, like it, aimed at moulding personality towards public life, was the book written by Peter Idley for his son Thomas in 1445–50. Idley was a substantial landlord with estates in Berkshire, Buckinghamshire, Oxfordshire, Middlesex, Surrey, Hampshire and Worcestershire. He benefited from several royal appointments, such as Bailiff of the Honour of Wallingford, and received in the 1440s several royal exemptions and favours. He was not socially exalted but was well connected (to the Earl of Suffolk and his wife), and was a shrewd observer of the vicissitudes of politics and the challenges of royal rule. His book of guidance provides political advice and moral counsel, as well as religious instruction. Above all, he recommends moderation in style and loyalty to carefully chosen friends. He describes in detail the many types of counsel and their givers, and recommends discretion in all: avoid advice of a drunk, of a fearful man, of a wrathful person or of those who had lost favour and then returned to it. His is a map of the many pitfalls which a man of standing might encounter in public life, an analysis of the political culture and social fabric of mid-century England, criss-crossed with vying loyalties, conspiracies and public challenges to authority.

Political life and much social interaction depended on an effective king and magnates whose intricate connections with their regions linked them with practically every person living there. Just as the quality of royal governance trickled down and affected the political body, so did that of magnate power. Magnates could support the proper provision of justice, but their neglect or active partisanship could breed a sense of lawlessness and corruption. Gentry families of varying degrees of wealth and status were enfolded within the magnate's affinity. When such men fell out, and consequently feuded, magnate authority could encourage resolution, even peace. When this failed, local repercussions were quick to follow, and in turn a wider disaffection born out of disappointment touched the whole political community. During the Fanhope–Grey dispute between two major families in Bedfordshire, which began in 1437, Lord Fanhope and Lord Grey appeared in the county court sessions, accompanied by armed followers. This forced local political society to take sides, and unsettled title to land among tens of families. In Wales, gentry families were particularly powerful in this period, in the almost total absence of resident magnates. Administrators and office-holders and many ex-soldiers rose to high administrative and honorific titles for the first time since the Glyn Dŵr rebellion.

Scholarly and forensic works reflected local political awareness of these complexities. We may call such work 'antiquarian', studies in search of title and precedent, in support of contemporary claims. This was not a new practice, but as law required more written evidence than before, a forensic antiquarianism developed, by secretaries for titled masters. Following his research, John Rous developed a unique argument against enclosure which he brought to the parliament of 1459 at Coventry, seeing it as harmful to the architectural heritage of England.

He showed that in Warwickshire depopulation followed enclosure, and that buildings on enclosed lands suffered decay, like the 'splendid gate-house which Joan, Lady Bergavenny had built for her husband'. Whereas religious houses had always been careful to maintain their archives, this period sees the gentry families doing the same. Sir John Byron of Clayton in south Lancashire kept some 300 deeds in his treasury, while Sir Geoffrey Mascy of Tatton (Cheshire) mentioned in his will the bequest of his archive to his heir. This is not to say that deeds were not kept before, but rather that archival awareness and order, often provided by the services of clerical secretaries, became part of the magnate and gentry household.

In some cases this research was enabled by skill in Latin, and from reading of Roman history and the acquisition of rhetorical skills. When he visited England in 1419 the peripatetic Florentine humanist Poggio Bracciolini declared that the English were 'barbarians' and that in their country one must give up all hope of finding a book, meaning a humanist book. But by 1440, the Benedictine monk John Walthamstead, who later become Abbot of St Albans, reported that a 'Cabalinian fount' gushed in Oxford and a 'Cirren stream' ran through Cambridge, where 'we join with the Muses in the singing of extraordinary melodies'. These muses inspired men such as William Gray, who gained his MA at Balliol in 1434, to a life of scholarly travel which took him to Florence, Padua, Ferrara and Rome before he became Bishop of Ely. When he died in 1478 his substantial library passed to Balliol College, the place where he had first learned to love books. Gushing rhetoric was deployed by Oxford University in the sycophantic missives which it poured on Humphrey Duke of Gloucester, in pursuit of his patronage and the bequest of his books. Aristocrats and scholars shared the taste for humanist letters; in 1453 the university elected its first aristocratic chancellor, the twenty-year-old George Neville, a lover of books, who was also the younger brother of the Earl of Warwick.

Participation in European styles and use of continental artists involved discerning application of modes and styles to an English context. The Book of Hours of Henry Beauchamp Duke of Warwick, of sometime between 1439 and 1446, displays the accomplishment of French illumination, but it is also recognizably English in style: a scene of King David facing God, at the beginning of Psalm 26, is set in an English pastoral landscape, with windmills and walled towns in the background. Alongside the scriptural texts is a whole-page figure of

St John of Bridlington, a very English prophet. Similarly, c.1430–37, Humphrey Duke of Gloucester had his likeness inserted into his Psalter. This is a magnificent English ducal figure, kneeling in front of Christ, who is presented as the Man of Sorrows, rising from his tomb and bleeding into a chalice. Education, wealth, a deep acquaintance with French culture – fostered in England by prisoners such as Charles of Orléans and, through marriage, by Margaret of Anjou – and Italian learning produced in this generation a group of English magnates of great cultural influence, with the power to set trends among artists, writers and musicians.

TRADE AND LIFESTYLE

The trends in religion, literature and learning were matched by movements of goods and money. Tracts about travel and routes for navigation were the subjects of contemporary writing, while the highly sophisticated tract *Libelle of English Policy* of c.1436–8 was an exercise in political economy. It analysed England's well-being as the product of its commerce, over which the king and council had such great influence. Here was a document aimed at policy-makers, one which recommended a shift in English political priorities. It advised vigilance over Wales (always a potential flashpoint for rebellion) and that Ireland be secured as a source of untapped wealth, away from dependence on links with western Europe.

Here is integrated thinking which linked policy, economy and political stability, and which recognized the ethnic and regional variety of the king's subjects. For regional differences and variation in wealth determined degrees of safety, mobility and lifestyle, habits in consumption and even susceptibility to disease. Informed attention to lifestyle choices is evident in all areas, although least among rural working people, who still ate bread, vegetables and dairy products, and meat only rarely. There was a truly regional set of diets, with trans-regional trade in delicacies and in cereals. Rye was the main bread-corn in parts of Norfolk and Worcestershire, barley in north Suffolk. Game was available in forest areas, cider and perry was drunk in Herefordshire.

Although associated with medieval diet in the modern popular imagination, the sucking pig was a great rarity, for pig was not the animal it later became: it was small, hard to feed in the winter, and it was a delicacy. People were eating more fish; monks already had well-stocked fishponds, and now great landlords were investing in the creation of ponds as they moved away from arable. The Duke of Norfolk, for example, restocked six of his ponds in 1460 with pike, perch, roach, tench, bream and carp. Fish could also arrive from abroad; indeed it was the only merchandise which ships could bring back from many Scandinavian ventures. In May 1457 the *Valentine* left Newcastle-on-Tyne for Iceland, with goods of Thomas Castell, William Haysand and eight of their associates. It carried wool cloth, butter, meat and beer and returned with salted herring, eels, monkfish, salmon and oysters.

Food was cheap, and took up a small proportion of household expenditure. The rest was used on other goods. A proliferation of manufactures and services was increasingly evident in hundreds of small towns and even in villages. The leather industry was the second largest after textiles, and it provided a whole series of goods from buckets and belts to saddles and bottles, which were modestly priced. While 1423 saw the foundation of the College of Physicians and Surgeons in London, with the patronage of Humphrey Duke of Gloucester, medical services were also dispersed throughout the land in villages and towns. Thomas Fayreford offered treatment in Somerset and Devon in the 1440s, and was in demand by a wide social range of patients. He wrote up at length his case-notes about the treatment of Lady Ponynges, but he also served less exalted figures. On his extended tours in the countryside he cared for a miller and a cook, some priests, and several patients whom he treated in their village homes. Thomas Fayreford offered not only his personal ministration, but sold ointments of his own making. He may even have dispensed amuletic cures, like the piece of inscribed parchment which hung around a patient's neck, its efficacy enhanced by masses and the eating of paeony root. Medical services were purchased from professionals, but traditional charms were recommended by relatives or neighbours. A popular charm for the staunching of bleeding was

> Christ was born in Bethlehem
> And christened in river Jordan.
> And as the river stood like a stone
> the blood of N. may stand.
> *In the name of the father and the son and the holy spirit Amen.*

In medical care as in religious life variety allowed people to make choices. Those who offered services and produced goods aimed to establish themselves in protected niches which secured employment and profit. Professionals, such as John Somerset, royal physician and Chancellor of the Exchequer, combined medical provision and the search for prayer: he founded in 1446 at Brentford End (Middlesex) the Hospital of the Virgin and Nine Orders of Angels, for nine sick persons. Hospital foundations of the period tend to specify medical aims more clearly and provide for treatment, where earlier houses tended to concentrate on shelter and hopeful prayer.

TOWNS

Most urban manufacturers and service providers worked and traded from within guilds. In face of the recession of the mid-century, each guild attempted to regulate its numbers, dominate supply of raw materials, and maintain profits sufficient for all members. Guilds supported members and demanded loyalty. The Grocers' Company of London enrolled its ordinances in 1444, with the huge penalty of £20 against any member who divulged secrets or harmed another member. Guilds offered advantages by developing collective awareness of demand, fashions and market-niches for their products, but also through the nurturing of patronage and the acquisition of political power. Some guilds saw an influx of immigrant workers, as, for example, the Goldsmiths, who annually admitted tens of 'Dutchmen' – a catch-all adjective for northern Europeans – into their company in the 1440s. As we have seen, the cities within which guilds operated were governed by oligarchies of councilmen and headed by annually elected officials, such as aldermen, chamberlains and mayors; election to these bodies and posts was operated through and for the guilds.

In London a political struggle was at play between artisans and merchants, between those who produced and those who bought, distributed and sold at great profit. Through a subtle interplay of their wealth and court patronage, the guilds of tailors and drapers tussled over primacy as governors of their city. When the experienced, if outspoken, Ralph Holland, tailor and draper, was passed over twice for election as mayor of London in 1439 and 1440 (election which was made by the incumbent mayor out of two names put to him by the Council of

Aldermen), an armed political force of artisans came together, even as the guild's lawyers were arguing their case in council and Chancery. The struggle over political power and the right to assess and examine the quality of cloth sold in London and its fairs dealt with real economic advantage, which in a period of economic stagnation mattered greatly. It is out of such sensibilities that a political sentiment emerged, one which led men to argue about rights of representation in urban government and the force of royal writs, and to attack directly London politicians such as John Paddesley, goldsmith and mayor, who was chosen over Holland in 1440. Indeed, in the following year, Ralph Holland was promoted and unofficially pronounced mayor against Paddesley's own candidate.

Sons were allowed to replace father, and thus inherit the right to be freemen, in York as in London. At the same time, internal guild politics led to constant assessment of the remits of membership: in 1434 journeymen blacksmiths were welcomed back to the blacksmiths' social and religious club, the fraternity of St Loy, where the group's cohesion could be promoted by the master blacksmiths, the employers. Tailors sought a large and strong membership, even allowing those not in the craft to join their social and religious grouping, the fraternity. Every aspect of social and political organization in London was scrutinized in a contracting economy and an uncertain political climate. Even magnates were drawn into the circle of London politics, as they had been during the 1390s: Humphrey Duke of Gloucester probably paved the way to the tailors' acquisition of a royal charter, while his wife enrolled in the company's livery, a sort of honorary membership, in 1434.

While many towns and ports experienced serious contraction in trade and population, London fared better than provincial towns in the fifteenth century. It had the advantages of buoyant demand generated by a political centre and the international stream of visitors which displayed its importance and taste. London attracted people of talent, those who sought to benefit from opportunities in training and advancement. Men could enter into positions of influence and prestige in London and its surroundings. Such a man was Alexander Anne, younger son of a Yorkshire gentry family, who, as a lawyer, became a member of the drapers' company, under-sheriff, escheator, recorder, and served three times as representative in parliament for Middlesex. Conversely, Londoners maintained links with their places of origin, and are found holding land in small communities, such as the London merchant who owned a house in Buntingford (Suffolk).

Such mobility through professional service made the categories of social status quite porous. The term gentleman applied to those who held substantial tracts of land, generating income, according to the Statute of Additions of 1413, but the variety of avenues which endowed status and reward created ambiguity over precedence and honour. Brothers pursued different careers and gained connections in different spheres. How are we to understand the case of two brothers, the Barets of Bury St Edmunds, one gentle and the other not? John Baret held land outside Bury, which his brother, a merchant, inherited upon his death. The survivor remained in Bury while holding the land; was he a gentleman? In London such questions were perhaps less important, as the city generated its titles and offices, but in provincial society it mattered more. The move to the city did not necessarily mean loss of gentle connections and aspirations. Robert of Ardern, to take another example, was not a knight, but he was the second largest landlord in Warwickshire, with £113 annual income in 1436, and therefore was seen as a leader among the 500 or so men who constituted gentle society in the county. Local landed men of substance made their views known. In 1439 a turbulent meeting of the Norfolk county court saw the sheriff exit in a huff, protesting against the presence at the gathering of some 500 men, not the 40 who had been summoned as qualified members of local political society. There were clearly more men who were interested and involved in politics, beyond the group of knights alone. In 1445 parliament grappled with this reality and produced the statute which restricted eligibility for election to parliament to substantial men with £100 or more in annual income.

London's wealth, the ambition and influence of its leading groups, were also displayed in the incessant activity of rebuilding of public edifices, especially churches: All Saints, Fulham, became distinguished by a Kentish-type perpendicular style; St Michael's, Wood Street, boasted a bell-tower from 1429, and an aisle was added to St Olave's Jewry in 1436. This was not the splendid rebuilding that the wool-churches of East Anglia and the Cotswolds underwent, but a well-planned campaign of extension and decoration, aimed at catching up with styles and displaying prosperity. The effort was both collective and individual, for the parish retained its place as a favoured space for display: parishioners hung their arms from roof beams in All Hallows, Staining, St Mildred's Poultry, St Peter, Cornhill, and St Olave, Hart

Street. In neighbouring Westminster some building work was always in progress. Then, as now, a good craftsman was to be cherished. Westminster Abbey showed its appreciation of good masons by providing them with maintenance packages and thus securing their services. The mason William Thornwerk and his wife Elizabeth were granted a corrody – lifelong maintenance – in the abbey in 1445–6; John Randolf, who was granted his corrody in 1450, lived on to enjoy it for forty years.

Within communal buildings – churches and guildhalls – texts and ideas circulated, reflecting contemporary political preoccupations. Urban chronicles regularly reported and interpreted national events. The records of London companies display a particular fascination with pomp and pageantry. Such events which passed through London streets were important in several ways: they reflected some of the affairs of magnates and royals, while their very shape and colour were the product of extensive purchasing from mercers and goldsmiths, and employment of the City's carpenters and painters. The continuity of corporations also meant that recording the events of the day – such as Margaret of Anjou's pageants of 1445 described in the Goldsmiths' book – meant that they were there to be studied by the Goldsmiths of the future.

English towns were home to diverse groups of people: long-standing burgess families and civic leaders lived side by side with recent arrivals from the country, southerners and northerners, as well as with migrants from France, Germany and the Low Countries. A city which was well governed and offered decent accommodation could attract traders. Even small towns, such as Coleshill (Warwickshire), boasted four inns; the construction of an inn built in Andover (Hampshire) in 1444–5 cost £300. In the west Midlands and Welsh Marches English and Welsh mixed, and in the north, Scots and Irish; there were German shoemakers in Truro (Cornwall) and Maldon (Essex). Such mixed environments, in which neighbours might be known as 'Scott', 'Pycard' or 'Brytan', were shattered during hostilities between home countries or regions. Following the rupture in Anglo-Burgundian relations, there were anti-Flemish riots, above all in London, and a requirement that some 1,800 Flemings take an oath of loyalty. A Frenchwoman felt sufficiently at home in 1448–9 to leave 12d. as a gift to her parish church of St Mary's, Sandwich (Kent), and a Dutch woman left 6d. for its wainscoting. But the French raid on Sandwich in August 1457 – an attack 4,000 men strong – hit churches and dwellings, and must have changed attitudes to French people, at least for a while.

In areas of intense ethnic awareness, a slur on identity could result in real harm, and thus people sued those who defamed them with suggestive ethnic labels. In the Peculiar Court of the Bishop of Durham in 1453 two women were charged with claiming that a Durham monk had been born in Scotland, and between 1453 and 1456 cases were brought for such malicious defamation as 'Scottish priest's whore' and 'Welsh priest's son'. The shifting political realities in a border region faced people with legal and personal dilemmas. In 1442 Robert Lynton attempted to prove that he was English since he was born in Jedburgh at a time when it had been English. The subsidy which was imposed on aliens in 1440, 1s. 4d. per head, was exacted in the north from those deemed to be Scots, usually servants and labourers, and from Anglo-Irish, who protested about this to parliament in 1441. To the intricacies of status, privilege and prejudice in English and Welsh towns can also be added claims to special treatment for the enclaves created by religious institutions. The history of cities like Exeter or Norwich is a story of struggle between townsmen and cathedral over jurisdiction, over the exaction of contributions to the defence of the town, and over the right to try criminals who might have only a tenuous link to such an institution, yet sheltered under the immunity which it offered.

Like London, middling towns elected citizens into offices which were meant to promote the general good. A glance at the accounts of the treasurers of Cambridge for the year 1445–6 shows an array of minute regulations which aimed at control of the quality of goods, and the generation of civic income: fines for unlawful sale of ale, for trade in Rhenish wine, for sale of Irish yarn. Licences for workers were sold at 1s. 8d. for a cordwainer or a huckster, 2s. 4d. for a shearman, 3s. 4d. for a master-glover. Over the century which followed the Black Death, and all over Europe, special attention was paid by officials to provision of clean water, removal of noxious foods and materials from public spaces, and dealing with persons considered anti-social. In Coventry in 1442 local prostitutes were required to wear furred hoods, and in 1448 ordinances dealt with obstruction of the common ditch which flowed through the town, and with the removal of animal intestines deposited behind the butchers' row. Perhaps in response to repeated petitions in parliament about people who became rich by owning 'stewes', or brothels, in 1445 ordinances were promulgated for Southwark, by its lord the Bishop of Winchester (Henry Cardinal Beaufort). These attempted to regulate prostitution and especially the coercion of women into it because of poverty.

WOOL AND CLOTH

This period saw a dramatic shift in the role which England and Wales played in European trade in wool and its products. Between 1420 and 1460 the balance of trade shifted, with the 1430s as the point at which cloth exports overtook those of wool. Whereas in 1420–24, 4,628 sacks of wool were exported from Hull, only 2,062 were exported in 1430–34, a decade later. At the same time the overall export of cloth grew from £41,750 worth in 1421–30 to £89,660 worth in 1441–50. A reorientation of the wool economy was under way, shifting the emphasis from production and distribution of the wool clip, already in place since the twelfth century, to the creation of networks of production, collection and sale of cloth which depended on the involvement of thousands of small manufacturers. Hectic diplomatic activity fostered the trading treaties which linked England not only with Italian merchants – well-established and situated in London – but with the Hanseatic cities and trade ports in Zeeland. The great merchants were pleased with the advantage allowed them as they traded as a staple from Calais, a city with a vast hinterland protected and patrolled by English garrisons and troops.

Much of the wealth produced and circulated in towns and cities was linked in some way to wool, England's main source of income. The taxes imposed on wool sales and on finished woollen cloth provided the crown with a substantial part of its income. In the making of wool into cloth several interlocking processes of production were involved, and a wide range of expertise went into the final product. By mid-century English wool had lost ground to Italian and even Spanish produce, but demand for woollen cloth of high to medium quality remained buoyant. A Commons petition of 1455 claimed that foreign merchants bought cloth for ready money all over the country and thus forced prices down, to the detriment of native cloth merchants. The *Libelle of English Policie* similarly recommended that the terms of credit to alien merchants be limited to six months, combining a monetarist argument with an aggressive view of national economic well-being. The benefits from this trade varied greatly by region, as did resulting losses when production was affected by war or by natural calamity. The endemic murrain caused the death of cattle and sheep in Staffordshire, Dorset and Herefordshire in 1439, and in Lincolnshire in 1442. Yet in areas such as

Wiltshire and the Cotswolds those who invested in the making and the sale of cloth prospered: in Castle Combe in Wiltshire, whose river turned a fulling-mill, fifty new houses for clothiers were built in the first half of the century.

The best wool to be had in the fifteenth century came from the sheep of the Cotswolds and Lindsey in Lincolnshire. Religious houses with large flocks were in many ways favoured producers, as they sold directly to wool merchants, in some cases Italian merchants. As the market now favoured cloth over raw wool, a whole array of skills and crafts developed in the towns of wool regions: jobs were plentiful in Yorkshire and the Cotswolds for spinners and dyers, crafts in which women's work was much favoured. Work in towns was organized within guilds, to which women had little official access, but under which their work was organized. Villages were becoming centres of production, and clothiers employed agents to deliver the wool and collect the product from rural workers. One such was Robert Collinson of York, who, in his will of 1456, asked the poor workers of many villages of the West Riding to forgive any excessive profits he may have made out of their labour. Such awareness of the ethics of business coincides with contemporary pastoral treatises, which listed types of usury, analysing the many injustices and sins inherent in the habitual forms of exchange, profit-sharing, lending and investment. One such text opens with the words: 'usury shows itself in many manners', and lists twelve types of lucre.

CHURCH BUILDING

Nowhere was the wealth from wool and cloth so publicly evident as in Suffolk and parts of Essex. Even today one is struck by the ambition, quality and sheer size of the communal enterprises initiated by wool towns. Guildhalls and, above all, churches were rebuilt on a large scale, though towns complained about the cost of maintaining walls, buildings and communal halls. The building of a Blythburgh, a Walberswick, a Lavenham or a Long Melford church required the interest and local attachment of a few prosperous families and dedicated individuals. These vast enterprises of real-estate management, building, employment, patronage and taste brought work to the community. Agents hired skilled masons, carvers and painters for their expertise, and imported objects and images which might never have been seen locally before. The purchase, hire, planning and accounting were the business, privilege and duty of churchwardens – community officials whose role was growing in prominence and weight. Chosen from the ranks of substantial tenants of the village, or well-off and respectable worthies in an urban parish, they often had to dip into their own pockets to plug the gaps in budgets, but above all they were charged with authority and enjoyed the related prestige. The churchwardens' task of providing the parish with the wherewithal for worship – vestments, plate, props – was complemented by the expectation that they cast an ever-vigilant eye over parishioners in their business, high and low. Parishioners frequently chose them as executors for their wills; many testamentary bequests were left towards the fabric of parish churches.

The chronology of building differed by region: in Yorkshire there was little new building after 1450, Suffolk peaked in the later fifteenth century, and Somerset in the sixteenth. Styles were regional too. Clerestories – registers of clear windows high above the nave – aimed at letting in as much light as possible. That particular magnificent feature of Blythburgh church was characteristic of Suffolk, and was never found in Kent or Cornwall. Similarly, the east of England developed the octagonal font – the font with eight carved stone panels, seven showing a sacrament and one the crucifixion – a catechism in stone. Specifically East Anglian too were the painted rood-screens with rows of saints and martyrs. In 1436 Litcham parish commissioned its own, with female saints on the north side and male ones on the south – twenty-two figures in all, ranging from universal Christian heroes such as St Helena or St Agnes to the very local William of Norwich, a boy believed to have been killed by Jews in the twelfth century. An erstwhile mayor of Norwich, Ralph Seagram, commissioned two panels for his parish church of St John Maddermarket around 1445. Their warm reds and golds depicted Saints Agnes and Laurence and Agatha, and, among them again, William of Norwich.

Local achievements inspired imitation, which in turn created local styles: the document commissioning the building of Walberswick's tower over the period 1426 to 1441 stipulated that it should resemble that of Halesworth. The tower of the church of Wymondham in Norfolk was meant to rise above the central tower of Wymondham Priory. The rood-screen area was elaborated, with additions of rood-lofts and ubiquitous staircases leading up to the rood, with some generous examples in the Cotswolds and the west, as in Burford (Oxfordshire) and Wimborne Minster (Dorset).

Early or late, elaborate or modest, the projects of building were remarkable for the prudence which collective scrutiny brought to them. The accounts of the rebuilding of the chancel of Hardley church (Norfolk) in 1457–8 record the employment of a master-carpenter by the church's rector; he was to provide the timber, the expertise and the labour. The chancel building was put in the hands of a Norwich mason, Robert Everard, who in turn provided the labour and the stone, building material which was to be shipped from Norwich on a barge. Four workers supported the master-mason at 3½d. a day, and they were also fed while working. A plumber joined the works in 1460–61 once the roof was up, and in the following year William Glayster worked on four windows for the chancel: in 1462–3 he also undertook the glazing of the east window for 33s. 4d. Over six years £21 9s. 1d. was spent, distributed in keeping with seasonal rhythm, stage by stage. A mason such as Robert Everard had a flourishing business in such repair and extension in Norfolk parishes, with additional responsibilities for work in Norwich Cathedral. Similar care and progress, step by erected step, was evident in the building accounts of St Martin's church in Coney Street, York, of 1447–52. Robert Seman, local vicar between 1425 and 1443, had left in his will funds for the completion of the rebuilding he had begun in his lifetime. Here too executors' vigilance and regular and relatively small periods of payment – fortnightly to masons – are in evidence. Executors, craftsmen and parishioners saw the dead vicar's bequest turn into a reality.

The small enterprise of a single parish brought together regional talent and trans-regional wherewithal. The stone was quarried in Northampton and travelled on barges through the Wash to Yarmouth and from there to Norwich, then to Brandon and finally by road to Hardley. Northamptonshire exported not only stone, but masons; those who helped rebuild Harston church (Cambridgeshire) around 1445 were men of that region. The roof for this church was probably made on site, but such roofs could be imported from centres of high-class building such as Essex and Cambridgeshire. Yet despite imported talent and materials, building it was a local affair. The churchwardens were the people on the ground; they lived near the church and were able to monitor its progress. Within the communal space of the church it was still possible for individuals, families or groups to mark out areas or times of special significance.

Churchwardens may have been public-spirited but they were often intrusive and heavy-handed. They supervised the provision of parish charity through the management of parish almshouses, as in Elsworth (Cambridgeshire) in 1451, but they also reported on parishioners' behaviour. What was high-spirited to some seemed downright anti-social to others. It is probably such parish worthies who brought offenders to the attention of constables or church authorities, like the men who repeatedly presented to the manorial court of Ramsey recidi-vist tennis players in the 1420s. The churches whose improvement they supervised are a more pleasing trace of their activities than is their informing and reporting on private conduct and speech.

COUNTRY LIFE

Most people lived on the land, and the living was not bad in the 1420s and 1430s, though it was to deteriorate soon after. In the south-east pastoral economy flourished, as it did in the Cotswolds and Oxford-shire. A map of Boarstall (Buckinghamshire) survives from around 1444, and it shows clearly the structure of the manor: the common fields, the church, the gatehouse to the manor house, and some 200 acres of deer park. In Shropshire, Herefordshire and Gloucestershire the torn fabric of exchange, travel and work, the legacy of Glyn Dŵr's decade, was being painstakingly rewoven. Although many peasants still held customary lands, few lived as unfree persons. Manumission was a common feature of the first half of the fifteenth century: in 1439 fellows of Merton College, Oxford, lords of Kibworth Harcourt (Leicester-shire), stopped using the term *nativus* (serf by birth) of their tenants there. In 1447 Richard Duke of York freed all bondsmen in his Cydewain lordship (Powys) for the sum of 1,000 marks, thus generating income for himself and providing the benefits of legal freedom to the men and their families.

A flexible attitude developed to adjustment of rents and services where lords sought to secure continued settlement and production. Yet some lords were more intent on monitoring change and enforcing their rights. In the records for Aldborough, in the bailiwick of Knaresborough, part of the Duchy of Lancaster, a return to the old rent is noted, after a reduction agreed during 'these mediocre years'. In 1449–50 accounts of the soke of Winchester recorded that the lord allowed a tool-sharpening mill to be built as long as it did not compete with his own seigneurial fulling-mills.

The mark of unfree birth remained on hundreds of manors until the sixteenth century, but most of its practical daily implications – curtailment of movement, occupation, work – were felt no longer to apply. Peasant holdings were diverse affairs, with a growing emphasis on cottage production and the rearing of livestock. Many households held more than one tenancy, with all the related responsibilities to maintain buildings and appurtenances. In Watford (Northamptonshire) in the 1430s the lord of the manor even paid his tenants to maintain the housing stock. On the Pelham estate of Laughton (Sussex) tenants carried wood and grain, stacked hay and ploughed demesne land. Such households were headed by men or by women, but in either case they blended into the routines of husbandry and village cooperation.

Cooperation remained vital to the maintenance of livelihood, and manorial courts were used to monitor it. In Havering (Essex) those who failed to dig out their ditches, or keep culverts open to allow the easy flow of water in this area of the Thames estuary, were presented to court and fined. If a protective wall collapsed, the fields would be flooded, and so procedures for monitoring and enforcing obligations still remained crucial, even if these were no longer attached to notions of personal servility. A wider range of offices for surveillance was in place within rural communities, and these brought most men – even modestly landed tenants and lessees – into the ambit of public action and authority.

The extent to which local office-holding impinged on the lives of men and women is made clear from the survey conducted in 1452 of the work and privilege of the forester of Bernwood Forest (Buckinghamshire). The job description had evolved over the preceding 200 years, from the period when payments for pasturing livestock were made in hens and eggs. By the mid-fifteenth century the forester was supervising the use made by those with common grazing rights, and punishing those who infringed them. He collected the dues by season: from Ambrosden and Blackthorn in Oxfordshire came 24 hens at Christmas, 24 bushels of oats at Easter, together with 240 eggs and 240 autumn work-days. The men of Brill paid 'smoksylver' of a penny a year for the right to collect dry wood in the forest, while those of Boarstall did an autumn day's work in return for the privilege. The forester's duties entailed the holding of a meeting, the *swainmote*, at which infringements were investigated and punished.

Around the royal forester were a whole series of local men serving the king in this manner as verderers and woodwards. Such appointments – and some men held several – created webs of authority and power that touched on a plethora of activities, as essential to the quality of life as they were mundane. In this manner royal privilege and presence were locally felt. The abundant resources of river and forest provided necessary food for smallholders and were a pleasurable pursuit for comfortable countrymen. The *Treatyse of Fysshynge with an Angle* was composed after 1413, a guidebook for the beginner and enthusiast alike, with instructions on making hooks and placing bait; lines were made of white horsehair. Men were fined for over-fishing, fishing with baskets and poaching, while others fished for sport.

MARRIAGE, WIDOWHOOD AND INHERITANCE

Lives everywhere were marked by the institution of marriage and by related widowhood. Marriage underpinned the ability of local men to undertake the many public tasks that were their privilege and their ambition. Because it was so central, it was also the subject of constant review. The canon law of marriage, which emphasized freedom in entering the marriage bond, stood in stark opposition to the patriarchal framework of family life and property-holding. Clandestine marriage, when it could be validated, was a binding marriage, and this opened many possibilities for transgression of parental preference: in Ireland there were many cases of clandestine marriage between people of English and of Gaelic origins. A case which reached the court as abduction, following a father's complaint against his daughter's man, might be described by a less disapproving witness as elopement. Violence within marital relations was present both in the poetical imagination, which presented it frequently and vividly, and in practice. As Chaucer had been before him, Sir Thomas Malory, the author of *Morte d'Arthur*, was twice presented to court for *raptus*, or abduction (from which the modern word rape has developed). On two occasions in 1450 he was accused of seizing Joan Smith, having broken into her husband's house, and of stealing goods. He was tried for neither case.

The ease with which marriage could be contracted by consenting people often brought a legal as well as a physical response from angry fathers and brothers (Plate 24). Court cases record the mundane circumstances which produced marriages: meetings in kitchens and barns, taverns and warrens, away from parental eyes. John Brogeam, an Englishman, worked for an Irishman, whose daughter Mabina Huns he married clandestinely. In 1448 Mabina sought annulment of this marriage on the grounds that John had already been married to another woman. The evidence which ensued showed just how displeased his friends were at his liaison with an Irishwoman. The couple did finally (re-)marry years later, a union celebrated in the local church of Stackallan (co. Meath). In 1455 in Drogheda a witness confirmed that consent had been pronounced in English in a barn 'on a clear day'.

In Ireland, as in Wales and England, marriage produced most of the business for ecclesiastical courts, displaying not an absence of adherence to church law, but rather a knowing use of the possibilities which it offered in defiance of parental choice and family expectation. Yet parental choice was most often coercive and all-controlling, bound up as it was with the fortunes of families and their lands. Sir William Plumpton of Plumpton in West Yorkshire arranged child-marriages for his offspring: his son Robert was betrothed in 1446 to the six-year-old Elizabeth, daughter of Thomas Lord Clifford of Skipton-in-Craven. When Robert died before the marriage was realized, his brother William replaced him, marrying Elizabeth in 1453, in keeping with a clause which their father had knowingly inserted into the earlier marriage contract. After William died, probably at the Battle of Towton in 1461, his father also arranged the marriages of the fatherless infant grand-daughters, Margaret and Elizabeth.

Canon law also controlled probate of wills, and here too a question touching women's rights was open to discussion, namely whether a woman could make a valid will while married. Canon law allowed women the right, which could be upheld in ecclesiastical courts; common law emphasized the husband's control over the wife and her property, probably with more success as the fifteenth century progressed. Women of the landed classes became embroiled in lengthy legal processes, as their inheritances and widow's portions were fought over by heirs. This turned women to cooperation with lawyers and male kin, but also, as the ample family papers of the Amburghs show, involved them in legal correspondence, hospitality and consultations during their widowhood and even into subsequent marriages. Joan Amburgh was called in 1443 to deal with the release of her late husband's prisoner, several years after her spouse's death.

WOMEN'S WORK AND COMMUNITY LIFE

While we have seen women act independently and effectively in many spheres of life, visual and textual representations of them as scatty, chatty, unreliable and frivolous nevertheless continued to be produced, the fantasies of learned and less learned minds alike. Although these accorded little with the lived experiences of most people, they were demeaning and demoralizing to women. A maxim which recommended that women '*penses molt et parles pou*' (think much and speak little) adorned the walls of Whalley parish church (Lancashire), just as the figure of the little devil Tituvullus, who recorded the idle chatter of women in church, appears on a misericord in Ely Cathedral. Another misericord, in St Lawrence's church, Ludlow (Shropshire), depicts a woman in a horned headdress and a bridle, which marked her as a malicious gossip.

Such representations were unpleasant, but they reflected little of a reality in which women were central to routines of work in homes and workshops. Most households which worked the land, manufactured goods, rendered services or administered manors depended at all levels on women's labour, family connections and initiative. The barber John Stubbs, who ran a 36-bed inn, a brewery and a grain store in York in 1450, could not have done so without the full participation of his wife. Although excluded from guild membership, women worked in family workshops and trained apprentices. In her will of 1458 Emmot Pannal, the widow of a saddler of York, bequeathed her tools to the servant with whom she had worked, Richard Thorpp. Women's work was crucial at every level of production. Among 153 widows identified on Sussex manors between 1422 and 1480 only 7.3 per cent remarried. As heads of households they had to hire and fire and plan agricultural routines with family members and hired hands. In 1453 in the Sussex Weald four widows attended the annual pig-fair – each with her herd. Women's social contribution was central to maintaining community bonds: exchanges of gifts and goods and assistance between and within families were clearly vital in both towns and villages.

Law affected marital affairs, relations of parents and children, the disposition of neighbours towards each other, and the exchanges between land-holders and their tenants and labourers through the offices of manorial administrators. The law operated in many spheres, but most mundanely and minutely it enlisted the energy and time of better-off peasants, those who held a sufficient amount of land to provide a comfortable surplus, some of which might be reinvested in the community. Such people, as long as they maintained good reputations, were entrusted with a wide range of responsibilities: they were tax-collectors, agents of the manor court, jurors in courts of hundred or county, churchwardens, and active in village forums for debate and the enforcement of by-laws. They were accustomed to deploying legal formulae, even in Latin, and to reflecting on affairs regional and national too.

Similarly highly integrated were the economic, social and political spheres of the lives of free and landed families of parish and county gentry, and the aspirations they maintained. Such was the case, for example, of the family of a prominent civil servant and bishop whose activities spanned the life of Henry VI: Dr Richard Andrew, first Warden of All Souls College, Oxford. He reached this position through a sparkling educational career, which took him from the Oxfordshire hamlet of his birth to Winchester College for his grammar school education, and then to New College, Oxford, for his BA and higher degree. How did he come to benefit from the patronage of these august academic and charitable institutions? He was born at Adderbury, a manor of the Bishop of Winchester, in north Oxfordshire. Richard's father held some land in that manor, but his uncle was a London grocer, prominent in Oxfordshire affairs. With his London links and a tenancy in the heart of wool-producing country, Richard Andrew's father lived prosperously from a combination of husbandry and trade. The London connection may explain how his bright son came to the attention of the bishop's circle. The country was criss-crossed by such networks of patronage, which often followed trails of business connections, regional origin, or shared experience in battle or civil service.

The appreciation of talent and the close monitoring of material resources were facilitated through rituals of hospitality and exchange which linked servants, neighbours and dependent clergy ever more closely to landed households and their spheres. Even the modest household of the priest William Savernake (d. 1460), who in the later part of his life served the Munden chantry in Bridport (Dorset) and whose weekly household accounts have survived, observed the rhythms of festivity and hospitality in the hard years of the 1450s. In January 1455 Twelfth Night was celebrated with a feast of sucking pig and goose, washed down with ale and garnished with pies from the local baker, all under the supervision of two cooks hired for the occasion, who used raisins aplenty in their cooking. Circles of friends were marked out for his favour: the rector of Bridport, two worthy local couples, the prior of St John's, Bridport; and his party was joined after the meal by a group of tenants and neighbours. On such occasions links of work were solidified, information exchanged and loyalty celebrated.

EDUCATION AND VERNACULAR RELIGION

The lifestyle of parish gentry was not so different from that depicted in the novels of Jane Austen. Regions were not isolated, but they did develop their own styles and trends. Local versions of the Christian story and local devotional styles developed too. Taste in religious patronage in mid-century Suffolk, for example, was consciously English: English saints, English texts and English style were their hallmark. Exalted women such as Isabel Bourchier, sister to Richard Duke of York, commissioned local men to compose suitable reading material in the English language. On Twelfth Night 1445 she requested that Osbern Bokenham (c.1392–1445), an Augustinian friar of Clare Priory (Suffolk), and a guest at her celebrations at Clare Castle, write the life of St Mary Magdalene in English for her edification. We gain here a glimpse of the local interaction of female patrons and religious writers, within the comfortable context of conviviality. Osbern could hardly have refused his hostess. For another woman, Katherine Denton, half-sister of the great clothier John Clopton, he wrote the life of St Katherine of Alexandria, a very popular early Christian martyr. He also wrote the holy biography of the fashionable St Anne, after whom Katherine's daughter was named. Osbern developed some expertise in writing of pious women for pious women and, after his death, his lives of thirteen holy women, in Suffolk dialect, were collected and spread as *Legendys of Hooly Wummen*.

Similarly conscious of vernacular and local traits was literary production in Welsh: saints and visionaries were celebrated, as in the poem by Rhys Goch Eryri (*c*.1385–1448) on the death and vision of heaven experienced by Beuno of Clynnog Fawr in Arfon. The interest in local martyrs was enhanced by the witness and poetry of those who visited Christian shrines in more distant locations. Such visits sometimes inspired texts which could be read in the comfort of home. The jubilee pilgrimage to Rome in 1450 inspired Robin Ddu to describe it in Welsh, just as it inspired the Carmelite friar of King's Lynn (Norfolk), John Capgrave, to write his *The Solace of Pilgrims* in English.

Gentry folk like the Stonors and Pastons habitually corresponded in English with great expressive ability and a richness of register on all matters of life: business, politics, family gossip and faith. Fifty years after Langland and Chaucer, English had become the language for most areas of work and play, and it resonated in unwritten forms of hymn and prayer, song and dance. Court poetry in elegant verse flourished in the works and then the heritage of Hoccleve and Lydgate, and new forms of expressive writing were turning romance from verse to prose. The prose romances, best exemplified in the work of Sir Thomas Malory and his *Morte d'Arthur*, were troubled literature for troubling times. The flow of verse allowed narrative to develop and touch the anxieties of readers' lives – family strife, betrayal, sibling rivalry. This prose was roughly textured and was less stylized than the poetry of the 1420s and 1430s.

Anything could be expressed and written in English. Nuns learned their rules of conduct from English texts, surgeons their intricate operations, lawyers their law; and royal officials now deliberated in English. While people spoke English before, they now also saw it defining, expressing and inspiring all aspects of life and authority. They encountered it in public, displayed on bills and signs, delicately traced on the pages of books of hours, and less delicately on amulets worn hanging from a leather strap around the neck. Such written vernacular objects in aid of devotion were many and varied and came at a variety of costs and in different sizes and shapes. Small, handy pocket-books were made for domestic use, personal use. A book, 16 cm by 30 cm, which included the lives of Saints Margaret and Dorothy and a treatise on the Virgin Mary, may have been made for a busy woman's pocket. Such reading gained occasional reinforcement from other forms of narrative display. Parishes pooled funds and hired players to enact sacred drama alongside the tales of Robin Hood: New Romney (Kent) had a play of the Resurrection in 1456, attended by people from other villages and towns.

Yet there were domains which seemed threatened by the cadences of the English language – a language not tethered by strict grammatical practice or uniform orthographic convention. It sometimes seemed too close to the local, the ephemeral, the passing, the regional, the factional, and so open to misunderstanding and imprecision, even error. There were sustained efforts to withhold whole areas of discussion and inter- action from the English tongue, in keeping with Archbishop Arundel's Constitutions of 1407 and 1409. Thus the sacrament of the mass was not to be discussed in vernacular parish instruction, Bibles in English were to be kept only for authorized use by monks and scholars, and Christ's death was best contemplated through a few English authorized devotional texts. At the same time, those whose vocation forced them to reflect on the language and its capacities – such as preachers – expressed pride in its growing powers. John Lydgate placed himself in Chaucer's tradition. In his poem *The Life of Our Lady* Lydgate called Chaucer 'my master', 'a noble rhetor, poet of Britain', who took the 'rude speech' of England 'only to illumine it'. A lavish copy of Chaucer's *Troilus and Criseyde*, with ninety illustrations to the text, was made in these decades, and was later owned by the writer John Shirley (d. 1456) (Plate 10). The frontispiece presents an imaginary scene of lords and ladies in rich attire, sitting in a rocky outdoors, around Chaucer, shown reading from his book at a pulpit. Arthurian lore was more pervasive. The epitaph inscribed on Arthur's tomb at Glastonbury was copied into a book owned by Shirley. Humbler men, such as Henry Lovelich (*fl.*1425), a member of the London Skinners' Company, developed writing into a hobby. He translated from French two Arthurian favour- ites: the history of the holy grail and the story of Merlin, probably for the delectation of his fellow craftsmen.

Intervention in reading matter and the matter of devotion was by the mid-fifteenth century decades old. Bishops were there to supervise teaching, license preaching and scrutinize the books in circulation. Mechanisms for detection of heresy were at work; Archbishop Chichele disseminated a standardized set of questions for interrogation of sus- pected heretics. These were used in individual cases as well as in occasional proactive campaigns of interrogation, such as that of the Bishop of Norwich between 1428 and 1431. Bishop Chedworth of Lincoln examined suspected Chiltern heretics in 1463 and 1464. The latter group displayed some cohesion in claiming to have learned a lot from James Wyllys, a 'lettered weaver' from Bristol. Adherence to the ideas disseminated by a charismatic preacher may well have created certain niches in belief. Like the religious ideas and practices deemed orthodox, much religious style and taste was regional and local in its appeal.

Orthodox pronouncements were regularly available from parish pulpits, but the more adventurous words were those of scholars, who committed ideas to writing. In the 1440s and 1450s Reginald Pecock (d. 1460), as Bishop of St Asaph and later of Chichester, wrote with polemical fervour against the removal of the Bible from the laity, and against the shutting down of religious debate. He studied the example of Bohemia, a kingdom torn by civil war over religious dissent and ethnic identity, and warned against the eruption of such strife in England if a heavy-handed religious policy persisted. The state's involvement in decreeing what could and could not be read only led to hypocrisy among believers, claimed Pecock; it stifled engaged discussion and the application of reason to important religious matters. His works in turn inspired debate and polemical retort, like *The Sword of Solomon* by the Oxford theologian Thomas Bourchier. Pecock's views were also examined by the king's council, which ordered the destruction of his works, while Pecock himself was sent in 1459 to spend his last days under house arrest in Thorney Abbey (Cambridgeshire). Similar, if more subtle and prudent, were the views on state intervention in religious life expressed by the Carmelite John Capgrave in his *The Solace of Pilgrims* of *c.*1450. Among his descriptions of the shrines of martyrs in Rome was that of St Cecilia's church. The martyr was renowned for her habit of carrying the gospel in her breast: here he held up the example of an independent reader, a woman and her Bible, of the type that by the 1450s the church and state feared and condemned.

The most widely circulating 'safe' text for religious instruction remained Nicholas Love's *Mirror of the Blessed Life of Jesus Christ*, still in wide circulation two generations after its composition. But for the daily use of parish priests, bishops continued to provide useful handbooks. Bishops led the pastoral thrust and the provision of support for priests: John Stafford, Bishop of Bath and Wells (and later Archbishop of Canterbury), disseminated in 1435 a translation of the syllabus for parish instruction which had been formulated 150 years earlier by Archbishop Peckham. Several fifteenth-century manuscripts contain the *Memoriale credencium – The Memorial of the Faithful –* a handbook for the instruction of layfolk. Typical of the guidance imparted was the scheme of the works of mercy: feed the hungry, give drink to the thirsty, clothe the naked, harbour the traveller, visit the sick, comfort the sorrowful and bury the dead. This scheme of works was reinforced in some parishes by visual representations: feeding and clothing appear in Little Melton church (Norfolk), and on the south wall of Toddington church (Bedfordshire) the seven works of mercy are accompanied by images of the seven sins. Similarly, and somewhat later, in Blythburgh church (Suffolk) the carved poppy-heads at the bench-ends expressed visually the teaching on the seven deadly sins: avarice sits on a money-box, slander sticks out her tongue, hypocrisy prays with prayer beads but with open eyes.

The vernacular came to encompass more and more of the space previously filled by Latin and French. But here was not solely a process of replacement; there were also more texts and genres about, and in them a variety of modes for religious expression. While the doctrines to be taught were never more clearly expounded, and the efforts to present them visually and spatially never more intense, their expression of personal taste was also sustained. Innovation and experimentation in form and content necessarily developed when so much was at stake in the formulation of religious opinion. The interiors of churches were habitually adorned with Creed windows, which were meant to remind people of Christian truth, as in Ludlow from *c.*1445–50. Doom scenes were painted to remind beholders of the punishment which might befall those who died unrepentant, and the Wheel of Life, like that in Kempley (Gloucestershire), interpreted the stages of the life-cycle and their concomitant moral dilemmas. Past and present were affected by worldly fortune; security and solace were only to be found in and through the church. It was back to basics according to the leading bishops, and those who wrote for lay people kept things simple: the Lord's Prayer was the basis of all, the fount of all prayer. Or, even more simply, every good deed and good thought could be a prayer, a link to God, as the *Disce mori (Learn to Die)* taught: long or short, prayer was the touch of the Holy Spirit. Through prayer one was bound in a knot 'so fast' that it could never be severed.

By the mid-fifteenth century there even existed small parochial libraries, with collections of pastoral books as well as statutory service books. Rectors often left books to their parishes: John Edlyngton, rector of Kirby Ravensworth (North Yorkshire), bequeathed in 1457 to the library of Boston parish church a bible, a history and devotional texts.

In 1439 the vicar of Hornby (North Riding) left a breviary to his church on condition that little boys did not soil it. A great interest in preaching materials is evident, not only in long-standing traditional collections, but in new translations from the Latin, and original contributions, such as the sermons of John Felton (d. 1434), vicar of St Mary Magdalen, Oxford. These vernacular collections served the parish clergy, especially those of urban churches. They were also avidly read by people who wished to keep abreast of new trends in religious instruction, such as the monks of Norwich and Worcester Cathedral chapters, who occasionally preached in parishes under their tutelage.

Parish clerks, those hired by the parish priest, or those attached to a chantry, or charged with private arrangements for commemoration, were also involved in other activities in the parish: education of the young, scribal services, and musical embellishment of the liturgy. Poly-phonic settings created for the exclusive space of St George's Chapel, Windsor, in the 1430s, provided material from which widely known Christmas carols developed. These decades saw the incorporation of music into the provisions made by parish churches. Churchwardens' accounts of these decades mention the purchase of organs, music books, and payments for refreshments offered to singers after particu-larly festive – hence musically demanding – services. Musicians were rewarded and could become prominent property-holders: at his death in 1453 the composer John Dunstable held tenancies in thirteen London parishes.

Some parish statutes specified the duties of care which priests and clerics were meant to observe. Those of c.1442–83 from St Stephen's, Coleman Street, London, demonstrate just how much routine mainten-ance went into the preservation of decorum and the flow of services. The parish clerk assisted the priest in several liturgical and housekeeping tasks: ringing bells, preparing bread for the mass, visits to the sick, copying out music. The clerks were to avoid discord with each other or with the parishioners. The latter were to be addressed decorously, and their payments were to be requested 'amicably'.

Among the many services rendered by clerks, education was in great demand, especially the teaching of Latin to the sons of merchants, lawyers and gentry. The workbook of Thomas Schort, a respected cleric and teacher in the diocese of Exeter between 1427 and 1465, contains examples for the demonstration of good Latin usage. At Bristol Newgate School his charges were sons of gentry families as well as of

Bristol merchants. Their translation work reflects mundane and daily affairs: 'I am sleepy for the weather is sleepy', or, more puzzlingly, 'The nearer the church, the further from God', two sentences among tens for training in translation into elegant Latin. Similarly, John Elwyn, a clerk of Holderness, bequeathed in 1465 all his grammar books to the chapel at Hendon for the edification of the children studying at the local grammar school.

Education could provide the basis for a multitude of secular and religious careers, through the entry it provided into the acquisition of rhetorical and legal skills. For a privileged and fortunate few – those who secured patrons willing to support their education, and above all those who benefited from membership in a college – education at Cambridge or Oxford, and after 1410 at St Andrews or 1451 in Glasgow, was an opening for further advancement. Bishops, who were often also involved in royal administration, increasingly boasted higher degrees in law or theology. The higher university degrees – in Roman and canon law, in theology and medicine – led to careers in royal administration, diplomacy, high-level legal work, or even in academic scholarship and teaching. The hundreds who passed through university every year, many of whom never took a degree or completed a course of study, later found a place among the many occupations in England, Ireland, Wales and on the continent which required literacy. Indeed, when reflecting on the profusion of unlicensed and heretical opinion in England, Reginald Pecock opined that too many unsuitable people had access to universities, sowing confusion when they spoke publicly and authoritatively on complex religious issues. He preferred fewer degrees more sparingly given.

The religious life of the parish did not suffice for all. While Henry IV had concentrated on maintaining orthodoxy's upper hand, Henry V used religious imagery for the exaltation of Englishness. In Henry VI's years, under the guise of orthodoxy, a great production of styles and opportunities was under way. Women of gentry and aristocratic families lived active and edifying lives in nunneries. The nuns of Barking (Essex) enjoyed a high level of learning, to judge from the regular stocks of books and the broad range of texts which their library contained at this time. Enclosed religious life marked a woman's elevated social status and offered an alternative to a marriage dictated by her father's social and political ambitions. The women who served in the administrative offices of nunneries were faced with a wide range of challenges and contacts with the world. The records of visitations of nunneries tell us not only of the many lapses from monastic discipline – meeting lay people, chatter and dancing, irregular dress – but also of the administrative tasks which running a nunnery entailed. Nuns kept in close touch with family and friends in this period, and adorned their cells with keepsakes and personal belongings.

Men's religious quests were more likely to take them far from home. Joining an order of friars – Franciscan, Dominican, Augustinian or Carmelite – was like joining the army: a friar might be posted anywhere in his native country or in his order's service abroad. Male religious enjoyed more freedom than women in reinventing their physical appearance. Thomas Scrope, an ex-Carmelite, was known in Norfolk c.1425, in his hair shirt and sack, wearing an iron chain, preaching the gospel and proclaiming the new Jerusalem. Two former monks of Goldcliff (Gwent) served Bridgwater parish church (Somerset), and supported themselves by saying masses for the dead.

1450 – ANNUS HORRIBILIS

In 1450 a whole series of long-term tensions and aggravating events combined to produce instability and violence of unprecedented diversity and range. It followed a year in which royal finances collapsed and the Exchequer no longer paid the salaries of state officials; and in which after the cession of substantial English holdings in France Charles VII continued his reconquest of Normandy. Those involved in policy and its execution – above all the most powerful man at court, William de la Pole Duke of Suffolk, and officials of his administration – were made to carry the blame. *Ad hominem* political attacks and humiliations followed: the estates of Reginald Boulers, Abbot of Gloucester were attacked, as he was pilloried for his role in the negotiations in France; the king's chief adviser, Adam Molyens, Bishop of Chichester – a man who had risen from a humble Chancery clerkship – was murdered for his diplomatic role; Suffolk was accused of abuses of power and exiled, but was brutally murdered by sailors on the ship taking him to exile in France, and his body thrown overboard. There were storms too, and an accumulation of hardship caused by repeated taxation and provisioning of armies. Agricultural production had passed its worst decade, in the 1430s, and was probably improving. The conditions were ripe for unrest and political action, for men rarely march when the situation is at its worst, but rather vent their frustration when the family's livelihood is more secure.

The sense of disorder touched not only the political classes but the country more widely. Sentiment was not so much directed against Henry VI, but pleaded for his vigilance and responsible engagement with those around him. Bills and political ditties warning against conspiracies appeared: there were traitors about, sworn into bands and the king should 'let them drink as they have brewed'. More caustic was the Latin alliterative refrain:

> O king, if you be a king, rule yourself, or be a king of nothing;
> If you do not rule yourself well, you will have nothing but a name.[*]

Since the king did not act, others did.

Rulers are not blamed for the advent of bad weather, nor even for the recurrence of disease; people sought providential and moral explanations for those. But kings were weakened by bad management and corruption, by a failure of governance, and, as the events since 1381 showed, communities had a clear idea as to who the culprits were. Grassroots political culture nurtured an extraordinary loyalty to the king, and preferred to blame bureaucrats and advisers, whose evil influence was felt not only in court but in the management of their regional fiefdoms, thus affecting the life of modest people. There was not a single area in which the king's advisers were doing well. Royal debt was worse than ever: at £372,000 more than double the £168,000 which had worried parliament in 1433. In Kent a movement of complaint stirred which called for the king's repair of bad governance. A Welsh tradesman, Philip Corveser, was accused of calling on the Welsh to rebel against the English mayors of towns with which they traded at a disadvantage.

As is often the case, the sense of discontent came to be associated with a figure who attracted a great deal of blame and hatred – the culprit in 1449–50 was William de la Pole Duke of Suffolk. A veteran of Henry V's wars in France, active on the royal council and then a prominent diplomat and courtier, Suffolk led the court which sought accommodation with France and an end to war. He was thus associated

---

[*]   *O rex, si rex es, rege te, vel eris sine re rex,*
    Nomen habes sine re, nisi te recte regas.

with the cession of lands to France in 1447, and to the loss of purpose in foreign affairs, together with mismanagement of the vast sums which had been allocated towards maintenance of French outposts and garrisons. When he sought parliament's support and confidence in him in 1449, he found that gathering intent on impeaching him. Henry VI was able to commute the punishment to one of five years' banishment. But Suffolk was never to return – murdered by sailors on his way into exile in France. Yet the men who killed him flew the banner of St George, loyal subjects of the king, doing dirty work on his behalf. In the territories once influenced by the Duke of Suffolk – East Anglia, the Thames Valley, Kent – his followers and relatives were exposed to ridicule and violence.

Discontent, violence and disorder were brewing in the south-east, and detailed accounts of the movement known as Cade's Rebellion have survived. Unlike the events of 1381, it received a somewhat sympathetic depiction in London chronicles. In May 1450 Jack Cade led his men of Kent – joined later by a contingent from Sussex – on a parody of a royal entry into London. He was dressed in a blue velvet gown lined with fur, and crowned with a straw hat. He processed to London Bridge, Southwark and then back to Cheapside, while rumours abounded about rampages by disbanded soldiers in Southampton, and the beheading of royal advisers – all true. Cade and his men pinned their hopes on a champion, Richard Duke of York, who would help shore up royal rule. They claimed, 'We blame not all the lords . . . nor all men of law, but all such as may be found guilty by just and true inquiry by the law.' Like the rebels of 1381, they possessed a familiar as well as utopian idea of law as a tool for justice, and as a tool for social and economic redress in the hands of to modest people.

While the men of Sussex were contemplating action, a more radical group emerged with slogans such as 'the king is a fool'. They gathered in groups in market towns, demanding the lowering of rents below 2d. per acre. The autumn of 1450 saw these groups, composed mainly of artisans – tanners, shinglers, thatchers, dyers, masons, cappers, smiths – mostly young and unmarried men, gather to hear speeches and occasionally threaten tax-collectors, stewards, sheriffs and under-sheriffs. By 1451 rule had been re-established and judicial inquiries had sought out perpetrators, although almost all were pardoned.

THE END OF THE HUNDRED YEARS WAR

What did the losses in France mean to the English crown and its people? A smaller number of captaincies, loss of life, and loss of prestige among magnates, whose reputations controlled regions in France, as well as in England and the Marches. Beyond the tens of magnates, there were thousands of gentry; loss in France created scenes which touched them, scenes such as those enacted in Paris, following the Siege of Pontoise of 1441, when English captives were processed in rags through the capital, fifty-three of them tied together and plunged into the river to drown. France had represented opportunity and fostered an ethos of service. While the military challenges of the 1430s and 1440s had exposed competition and divergent policies among England's magnates, first between Beaufort and Gloucester, then between York and Somerset, France remained the central royal project. Defence of the royal title and lands there blended seamlessly with the very essence of the king's expectation of loyalty and gratitude. As for the people of Normandy, they no longer feared English reconquest and opened their gates to French forces.

Shakespeare's image of John Talbot Earl of Shrewsbury and his dramatic death with his son in the battle of Castillon (1453), the last battle of the Hundred Years War, is wholly inaccurate. Yet Talbot is a good example of an effective, loyal and responsible soldier and administrator, and there were others. The message he penned into the book which was his wedding-gift to Henry VI and Margaret of Anjou declared: 'My sole desire is to serve the King and you well, even until death. Let everyone know: my sole desire to the King and you.' Men like Talbot had been born into a kingdom which posed clear objectives and opportunities for military exploits, high-level military administration, and the related tasks of diplomacy. For lesser men there were many posts as captains of garrisons, under the direction of magnates appointed as lieutenants-in-chief. A man like Sir John Cressy, who died in 1445, is a good example of the numerous possible careers created by Henry V's conquests and available under Henry VI, until 1453. In 1430, at the age of twenty-three, Sir John formed part of the coronation expedition, as a man tied by indenture to Thomas Lord Roos. In 1432 he moved on to the next official, the Earl of Arundel, and in 1435 led his own company of twenty-eight men-at-arms and ninety archers in that year's expedition. He experienced defeat as commander of the garrison of Eu, taken by the French in 1436, and moved to the service of Richard Duke of York at Caen later that year. In 1441 he led another retinue which was part of the effort to defend Pontoise, and was appointed captain of Gisors in 1442. The last year of his life saw him in charge of three garrisons, until his death in March 1445. He was buried in his parish of Dodford in Northamptonshire.

Families extended their local links into the enterprise in France, maintaining abroad the loyalties and relations they harboured at home. The Standish family, for example, developed a link with the garrison of Pontoise: in 1437 Henry Standish was captain of the garrison, and several men-at-arms and archers bore that same family name. In the Welsh retinue of Griffith Don at Tancarville in 1438 half of the archers were Welshmen. Conversely, the reality of death, injury and dispersion, as well as of being taken captive or going native, meant that once in France retinue ranks had often to be filled by whoever might be willing and available. Men who had earned ransoms in France could retire with great homes, such as that of Sir Roger Fiennes at Herstmonceaux in Sussex, built in 1441. He used Flemish treasure as well as Flemish brick and workers to build this magnificent moated home, befitting a veteran of Agincourt, who also served as Treasurer under Henry VI. A whole legal and financial system supported the efforts of such men. Financial services developed to assist wartime transactions. For example, Filippo Borromei and Co. transferred £1,631 4s. 11d. from an account in their London branch in 1436 for the final payment of Sir Thomas Rempston's ransom, incurred after the Battle of Patay in 1429.

The garrison system established under Henry V was effective for about a decade, but from the 1420s it came under pressure from the new technology of artillery, adopted by the French with the aid of foreign, mostly Italian, experts. The French efforts of the 1430s were patchy, but rather than passive defence they saw the action of ad hoc detachments – often with familiar Scottish soldiers – aimed at harassing a single town and its garrison. By the late 1430s English superiority was seriously challenged: Henry VI wrote after the fall of Castelnau-de-Cernès to the French: 'it had been broke down during siege . . . by cannon and engines'. By 1450 it took only sixteen days to dismantle the walls of Bayeux. The initiative was with the cannons of the attackers, hardly matched by the tenacity of the defenders; in 1451 Bourg-en-Bresse (Normandy) surrendered after six days of heavy artillery action. John

Talbot's last battle, at Castillon, was similarly lost by the English to French gunners 'through breaches made by artillery'. Reflections on the new technology were penned in English in the form of a paraphrase of Vegetius's classic text on siege warfare.

The military resources of England and Wales in France had to be rethought and by 1452–3 men from garrisons in Normandy were redistributed among the seventeen garrisons of Gascony. It is this type of action which bred disappointment in leadership, sharpened by the collapse of future prospects. To these were added the hardships caused by incursions in the northern Borders, and the unsettling effect of news about them. Nor were there economic prospects to gladden the heart. A large variety of indicators bears witness to a decline in the incomes of big landlords – religious institutions and magnates – and there was a dearth of food in some years, especially the 1430s, exacerbated in the west Midlands by an outbreak of plague. No noble family collapsed because of economic hardship, nor even through the more frequent demands to pay ransoms. It was probably the gentry, the parish gentry, and smaller religious institutions that felt the collapse in demand for land and the price of produce most acutely. In north-east Kent, a good farming area, the falling demand for foodstuffs meant that lower seeding ratios were applied: on the Christ Church, Canterbury, estates in 1444, there was a drop from four to three bushels per acre for wheat, five to four for barley, and then for oats from six to five in 1444, four in 1447, and five in the 1450s. In parallel, livestock flocks were reduced, and fattened rather than kept for their milk and wool, produce hard to sell even to the markets of London and the Low Countries.

The faultlines which characterized groups and communities were exacerbated in an atmosphere of despair and distrust. Welshmen in English towns were arrested for suspected sedition, and tenants refused to provide services and in some cases disrupted work. There were real complaints and misery in the 1430s and 1440s, a rise in prices of the vital commodities which fed peasant families, sustained the income of land-holders large and small, and maintained the trading classes and their dependants, the providers of services and goods in cities. The export of broadcloth fell from 55,000 cloths on average in the years 1438–48 to 34,000 in 1448–71. The boom which had seen thriving cattle herds in the north-east in the 1430s and early 1440s ended with disease and the collapse of demand in the late 1440s. The sheep farming of Horsley Manor (Gloucestershire) brought little profit to Bruton Priory by 1444–52. Properties in towns fell in value; thus Oseney Abbey outside Oxford saw a decline in its income over the 1440s from £201 c.1435 to £170 in 1449. In town and country a chronic inability to collect rents and the resulting fall in rental income is apparent on the pages of letters, such as the correspondence of the members of the Paston family in Norfolk, and in the account rolls of manors. The accounts of the estates of the Bishop of Worcester demonstrate that resistance to payment of dues was organized, the result of real hardship. The European bullion crisis further made the payment of dues difficult, because of the absence of suitable coin. In the 1440s royal mints were producing only 5 per cent of the coin minted in the 1420s. Economic cycles and political inadequacy made the 1440s and 1450s very trying times for those who already had land and status, and miserable for those who depended on a fine balance of subsistence agriculture and small-scale exchange.

POLITICAL CHALLENGE: THE DUKE OF YORK

Out of the desires of the men of Kent, the power of dynasty, the confusion of magnates and the inability of King Henry to offer leadership arose a challenge by a most potent magnate, the king's kinsman, Richard Duke of York. The petitions of the men of Kent singled out the corruption of royal officials, but Jack Cade also claimed to be associated with the Mortimers, and thus with the Yorks. By 1450 popular prophecies were circulating with an explicit demand to replace the king by the Duke of York. York had held a series of important and testing positions: Lieutenant of France and, most recently, since 1447 Lieutenant of Ireland. He had the lineage, the talent and the experience to make him an effective ruler, even an heir apparent.

York gained his experience in France, where his wealth often subsidized a large segment of English expenditure, debts which were never repaid. When Henry VI sent him to Ireland, an arena ripe for influence was opened to him. In the decades leading up to his arrival, English ambition in Ireland had all but crumbled, with effective rule over only a third of the nominally Anglo-Irish region. Rule was patchy outside the four counties of Dublin, Louth, Meath and Kildare. Ireland was different from Normandy, inasmuch as it had a political community integrated deeply into the English one. The initiatives for self-defence and tower-building of the 1420s, which offered subsidy for fortification, still remaining in Kilchief (Down) and Kilmallock (Limerick), had been all but abandoned in the years of Henry VI's majority.

York was heir to substantial holdings in Ireland. Upon arrival there with 600 men in 1448 he led a force into county Wicklow and succeeded in restraining the O'Neills. In Ireland there was proof of dereliction, and it offered York the motive for and the means of organizing in relative autonomy. In 1450 he crossed the sea to his castle at Denbigh, and then marched through Wales and the Marches and on to St Albans and then to London, where he presented bills of complaint and grievance. His party used pamphlets and legal challenges in parliament, and always presented the duke as acting in the common good. In the parliament of 1450–51 Thomas Young of Bristol petitioned that York should be made the king's heir, a step too soon and too far, for which he was arrested. But York came out the winner from his feud with Edmund Beaufort Duke of Somerset over policy in France, which resulted in his denunciation of Somerset as an evil counsellor, a greedy administrator in France, and unworthy of the king's trust. As to York's own qualities, these were made clear in the 1452 Shrewsbury Manifesto: he was full of worship and honour and manhood, and loyal to the king. When Henry fell ill in 1453 – and it is unclear what ailed him, but it affected his mind as well as his body – reforming York was the man most suited to the task of Protector. The Clare Roll, that genealogy of virtue and fecundity penned around 1453 by Osbern of Bokenham, led inexorably from Edward III's loins to those of Richard Duke of York. It was a line presented through continuous progeny reared by good women, through Anne, York's mother, back to Lionel, Edward III's son (d. 1368). When it came, York's claim was made to seem stronger than Henry IV's had been: it had full dynastic force and was underpinned by demonstrable capacity and experience.

Protector York had the support of a large affinity: the Nevilles, his kin in the north, and the Earl of Salisbury. In 1454 he marched north to put down the Yorkshire rebellion led by the Duke of Exeter. But when the king regained his health, York's control of council and position as deputy was revoked. This was a test of York's ambition and loyalty. Would he step down and accept a more modest political role? He did not, and an encounter was forced between Yorkists and Lancastrians at St Albans in May 1455, in which Somerset lost his life. This was not a rebellion but a feuding confrontation, and after it the queen's leadership was marked by the fear of York, who had emerged as all but heir apparent. In the next few years York and his son, Edward Earl of March, withdrew to Ireland and to Calais respectively, building up armies and avoiding confrontation until their forces and alliances were ripe.

In 1459 York was deemed a traitor, an accusation moved by Margaret of Anjou in fear for her son's inheritance, and the Act of Attainder of the Coventry Parliament stripped him of land and office. York returned to England in 1460 to fight his case, landing at Redbank at the north-west tip of the Wirral on 9 September 1460. He travelled through the Marches to join his wife at Abingdon. The aim was to demand redress, for a second time. The Act of Accord of October 1460 did just that, and more. For it granted that after Henry VI's death the Duke of York would inherit the crown, rather than Edward, the seven-year-old prince. The desire to replace an incompetent king with an able ruler was fulfilled at the expense of the sacred principle of dynastic continuity which all magnates greatly cherished in their own lives. It is easy to imagine the outrage and anxiety that such an accord prompted: the displacement of the hereditary principle, the dispossession of a prince. The chronicler of St Albans Abbey, among others, claimed that York had aggressively made his claim in parliament, disregarding the king, first demanding the crown and then settling for the accord. His real enemy now was no longer the king, but the queen, the mother of the dispossessed prince. Her forces were in the north, where the real opposition had concentrated. Marching northwards, York and his supporters encamped by Wakefield on 30 December 1460, where they were surprised by Margaret of Anjou's force: York was killed in the battle.

The bills posted on the gates of York, where the Duke's body was taken, were penned in a ripe political idiom, and the public humiliation of his corpse was political theatre in the round. Recounting the events, the monastic chronicler John Walthamstead inverted the story of Christ's mocking and crucifixion: the body was crowned with a paper crown, and he was mocked: 'Hail, King, without kingdom. Hail, King, without inheritance. Hail, Duke and Prince, without people and possession.' After this mocking, York's head was cut off and displayed on the gate of York, the city which had been his home, an act inspired by a Devon squire, James Luttrell. Here was a sorry end to the Yorkist claim, as Salisbury was executed on the next day at Pontefract, and York's son Rutland was killed in battle.

But York's ample progeny was moved to continue his claim, now spurred on by the deaths and humiliation of father and brother. Henry VI was still in London, alone, and it was to London that York's son, Edward Earl of March, with the Earl of Warwick at his side, directed his 'great force' in February 1461. A London chronicle describes his triumph as an act of acclamation supported by magnates and the Archbishop of Canterbury, who did not believe that 'Harry were worthy to reign'. On 4 March a gathering at St Paul's declared the Earl of March King Edward IV, in a religious ceremony accompanied by sermon and litany. Henry VI went into exile in Scotland, while Margaret of Anjou and her son sought succour in France with a group of Lancastrians. London and the Commons hailed the new king.

6

Little England and a Little Peace, 1461–1485

When Richard Duke of York was named Henry VI's heir in October 1460, this seemed to many a mockery of the principle of lineal inheritance, but it may also be seen as an affirmation of the dignity of kingship. Kings had to act like kings, and if they failed to do so, failed spectacularly, their authority was questioned. Henry's failure was not the sole basis for the Yorkist claim. Even as they criticized the policies of Henry's rule, the Yorkists also made a strong genealogical claim for inheritance, through the dynastic link offered by Philippa, daughter of Lionel, son of Edward III (Plate 23). As we have seen, Richard Duke of York ended his life on the battlefield and finally became a subject of mockery for all to jeer at outside the gates of the city of York. But he also gained a victory: within months of his death at Wakefield, his son was crowned King Edward IV. The rise of his other sons, George and Richard, was also secured, and they garnered some of the greatest titles the kingdom had to offer. As to posterity, Shakespeare's dramatic poetry turned the Duke of York into a martyr in *Henry VI Part 3*.

Following the battle of Mortimer's Cross near the Welsh border in February 1461, and that at Towton, half-way between Leeds and York, in March, the Yorkists ascended to power. The eldest son of Richard Duke of York – Edward Earl of March – became king. Margaret of Anjou, the Prince of Wales, and their supporters (Devon, Northumberland, Somerset) failed to secure London. Edward did. George Neville, Bishop of Exeter and future Archbishop of York, proclaimed the Yorkist case on 1 March at St John's Fields, and then preached in the traditional speaking corner of London, St Paul's Cross, expounding Edward's legitimacy. This public acclamation was followed by a coronation, a sumptuous affair, as the consecrations of usurpers often are. A ceremonial of praise was reinstated after decades of oblivion. Edward was then crowned and anointed with Becket's oil in a ceremony that restored sections of the coronation ritual long unused. The king was welcomed with hymns such as the *Laudes regiae* that had been left out since the time of Richard II:

> True King Edward, upright King Edward
> Just, law-worthy and legitimate King Edward
> To whom we all wish to subject ourselves
> And to whose yoke of rule we wish to admit ourselves humbly.

Every aspect of court ceremonial was soon mobilized to support the image of stability, good sense, royal authority, and an unassailable British tradition. Grassroots political aspirations and vernacular prophetic impulses were conjoined with a political inclusion of erstwhile foes once they offered their loyalty. In his first parliament Edward put the historical record right and exculpated his forebears; that parliament annulled Richard of Cambridge's condemnation for his part in the Southampton Plot against Henry V, of 1415. In 1461–2 Edward faced the fear of invasion from the alliance created around Margaret of Anjou and Henry VI in the court of France. One spy reported an international conspiracy including the King of Denmark and the Dukes of Brittany and Burgundy. There was still some unrest at home, but by the end of 1462 London had been pacified, and Lancastrian supporters in the north were routed in 1464 at Hedgeley Moor and Hexham; Edward won most of the battles he fought. Foes from across the channel remained quiet for the time being.

Edward's own behaviour caused a threat to this new-found stability by his clandestine marriage in 1464 to Elizabeth Woodville Lady Grey, the widow of Sir John Grey, son of Lord Ferrers of Grosby, who had died at the second battle of St Albans in 1461. The marriage to this mother of two sons was a match which brought neither fortune nor diplomatic advantage. It was even politically injurious, since it spurned the advanced plans for an alliance between Edward IV and the sister of Louis XI, King of France. The liaison began secretly, at the house of Elizabeth's father at Grafton, and a low-key coronation followed in May 1465. Some even claimed that the match was so unwise that it must have been the result of malign magic. During the crisis of 1470 Edward IV's mother-in-law Jacquetta of Luxembourg, Dowager Duchess of Bedford, was accused of having used a figurine, 'made like a man of arms', to cast an incantation on the king and lead him into the impolitic union.

With Elizabeth Woodville and her kin – and then with the ten children they had together – Edward turned the expansive court of Margaret of Anjou and Henry VI into a cosy and close-knit household. His courtiers spent evenings 'in talking of chronicles of kings', in the king's chamber. Edward IV was loyal to members of his household, and took care to provide for them in old age. The *Black Book* of Edward's household shows, *c.*1472, the efforts to keep the household on a sound financial footing. Edward IV planned the court's life to its utmost detail; he planned the budget minutely down to items in the diet offered to its members. He who could rule his household, could rule his country – this was the message of the Yorkist spin-doctors. After terrible bloodshed, Edward IV had brought peace to a war-torn country, and was likely to seek taxes only in support of the most urgent tasks. This image of modest domesticity was a powerful political platform for Edward IV's first reign: here was a king who lived a simple life, whose wife was more modest in her tastes and expenditure than her predecessor had been. Elizabeth was not a well-connected French aristocrat, brought up on the finest of European art and romance, but a woman who fitted comfortably into the life of London. Indeed she would have felt at home among the Skinners, who honoured her with membership and an image, as Virgin, in their Guild Book. The Guild of Luton equally delighted in placing the royal couple alongside the Trinity in the frontispiece to its book of *c.*1475.

The courts of Henry VI and Edward IV differed in many ways. Henry VI enjoyed, above all, decorous religious display. When he participated in events which smacked of boastful chivalry he did so half-heartedly and awkwardly. His father had been famed for his prowess in battle; yet the court of Henry VI had in fact been strangely austere, without the habitual bombast of jousts and the excitement of anticipation before duels of famous champions. When the English court staged jousts as part of the entertainment in Paris around Henry VI's coronation, these were miserable events. A chronicler of Paris commented that they were not even worthy of the wedding of a Parisian merchant. Henry VI saw, in the ceremonial of the Garter, religious ritual rather than courtly display.

Conversely, Edward IV enjoyed and promoted the chivalric aesthetic as the cultural frame within which bonds of loyalty and camaraderie were cemented. Here were echoes of Edward III rather than of Edward the Confessor. Edward IV seized the occasion of his first Garter ceremony to make a dozen new members: foreign dignitaries – a Sforza, a Douglas – and peers such as William Lord Hastings and John Lord Scrope of Bolton, but also famous knights like Sir William Chamberlain, who had displayed courage in battle in France, and Sir John Asteley of Nailstone (Leicestershire), a famous champion jouster. The queen's brother Anthony Woodville wrote about chivalry, and practised it too. He challenged the Bastard of Burgundy (the Duke of Burgundy's illegitimate son) to a competition of arms in 1467, an occasion for enhancement of the renewed Anglo-Burgundian alliance on which peace and prosperity depended. The Yorkist court was small, with only a few tens of close associates around the king, but it had a single and clear centre, and it enjoyed and revelled in its success and good fortune, for a while. Gabriel Tetzel, a Bohemian diplomat who visited in 1466, commented on the court's decorum; he particularly noted the strict precedence observed in the queen's eating arrangements.

Edward passed the Act of Attainder in November 1461, which affected those magnates and gentry who had fought on the Lancastrian side. Their lands fell into Edward's hands in great regional blocks. The Thames Valley, where Margaret of Anjou had developed a solid base of support (the participants in which were now in exile), became crown land. In Ireland the lands of the Earls of Ormond, tenacious Lancastrian supporters, were confiscated. Edward IV was then able to use the lands forfeited by diehard Lancastrians to reward those who had stood by him. He chose to promote relatives, rewarding his brothers generously: Richard of Gloucester in the north, George of Clarence in Ireland and, from 1462, in the Midlands. After his marriage to Elizabeth Woodville Edward IV embraced a whole new group of kin, the Woodvilles. Elizabeth had five brothers, whom he advanced and rewarded. The Woodvilles took to court life like ducks to water.

Edward was presented and thus imagined as a very British king. In the first decade of his rule his preoccupation was drawn little to France, the first king in over a century who was not forced to think constantly about Gascony or Normandy. This new reality was acknowledged in the habitual use of the sole title 'Roy d'Angleterre' or, at most, 'Roy d'Angleterre et Seigneur d'Irlande', by most European princes when addressing Edward IV, although Chancery still used the fuller, more ambitious title. The loss of continental territories occasioned an assertion of the value and prestige of those in the British Isles. An emissary of the Irish parliament in 1474 described the Irish territories:

'His land of Ireland . . . is one of the members of his most noble crown and eldest member thereof.' The king was reminded that he was 'bound to the defence of his land of Ireland'.

The rich vernacular and Latin traditions of prophecy – such as the Bridlington prophecies – were rewritten to match a Yorkist king and a British kingdom. Prophetic writings and court ritual all aimed at making a virtue of the new geopolitics. The Yorkist sense of dynasty and history was different from that which prevailed before it: Yorkist fortunes, it was now claimed, were won not through conquest, but through dynastic right and good governance. Welsh bards responded with enthusiasm: here was the fruit of a Mortimer–Llewellyn marriage. Rhymed chronicles and prophetic effusions depicted in words and diagrams the arrival of a rightful king and his lineage. An anonymous chronicle from the west Midlands figured seven ways by which Edward's claim could be made, and ended with the hope for a long, peaceful rule:

> That he may long abide in holt, hill or plain
> In court or in coast where he likes to abide.
> The fox is fled, and fallen is pride.

Edward IV's coin of 1465 showed the ship of state, majestic, and with the cross as its mast. This image of a well-steered vessel was confirmed by the approval of parliament: the Commons were so delighted with Edward's peace that it voted three subsidies to support war in Scotland in 1462 and 1463, and a planned invasion of France in 1467, a project which was never realized, but the threat of which facilitated the signing of a treaty with France. All this effort was directed at shoring up a king whose advent had been steeped in blood, and whose rule was irritated by the existence of another, living king and an active queen, mother to an heir.

Exhaustion with the turbulence and uncertainty of politics favours the last man left standing. This was Edward IV, even as Henry VI lived in Scotland and, later, with his queen, at St Mihiel, in the Bar, a French county between Champagne and Burgundy which was held by René of Anjou. Around the ousted royal couple developed courts in exile, a combination of those who were utterly dependent, the opportunistic, and the idealistic. John Fortescue, chief justice, went into exile, first with Henry VI in Scotland and then at Margaret's court in France. There, in the late 1460s, he wrote a tract, *The Governance of England*, that was more ambitious than any previous attempt at analysis of the English political system. According to Fortescue, Edward IV was 'barred' both by law and by reason from any claim to the throne.

Margaret of Anjou still had connections, and she toured France and Burgundy in search of support for the Lancastrian case. A medal designed in her honour in 1465 shows her still regal, in a formal continental style. In 1463 Margaret turned to Philip the Good, Duke of Burgundy and Count of Flanders, for support, but the attitude to the Lancastrians in the Burgundian court had always been at best lukewarm. In France sentiments towards them were also mixed, since Charles VI of France had been appalled by the deposition of Richard II. York's rise and aspirations were seen by Thomas Basin, Bishop of Lisieux, as justified responses to Richard II's deposition and murder, creating a positive disposition towards Edward IV in the 1470s. Conversely, a reorientation in European politics saw a withdrawal of Flemish interest from alliance with the French crown, and a move towards a more independent policy, sometimes friendly towards England. The marriage of Edward's sister, Margaret of York, and Charles the Bold Duke of Burgundy, in 1467, solidified the existing links between the two countries and dynasties. It had been carefully prepared by the queen's able brother, Anthony Woodville, with William Lord Hastings. If the Lancastrians were seen as the conquerors of large parts of France, continental historians remembered this too, and favoured the son of York, who had deposed them.

For all this progress in pacification at home and diplomatic affinities abroad, the tale of dynastic unrest was not over. A serious defeat was in store for the Yorkists at the battle of Edgcote, near Banbury (Northamptonshire) in 1469. Following the extensive support which Edward IV had amassed and the loyalty he had fostered among his household, a new rhetoric had to be created to vilify him in 1469. A manifesto publicized by George Duke of Clarence (the king's now alienated brother), Richard Neville Earl of Warwick, and his brother George Neville Archbishop of York, likened Edward to a string of inadequate rulers who had made the land suffer: Edward II, Richard II and Henry VI. His court was said to be one of 'mischievous rule'; and there is some evidence of popular discontent with the continuation of years of taxation, and of plans for campaigns abroad. By 1468 John de Vere Earl of Oxford turned and gave evidence against the group, revealing the scope of its ambitions. There followed a judicial commission led by Richard Duke of Gloucester in January 1469, to investigate the extent of planned treason.

Edward IV had perhaps been both too lenient and too grasping in his first years. Some of the ways in which he managed patronage meant that the balance of influence between York and Lancaster was being unsettled at the level of local land-holding. In a county such as Lincolnshire, traditional Lancastrian estates had been handed to Yorkist supporters. Similarly, in the Midlands, Lord Sudeley, a stabilizing and reliable figure, was made to hand over his castle to Gloucester in 1468. Fear of the loss of hereditary title and the unsettling of spheres of influence rekindled the animus of the 1450s in the shires.

One might ask why – in a country which saw relative prosperity and peace, with a king who was almost self-supporting, if somewhat brutal, with an economy recovering its ability to trade and sustain stability in prices, and with a flourishing array of religious forms and public displays of piety – such disorder and bloodshed followed. Discontent lingered among magnates and their supporters. Warwick's grievance seems to have been personal and dynastic: the king stood in the way of his ambition to marry his daughter to Clarence, and thus to elevate his kin into the royal family. Warwick held important appointments, such as keeper of the royal forest in the north, and controlled vast tracts of land in the Midlands and the north. These did not produce a satisfied and loyal subject, but an ambitious and restless one. Throughout the late 1460s his discontent moved like a shadow behind Edward's initiatives: he argued for peace with France just as Edward was planning the marriage of his sister in Burgundy, and he petitioned secretly for papal dispensation for his own daughter's marriage. He spread his generosity knowingly upon his entry into London in July 1469, when he took over government, securing it through the battle of Edgcote, after which rebel victory King Edward was kept prisoner in Warwick Castle. Edward IV's surviving army regained London in October and forced Warwick into exile. When Warwick returned from Calais with an army in October 1470, through French support, he was joined by the king's brother, Clarence, and the remnants of Margaret of Anjou's supporters. Those who turned up for the Lancastrians were, like most political alliances, a collection of diverse groups of supporters and Yorkist dissenters.

The result of the Lancastrian triumph of 1469 was a restoration – known as the re-adeption – of Henry VI to the throne. Yet this was a short reversal. In Bruges, in an exile spent in one of the most gracious and artistically refined households of Europe, that of Louis of Bruges,

Lord of Gruthuye, Edward planned his reassertion as king. It was not so much that he relied upon mass support – no such overwhelming enthusiasm was ever displayed for either side in the battles of these decades – but rather that he expected to face only little resistance. He landed at Ravenspur at the beginning of spring 1471, and marched through Yorkshire and into the Midlands. Well-circulated bills prepared the way and a first-hand account, *The Arrivall of Edward IV*, by a member of Edward's household, traces the march to Barnet and then Tewkesbury, a royal entry full of portents and wonders, which foretold his victory in the month of May. As Edward and his followers attended the Palm Sunday service at Daventry church, a miracle was said to have occurred: the wooden casing which surrounded an image of St Anne – images were covered during Holy Week – 'gave a great crack, and a little opened' and then closed, all without human touch. All were amazed, and agreed that St Anne was 'a good prognostic' to Edward's political reinstatement. At Tewkesbury the Yorkists overwhelmed their opposition and, most importantly, killed the Lancastrian heir to the contended throne. Desperate Lancastrians sought refuge in the ancient minster, but were dragged out and cruelly hacked to pieces. Yorkists delighted in turning this place from a site of trauma to a site of memory: the abbey's ceiling was soon painted with images of the 'sun of York'.

RESTORATION AND RECONSTRUCTION

After 1471 Edward was more confident, and could count on the support of quite a number of powerful advisers and supporters. His brother Richard Duke of Gloucester emerged as a true lieutenant, who captured and tried opponents and led the commissions of array in southern England following the regime change. He probably did even more, and worse, for his brother, by arranging the killing of Henry VI in the Tower. Gloucester no doubt judged, as Shakespeare once assumed, that

> The presence of a king engenders love
> Amongst his subjects and his loyal friends,
> As it disanimates his enemies. (*1 Henry VI*, III.i.185–7)

Official accounts, however, claimed that the once king died of 'displeasure and melancholy'.

As the Lancastrian enemy was destroyed, cracks began to emerge within the ruling family, as the ambitious brothers vied for spheres of influence and lived the legacy of violence. George Duke of Clarence, now a repentant rebel, was rewarded for his late return to the family fold. He held much of the land which Warwick and his followers had forfeited; he was, after all, married to Warwick's daughter, Isabel, and through her claimed the Beauchamp and Despenser inheritances too. By 1471–2 Gloucester and Clarence were in dispute over large tracts of land, so much so that they were summoned by the king to air their discontents before the royal council. In 1472 the stakes rose as Richard married Anne Neville, who had been betrothed to Edward Prince of Wales, son of Henry VI, by her father Warwick in 1470. Richard had to kidnap Anne, his enemy's younger daughter, who had lost her father at the battle of Barnet in April 1471 and her husband-to-be soon after at Tewkesbury, from the Neville/Clarence household, where she lived under the tutelage of her sister Isabel and Clarence. Richard placed Anne in sanctuary while he argued her case for some of her family lands in the Midlands. Clarence and Gloucester were neighbours in the Midlands, and had resolved many disputes over land quite amicably in the mid-1470s. But Gloucester was never fully reconciled to Clarence's return, and nor was the king, their brother. In 1477 a confession was coerced out of a friar who dabbled with magic, which incriminated a member of Clarence's household in acts of magic and divination aimed at hastening the death of the king and the Prince of Wales. Here are echoes of the case against Eleanor Cobham thirty years earlier; when Clarence broke into a session of the king's council to complain, he was arrested, his lands attainted, and he was forced to await the next parliament for a trial of his peers. Clarence had failed to mask the ambivalence he felt towards his crowned brother and his progeny; his ambition was made too public too often. Nor did the Lords beg for mercy towards him or challenge the unfolding family drama; and so on 18 February 1478 he was executed in the Tower, strong rumours suggesting that he had been drowned in a barrel of Malmsey wine. Fratricide now tainted Edward IV's name; and although there was little political opposition to his well-ordered government, nor was there evidence of warmth towards the king and his family.

Around Edward's tragic opponent Henry VI, on the other hand, a cult was being formed. In life, between 1469 and 1470, those who drew power from proximity to him, and thus in effect acted in his name, had unseated Edward IV for a while. But in death his body was more effective than it had ever been in life. It was buried simply in Chertsey Abbey in Surrey, and around it reports of miracles were soon recorded. Edward IV attempted to halt the cult which was developing around the dead king; in 1479 the Archbishop of York refused offerings to Henry VI's statue in the Minster. Edward similarly considered the suppression of Eton, Henry's cherished foundation.

Around 1484 John Blacman, Henry VI's chaplain and long-time confidant, a member of the favoured circle of Eton Fellows with whom the king had felt at ease, wrote a hagiographical *Life* of the Christ-like king. As in all hagiographical writings about a lay person, intimations of sanctity are identified even in mundane activities: Henry had never played with hawks, never carried a dagger or a sword; he prayed a lot and read scripture and chronicles, never frivolous literature; he supervised the life of the youths of his household to keep them from sin; he shunned nudity in both men and women, and founded the pious foundations of Eton and King's. When he lost all – his kingdom, his lands – he also won all, namely life in Christ. Reversing his brother's policy, Richard III later had Henry VI's body moved to Windsor Castle, where it could be visited more conveniently and by many. Here was a martyr in the making, and before long the cult of his suffering and death was confirmed by reports of miracles: a mad woman from Ashby St Legers in Northamptonshire was cured, as was a blind vicar from Hollington in Sussex; three stolen pigs were restored to their owners after the invocation of the saintly king's name. Prayers to him were copied into books of hours, and his figure was included in rood-screens featuring ranks of Christian martyrs, such as that in Gateley (Norfolk). Offerings were made to his image in Walberswick and Horstead in the same county in future decades, and elsewhere in the country.

Dynastic opposition appeared all but crushed with the death of Warwick at Tewkesbury and the return of Clarence. A fairly relaxed policy of patronage and promotion emerged around the king in the 1470s as Lancastrian families entered into lands and holdings. Famously, after the death of the Duke of Norfolk in 1477, John Paston was allowed to hold Caister Castle, a much disputed prize, although he had fought against the king at Barnet. Edward IV was now able to turn his attention to parts of his kingdom, such as Ireland, previously all but ignored. As was usually the case, years of unrest in England saw the intensification of raids upon settlements in Ireland, and so it was in 1470–72. In 1474 Edward attempted to revitalize Anglo-Irish magnates with the creation of the Brotherhood of Arms of St George, with its power to elect a captain and maintain a force. When his son George was born in 1477, Edward appointed him Lieutenant, a nominal gesture to be sure, yet symbolically potent, with the experienced Lord Hastings as the active deputy.

THE PARISHES AND THE CLERGY

Most religious life took place in the safety of the parish church. Parish priests were familiar figures, and familiarity often bred contempt. More priests than ever before had some university education, and in this part of the century books abounded, still mostly in manuscript, but with a growing presence of printed books in the 1480s. Books aided priests in all areas of their practice. A variety of orthodox and user-friendly pastoral manuals further aimed to support the parish priest – often a poorly paid vicar – in his demanding and many-faceted job. A notebook which belonged to a priest of York in the 1470s contains summaries of doctrine and practice on the central issues which faced parishioners and their priests: penance and the priest's function at the mass, and basic rules about Christian marriage. A set of questions is answered, for example: 'Why do people not eat meat during Lent?' 'Because God cursed the earth on account of Adam's sin, but did not curse the fish, hence fish are purer'; or 'Why does Christ's body remain in the appearance of bread and wine at the altar?' 'Because if it were not the parishioner would be afraid to eat it.' To the question 'What is woman?' the answer is 'Man's confusion', while man is 'a spirit incarnate'. These answers are pithy formulations based on centuries of theological and scholastic discussion, here parcelled into neat packages for instructive exchanges, which by the 1470s reached northern audiences of parishioners.

A great deal of effort was still invested by scholars and bishops in providing guidance to the clergy, writing useful handbooks for their edification, and helping parishioners too. This had always been a strong English tradition. The material on the sacraments was reinforced in some fortunate parishes by representations in other media, such as the seven sacraments window at Tattershall (Lincolnshire) made in 1482, which tenderly demonstrates scenes like baptism, with a baby being lowered into the font. There was preoccupation with the quantity and quality of the clergy, upon whom the whole ecclesiastical structure depended. To prevent the proliferation of poor clergy without support, a system was devised whereby each candidate had to demonstrate before ordination access to sufficient income: with private means, a parish living, or support of a religious institution. Such provision was called 'title' and although the relationship was often a nominal one – with a monastery, a religious house, a college – it associated clergy, men without family and home, with some useful frame of reference. Lay people offered some 15 per cent of such titles, to encourage the ordination of relatives, friends or well-trained associates. The ordained were then expected to enter many possible occupations – in the cure of souls, teaching, chantry ministration, or clerical work.

Bishops, who were usually hard-pressed by demanding offices of state, local and national, were assisted by an army of helpers known as suffragan bishops, who undertook many of their routine tasks in the diocese. Most rural parish priests enjoyed the assistance of a chaplain, a junior cleric who could stand as deputy for only some of the required tasks. Parish priests were also habitually involved in the management of their church's patrimony – lands, rents, flocks of sheep – in order to sustain the level of income they hoped to extract from it. At the comfortable end, a well-endowed parish with active patrons could be a worthwhile prize: Oxnead parish, a living in Norfolk, was described in 1478 as being worth £8 16s. a year. While the church was small, the buildings and lands related to it were extensive: a parsonage with halls and chambers, a barn and dovecote, two fruit gardens, twenty-two acres of pasture, a fishing river. The church served only twenty persons, but its maintenance rivalled the business of a modest yeoman. The new incumbent was a fortunate university-educated man, who was presented to the living by Agnes Paston. He was to become immersed in local land-holding affairs just as much as in the cure of souls.

When, in the following year, Margaret Paston attempted to promote her son Walter – a young man who met neither the requirement of age nor that of clerical status – to a living in the diocese of Norwich, she was rebuffed by a family friend, William Pykanham, chancellor of the diocese of Norwich, who chided her for the attempt to promote so unsuitable a candidate. There was great awareness in fifteenth-century England that the clergy were under observation and that parishioners were quick to note deficiencies, and were active in bringing such complaints before ecclesiastical courts. Demands on parish priests were diverse. A late-fifteenth-century addition to the parish book of Wisbech

(Cambridgeshire) shows the many types of business which occupied a priest: there were notes on the law of marriage, a list of feast-days, a prayer, and extracts from wills noting bequests to the parish.

But priests could not answer all questions; they got things wrong, and sometimes behaved badly. A London vicar was prosecuted in 1472 for having preached that excommunicated persons could come to church on feast-days and hear the divine word. In 1484 parishioners of Burmington (Worcestershire) complained to the Warden of Merton College that the vicar he had appointed to serve them removed their candles and wax tapers, abused the churchwardens, and grazed too many cows on the common meadows. Even worse, he revealed what a parishioner had told him in confession and, according to his sister-in-law, who acted as his housekeeper, he wished to have a relationship with her sister. The college dismissed the complaints. Yet this case reflects dissatisfaction noted in hundreds of other records, and establishes some of the issues around which vicars and parishioners frequently fell out.

The deep mid-century economic crisis having passed, cathedrals and communities of parishes were willing to undertake necessary, and sometimes even superfluous, works on their churches. Following the destruction caused by a lightning strike in 1463, Norwich Cathedral Priory undertook in 1470 to rebuild the roof, decorated with stone vaults sporting some forty-seven carved bosses. These bosses were painted with colourful images of biblical tales, including that of Delilah cutting off Samson's locks, and Joseph standing like a proud reeve in front of bags of grain bursting at their seams. Similar decisive action after disaster is recorded in the Church Book of All Saints', Bristol, in 1464. On the night of Whit Monday fire destroyed parish buildings on Corn Street, and on the morrow four men, at twopence each, were hired to remove the charred timber and salvage the valuable lead, probably for future use in the repair of the roof. In London, St Sepulchre was rebuilt thanks to a bequest of 1473; the north side of St Michael, Cornhill was repaired in 1474, and decorative battlements were added to St Mildred's Poultry.

Rural parishes sported new towers or had windows inserted, each reflecting local taste and the availability of patronage and funds. Thus the rood-screen in the parish church of Gateley (Norfolk), bequeathed to the parish in 1485, was made of eight panels: four depicting male and four female saints. On these panels universal figures met English ones: the Virgin and Henry VI as martyr, St Elizabeth and probably

Christina of Markyate (a twelfth-century saint connected with St Albans). In Tatterford church (Norfolk) a panel, part of a screen, contains two images: one of a nun, perhaps a woman of local renown whom we can no longer identify, and the other of St Helen, with crown and scarlet cloak. The church of Santon Downham (Suffolk) acquired a plinth and tower through the combined efforts of a group of local benefactors. The stone and flint motifs create still legible patterns of letters: the monograms of the Virgin and Jesus (M and J) on the north side, those of the benefactors on the west and south sides.

The repertoire of images was constantly replenished by local elaboration or by experimentation with imports from abroad. A moralizing image against work on Sundays and feast-days (of which there were over 100 in the English calendar) was the Christ of Sundays. In this image Christ, dressed in a loincloth, bleeding from gashes and wounds all over his body, is surrounded by the implements of craft and agricultural work which had caused them: metal wool-combs, scissors, hooks, knives, shears. The message was – as the people of Breage and of St Just in Penwith (both Cornwall), of West Chiltington (Sussex), of Ampney Crucis (Gloucestershire), and others, no doubt appreciated – that Christ's modern-day tormentors were those who ignored the commandment and worked on feast-days, rather than go to church. A unique version of this theme at Broughton (Buckinghamshire) substituted breakers of the Sabbath with women who chatted in church – each idle word was a blow to Christ's suffering body.

In English churches architectural styles and manners of adornment from a variety of origins coincided, a cumulative palimpsest of initiatives great and small. Porches were added to churches, and the room above the entrance level served as a convenient classroom for instruction in religion and Latin grammar. Pews were more widely introduced in mid-century, as churchwardens' accounts begin to record related expenses. At St Michael, Cornhill, eight shillings were paid to a carpenter in 1460 for the flooring of a pew; at St Mary at Hill, London, 'new pewes' were installed in 1476. Some pews were highly embellished with carved ends, like those still to be seen in Fressingfield (Suffolk).

People made contact in parishes with interesting and informative fittings. Parishioners of Hook Norton (Oxfordshire) baptized their children in a Norman font on to which were carved Adam and Eve and the Tree of Knowledge but, thanks to the Earl and Countess of Suffolk, the space in which they worshipped had entered the Perpendicular age.

These active and interested patrons, whose efforts were evident in the endowment of the Ewelme (Oxfordshire) almshouses, supported the remaking of the church's nave to match a new tower in rich green stone with a doorway from the west and finely cut stairs and eight pinnacles.

The desire for commemoration expressed by the rich in the foundation of chantries was shared by more modest people, who did not found new institutions, but inserted a tomb within their parish churches. These insertions often altered the shape of the church: Sir John Say's tomb in the south aisle of Broxbourne church (Hertfordshire) caused the lengthening of the aisle in 1476. Such insertions also reshaped what parishioners saw in areas central to the performance of liturgy: John Flaxall's chantry in the chapel of Our Lady at Wassall (Staffordshire) was placed under the rood. A single bequest could enrich performance substantially. Margaret Chocke, widow of Sir Richard Chocke, managed commemoration of her husband in her will of 1484: she left rich fabrics of velvet and damask, and tapestry, and endowed a window at Ashton church (Somerset), which displayed their arms in the centre and figures of saints either side.

The evidence of wills and churchwardens' accounts demonstrates that the late-fifteenth-century parish church was accommodating a growing array of furnishings, which reflected diverse new functions. Marian devotion was observed everywhere. The churchwardens' accounts of Walberswick (Suffolk) recorded in 1466 some concerted efforts: expenditure of 5s. for a painting of the Virgin, 8d. for a base to carry it, and 6s. 10d. for a tabernacle within which it was encased. At All Saints church, Tilney (Norfolk), in 1474, 13s. 7d. was spent on the tabernacle, within which an image costing £1 6s. 8d. was placed. New foci for devotion, whose origins were on the continent, were quickly absorbed by English and Welsh parishes – the cult of St Anne, for example. A popular new choice for commemorative masses was, from the 1460s, that to the Name of Jesus, following the creation of a new universal feast of the Name in 1457.

The whole range of current religious practices – prayer with images, devotional meditations, books for lay instruction – was followed by the family of York. In all ways their piety was extremely orthodox. Edward IV sent to Rome for an indulgence from the Marian chapel of Scala Coeli, to boost the attractions of St Stephen's chapel, Westminster. Yorkist women were some of the first in England to use the rosary, an aid to reflection on the life of the Virgin and Christ's Passion. Though no longer obsessed by the danger of religious dissent, they none the less supported such bastions of orthodoxy as King's College, Cambridge, and doubled the endowment of the new foundation of St Catharine's College there, to house a master and three fellows whose aim was to produce and spread orthodox theology. Theological debates nevertheless continued to take place, in decades which saw strong currents of reform on the continent over ecclesiastical authority, suitable forms for lay instruction, and the value of vernacular use of the Bible. The liturgical prayers of priests were much prized, but so were the personal experiences of prayer with or without the aid of books, beads and images. People prayed for their own illumination and good life, as well as for their dead loved ones. This was a period of extensive and varied possibilities for prayer.

The Yorkist home style was of household piety in the Netherlandish manner that they knew well from their boyhoods and exiles: lavish sacramental liturgy and a lot of private prayer with the aid of magnificent books. Elizabeth Woodville's Book of Hours is typical of aristocratic women's domestic books of prayer. Small in format, with a short paragraph on each page, it opened with a presentation image of the female donor, and contained a multitude of prayers to female saints. The Hastings Book of Hours may have been in the hands of Edward V in the Tower; its images, vivid illustrations to the text, with few marginal distractions, made it an attractive and useful book. Aids to prayer were sometimes luxury items. Such was the Middleham Jewel, found near Richard of Gloucester's residence in North Yorkshire, an exquisite lozenge-shaped gold pendant of c.1450–75, mounted with a sapphire and pearls, and inscribed with blue letters. In it is combined the high-class workmanship which members of the family could expect, together with inscribed invocations for protection phrased in the language of prayer, but also in that of charms and the occult.

The cultural resources available in the Yorkist court did not belong to a separate and rarefied world of religion, art and letters, such as that of Richard II or even Henry VI. It was much more 'middle-brow' and thus shared in the enthusiasms of merchants, yeoman farmers, gentry, religious fraternities and parishes, though court patrons could have cast in gold and jewels what others did in wood or silver. The verses inscribed on the Middleham Jewel are all but identical to those copied into the commonplace book of Robert Reynes of Acle (Norfolk) – a farmer and local official – for protection from evil. Similarly,

Edward IV's interest in alchemy was not far removed from the metallurgical experiments which his officials of the Mint conducted in their attempts to cure the deficiencies of English coinage (Plate 25). Some of Edward's success in stabilizing politics and reducing social tension may be explained by his gift for making himself into 'the people's king'.

A developed cultural sphere which offered a recognizable and accessible style was that of church music – organ and choral music alike. Cathedrals such as York, Winchester and Wells boasted well-established choirs to which were attached schools, and over which presided choirmasters, who also composed and arranged the music. The responsibility of training boys in music led to the provision of education and thus choir schools. The royal chapel had in 1471 twenty-six chaplains, eight choristers and a grammar teacher for the boys. Court musicians composed elaborate musical settings for the liturgy, but these also spread widely. Parish churches owned copies of an elaborate mass used at St Margaret's church, Westminster, which was composed in mid-century but was still being copied in the 1480s. A parish church like St James Garlickehithe, London, owned choir-books into which the work of leading composers had been copied. So even more modest venues could provide musical embellishment. In his will of 1482 Robert Morley of Hingham (Norfolk) bequeathed seven surplices for choir members and seven 'rochettys', or surplices, for the children; he expected them to sing on the Sunday following his burial. The presence of many chantry priests in parishes added to the elaboration and continuity of services, the sounds and sights of which penetrated beyond the altar or even chapel in which they fulfilled their liturgical duties. John Motram, chantry priest at St Mary at Hill, London, owned an antiphonal so precious that the churchwardens preferred to have the proceeds from its sale rather than own and use it as a gift. This and other parishes often hired singers from St Paul's for their services. London was, of course, particularly well endowed with music and musicians. Chaplains and priests of great households, of royal institutions, of St Paul's, also offered their paid professional services to parishes, hospitals and chapels.

Drama was highly prized for its didactic quality and for the entertainment it brought to hard-working villages. The dramatic offerings varied in professionalism, length and elaboration. In Thame (Oxfordshire) in 1481 a play about Jacob and his twelve sons was performed, an occasion also important for fund-raising in the parish. Easter sepulchres formed the focus of the dramatic vigil at Christ's tomb, in anticipation of the Resurrection on Easter Sunday. The parish also marked the liturgy with drama, with a play of the Burial and Resurrection of Christ between Good Friday and Easter Monday. Thame parish also had a St George play performed in 1482–3. The frequency was determined by the state of parish funds and the availability of troupes of itinerant players.

Alongside the hundreds of annual dramatic events in rural and urban parishes, and the many occasions for dramatic embellishment at aristocratic feasts and tournaments, entries and banquets, a unique type of biblical drama, sometimes known as Corpus Christi cycles, emerged in a number of cities. The best known is probably the cycle from York, which contained forty-eight episodes, a survey of Christian history performed in English by lay people. (The cycle was revived in York for the Festival of Britain, and now receives regular stagings.) The play-text of c.1470 survives in the muniments of the city of York, and this is no accident. The ambitious cycle was an important urban event, performed by the city's defining corporations, its craft guilds, each with a scene to stage and enact. Another cycle of thirty-two episodes from the Creation to the Last Judgement has survived from the West Riding of Yorkshire (the Towneley Plays), and another from East Anglia, with twenty pageants. These elaborate productions are a testimony to the buoyancy of vernacular idiom in religious instruction, to the sophisticated capacities of urban corporations and craft guilds, and to the effective collaboration between clerics (who composed and directed) and lay people (who financed, performed and viewed the plays). Performers and spectators alike were involved in a complex religious and social activity: mocking Noah or Joseph, scourging a neighbour playing Christ, seeing the avenging terror of the Mouth of Hell.

The plays were amusing, informative and exhortative. Like all religious instruction they reminded people of their end. This is evident in the macabre creations of the 'cadaver' tombs which combined an upper effigy of the deceased, and a lower figure of the rotting cadaver, like the Brigge tomb in Salle (Norfolk) or that of Thomas Beckington in Wells Cathedral (Somerset). In parallel, there was a literature on 'how to die well', which proliferated in this period and was produced in abundance by early printing presses. A misericord in St George's Chapel, Windsor, depicts the Dance of Death: a rich man is taken by Death. Death and the afterlife were visualized in 'doom' scenes, often over the cross, which faced the congregation above the chancel arch. Around 1480, it was probably a monk from Blythburgh who painted on wooden boards the scene of the Last Judgement still at St Peter's church, Wenhaston (Suffolk) (Plate 26). The bright colours and vivid scenes still have the power to arrest. Christ, seated on a rainbow, presides at the top, over the fortunes of humans. There is the liberation of the saved – a king, a pope, a cardinal – from purgatory, and the operations of devils dragging the damned into the monstrous mouth of hell. Its original location, above the entrance to the chancel, meant that it could have been used as part of an unfolding sermon, for instruction. It ominously framed the view of the celebration of the mass. Death and its aftermath were a constant preoccupation of most people, and a bad death came to a person who had not prepared. Preparation included reflection, settling of affairs with friends, neighbours and business partners, an investment of time and money in good works, and the setting-up of arrangements for prayers after death.

The preoccupation with death touched all, and the lore which reflected its logic was common. Chantries were founded by those who could afford to part with lands and rents, a not insubstantial section of English society. Richard Duke of Gloucester founded Middleham College (Yorkshire), a chantry at Barnard Castle (co. Durham) and, in 1483, as King Richard III, the College of St William, with a hundred chantry priests, at York Minster. Similarly, yet more modestly, in 1482 Sir Richard Chokke, a Justice of Common Pleas, whose widow's efforts on his behalf we have already encountered, established a chantry with a single priest in the parish church of Bridgwater (Somerset).

Chantries, large or small, established sources of income to support priests whose duty was to celebrate daily masses for the commemoration of the souls of founders, often husband and wife, for their parents, and for their progeny after them. In order to ensure that the income continue to be generated and the duties fulfilled, founders sought the supervision of executors, and often entrusted their foundation to a perpetual, reliable institution. Thus in 1469 John Codrington, lord of the manor of that name in Gloucestershire, and his wife entrusted their foundation to the Dominican friars of Bristol. The will made by John Cobbes of Newchurch (Kent) in 1472 stipulated that lands in Newchurch be transferred to twenty-four of the wisest men of the county for the maintenance of four priests to sing in his memory in Newchurch church.

In giving to the parish, donors had in mind practical use and centrality to cult: most of the gifts to Kent parishes in this period were linked to the needs of celebrating the mass, half of them in the form of cloth, canopies, cross-clothes and linen for use during the mass. In 1482 William Kenett bequeathed a silver ring, to be melted down and used to make a chalice. Parishioners used their testaments to bestow necessary items, or to support particular activities. In the parish of St Andrew Hubbard in Eastcheap, London, in 1459 Joan Reynold left forty shillings for repair of the bell-tower, while in 1479 John Brugge contributed towards the making of a new cope for the parish priest, and John Harpham left forty shillings for a new chasuble. This is informed giving to meet local needs, and with a clear sense of the life of the parishes. Women often offered personal garments and adornments for favourite female images, carved or painted.

The physical and artistic heritage was managed by tens of thousands of churchwardens, usually working in pairs and elected annually from among the respectable and better-off members of towns and villages. They kept inventories, managed funds and donated money for the maintenance of lights in front of images and altars of saints. They rendered accounts as well as they wished or could, recording the many little gifts of wool, wax, cash, vestments, cloths, books and vessels which parishioners habitually donated in their lifetime or bequeathed to the parish in their wills.

The men who were elected for such tasks were usually those who had already proved their ability or willingness in other public offices. Churchwarden John Chapman of Thame was a burgess who served eleven times between 1449 and 1482, and who, as a tenant of the Bishop of Lincoln, was summoned to act as a juror in court. He also worked at the useful crafts of chandler and fishmonger, and his wife probably brewed ale, since he was fined for infraction of the assize regulating its production. Robert Reynes of Acle in Norfolk, who was a reeve as well as a guild officer and tax collector, had a similar career, which involved him in the management of local religious foundations, law and administration.

The skills needed in all these spheres were transferable ones: good literacy in English, some acquaintance with Latin terms of accounting and law, understanding of spheres of jurisdiction, and a sense for investment and risk through an acquaintance with the operation of the local and regional markets in basic foodstuffs and cash crops. Robert Reynes's unique commonplace book, a work-diary in which he copied a wide range of texts – prayers, proverbs, legal formulae and accounts of contemporary events – reflects the scope of his interest and duties. He was able to work his way through a short list of the sacraments in Latin, but most of the proverbs and maxims were in English, like the sardonic: 'Law is laid down, love is very small, charity is out of town, truth is "go withal".'

Such were the men who also mediated between the officials of royal and church courts and the localities, by citing felons or criminals. The lower church court which met in 1462 at Wisbech (Cambridgeshire) dealt with business ranging from accusations of sorcery to complaints of Sabbath-breaking by the town's seven butchers. The fines were divided between alms to the poor and the upkeep of the fabric of the church. It was men like Chapman and Reynes who scrutinized their neighbours and passed on information about suspects to the courts.

Their efforts also formed a network of social regulation which spread increasingly tightly over England. Small communities, like Fordwich in Kent, presented people for anti-social behaviour: for assault, hedge-breaking, scolding and gaming. They were particularly attentive to the verbal abuse pronounced by women, and women were eight times more likely to be presented to court for bad language. The women presented were married women, who were expected to comply with social etiquette and who were punished when they failed to live up to this standard. If a woman lashed out and called someone a thief or a whore, she was made to walk through town, mockingly heralded by a piper. This was meant to deter, though some towns allowed women to pay the fine rather than undergo public humiliation.

Leisure activities were increasingly scrutinized by activist groups of parish worthies, people prominent in running the parish, manor or ward, who held judicial and fiscal roles, which often ran in families. In Romford (Essex) masters were fined when their servants were found in ale-houses after hours, and in 1477 the keeper of the Vine Tavern was fined for keeping the house open late. Ambivalence about outdoor and popular pastimes is evident in attitudes to the popular sport of camping or 'campball', a hybrid of what we call football and handball. Whereas a century earlier statutes had banned games, including tennis, quoits and football, by the 1470s such play was afforded space and regulated. In 1474 Dr Jon Botwright of Swaffham (Norfolk), local rector and Master of Corpus Christi College in Cambridge, bequeathed camping-land to the parish. This was to be a place in which 'they may play their games, such as involve running, shooting . . . and other honest games'

(Plate 21). Flat East Anglian villages and towns, such as Saxtead and Stowmarket, had camping closes and greens. The attitude displayed by Dr Botwright displays a combination of scrutiny and concession: 'they' will play their games, so let there be an allocated space, and a clear notion of appropriate sports.

Multiple jurisdictions reinforced and repeated tasks of surveillance and punishment. In late-fifteenth-century London proclamations against prostitution were made by the mayor and aldermen, as in 1483; they denounced fornication, a crime which fell under spiritual jurisdiction. London's ecclesiastical courts were used mostly to regulate sex and marital life (over 60 per cent of their cases), while just under a quarter of cases concerned defamation: in 1471, 980 cases were heard, and in 1484, 764. Yet other jurisdictions claimed an interest in these issues too. The enforcement of marriage discipline was also a local business: when in 1471 Thomas Wulley's son refused to break up a pre-marital relationship, the father turned to the local constable in the hope that his son might be persuaded by a civic accusation for fornication. Similarly, when Jane Kydde was harassed by the friends of the Cooke family, the family of a leading London draper, who hoped to unmake the commitment young Philip Cooke had given her, Kydde chose to petition the king (in 1478–84) and plead for his mercy, rather than use the church court to claim that a promise of marriage had been made. Marriage and lineage, women and property, all emerged in the many protracted matrimonial cases which kept lawyers and judges – secular and ecclesiastical – busy all over England.

Although the previous 100 years had seen the gradual erosion of aspects of servility for many English families, as they migrated or were freed (manumitted) by their lords, and came to hold free lands in free status, there were still some benefits – financial and political – to men who could prove their lordship over land and people. That servility mattered is evident from the frequency of court cases which dealt with an accusation of defamation, concerning one person calling another 'serf'. To the church court which assembled at Wisbech in 1461 witnesses came from Spalding in Lincolnshire to swear to the freedom of a family which had been claimed as servile. The survival of serfdom was uneven over English regions, but there was much of it on Norfolk estates. Personal status was often linked to a duty to pay certain personal dues: like the craftsmen labourers of the manor of Salle Kirkhall (Norfolk) – a lantern-maker, a pedlar, a shepherd and a tailor – who paid a few pennies a year. Enforcing such minute duties required lists and records, a few of which have survived. The manor court of Spalding Abbey (Lincolnshire) possessed in 1476 a register compiled by its librarian Laurence Myntling, a book of genealogies of servile families on the abbey's estates, going back several generations. Of similar nature, though within a different social class, was the collection of genealogies prepared by the Abbot of Whitby, Thomas Pickering, between 1462 and 1475. Some thirty-five such 'histories' of local gentry families were meant to assist in the legal work of probate attached to the working of the ecclesiastical court of the diocese of York. Some records could assist not only those who wielded lordship, but individuals in pursuit of claims and rights. On the manor of Topsfield Hall, Crouch End, they helped Nicholas Kingsden – thought to have been killed at the battle of Towton in 1464 – to return and assert his prior claim against that of his sister, who had been admitted to their father's tenancy in his absence.

LAW AND LEGAL TRAINING

The kingdom was bound by statute law, acts of parliament which could override common law and law-merchant. This produced a growing demand for legal services, and a greater specialization in tasks, all of which resulted in substantial promise and reward for those who pursued legal careers. Training in law began early in life, after attendance at a local grammar school; by the age of fifteen a promising and well-supported young man was sent to work his apprenticeship in the Inns of Court. Like university colleges, the Inns of Court possessed regional and social characters: it was thus fitting that Roger Townshend of East Raynham in Norfolk was sent by his father to Lincoln's Inn in 1454, an East Anglian stronghold. Chief Justice John Fortescue opined that the Inns were as much schools of gentility as they were schools of law. The Inn was an institution which offered and expected immersion in training, sociability and discussion of law. The curriculum was dense, and learning it was hectic. Many of the didactic methods used then still prevail in training for the Bar today – learning of case law and the form of writs by rote combined with mock trials staged by trainees, and much attendance at courts to absorb their workings and style. As in the university colleges, seniors taught juniors in a system of personal supervision or pupillage. With so many aspiring young men living, working and competing, there was also a lot of hilarity, with dances and long festive periods. Furnivall's Inn began its Christmas session of 1471–2 on All Hallows and it lasted until Twelfth Night. The Inns of Court became discerning and spirited artistic patrons in the capital. This tradition endured. Shakespeare's *Twelfth Night* may have been first performed at Middle Temple in January 1602.

In length and applicability training in the law was a secular equivalent to clerical university training. The contacts made within the Inn structured the business, and subsequent 'winnings', which men had from their practice. It was common for well-connected and experienced lawyers to be selected for judicial office as justices of assizes. The same Roger Townshend was thus chosen in 1482 and sent first to the arduous northern circuit – which involved a great deal of travel and long tours – and later to the southern home circuit. Appointment as a common law justice was a useful marker of approval, but real advancement was to be had from specialization in niches of practice, expertise that was regional as well as technical. In general, the latter part of the century saw the decline in the amount of civil business heard by common law courts to the advantage of the Chancery court and courts-merchant. The Chancery court – the court of equity which developed around the chancellor – had seen a prodigious rise in the fifteenth century. It all but doubled its business during the Yorkist decades, with 243 cases per annum before 1475 and 553 cases per annum on average between 1475 and 1485. It emerged as the court of choice for merchants and smaller land-holders, standing apart from common law, with its own traditions and know-how. Roman law was practised by experts in Doctors' Chambers in the City of London, for cases relating to navigation and admiralty. Roman lawyers, also known as civilians, came to prominence in royal administration. Such was Dr John Morton, the first expert in Roman law to become Master of the Rolls, following a career of lucrative consultancies in the court of the Chancellor of Oxford, of George Neville (later Archbishop of Canterbury), and in the Court of Arches at St Mary-le-Bow, the supreme ecclesiastical court of the province of Canterbury.

The law became the good practitioner's social ladder, with phenomenal examples of movement from modest yeoman status to safe membership of the gentry even over a single generation. Several families in Norfolk have left good sources: the Pastons, the Hoydens, the Clears and the Townshends. Through the administrative services rendered by him to magnates and gentry in Norfolk, John Townshend (d. 1460) had amassed leases and manors and connection with the Scales and Woodvilles, sufficient to allow him to send his son to Lincoln's Inn and make good gentry matches for his children. His son, Roger, among his other appointments became a legal adviser to Elizabeth Woodville. Good lawyers were so essential to the working of a social system based on landed wealth, and a kingship based on the provision of justice, that as long as lawyers kept out of public politics they could weather almost any storm. Roger Townshend did so; he lived on to serve Henry Tudor, Elizabeth Woodville's son-in-law.

Law was the vehicle for such advancement since it was an expertise which almost every man and woman in the country made use of at some moment in life. London lineages were created by sons of country yeomen and country lawyers. These dynasties were fostered by close management of careers and direction of training, studies and marriage, in a manner easily learned from gentry families. Sir John Sulyard, for example, a lawyer with an estate in Suffolk as well as urban properties in Ipswich and a flourishing provincial as well as London career, in 1474–5 allocated rent income towards the education of his son in a local grammar school, the still excellent Ipswich School, a school to which Suffolk gentry sent their sons.

Their association with powerful families forced the more successful lawyers to steer a careful course between the many loyalties upon which their careers depended, but which could also turn menacing in politically tumultuous times. Miles Metcalfe of Wensleydale (Yorkshire) was a lawyer in Neville patronage, who worked for all three Yorkist brothers. He was part of a northern (North and East Riding) circle of lawyers which sustained Gray's Inn. Metcalfe's training and work was in London and Westminster, but he toiled hard at maintaining social and familial links in the north. His work also brought him in touch with the estates of his patron, as auditor-general of the estates of the Earl of Warwick. He and his wife joined the prestigious Corpus Christi guild of York, and he managed to survive the fall of Warwick by attaching himself to Gloucester's household, where ultimately his son, too, found patronage. He wisely, or perhaps just luckily, was absent on business in Yorkshire during the few days of Edward V's reign in 1483, and thus was saved from the anguish which those days caused to many decent people.

LANDED SOCIETY

The entry of modest families to gentle status always causes complaint from those already established and privileged. Families like the Pastons and Townshends and Metcalfes were similarly the subjects of contemporary comment and complaint. But they were also essential to the maintenance of the vast landed interests of those magnates who concerned themselves with politics, and who were, of necessity, absent from most of the tracts of country which they held and ruled. A magnate such as John Howard Duke of Norfolk (d. 1485) spent his time between his country residence, Tendering Hall, at Stoke-on-Nayland (Suffolk), and a London house in Stepney. The more unsettled the politics, the more important frequent presence at Westminster and court became to men such as Howard.

Defining categories of social status is always difficult, but this was none the less attempted: the Coventry Parliament in 1474 defined a gentleman as someone who 'inhabits a livelihood' of £10 per annum. Demarcation was observed within larger and grander households by allocation of graduated placements and slightly differing menus at table. In the great household of Sir Henry Stafford and his wife Lady Margaret Beaufort at their palace at Woking (Surrey), in 1469, most meals comprised generous portions of beef and mutton, bread and ale, but about a quarter of the members feasted on finer foods: veal, capons and pullets. Above all, notions of 'good lordship' made or broke relationships of trust and loyalty: among the accusations against the Duke of Somerset, attainted in 1465 in parliament, were his failing in the 'very gentleness and the noble honour that ought to be grounded in every gentleman'.

The organization of magnates' wealth and power was carried out by ranks of professional and well-remunerated servants, clergy, lawyers, estate managers and men of the land. Their households now included men who could produce visual, historical and cartographic support for dynastic rights. John Rous, an Oxford graduate and antiquarian scholar, was chaplain at the Earl of Warwick's chantry chapel at Guy's Cliff, Warwick. He also wrote a glorifying history of his patron's family, for which several genealogical rolls survive from the 1470s. Even towns and cities sought to establish heraldic and historical credentials through seals and coats of arms. Around magnates coalesced complex networks of gentry families, ready and able to receive positions which were at once honorific and challenging, at the apex of management of people and land. Margaret Beaufort, for example, mother of the future Henry VII, was served by the Shirleys, Parkers, Brays, all of whom supported her vast landed interests in Devon, Somerset, Northumberland, Northamptonshire, Lincolnshire and Westmorland.

The term 'yeomen' came to describe the social group from which many lawyers and servants to such magnates emerged and out of which several of the more ambitious and driven members ascended to social and material rewards. The literature of Robin Hood captures an awareness of the dignity, almost heroism, of the yeomen in charge of vast areas of park and forest. These were great environmental and economic endeavours, aimed at generating income and sustaining the unique lifestyle of a noble class. Forest staff were charged with maintaining the vegetation, sustaining the animals for hunting prey, supervising boundaries, and punishing incursions. A whole hierarchy of officials worked under a chief keeper; they were local free men, of some standing and reliability. This occupation gave rise to a profusion of local names, such as Hunters and Foresters in Wensleydale. When the royal or aristocratic hunt was under way their tasks included hunting rituals such as the handling of dogs and butchering of carcasses. A moral economy governed the rewards and the sharing of such bloody prizes among the varied social groups that comprised the hunt.

The administration of landed and commercial interests, as well as leisure and social pursuits, brought people of very differing status into contact on terms which were usually well understood. For the whole system to cohere and make sense, it required the exemplary endorsement of the king, the magnate of all magnates, good lord, provider of peace or leader in war. The instability of our period is deeply related to the failure of such security, to dynastic competitions, which became the major preoccupation of families and regions, but also of lowlier subjects everywhere. Edward IV attempted for a while to reassure his subjects by living what seemed a household-bound existence, neither fighting far from home nor indulging in magnificent display. His dwelling at Eltham (Kent) was an impressive traditional structure around a great hall, built in brick and wood; he built no great palaces and commissioned no great art. He invoked only gently the example of Edward III: the *Black Book* of 1478 required that the treasurer of the household search 'good, old, sad, worshipful and profitable rules of the court used before time'.

Inspiration might come from Edward III, 'first setter of sentences among his domestic household', a king whose example Yorkists consciously aimed to follow.

BOOKS AND READING

All those involved in securing order and peace, in parish, town or court, were assisted and challenged by the proliferation of writing and literacy. For many, writing and literacy were primarily working tools, but these skills also allowed people to benefit from the wide range of reading materials that circulated in late-fifteenth-century England, Wales and Ireland. With the technology of print came new groupings which struggled to find their place among and within traditional guild structures: the freemen admitted in the city of York in these years included a text-writer and book-binder; while the girdlers of the city produced not only harnesses and dog-collars, but book-clasps. In these years the stationers of London came to be organized and recognized as a guild, with the core of their activity in the tenements of Paternoster Row and London Bridge. Within these workshops, like the Moulton workshop that produced the books of Sir John Fortescue, the new technology of printing was being absorbed. By the 1470s its potentialities were being realized in the production of traditional texts. One of the earliest products of William Caxton's Westminster press was a papal indulgence of 1476. It was what we would call a form; to a sole surviving copy the names of the recipients, Henry and Katherine Langley, were added by hand. They were promised remission of the punishment due for confessed sins. Income from this indulgence was to flow to the coffers of Westminster Abbey in support of its rebuilding projects. In Caxton's tenement in Westminster the first edition of Chaucer's works was produced, as was the national epic of the *Brut* chronicle, as well as vital and widely used liturgical books. Here was a new and exciting elaboration in the workshop practices of Caxton, a London stationer with continental knowledge gleaned from his training at Bruges.

Printed books took a while to come into common usage among traditional book-owning sections of society, and beyond. The books most likely to appear in print were prayer books and catechisms. The liturgical scheme most commonly used in the south of England, the

Sarum Hours, was first printed in 1475, and had gone into twenty-nine editions by 1500.

At this early stage books were hybrids of old and new: a traditionally hand-painted and coloured miniature shows the printer Guillaume Fichet offering to Edward IV a copy of Cardinal Bessarion's prayers, a book printed in Paris in 1472, but to which an illustration was added in England. Printed books coexisted for decades with affordable hand-written books, mass-produced and quite uniform, like the thousands of Books of Hours for English use which were imported in these decades from the Low Countries, especially from Bruges. Alongside the liturgy were the needs of pastoral care in thousands of churches; these were served when Caxton printed in 1483 an English translation of the *Golden Legend*, the authoritative collection of the lives of Christian saints. Refined taste continued to prefer richly illuminated fine parchment books, each copy unique and styled to the owner's desires. Anthony Woodville, Lord Scales, translated, and had his work copied and produced in great style. He presented an English version of Christine de Pizan's philosophical vignettes as *The Dictes and Sayings of Philosophers*, and her *Livre du Corps de Policie*, a mirror for princes, to Edward IV for the use of his son, as well as for Edward's own edification.

The secular literature was above all romance, classical poetry, and history, all read very widely. John Paston lent his copy of Ovid's *Ars amatoria (Art of Love)* to a friend at court, who promised in a letter to return it; while he lent his son, also John, John Lydgate's poem *The Temple of Glass*, and in turn the son inquired about that poet's *The Siege of Thebes*. Caxton printed a stylized study of the game and politics of chess, *The Game and Play of Chess*. This was middle-brow literature for the gentry. Edmund Reed, Esquire, who inherited the estate at Boarstall (Buckinghamshire), was similarly a reader of chivalric romances, the poetry of Lydgate and Gower and, fittingly, books on estate management. Among the bestsellers were also books for the edification of the young of such families. One of Caxton's earliest products was a table-manners book for children, a poem by Lydgate, produced in clear and bold letters in 1476 and accompanied by an ever-useful hymn to the Virgin Mary, the *Salve regina*.

These are the decades of school foundations, almshouse building, and the investment in books, even mobile libraries. Most initiatives were local and related to the parish: in 1473 Margaret Fawkner, widow of Roger, founded a house for poor men and women in St Mary's parish, Cambridge; she endowed it with tenements invested in the person of the parish chaplain. John Alcock, Bishop of Rochester, founded in 1479 a small school in the parish of his youth, in his parents' house in Hull. In the province of York twenty-five new schools were founded in the half century after 1450, and twenty-six in the west of England. Education was linked with the inculcation of habits of obedience and respect. Some of the more tender lines directed children towards good table manners, and sound very familiar even to our ears:

Set over your dish your head you should not hang and with a full mouth do not drink. Your nose, your teeth, your nails, from picking keep at meal time . . . Answer and speak when men speak to you.

Books and trade were allied ventures in many ways. The keepers of London Bridge toiled over customs and tolls but also monitored the entry of books into the country. When the crown attempted to curb astrological calculation of a dubious and possibly seditious nature, it turned to the keepers of London Bridge and stationers in pursuit of dangerous texts and practices. But control was modest; dispatches on politics were regularly seen by Londoners, and Lancastrian supporters – such as the Cookes in London – also communicated regularly with Margaret of Anjou in exile. In London, new types of writing recorded the events of public life with a deftness, colour and involvement that distinguish them from the traditional monastic histories and annals. Henry VI's restoration was described in a London chronicle, now in the Guildhall Library, as an occasion orchestrated by others around a king who was 'spiritual and virtuous', and whose 'kingdom was not of this world'.

POLITICS AND PARLIAMENT

The taxes raised in the 1460s were hedged with conditions, and the king undertook no truly ambitious projects in those years, though parliament supported him in new adventures in the 1470s. In 1472 parliament was opened with a bravura performance in Speaker Stillington's State of the Nation speech: the king sought the support of the Commons in promoting the joint aims of defending England's external borders and securing its internal peace. Echoing the experience of Henry V's years, a deft linkage between violence abroad and peace at home was being offered to potentially unruly sections, who were attracted by wages and action in the service of the king abroad. Among those standing to benefit from the king's war in France were younger members of gentry families, future captains of newly gained garrisons, and merchants, whose trade would flow through the reconquered ports of Gascony and Normandy. Robes of gold and crimson were prepared for Edward IV's ultimate coronation in Reims. To every part of the nation were offered advantages and hopes within this royal project. This was not to be dynastic war, but rather a war dictated by the reasoned requirements of political economy; or so Edward wished his Lords and Commons would see things.

And they did. Another result of Yorkist restoration was a parliament packed with loyalists: 14 per cent of representatives were royal servants, with many retainers linked to Edward IV by blood and marriage. There was no one, for the time being, who could mount a credible challenge to the king. The Commons were being taxed, but there was loyalty to the king who had brought an end to the bloodshed of the previous two decades. It was a time for consolidation. Edward processed the country, and those who had remained Lancastrian loyalists during the 1460s made their peace in the 1470s, having buried the subject of their previous allegiance. A great royal servant, thinker and writer such as John Fortescue is a good example. He had exhibited his loyalty beyond doubt during the years of exile in Scotland and France with Henry VI and Margaret of Anjou, advising, writing, polemicizing and composing pro-Lancastrian treatises. After Tewkesbury he was faced with a dilemma: were he to join the Yorkist cause he would again be at the centre of politics, having regained his confiscated lands. So he recanted, and rewrote several of his genealogical arguments in his *Declaracion upon certain writynges sent oute of Scotteland* of *c.*1473, and became a trusted and extremely able royal propagandist. His spirit and his arguments are reflected in the works emanating from the Yorkist court in the 1470s. These works supported war with France, the legitimacy of the Yorkist family, and the sense of a fateful coincidence between Edward IV's kingship and the general weal of England and its dominions.

These political vicissitudes took their toll, although the human cost is hard to assess. Where so large a number of magnates and their sons were killed in battle, where loyalty was tested and maintained at the highest possible cost, life-choices and priorities were under constant reassessment. As ever, the most privileged members were most at risk, but equally they had a fair number of scenarios at their disposal. Forty-nine members of the peerage died in the dynastic wars, which Shakespeare named the Wars of the Roses, thirty-four falling in battle and fifteen being executed. Of the resulting forty-four widows, about half remarried. Several aristocratic and gentry women chose to remain in their widowhood, defying the expectation that they continue to be enmeshed within dynastic and marital webs. Famous women whose closest kin were killed sought immunity and a space for mourning in their widow's weeds, to which the blessing as a 'vowess' added religious approval in quasi-sacramental manner. These years produced a considerable number of women of high status in that role. Elizabeth, widow of John Talbot Earl of Shrewsbury, received her licence to become a vowess a mere nine days after her husband's death at the battle of Northampton in support of the Lancastrian king, though she sought dispensation to remarry in 1464. In the province of York the number of vowesses practically doubled in the 1480s. The networks of kinship and friendship encouraged this choice among women in households which favoured religious engagement.

TRADE AND URBAN LIFE

Edward's peace benefited trade and this touched almost every household in England and Wales. The times were changing: sailings from Newcastle-upon-Tyne averaged two or three per annum in the 1450s, but were up to seven in 1465–6. The disruption of trade with France and the Low Countries in the 1440s and 1450s had made all imports dearer and created more prudent habits of house and larder. The consumption of luxuries was reassessed, although those who could afford them still sought a varied and tasty table. So Durham Cathedral Priory halved its consumption of wine around the middle of the century, but continued to flavour its food with ginger, cinnamon, nutmeg, cloves, mace, pepper, figs, raisins and sugar, imports all.

By Edward IV's accession a fundamental shift had taken place in England's export trade, moving from a predominance of wool to one of cloth, in a market which saw more stable demand for cloth. And yet a reversal in fortunes is notable, with a marked recovery in incomes from wool in accounts from Worcestershire, Durham and Derbyshire. Far-sighted landowners followed the trend: the Townshends in Norfolk enclosed fields and renewed their flocks. And when big landlords, among them several religious houses, recovered their income from wool, they were able to build and expand. When this happened at St Swithin's Priory in Winchester, building projects brought employment and wages to the townspeople. Regional specialisms were being revived, especially the mining of lead and of tin so vital for the making of pewter, from which most household and cooking utensils were crafted. But towns' fortunes varied greatly. Not all were positioned to benefit: Cambridge was but a small town with no clear commercial or occupational specialization, a market town which supplied a university's basic needs. Its decline began in earnest in the early fifteenth century, and in 1463–4 it pleaded for exemption from its annual fee to the king and from contribution to taxation.

The more extended the peace and the more extensive the diplomatic efforts and their fruits – such as the Treaty of Utrecht with the Hanse in 1474, and the Treaty of Piquigny with France in 1475 – the greater were the risks merchants were willing to take in broadening their horizons of investment. In Portugal English merchants were encouraged by protection, and the ability to create a distinctive local quarter, and even found their own religious brotherhood. Protection of convoys with soldiers and arms added to the price of every tun of wine and every sack of peppercorns. By raising taxes Edward IV aimed at the wealth of the landed, not the stock and bullion of merchants and manufacturers. Between 1472 and 1475 he managed to raise as much tax as Henry V had done before his invasion of France. The renewal of legislation against sumptuary excess fitted well with the policy of provident investment. In 1463 it set patterns of adornment according to estate: gold to be worn only by great lords, as were patterns of velvet upon velvet; and no person lowlier than a knight should be seen in damask or silk.

As before under Henry V, towns attracted the king's attention as sources of wealth and support. Edward IV intervened in 1464 and again in 1473 in the composition of the franchise in mayoral elections in York, and personally approved the results of 1482. He understood that the institutional framework of city life could do much to enable or discourage trade. The men who ran the towns were now usually involved in a wide range of activities, among which the wool trade often dominated. Thus, in the 1470s, Geoffrey Dormer, 'woolman' of Thame (Oxfordshire), was the richest man in Thame. As we have seen, men like him involved themselves in parish affairs and local politics, law and pageantry. In the fifty years after 1453 twenty of the twenty-two men elected as mayors in Newcastle were overseas merchants. Northern merchants were exploring the North Sea as far as Bergen; and mayors promoted trade abroad, as well as when at home.

The objects used in daily life and some vital services were circulating more widely than ever before. These extended the scope of aspiration and created wide participation in patterns of consumption and taste. Medical services were widely available. Modest practitioners won the right to organize: first the surgeons of London, who boasted the king and the Duke of Gloucester as honorary members, were incorporated in 1462, and then barbers followed. In 1474 the court of Bury St Edmunds recognized the right of *barbitonsores* of the town to choose their wardens and process in the civic parade of the Corpus Christi feast. Religious houses had always provided good medical care to their members, and now retained physicians who were also required to treat the poor living in monastic almonries and almshouses. Hospitals themselves were turning towards more professional assistance.

In their travels in the British Isles and elsewhere merchants sought to secure their safety, both physical and spiritual, by joining fraternities, securing prayers in the case of death away from home, and extending social links with like-minded merchants of other towns. A literature for mariners was developing, like the 'rutter' (*routier*) of the time of Edward IV which guided an English captain around the coasts of Ireland, Wales and England and on to the Bay of Biscay. Towns such as Newcastle, Hull, Boston and King's Lynn struggled to compete with London's predominance in all areas, and especially in trade by foreign merchants. Their secure niches were only small portions of overseas trade: Newcastle had 3 per cent of wool exports, and a trade circle which was predominantly Flemish and Netherlandish. London was drawing business away from other cities; it acted as a clearing-house where imports were unloaded, and London merchants controlled the distribution of many goods. Edward IV encouraged foreign merchants as urgently needed stimulants to the economy.

London was growing in size and demand, and sprouting new suburbs and industries, even though its population grew slowly, reaching no more than 40,000 around mid-century. Running it was increasingly a complex business and its officials were full-time magistrates and leaders. In 1478 London appointed its first city surveyor, and its twenty-four officials were paid a total of £200 in salaries in 1485. There were, in addition, many worthies who worked for London for the sheer honour and useful connections that such civic activities brought with them. It is striking to observe the number of London merchants who aspired to, and achieved, knightly status, a position which was increasingly understood as one which could be honestly earned by services other than military. This period produced the merchant families who were to shine through law, trade and service in the Tudor period, chief among them the Boleyns.

The long periods of uncertainty in prices, the visitations of mortality, and the absorption of many magnates into national politics meant that the 1440s and 1450s had been years of uncertainty even at the manorial level. Now, on many estates there was continuity in sowing patterns, reflecting greater stability. The more enterprising estate managers attempted to bring in extra income from exploitation of customary rights over their serfs, or from a particularly marketable produce. Timber was appreciated in this way; trees were leased in batches of a hundred and on some estates could account for about 10 per cent of income. But by the 1470s attitudes became more proactive. In Kent there is much evidence of ditching, enclosing, clearing of trees and even re-acquisition of land previously leased out. With the surge in prices, growing wheat and oats was now profitable. Those with disposable income were able to invest in land very cheaply and with little risk. Many a gentry fortune and related estates and homes were built from the riches of the last quarter of the century. The Sulyards of Suffolk are a good example – first distinguished by John Sulyard, who entered Lincoln's Inn in 1451, and became one of its most prominent barristers, being named Justice of the King's Bench in 1484. He invested every spare penny in land, combining even parts of manors wisely in the 1460s and 1470s in painstaking accumulation, entering into carefully thought-out crop-sharing agreements with local farmers. He also owned many sheep: 400 at Wetherden, 400 at Pulham Hall. In this economic climate he was able to increase these manors' income from around £35 in the 1470s to around £54 in 1483–5. The manor of Wetherden was to be his home and seat, and he continued to purchase small parcels of land all around it. He died a knight and a lord of many manors.

The language and images of devotion were used to great effect in Yorkist display and dynastic assertion. One of the grandest occasions was the reburial of Richard Duke of York in July 1476, a ceremony designed by his son, Richard of Gloucester. Here was filial piety and dynastic proclamation. In December 1460 York's and Rutland's bodies had been displayed on the walls of Micklegate Bar in York after their deaths at the battle of Wakefield. After the battle of Towton in 1461 Edward IV had them recovered and buried at the church of Pontefract Priory, and in London had commemorative rituals celebrated at St Paul's. But the ambition of the 1470s, and Richard of Gloucester's own flair, inspired desires and imagining of more. It was to the family's collegiate church at Fotheringhay (Northamptonshire), with windows reglazed and walls redecorated, that the remains of Richard Duke of York were to be carried in ceremony on the summer days of 21–30 July. The stately progression gained on average twenty miles a day. Bishops and abbots, earls and barons, all processed behind the cortège, led by Gloucester, the chief mourner. Within the church the reburial was conducted by bishops. The life-sized effigy of the long-dead magnate, dressed in ducal blue trimmed with ermine, was surrounded by poor men with torches and by mourners. The epitaph on his tomb recounted his many exploits, and told of the king that should have been: hero of Pontoise and Normandy, pacifier of Ireland, scourge of the King of France, rightful heir of many lands, father to a long line of children, one of them the king.

The upheavals of fortune, the unjust deaths, produced for both Yorkists and Lancastrians political martyrs, figures around whom loss, memory and identity were expressed. Archbishop Scrope became a Yorkist hero; a contemporary poem saw in his execution evidence of 'tyranny and violence'. Indeed, in 1468 Edward IV reinstated the custodian of the shrine at Archbishop Scrope's tomb. These concerns inspired an explosion of new expressive forms, much of it poetry, laments on the instability of human affairs. The image of the wheel of fortune was seized on by the illuminator of the *Life of Edward IV*, who chose to place the king enthroned upon a wheel of fortune, which had turned in his favour. A typical poem declares:

> This world is variable,
> No-thing therein is stable,
>   Say now who so will.
> Since it is so mutable,
> How should men be stable?
>   It may not be through skill.

The poem ends with an appeal to God, 'Deliver us out of this world and grant us a good end!' Alternatives to worldly affairs might well have been attempted by some of those closely affected by civil war and strife. Writing about the contingency of politics – in poetry, in political and legal tracts – flourished in these years much more than philosophy or even the writing of history.

Intellectual reflection on government was extensive and fed off a variety of sources: classical, early Christian and many original new compositions. Some in England had had enough of peace and domestic bliss, and sought in the king a martial leader, but this was not his own mood. The *Book of Noblesse*, rededicated by William Worcester to the king in 1473, encouraged Edward to lead an army into France and achieve revenge for ignominious treaties and concessions. Although Edward raised taxes for it and commissioned doctors and surgeons for the campaign, the invasion of 1475 was a half-hearted affair. With little support from Edward's Burgundian ally, it achieved no military end. It ended with the Treaty of Piquigny, according to which Louis XI paid £10,000 per annum for the suspension of Edward's claim to France. The marriage of Elizabeth of York and the French prince, the Dauphin, was also discussed. This aborted case of martial leadership allowed a breach to become more apparent between Richard Duke of Gloucester and his crowned sibling.

Richard Duke of Gloucester was in many ways the real heir of York's heritage of activism and leadership. He had proved his qualities in the lordship of Yorkshire, in his political deftness as the king's enforcer. Richard had also proved himself in battle, he had been at his brother's side at Tewkesbury and Barnet, he had controlled the northern border, and had seen repeated action there, culminating in the relief of Berwick in 1482. Richard was interested in the mechanisms of government, and became involved in the local affairs of cities and regions under his rule. York was especially close to his heart, and the city's records attest to his arbitration even in disputes over illegal trapping of fish, which affected York's fortunes. From York he commanded the northern marches, and recruited and sent men to Scottish campaigns. He was in close contact with the city through gracious entry ceremonies, and the flow of reciprocal gifts of food, plate and wine.

RICHARD III

At Edward IV's peaceful death in 1483, Richard Duke of Gloucester was poised to become an elder statesman, the helpful uncle to a new young king, Edward V, aged twelve, and to his brother the Duke of York. A few days after the death, Richard assembled the northern magnates for a memorial service, at which their loyalty to Edward IV's heir was secured by oath. The uncle, who oversaw the coronation on 9 April, arranged for a rather heavy-handed entourage to bring the young king and his brother to London. Here begins one of the most notorious chapters of British history: the murder of the princes in the Tower and Richard's ascent to the throne.

Within weeks of delivering his nephew to London Richard advanced a legal claim against his birth. In accordance with the precepts of ecclesiastical law, pre-contract was an impediment to marriage. Such an impediment, he claimed in parliament, disabled the marriage of Edward IV and Elizabeth Woodville, since his brother had been pre-contracted to marry Lady Eleanor Butler; it also tainted its issue. Like thousands of cases heard in the bishops' court in England and Wales, one party sought to invalidate a marriage – rendering it a form of fornication – by claiming that another contract pre-existed. Only here the claimant was not one of the pair, but the dead groom's brother. The claim was not simply of impediment to the marriage, which might have disappeared with the death of Eleanor Butler in 1468, but that the heir to the throne was a bastard. Edward IV's issue – so stated Richard's case – was born of a marriage that should not have taken place, from adulterous parents. Although it was a case for ecclesiastical jurisdiction, it was discussed in parliament as an issue of public interest. Parliament declared the marriage invalid; Queen Elizabeth became Elizabeth Grey, with an annuity of 700 marks.

What was on Richard's mind? It is hard to tell. He must have felt beleaguered when facing the young king and his extensive and close family, led by his mother Queen Elizabeth. He may have feared marginalization, or worse, at the hand of powerful men such as the king's uncle, Earl Rivers. He may have feared the re-enactment of the violence which Margaret of Anjou had visited on his father. He could have chosen a quiet life in the north, away from court and the arenas of princely action. By questioning the princes' birth and by accusing Elizabeth so openly, he justified all the fears and suspicion she had long harboured against him.

So Richard continued his political campaign. His supporters approached the main political actors – the Duke of Buckingham persuaded the mayor and aldermen of London on 24 June to lend their support to Richard, and two days later a gathering of lords and gentry, far from a proper parliament, asked Richard to take the crown. As Buckingham made his way to Westminster Hall, the two boys in the Tower met their death. A few days later Domenico Mancini wrote to his patron, the Archbishop of Vienne, that Richard had violated his kin and all ties of friendship. An ode by the Welsh poet Dafydd ap Llewellyn ap Gruffydd of Mathafarn clearly saw in Richard a base 'servile boar' who had slain 'Christ's angels'.

Shakespeare's heart-rending portrayal of the princes' death in *Richard III* was based on a long tradition of invective against Richard, in triumphant and disparaging accounts written after Tudor ascendancy – the truth is all but impossible to unravel. Sometime soon after the coronation Richard must have hatched a plan, and on 22 June Edmund Shaw, Doctor of Theology, proclaimed Richard's claim to the throne in a sermon at St Paul's Cross. A strange sort of parliament was summoned on the day of the new young king's death. John Argenteyn, Edward IV's physician, informed the Venetian ambassador Domenico Mancini that Edward V, on the eve of his murder (25 June 1483), had feared he might be killed. Argenteyn was the last to see Edward alive, and must have seen the princes' bodies after death. He was one of England's most prominent scholars, with a wide range of medical and alchemical knowledge, accumulated over years spent in travel and study abroad, especially in Italy. On his return to England he became Provost of King's College (Cambridgeshire) and soon witnessed momentous events at the heart of the Yorkist court. He was chosen by Henry VII and served as Prince Arthur's physician, and died peacefully in 1508; his brass is still to be seen at King's College chapel. Could a man such as he have done something to avert the boys' fate?

Richard's coronation took place on 6 July, and it was a grand affair, with a procession from Westminster Hall to the Abbey. The traditional components of sermon, oath to the king, anointing, vesting, crowning, investiture of regalia and blessing followed. But this was no ordinary coronation. There was rumour and fear about. The new king soon sought to reinforce his own confidence and to look regal by visiting the lands he loved best: he conducted a royal progress to the north. En route he aimed to win the south of England: he visited Windsor, the University at Oxford, Woodstock, his Chamberlain at Minster Lovell, and passed through the Thames Valley to Gloucester, Warwick, Coventry, Leicester, Nottingham and then York. He entered the city magnificently on 29 August and spent over three weeks there. There were gifts, and pageants – York was renowned for mounting biblical drama – and Richard's son Edward was invested as the Prince of Wales. All aspects of dynastic wealth were on display along the king's route, and some business was also conducted, for the progress was a good occasion for towns to seek favour: the city of Gloucester was incorporated as a county, and Lincoln's annual fee was renegotiated.

But Richard never achieved the normalization and acceptance he craved, and the ritual attempts he made soon proved to be empty. While in Lincolnshire in October 1483 he heard that in several parts of the kingdom magnates and knights had risen against him: in south-east Wales, around Exeter, Newbury, Salisbury and in Kent. The political coordinator of the uprisings was the Duke of Buckingham, Edward IV's closest courtier. But the rebels failed to release Elizabeth Woodville and her daughters from the Tower or to establish rule in London, and the king was back in Westminster by late November. The rebels had not unseated Richard, although they had greatly unnerved him, and pockets of disturbance persisted into January 1484 in Rochester, Gravesend, Maidstone, Guildford and Tonbridge. The Acts of Attainder against the rebels name some fifty-five men, leaders of the rebellion, all royal servants, from within the Yorkist network. Eighteen were intimates of Edward IV, knights and squires of his body. These were all men who had sworn an oath to Edward V. Whose men, therefore, were they to be now that Richard ruled? So they were rounded up, tried and punished in a variety of ways: attainders, fines, bonds for future peace. On the whole, those who had been good Yorkist servants were pardoned and tentatively accepted into the new king's favour. And when he pardoned, he took a moralizing tone, a self-justifying rhetoric, as if these were acts 'for reform of morals'. As he dispossessed Thomas, once Marquess of

Dorset, a political enemy, Richard III's letter cast him as 'deflowerer and devowerer and defouler of maidens, wives and women'.

Richard was forced to rebuild his present and reconsider his future. He carefully attached to his court men from a variety of affinities, and placed household servants in counties where they had no ties and pre-existing loyalties. Some of them continued from service to his brother: Richard Croft, Receiver of the Earldom of March from 1471 and charged with the household and council of the Prince of Wales, with its vast lands in the west Midlands, continued as Richard's treasurer. Sir John Wood was Speaker of the Commons in Edward IV's last parliament and also served as treasurer to Richard III. Richard brought men out of retirement, men such as Bishop John Russell, a great partron of university building, who became Chancellor

Richard's political struggle was compounded by the loss of his own son and heir, Edward. This fed the rumours that Richard planned to divorce his queen, Anne, and marry his niece Elizabeth of York, a view held by the Crowland chronicler by Christmas 1484. So strong were the rumours and so dense the atmosphere of mistrust that after Anne Neville's death Richard was warned by his confidants that the country would rebel if he attempted to marry the girl whose brothers' deaths he was believed to have caused. Indeed, several chroniclers expressed strong opposition to the union; some, like the priest in Neville service, John Rous, even claimed that Richard had poisoned his wife. It was not unknown in 1484 for seditious bills to be nailed at public places like the Cheapside Cross. It was, therefore, a self-deluding Richard III who commented to a German visitor in 1484 that without the princes he and his people would get on fine: together they could defeat even the Turk!

There was real substance to the discontent with Richard III. A government in waiting was supported by the Duke of Brittany and several refugees from the rebellion. All these pinned their hopes on Henry Tudor, who arose as yet unsullied, with the powerful landed support of his mother Lady Margaret Beaufort, benefiting from the crisis within the Yorkist household. Henry Tudor had lived in exile in Brittany since 1471, in the court of Duke François II, where he matured and trained and fostered links with Breton and French magnates. By October 1483 he was considered an experienced political player, into whose hands an army and the leadership of an invasion could be entrusted. Richard III attempted to undermine his position through diplomatic initiatives which offered the duke an Anglo-Breton treaty against France. Henry Tudor swiftly escaped from Brittany and moved in October to the court of France. There he received support which allowed him to invade England in July 1485. Only a month earlier Richard had reassured his ally the Duke of Brittany by ordering that a contingent of 1,000 archers be raised for his use.

Richard III's last year was a time of waiting, with few new initiatives and much rumour and anxiety. It is hard to imagine how a breakthrough and reconciliation of tensions and fears could have been reached among players who had known each other so long and so well. The dynamics were of weary dysfunction, within cycles of trauma and memory which were hard to heal and which were reinforced by followers and patterns of allegiance. As ever, Richard was interested in government in all its forms: he initiated meetings with experts, for example the judges of the Star Chamber in June 1485 with whom he reviewed procedures for trying clerks who falsified court records. In the personal domain Richard sought solace in the collection of books and the recitation of prayers. Into his Book of Hours were added during his years as king some new prayers. Although prayers are highly formulaic texts, the words he had added reverberate powerfully with penitential qualities:

O sweet lord Jesus Christ . . . who was sent from the bosom of the almighty Father into this world . . . to console those in grief and distress, deign to release me from affliction, temptation, grief . . .
Deign to free me, your servant King Richard, from every tribulation, sorrow and trouble in which I am placed . . .

Richard also read the history of kingdoms – he annotated his copy of Geoffrey of Monmouth's *History of the Kings of Britain* – and imagined a role of sorts for himself in more peaceful times. He also read Caxton's introduction to the printed edition of *Morte d'Arthur* of 1485 which recommended, for more peaceful times: 'Let the king arrange jousts and encourage the display of chivalry.'

On 11 August 1485 the king heard that Henry Tudor had landed at Milford Haven (Pembrokeshire). Henry had arrived with seven ships and up to 1,000 men four days earlier. He began a march towards the north, where Richard was strongest. Marching from Wales through Shropshire and Staffordshire, he attracted important new strength – some 5,000 men – in the contingent of Sir Gilbert Talbot and a large Welsh one led by Rhys ap Thomas. Meanwhile, members of the York household from the north joined the king. The eve of the impending battle saw both camps situated on Redmore Plain, between Shenton and Sutton Cheney, about two miles from the market town of Bosworth, most probably in Warwickshire and not Leicestershire, as has traditionally been believed. The king had superior forces, and he held two important hostages: the sons of Talbot and Thomas Lord Stanley, a Yorkist stalwart who was also (as Margaret Beaufort's fourth husband) Henry Tudor's stepfather. Much depended on the force Stanley and his brother Sir William Stanley led, some 3,000 strong. Later accounts described this night as an ominous dark experience, when Richard found himself assailed by demons. Dafydd ap Llewellyn's ode described Richard as 'the little caterpillar of London'.

On the morning of 22 August the experienced Richard placed his forces on a plateau overlooking the plain, Ambien Hill, an excellent vantage point, protected on one side by marshy ground. John Duke of Norfolk – a long-standing Lancastrian servant and king's carver since 1461 – led the vanguard of 1,200, followed by the mounted contingent of some 2,000, led by the king with his trusted guard; Henry Percy led the rearguard. This force faced below a similar contingent of archers led by John Earl of Oxford. After the first volley of arrows, Henry Tudor initiated a bold action which saw Oxford leading a force up the hill, through the marshy tract, and engaging fiercely with Norfolk's force, killing its leader. This exposed the next force, mounted on horseback and led by the king. Richard fought fiercely, battle-axe in hand, even after his horse was killed under him ('A horse! A horse!). Contemporaries described Richard's bravery. He refused the offer of a horse and escape; in Polydore Vergil's words, 'he was killed fighting manfully in the press of his enemies'. The August sun added to the discomfort and disorientation of his mounted men, and a terrible bloody crush followed. Once Lord Stanley joined on Henry Tudor's side, the battle was decided.

A new king, Henry VII, was hastily crowned on the battlefield by Stanley with Richard's crown. Henry Tudor and Elizabeth of York, daughter of Edward IV, were married. The union of their bodies was to create a new lineage – neither York nor Lancaster – and the possibility of a new grounding for politics too. A country tired of war, and appalled by recent bloodshed, was willing to trust in the new hybrid – the Tudor rose – neither white nor red, but both.

Here was a world of possibilities, not certitude, to be tested in the many minute decisions taken by the new king. Henry VII represented the desire for settlement felt by many people in England and Wales, in France and in Scotland, in the capital and in Flanders. But Richard III's awesome hegemony of the north was yet to be conquered. And Henry disposed of this task doggedly over the next decade.

Where there was uncertainty, there was also a great deal of good will. To a sumptuous pedigree roll made for Richard III, showing his putative heirs all linked with red ink, a thick black line was added, for the outsider, whose marriage secured new beginnings. The ambitions of communities, families and individuals never end, and the realms of heaven and earth were soon to be disputed afresh in the new world of the sixteenth century.

Epilogue

The Hollow Crown ends with the year 1485. This year was one of the
great milestones in traditional histories of England, a form of history
preoccupied with the rise and fall of kings. But this book has also
unfolded many other kinds of stories – about responses to famine and
war, about the efforts to seek spiritual security both in the present and
the future, about forms of social life in towns and villages, about
aspirations and their fulfilment through careers in law or the church,
in local government, military service, governance in France, trade and
manufacture. Prospects differed greatly – for men and women, for the
free and the unfree, for those educated in Latin letters or in administrative French, and those who functioned mainly in English, for those
trained to make and produce, and those destined to serve.

The patterns of many of the lives in our period sound much like the
challenges still facing people in the world today. And they are. Yet our
story is also firmly situated within the fourteenth and fifteenth centuries
and within the dominions of the kings who ruled England and Wales
and parts of Ireland and France. These lands have meaningfully been
called British, although they do not encompass the whole of the British
Isles. They were characterized by a political order, bound by law,
administrative units and the exchanges which occurred regularly
between them. Inasmuch as they were ruled jointly, the communities
of these lands also developed capacities to respond to that rule: to act
as local agents of its law – both secular and ecclesiastical – to seek
representation in parliament, to judge how the burden of taxation
might be spread, to manage parishes, maintain churches, to mourn and
occasionally to protest. They could also be inspired by affinity to a
regional magnate, and on occasion were aroused by the sense of patriotic
loyalty.

The generation with which we began experienced enormous hardship during the Great Famine, their sons and daughters then seeing a world halved of its inhabitants by plague – a mortality so far not even matched by the terrible HIV/AIDS epidemic in Africa. Their sons and daughters still feared it – less virulent outbreaks occurred in 1361, 1369 and 1371. That cohort also learned a political lesson of violent regime change, whereby a magnate replaced his cousin as king. The next generation was perhaps not fully convinced that this king was quite steady on his throne – though he put down rebellions effectively – for the country remained awash with rumours of sightings of Richard II. Fewer of them were called up for war – either in the north or in France – but the following generation of young men could easily be excited by war all over again. They were called to serve with a charismatic prince, now King Henry V, to conquer and then rule large parts of Normandy for the next generation.

The less populated lands of the fifteenth century were on the whole feeding people comfortably and sustaining a wide range of productive and manufacturing activities. The markets provided services and goods efficiently to all regions. Niche expertise meant that even modest parishes could hire skilled masons and artists from other regions to adorn their churches. Travelling physicians reached all parts of the country and entertainers travelled the same roads as did wool and cloth merchants and similarly affected the lives of almost every person. In the south of England much agricultural work was geared to feed the hungry metropolis – London – reinforcing that sense of involvement in the capital's life. London was also the natural centre for popular political complaint – as Cade's rebellion was to show in 1450.

The link between prosperity and peace on the one hand, and political action on the other, is a complex one; it challenges observers even in our own times. Political action can often take forms which are unlikely to enter into official documentation and public historical accounts – court records and chronicles, for example. We are thus bound to remain ignorant of the variety of political views and of the ways these may have been expressed or practised: only occasionally can we document rent-strikes, public disapproval of certain forms of rule, distaste for violent lordship or even abusive headship of families. When such views are accessible we have aimed to take note. People act not only when they are utterly miserable, when they can no longer feed their families, but also when their rights are infringed and questioned. The politics which turned into civil war and violence in the fifteenth century saw great blocks of lordship and the expectations of those who led them frustrated and foiled – from Henry of Derby's exile to Richard Duke of York's frustration with the king's rule. Those who followed them were drawn into an ugly set of confrontations: verbal, legal, in image and on battlefields. As we have seen in our own time in Bosnia, Rwanda and Iraq, such periods of confrontation also give licence to thugs and psychopaths.

The title of this book speaks of the crown – the frame of law, ritual and memory – which gave shape to many of the mundane activities of life on manors and in small towns, in parishes and neighbourhoods. The hollowness of that crown invites us to examine the making and unmaking of meanings. Those who wore it claimed rights over vast dominions, and the complex administration which acted in its name managed resources and people. Its potential power was enormous, but the competition over the idea of that crown – what it could claim to achieve and deliver, who was rightly its bearer – was the defining stuff of politics, which involved not only magnates and gentry, but those who depended on them for security of title or safety of limb.

Dynastic claims were repeatedly made in our period for a leading role in public affairs, the right to fill that crown with meaning, in a kingdom advised by parliament but ruled by kings and princes of the blood. These claims were made acute when a king failed to realize the qualities – ineffable and yet vital – which turned a dynast into a tolerable ruler. The great claims of lordship were at the core: when a king failed to act as more than a privileged magnate, then any other magnate might consider himself a better candidate. When alternative genealogical calculation could support such claims, then a Henry of Derby in 1399, a Richard of York in 1450, and an Edward of March in 1461 found their opportunity and their supporters too. Conversely, Richard III failed to convince of his right between 1483 and 1485.

The Hollow Crown offers encounters with the institutions of late medieval civil society: universities and courts of law, fraternities and craft guilds, town councils and libraries, manor houses, schools and Corpus Christi processions. Yet the existence of such institutions did not remove the problem of dependence on the qualities – real or perceived – of the monarch. The Reformation may only have deepened this dependence with the quite new weight it placed upon the monarch as guardian of a complex and many-shaded religious order. The late medieval order thus shares a great deal with the subsequent centuries as a British *ancien régime*.

This story stops at 1485. Historians have claimed that a 'new' monarchy arose with the coming of Henry VII, that a new age was inaugurated, vigorous in administration, ambitious in its European and global performance. But wise readers should be wary of the 'new'. Late summer 1485 brought relief to some, and great joy to others: hope for peace and dynastic union. 'New' is so often an adjective spun by professional illusionists, the makers of political slogans. While appreciating the verve of the 'new' politics, the reader will stop and ask whether it is not above all the fantasy of shapers of opinions – servants of power itself – which historians have been eager to endorse. Most change, deep change, occurs more slowly, experimentally, cautiously and through deliberation. It thus often goes unnoticed by those who live it and make it happen.

EDWARD II = Isabella of France
(1284–1327)   (1292–1358)

EDWARD III = Philippa of Hainault
(1327–77)   (d.1369)

Edward, 'the Black Prince' (d.1376)

Lionel, duke of Clarence (d.1368)

Blanche of Lancaster (d.1369) = (1) John of Gaunt (3) = Katherine Swinford
(d.1399) (Duke of Lancaster 1362–99)   (d.1403)

Edmund of Langley, Duke of York (d.1402)

Thomas of Woodstock, Duke of Gloucester (d.1397)

Anne of Bohemia (d.1394) = RICHARD II (1377–99) (deposed 1399; d.1400)

HENRY IV (1399–1413)

John Beaufort, Earl of Somerset (d.1410)

Joan Beaufort (d.1440) = Ralph Neville, Earl of Westmorland

Edward, Duke of York (d.1415)

Edmund Mortimer, Earl of March (d.1381) = Philippa (d.1382)

HENRY V = (1) Katherine de Valois (d.1437)
(1413–22)

John Beaufort, Earl of Somerset (d.1444)

Edmund Beaufort, Duke of Somerset (d.1455)

Cicely Neville (d.1495) =

*Anne Mortimer (d.1411) = *Richard, Earl of Cambridge (d.1415)

Roger Mortimer, Earl of March (d.1398)

HENRY VI (1422–61) (deposed 1461; d.1471)

John Beaufort, Earl of Somerset (d.1444) = (1) Owen Tudor (d.1461)

Edmund Tudor, Earl of Richmond (d.1456) = Margaret Beaufort (d.1509)

Elizabeth Woodville (d.1492) = EDWARD IV (1461–83)

*Richard, Duke of York (d.1460)

RICHARD III (1483–5) = Anne Neville (d.1485)

Edmund Mortimer, Earl of March (d.1425) = *Anne Mortimer (d.1411)

Edward, Prince of Wales (d.1471)

HENRY VII = Elizabeth of York
(1485–1509)   (d.1503)

George, Duke of Clarence (d.1478)

Edward (d.1484)

*Richard, Duke of York (d.1460)

*Richard, Earl of Cambridge (d.1415)

EDWARD V (1483)

Edward, Earl of Warwick (d.1499)

Richard of York (d.1483)

(see under Edmund of Langley, 4th son of Edward III)

*Appears twice

An Essay on Further Reading

The subjects of historical inquiry have never been more diverse. The historical landscape is now full of groups and individuals who only a generation ago might have seemed too insignificant for historical interest, or so ill-documented as to be 'hidden from history'. Whereas most histories – for leisurely reading as well as for the classroom – have traditionally concentrated on kings and queens, aristocrats and battles, historians are now able to complete the picture: peasants in their communities and alongside their lords, lower clergy alongside monks and bishops, young people among adults and their elders, Welsh as well as English. Most significant, because it touches all areas of life – women alongside men, as wives, daughters, business partners, co-workers and neighbours. With these moves there has been a vast expansion of materials which historians now habitually study. In religious life they seek not only the Latin records of theological and administrative activity, but vernacular texts – in English, Welsh, Anglo-Norman – materials used by wide social groups, and which were often prepared for the purpose of dissemination. The church-wardens' accounts are as important to historians as the records of church councils, for they allow pictures of local daily life to emerge, as it was experienced by most people. Similarly, historians of the economy and peasant life, the study of which was pioneered by Michael Postan (1899–1981) and Rodney Hilton (1916–2002), now study with relish the records of manorial courts, the accounts of those manors, and embed these studies in a close observation of environment and landscape. In cities, the rhythms of work are now more clearly understood through the study of guild records, many of which have been recently published, and by aligning these with the social and religious group – the fraternity – which so many crafts constructed for the promotion of cooperation, cohesion and mutual help among its members. The built environment has been rediscovered and major surveys have been conducted in Winchester, York and Cheapside in London. Archaeology and economic history, urban history and social history all combine to illuminate lives in which spheres of work and play, religion and family were intimately interlinked.

Material culture – food, clothing, household artefacts, public monuments and buildings – all fitted into the lives of, and were understood by, the men and women I have aimed to understand in this book. Hence there has been much mention of crops and food, spices and ale – and historians are becoming more knowing about their value: nutritional, social and symbolic.

By addressing a wider range of historical subjects, by introducing the daily and mundane (work, marriage, parish life) alongside the extraordinary and awe-inspiring (wars, coronations, depositions), historians have also come to use a wider range of materials, and to question traditional judgements on taste and style. To the art of the court, such as the Wilton Diptych (Plate 11), the sumptuous prayerbooks of princes (The Bedford Hours; Plate 18), have now been added the art of the parish, like the doom scene at Wenhaston (Suffolk), the screen at Welsh Newton (Herefordshire) or the vibrant wall-paintings at Pickering (North Yorkshire). Women's taste and initiative in patronage are now acknowledged and realized, not only those of queens, but of gentry women and townswomen also.

The following pages list some points of entry into the vast literature on all aspects of late medieval British life. They begin with a thematic offering of some titles for further reading, and then unfold chapter by chapter, covering themes discussed in them. The full list of works from which information has been used in this book is at http://www.history.qmul.ac.uk/staff/rubinbiblio.html.

BRITAIN: DYNASTIC DOMINIONS

A great deal of recent research and new conception has developed around the political relations within the British Isles, as in Robin Frame, *The Political Development of the British Isles, 1100–1400*, Oxford, new edn, 1995; and R. R. Davies, *The First English Empire: Power and Identities in the British Isles, 1093–1343*, Oxford, 2000. Some thought-provoking articles appeared in *The British Isles, 1100–1500: Comparisons, Contrasts and Connections*, ed. R. R. Davies, Edinburgh, 1988.

On Wales in our period see R. R. Davies, *Age of Conquest: Wales, 1063–1415*, Oxford, new edn, 2000; on Ireland Robin Frame, *Colonial Ireland*, Dublin, 1981 and Art Cosgrove (ed.), *A New History of Ireland II. Medieval Ireland 1169–1534*, Oxford, 1987; on Scotland A. A. M. Duncan, *Scotland: the Making of the Kingdom*, Edinburgh. 1978; Ronald Nicholson, *Scotland: the Later Middle Ages*, Edinburgh, 1974 and Alexander Grant, *Independence and Nationhood: Scotland 1306–1469*, London, 1984.

THE ECONOMY

For authoritative survey essays on agrarian life see *The Agrarian History of England and Wales*, ed. Joan Thirsk and H. P. R. Finberg, Cambridge, 1967–2000; volumes 2 and 3 are most relevant for our period; and on the circulation of money, *A New History of the Royal Mint*, ed. C. E. Challis, Cambridge, 1992.

A useful survey is offered in J. L. Bolton, *The Medieval English Economy 1150–1500*, London, second edn, 1985, which is always aware of the European context. Christopher Dyer has done most to explore the interaction of rural and urban life in the interlocking spheres of production, distribution and exchange. In *Making a Living in the Middle Ages: the People of Britain 850–1520*, New Haven (CN) and London, 2002, he presents the great regional diversity of the British Isles, and the long-term processes by which the interdependence between them developed. In *Standards of Living in the Later Middle Ages: Social Change in England c.1200–1520*, Cambridge, 1989, he demonstrates that use of markets – for selling and buying – touched the life of most people, and that a wide range of niches of consumption coexisted.

The Rural Sector

For a survey of shifts in the status of the unfree see R. H. Hilton, *The Decline of Serfdom in Medieval England*, London, second edn, 1983. For an introduction to rural life and social relations see Phillipp Schofield, *Peasant and Community in Medieval England*, Basingstoke, 2003. For a series of studies of manors, and surviving sources for manorial studies, with a strong demographic emphasis see *Medieval Society and the Manor Court*, ed. Zvi Razi and Richard Smith, Oxford, 1996; and on manorial relations in Wales, R. R. Davies, *Lordship and Society in the March of Wales, 1282–1400*, Oxford, 1978. For a selection of translated sources on rural life see *The English Manor c.1200–c.1500*, trans. and annotated by Mark Bailey, Manchester, 2002. An analysis of the emergent trends of the later part of our period, based on the study of Norfolk, is offered by Jane Whittle, *Development of Agrarian Capitalism: Land and Labour in Norfolk, 1440–1580*, Oxford, 2000.

Town and City Life

On urban life in a series of well-researched and detailed articles, see *The Cambridge Urban History of Britain, 1: 600–1540*, ed. D. M. Palliser, Cambridge, 2000. The best introductions are Susan Reynolds, *An Introduction to the History of English Medieval Towns*, Oxford, 1977; and Edward Miller and John Hatcher, *Medieval England: Towns, Commerce and Crafts, 1086–1348*, London, 1995.

TRADE

Unlike Italy, with its large and sophisticated cities, England, and parts of Wales and Ireland, developed early many small towns. This process is studied in R. H. Britnell, *The Commercialisation of English Society, 1000–1500*, Cambridge, 1993; Britnell's study of Colchester traces the vicissitudes of the economy through a regional study, R. H. Britnell, *Growth and Decline in Colchester, 1300–1525*, Cambridge, 1986. The discussion is extended to other towns in the same author's 'Urban demand in the English economy, 1300–1600', in *Trade, Urban Hinterlands and Market Integration, c.1300–1600*, ed. James A. Galloway, London, 2000, pp. 1–21. On London's mercantile life from the vantage point offered by an influential trade group see Pamela Nightingale, *A Medieval Mercantile Community: the Grocers' Company and the Politics and Trade of London, 1000–1485*, London, 1995.

ARTISANS AND GUILD LIFE

A useful survey is Heather Swanson, *Medieval Artisans: an Urban Class in Late Medieval England*, Oxford, 1989; and a close look at a single trade, which attracted many women, is offered in Judith Bennett, *Ale, Beer, and Brewsters in England: Women's Work in a Changing World, 1300–1600*, New York and Oxford, 1996. The accounts of the prosperous goldsmiths of London reflect all areas of craft-guild activity: training, discipline, recruitment, price-fixing and sociability: *Wardens' Accounts and Court Minute Books of the Goldsmiths' Mystery of London, 1334–1446*, ed. Lisa Jefferson, Woodbridge, 2003.

PARISH LIFE AND NEIGHBOURHOOD RELIGION

A number of local studies have explored the development of neighbourhood through the integrated growth of economic activity, administrative capacity and social institutions which enabled interaction, celebration and bonding. See, for example, Gervase Rosser, *Medieval Westminster: 1200–1540*, Oxford, 1989. The mixed roles of religious fraternities in these spheres is well appreciated and demonstrated in Virginia R. Bainbridge, *Gilds in the Medieval Countryside: Social and Religious Change in Cambridgeshire, c.1350–1558*, Woodbridge, 1996, and David J. F. Crouch, *Piety, Fraternity and Power: Religious Guilds in Late Medieval Yorkshire, 1389–1547*, Woodbridge, 2000.

RELIGION AND ITS DISCONTENTS

R. N. Swanson, *Church and Society in Late Medieval England*, Oxford, 1989, surveys most areas of religious practice and the ideas underlying them. Eamon Duffy, *The Stripping of the Altars: Traditional Religion in England, c.1400– c.1580*, London, 1992, presents the many forms of parochial practice vividly and with rich visual illustration. On sacramental religion and the many ideas and practices which it encouraged, see Miri Rubin, *Corpus Christi: the Eucharist in Late Medieval Culture*, Cambridge, 1991. A work which presents the variety of attitudes to images in worship is Kathleen Kamerick, *Popular Piety and Art in the Late Middle Ages: Image Worship and Idolatry in England, 1350–1500*, New York and Basingstoke, 2002. For a regional study see Andrew D. Brown, *Popular Piety in Late Medieval England: the Diocese of Salisbury, 1250–1550*, Oxford, 1995. All forms of parish religion attracted sustained criticism in this period, not least by those who came to be known as Wycliffites or Lollards: see Anne Hudson, *The Premature Reformation: Wycliffite Texts and Lollard History*, Oxford, 1988.

GENTRY AND ARISTOCRATIC LIFE

Our period sees the rise of the greatest family of magnates to the throne; on the Lancastrians the classic study is Simon Walker, *The Lancastrian Affinity, 1361–1399*, Oxford, 1990. On the many-layered social and political map of a single county see Christine Carpenter, *Locality and Polity: a Study of Warwickshire Landed Society, 1401–1499*, Cambridge, 1992. For an overview of aristocratic households see Kate Mertes, *The English Noble Household, 1250–1600: Good Governance and Politic Rule*, Oxford, 1998; and for many interesting insights which arise from the study of their household accounts, C. M. Woolgar, *The Great Household in Late Medieval England*, New Haven (CT) and London, 1999.

For conceptual guidance in approaching the gentry, see Christine Carpenter, 'Gentry and community in medieval England', *Journal of British Studies* 33 (1994), pp. 340–80; and for an example of a single man's rise to gentry status in royal service, Simon Walker, 'Sir Richard Adderbury (*c.*1330–1399) and his kinsmen: the rise and fall of a gentry family', *Nottingham Medieval Studies* 34 (1990), pp. 113–40. On the power of powerful local men to disrupt as well as ensure the peace, see Nigel Saul, 'Conflict and consensus in English local society', in *Politics and Crisis in Fourteenth-century England*, ed. John Taylor and Wendy Childs, Stroud, 1990, pp. 38–58.

The most famous of all gentry families are the Pastons of Norfolk, who have left tens of revealing letters which illuminate all areas of life. They have been treated in the trilogy by Colin Richmond: *The Paston Family in the Fifteenth Century*, Cambridge, 1990–2000. The letters are published as *The Paston Letters*, ed. with notes by Norman Davis, Oxford, 1971; a recent collection offers a unique glance at the female correspondents in *The Paston Women: Selected Letters*, ed. Diane Watt, Woodbridge, 2004.

WAR, WARFARE AND TRAINING

War can be studied through its technology, its social impact and its rituals. The classic study of chivalry is Maurice Keen, *Chivalry*, New Haven (CN), 1984, which draws on wide European comparisons. Rituals of violence regulated some areas of aristocratic involvement, as discussed in Malcolm Vale, 'Aristocratic violence: trial by battle in the later Middle Ages', in *Violence in Medieval Society*, ed. Richard W. Kaeuper, Woodbridge, 2000, pp. 159–81; but the changing social structure of the armies also affected their ethos, as shown in Maurice Keen, 'Chivalry, nobility, and the man-at-arms', in *War, Literature and Politics in the Late Middle Ages: Essays in Honour of G. W. Coopland*, ed. C. T. Allmand, Liverpool, 1976, pp. 32–45. Nicholas Wright, *Knights and Peasants: the Hundred Years War in the French Countryside*, Woodbridge, 1998, fills an important gap by considering the impact of warfare on the communities which suffered its effects.

On mobilization of forces for the French wars see Andrew Ayton, *Knights and Warhorses: Military Service and the English Aristocray under Edward III*, Woodbridge, 1994; and on some areas of naval technology, Ian Friel, 'Oars, sails and guns: the English and war at sea, *c.* 1200–*c.*1500', in *War at Sea in the Middle Ages and the Renaissance*, ed. John B. Hattendorf and Richard W. Unger, Woodbridge, 2003, pp. 69–79

GOVERNMENT AND THE LAW

The last decade has seen a return to the study of law, and a probing of its political and social contexts. A useful introduction is offered by Alan Harding, *The Law Courts of Medieval England*, London and New York, 1973; and a conceptual frame which links the two is found in G. L. Harriss, 'Political society and the growth of government in late medieval England', *Past and Present* 138 (1993), pp. 28–57. On the jurisprudence which prevailed in the many courts of England and Wales see R. H. Helmholz, *The Ius Commune in*

England: Four Studies, Oxford, 2001; and, on the professionals, E. W. Ives, *The Common Lawyers of Pre-Reformation England*, Cambridge, 1983.

On the operation of parliament the contemporary text is the *Modus tenendi Parliamenti* in *Parliamentary Texts of the Later Middle Ages*, ed. Nicholas Pronay and John Taylor, Oxford, 1980, pp. 13–114. On the working of parliament in our period see G. L. Harriss, 'The formation of Parliament, 1272–1377', A. L. Brown, 'Parliament, *c.*1377–1422', and A. Myers, 'Parliament, 1422–1509', in *The English Parliament in the Middle Ages*, ed. R. G. Davies and J. H. Denton, Manchester, 1981, pp. 29–60, 109–40, and 141–84.

POLITICAL CULTURE

This term is now used to describe a whole range of ideas and expectations, rituals and procedures, through which people participated in politics. This was politics in the broadest sense: parliament and court, but also local assemblies, negotiations of grievances with manorial lords, comportment in local courts, participation in civic councils and the holding of office. Political culture thus covers a wider area than 'politics' has in the past. It aims to engage with the ideas of social groups which wield little official power, and to discover them in materials – visual, poetical, vernacular – since official documentation rarely reflects them. John R. Maddicott's interesting studies of the long-term political 'memory' of Magna Carta is a good example – 'Magna Carta and the local community, 1215–1259', *Past and Present* 102 (1984), pp. 25–65. Another approach was taken by the late Simon Walker in his study of political 'martyrs': 'Political saints in later medieval England', in *The McFarlane Legacy: Studies in Late Medieval Politics and Society*, ed. R. H. Britnell and A. J. Pollard, Fifteenth-Century Series 1, Stroud, 1995, pp. 77–106 and Lesley A. Coote, *Prophecy and Public Affairs in Later Medieval England*, Woodbridge, 2000. The articles in *Political Culture in Late Medieval Britain*, ed. Linda Clark and Christine Carpenter, Woodbridge, 2004, explore the concept of 'political culture' in the fifteenth century. For some ideas about queenship, based on the coronation rite, see Joanna L. Laynesmith, 'Fertility rite or authority ritual? The queen's coronation in England 1445–87', in *Social Attitudes and Political Structures in the Fifteenth Century*, ed. Tim Thornton, Stroud, 2000, pp. 52–68.

Historians are currently debating the importance of constitutional ideas in motivating political decisions and informing practices. Some of the issues are raised in Edward Powell, 'After "After McFarlane": the poverty of patronage and the case for constitutional history', in *Trade, Devotion and Governance: Papers in Later Medieval History*, ed. Dorothy J. Clayton, Richard G. Davies and Peter McNiven, Stroud, 1994, pp. 1–16. On emergent views on contingency, virtue and fortune in determining political affairs – tantamount to a British 'Machiavellianism' – with particular emphasis on the fifteenth century, see Paul Strohm, *The Language of Politics between Chaucer and Shakespeare*, Notre Dame (IN), 2005.

SOCIAL RELATIONS

A useful survey of attitudes to different social groups for the later part of our period is *Fifteenth-Century Attitudes: Perceptions of Society in Late Medieval England*, ed. Rosemary Horrox, Cambridge, 1994. For a seminal discussion of family relations in rural communities, see Zvi Razi, 'Family, land and the village community in later medieval England', *Past and Present* 93 (1981), pp. 3–36, and for a more general study of marriage and family life see Peter Fleming, *Family and Household in Medieval England*, Basingstoke, 2001. On pervasive denigration, and occasional advocacy, of women in public utterance see *Women Defamed and Defended: an Anthology of Medieval Texts*, ed. Alcuin Blamires with Karen Pratt and C. W. Marx, Oxford, 1992.

Ecclesiastical courts were widely used for adjudication in cases related to marriage and its unmaking, promises of marriage and adultery. The rich sources which survive allow us to encounter ideas transmitted in testimonies of people whose lives are rarely recorded. These sources have been used by Richard Helmholz in *Marriage Litigation in Medieval England*, London, 1974; and by Goldberg in *Women in England c. 1275–1525*, trans. and ed. P. J. P. Goldberg, Manchester, 1995. In England, where marriage was usually late, people lived long periods in singlehood, and up to 20 per cent never married; on some of these young and single women see Kim M. Phillips, *Medieval Maidens: Young Women and Gender in England, 1270–1540*, Manchester, 2003.

WOMEN'S WORK

It may seem strange to separate women's work from the section on the economy, but it has been left out of so many authoritative surveys, and often requires unique methodological tools. Eileen Power (1889–1940) led the way in the study of nunneries as working communities, in *Medieval English Nunneries c. 1275–1535*, Cambridge, 1922, and in her portraits of women in *Medieval People*, London, 1924, the eleventh edition of which is accompanied by an introductory essay by Richard M. Smith, London, 1986. Good examples of more recent work are the survey by Mavis E. Mate, *Women in Medieval English Society*, Cambridge, 1999, and Barbara A. Hanawalt, 'Peasant women's contribution to the home economy in late medieval England', in *Women and Work in Preindustrial Europe*, ed. Barbara A. Hanawalt, Bloomington (IN), 1986, pp. 3–19; a dense regional study in P. J. P. Goldberg, *Women, Work, and*

Life-cycle in a Medieval Economy: Women in York and Yorkshire, c.1300–1520, Oxford, 1992; for a manorial study, Judith M. Bennett, *Women in the Medieval English Countryside: Gender and Household in Brigstock before the Plague,* Oxford, 1987; and P. J. P. Goldberg, 'Migration, youth and gender in later medieval England', in *Youth in the Middle Ages,* ed. P. J. P. Goldberg and Felicity Riddy, Woodbridge, 2004, pp. 15–19. A volume of essays on widows contains several examples of women acting independently in work and business: *Medieval London Widows, 1300–1500,* ed. Caroline M. Barron and Anne F. Sutton, London, 1994. For a wide-ranging collection of documents in translation from all areas of women's lives see Goldberg, *Women in England* (above p. 332).

PATRONAGE OF ART AND BOOKS

On writing in the British Isles see *The Cambridge History of Medieval English Literature,* ed. David Wallace, Cambridge, 1999. This volume is cast with capacious vision and includes all regions of the Isles, as well as a broad array of genres with attention to local and regional literatures. Our period sees a broadening of the use of English in several spheres. On this process see *The Idea of the Vernacular: an Anthology of Middle English Literary Theory, 1280–1520,* ed. Jocelyn Wogan-Browne, Nicholas Watson, Andrew Taylor and Ruth Evans, Exeter, 1999. For an anthology of women's writings see *Women's Writing in Middle English,* ed. Alexandra Barratt, London, 1992. On the many types of women's writing, see *Women and Literature in Britain, 1150–1500,* ed. Carol M. Meale, Cambridge, second edn, 1993 and *The Cambridge Companion to Medieval Women's Writing,* ed. Carolyn Dinshaw and David Wallace, Cambridge, 2003.

Courts set fashions in art, music, literature and attire; see the rich detail of Malcolm Vale, *The Princely Court: Medieval Courts and Culture in North-west Europe, 1270–1380,* Oxford, 2001. On patronage of art by women, see Loveday Lewes Gee, *Women, Art and Patronage from Henry III to Edward III, 1216–1377,* Woodbridge, 2003, and on family patronage Nigel Saul, *Death, Art, and Memory in Medieval England: the Cobham Family and their Monuments, 1300–1500,* Oxford, 2001.

Excellent descriptions of manuscripts are available for our period in Lucy Freeman Sandler, *Gothic Manuscripts 1285–1385,* 2 vols, London, 1986; Kathleen L. Scott, *Later Gothic Manuscripts, 1290–1490,* 2 vols, London, 1996; and on stained glass Richard Marks, *Stained Glass in England during the Middle Ages,* London, 1993.

CHAPTER I FAMINE AND DEPOSITION, 1307–1330

The Great Famine and Agrarian Life

William Chester Jordan, *The Great Famine: Northern Europe in the Early Fourteenth Century*, Princeton (NJ), 1996; for a regional study see the work of Ian Kershaw (who was a medieval historian before he became an expert on the Third Reich), *Bolton Priory: the Economy of a Northern Monastery, 1286–1325*, Oxford, 1973; and for another regional perspective, on the Breckland, see Mark Bailey, *A Marginal Economy? East Anglian Breckland in the Later Middle Ages*, Cambridge, 1989, Chapter 4. For background on agrarian life see Bruce M. S. Campbell, *English Seigneurial Agriculture, 1250–1450*, Cambridge, 2000, Chapters 1–5; as well as his 'Economic rent and intensification of English agriculture, 1086–1350', in *Medieval Farming and Technology: the Impact of Agricultural Change in North-west Europe*, ed. Grenville Astill and John Langdon, Leiden, 1997, pp. 225–49. On the aftermath of the Famine see articles in *Before the Black Death: Studies in the 'Crisis' of the Early Fourteenth Century*, ed. Bruce M. S. Campbell, Manchester, 1991.

The North, Scottish Wars and Ireland

For a masterly conceptual discussion of the matters of Britain and its regions see R. R. Davies, *The First English Empire: Power and Identities in the British Isles, 1093–1343*, Oxford, 2000, as well as R. R. Davies, 'Frontier arrangements in fragmented societies: Ireland and Wales', in *Medieval Frontier Societies*, ed. Robert Bartlett and Angus MacKay, Oxford, 1989, pp. 77–100.

A useful recent textbook is A. D. M. Barrell, *Medieval Scotland*, Cambridge, 2000, which should be read alongside the more detailed A. A. M. Duncan, *Scotland: the Making of a Kingdom*, Edinburgh, 1978; and the early section of James Campbell, 'England, Scotland and the Hundred Years War in the fourteenth century', in *Europe in the Late Middle Ages*, ed. J. R. Hale, J. R. L. Highfield and B. Smalley, London, 1965, pp. 184–216. The document which has animated Scottish patriotism and the attention of historians, the Arbroath Declaration, is presented in the pamphlet by A. A. M. Duncan, *The Nation of Scots and the Declaration of Arbroath*, London, 1970; and, on the long-term impact of the Declaration, Edward J. Cowan, *'For Freedom Alone': the Declaration of Arbroath, 1320*, East Linton, 2004.

On the Scottish invasion of Ireland see A. A. M. Duncan's 'The Scots' invasion of Ireland, 1315', in *The British Isles 1100–1500: Comparisons, Contrasts and Connections*, ed. R. R. Davies, Edinburgh, 1988, pp. 100–117. On the Irish contribution to the warfare style of Edward II see James Lydon, 'The hobelar: Irish contribution to mediaeval warfare', *The Irish Sword* 2 (1954–6), pp. 12–16; and on inter-ethnic contacts, Katherine Simms, 'Frontiers in the Irish church – regional and cultural', *Colony and Frontier in Medieval Ireland: Essays Presented to J. F. Lydon*, ed. Terry Barry, Robin Frame and Katherine Simms, London, 1995, pp. 176–200.

Kingship and its Discontents

The King is dead! Long live the King! Times of succession were fraught with hopes and fears, and gave impulse to the writing of oracular and prophetic verse, a traditional British genre. On it see Lesley Coote, *Prophecy and Public Affairs* (above p. 331). The book which places Edward II within the dynastic context, and which is authoritative on war and its finance, is Michael Prestwich, *The Three Edwards: War and State in England, 1272–1377*, London, 1981. On royal patronage and dynastic self-fashioning see Paul Binski, *Westminster Abbey and the Plantagenets: Kingship and the Representation of Power, 1200–1400*, New Haven (CN), 1995. For Edward II's friendship with Piers Gaveston see Pierre Chaplais, *Piers Gaveston: Edward II's Adoptive Brother*, Oxford, 1994, and on Edward II's conflict with the barons see the comprehensive history of the period through a biographical lens, J. R. Maddicott, *Thomas of Lancaster, 1307–1322: a Study in the Reign of Edward II*, London, 1970, as well as Michael Prestwich, 'The Ordinances of 1311 and the politics of the early fourteenth century', in *Politics and Crisis in Thirteenth-century England*, ed. John Taylor and Wendy Childs, Gloucester, 1990, pp. 1–18.

On Gascony, and Anglo-French confrontations which preceded the Hundred Years War, see Malcolm Vale, *The Origins of the Hundred Years War: the Angevin Legacy, 1250–1340*, Oxford, 1996.

For signs of popular discontent see Wendy Childs, ' "Welcome, my tutor": Edward II, John of Powderham and the chroniclers, 1318', in *Church and Chronicle in the Middle Ages: Essays Presented to John Taylor*, ed. Ian Wood and G. A. Loud, London, 1991, pp. 149–63. A detailed account of Edward's last few years is offered in Natalie Fryde, *The Tyranny and Fall of Edward II, 1321–1326*, Cambridge, 1979, and on Edward's end, Joel Burden, 'Re-writing a rite of passage: the peculiar funeral of Edward II', in *The Rites of Passage*, ed. Nicola F. McDonald and W. M. Ormrod, York, 2004, pp. 13–29.

Trade and International Contacts

See Wendy R. Childs, 'Anglo-Portuguese relations in the fourteenth century', in *The Age of Richard II*, ed. James L. Gillespie, Stroud, 1997, pp. 27–49.

Local Affairs and Local Government

A great number of governmental functions developed during these decades, such as the commissions whose documents are edited in *The Records of a Commission of Sewers for Wiggenhall 1319–1324*, ed. A. E. B. Owen, Norfolk Record Society 48, Norwich, 1981. The system depended on the service of prominent men from the counties who served in their localities and also as impartial brokers in other areas, as, for example, the men described in Edward Miller, 'A judge of the early fourteenth century and his Cambridgeshire manor', *Recognitions: Essays Presented to Edmund Fryde*, ed. Colin Richmond and Isobel Harvey, Aberystwyth, 1996, pp. 125–38.

Religion: Word, Art and Artefact

On instruction, see the Anglo-Norman work of a Franciscan friar in Brian J. Levy, *Nine Verse Sermons by Nicholas Bozon: the Art of an Anglo-Norman Poet and Preacher*, Oxford, 1981, and for English instruction, *The Poems of William of Shoreham ab. 1320 Vicar of Chart-Sutton*, ed. M. Konrath, Early English Text Society, ES 86, London, 1902.

On an impressive regional school of religious panel-painting see Christopher Norton, David Park and Paul Binski, *Dominican Painting in East Anglia: the Thornham Parva Retable and the Musée de Cluny Frontal*, Woodbridge, 1987; on women's involvement in artistic patronage see Loveday Lewes Gee (above, p. 333). This period also saw the foundation of several early university colleges, on which see Alan B. Cobban, *English University Life in the Middle Ages*, London, 1999, and *Medieval English Universities: Oxford and Cambridge to c.1500*, Aldershot, 1988.

For a book of advice for kings, based on classical texts and offered during Edward II's worst hours, see Adam of Murimuth and Robert of Avesbury, *Continuatio chronicarum* and *De Gestis mirabilibus regis Edwardi tertii*, Rolls Series, London, 1889.

CHAPTER 2 PLAGUE AND WAR, 1330–1377

A short general survey of the Black Death and its effects in Europe is David Herlihy, *The Black Death and the Transformation of the West*, Cambridge (MA), 1997; a longer one is Ole J. Benedictow, *The Black Death 1346–1353: the Complete History*, Woodbridge, 2004; an older chronological survey is still useful – Philip Ziegler, *The Black Death*, Harmondsworth, second edn, 1998. A collection of translated sources includes materials from all parts of Europe: *The Black Death*, trans. and ed. Rosemary Horrox, Manchester, 1994. On attitudes to death see Paul Binski, *Medieval Death: Ritual and Representation*, London, 1996.

For the effect on pastoral care see William J. Dohar, *The Black Death and Pastoral Leadership in the Diocese of Hereford in the Fourteenth Century*, Philadelphia (PA), 1995, and John Aberth, 'The Black Death in the diocese of Ely: the evidence of the bishop's register', *Journal of Medieval History* 21 (1995), pp. 275–87.

John Hatcher analyses the demographic and economic implications, with useful serial material on wages and prices, in *Plague, Populations and the English Economy, 1348–1530*, London, 1977. Several thematic local studies offer refining detail: Mavis E. Mate, *Daughters, Wives and Widows after the Black Death, 1350–1535*, Woodbridge, 1998; L. R. Poos, *A Rural Society after the Black Death: Essex, 1350–1525*, Cambridge, 1991.

Administrative responses to the mortality are most evident in the legislation passed through parliament, and above all in the statutes which aimed to fix wages, prices and the terms of service. To the classic study, Bertha Haven Putnam, *The Enforcement of the Statutes of Labourers during the First Decade after the Black Death, 1349–1359* (Columbia University Studies in History, Economics and Public Law 32, New York, 1908), have now been added Christopher Given-Wilson, 'Service, serfdom and English labour legislation, 1350–1500', in *Concepts and Patterns of Service in the Later Middle Ages*, ed. Anne Curry and Elizabeth Matthew, Woodbridge, 2000, pp. 21–37 – which is broader in chronological scope and seeks signs of the application of labour legislation over the rural population – and the articles collected in *The Problem of Labour in Fourteenth-century England*, ed. James Bothwell, P. J. P. Goldberg and W. Mark Ormrod, Woodbridge, 2000.

For a concise treatment of the wars in France see Christopher Allmand, *The Hundred Years War: England and France at War, c.1300–c.1450*, Cambridge, revised edn, 2001. On spying, see John R. Alban and Christopher T. Allmand, 'Spies and spying in the fourteenth century', in *War, Literature and Politics in the Late Middle Ages: Essays in Honour of G. W. Coopland*, ed. C. T. Allmand, Liverpool, 1976, pp. 73–101; on the consequence for the conquered population, see Nicholas Wright, *Knights and Peasants* (above, p. 330). For the most celebrated account of chivalric performance, see the *Life of the Black Prince by the Herald of Sir John Chandos*, ed. Mildred K. Pope and Eleanor C. Lodge, Oxford, 1910, and on chivalric culture more widely, Juliet Vale, *Edward III and Chivalry: Chivalric Society and its Context 1270–1350*, Woodbridge, 1982. On the institution of political patronage within the ethos of chivalry created by Edward III, the crown and political relations, see Hugh E. L. Collins, *The Order of the Garter, 1348–1461: Chivalry and Politics in Late Medieval England*, Oxford, 2000.

On French coronation treatises which refer tellingly to the English claim, see Carra Ferguson O'Meara, *Monarchy and Consent: the Coronation Book of Charles V of France*, London, 2001.

To support the efforts in Scotland and in France, a fiscal as well as a military bureaucracy developed on the foundations set up by Edward I, on which see Michael Prestwich, *War, Politics and Finance under Edward I*, Aldershot, 1991. War and finance in this period are studied by Gerald Harriss in *King, Parliament and Public Finance in Medieval England to c.1369*, Oxford, 1975; for a long-term view of fiscal developments, see W. Mark Ormrod, 'England in the Middle Ages', in *The Rise of the Fiscal State in Europe, c.1200–1815*, Oxford, 1999, pp. 19–52.

Patronage in the service of political stability is analysed in several articles by James Bothwell: 'Edward III and the "new nobility": largesse and limitation in fourteenth-century England', *English Historical Review* 112 (1997), pp. 1111–40; and ' "Until he receive the equivalent in land and rent": the use of annuities as endowment patronage in the reign of Edward III', *Historical Research* 70 (1997), pp. 146–69. Parliament was the venue for deliberation over taxation, and its working is surveyed in John R. Maddicott, 'Parliament and the constituencies, 1272–1372', in *The English Parliament in the Middle Ages*, ed. R. G. Davies and J. H. Denton, Manchester, 1981, pp. 61–87. On the arrangements for representation of the clergy in parliamentary deliberation, see Jeffrey H. Denton and John P. Dooley, *Representatives of the Lower Clergy in Parliament, 1295–1340*, Woodbridge, 1987. Edward III's last parliament, one which called for root and branch reform, has come to be known as the 'Good Parliament', and is studied minutely in George Holmes, *The Good Parliament*, Oxford, 1975.

This period experienced an intensification of religious instruction, and the production of several manuals for the clergy, as well as for the use of lay people. Archbishop Thoresby of York disseminated a guidebook for lay people: *The Lay Folk's Catechism*, ed. T. F. Simmons and H. E. Nolloth, Early English Text Society 118, London, 1901. A guide to penance for the laity was offered by Dan Michel c.1340 in *Ayenbite of Inwit*, 2 vols, Early English Text Society 278, Oxford, 1979. For the activities of another bishop see the *Register of William Bateman, Bishop of Norwich 1344–1355*, ed. Phyllis E. Pobst, Canterbury and York Society, 84 and 90, 1996–2000.

Church courts interacted with people even in small towns and villages, for which see the evidence in *Lower Ecclesiastical Jurisdiction in Late-medieval England: the Courts of the Dean and Chapter of Lincoln, 1336–1349, and the Deanery of Wisbech, 1458–1484*, ed. L. R. Poos, Records of Social and Economic History New Ser. 32, Oxford, 2001. There was also creative writing in an emergent mystical style, like the English devotional prose of Richard Rolle (*c.*1290–1349), which was widely known and appreciated; see Claire Elizabeth McIlroy, *The English Prose Treatises of Richard Rolle*, Woodbridge, 2004.

CHAPTER 3 AN EMPTY LAND AND ITS KING, 1377–1399

An interesting commentator on the period is Thomas Brinton, Bishop of Rochester, in his Latin sermons delivered to a variety of religious and learned forums. He excoriates sin and corruption with a great deal of comment directed at contemporary sources of abuse and discomfort: *The Sermons of Thomas Brinton, Bishop of Rochester, 1373–1389*, ed. M. A. Devlin, Camden Society Third Series, 85 and 86, London, 1954.

On diversification of the economy in the decades after the Black Death, Mark Bailey, *A Marginal Economy?* (above, p. 334) and L. R. Poos, *A Rural Society* (above, p. 337) offer interesting regional vantage points. New industries developed, like fishing, which was studied in Richard C. Hoffmann's articles, 'Economic development and aquatic ecosystems in medieval Europe', in *American Historical Review* 10 (1996), pp. 630–69, and 'Medieval fishing', in *Working with Water in Medieval Europe: Technology and Resource-use*, ed. Paolo Squatriti, Leiden, 2000, pp. 331–93.

The long-term effects of the Black Death and the subsequent plagues (1361, 1369, 1371) took the form of a general rise in the standard of living of workers, and this took shape in the more varied diets and larger portions of meat, fish and ale in them. London was a large consumer, and a research project at the Centre for Metropolitan History has revealed the patterns of its needs, and the manner in which these were met. The project resulted in several publications, such as James A. Galloway, Derek Keene and Margaret Murphy, 'Fuelling the city: production and distribution of firewood and fuel in London's region, 1290–1400', *Economic History Review* 49 (1996), pp. 447–72, and James A. Galloway, 'Driven by drink? Ale consumption and the agrarian economy of the London region, *c.*1300–1400', in *Food and Eating in Medieval Europe*, ed. Martha Carlin and Joel T. Rosenthal, London, 1998, pp. 87–100.

London's population had been depleted but it was still large and demanding. The 'biography' of the city is offered in Caroline M. Barron, *London in the Later Middle Ages: Government and People 1200–1500*, Oxford, 2004, which expertly explores the intertwined spheres of trade and politics. Paul Strohm brings to light several episodes in the life of London during these decades in his collection *Hochon's Arrow: the Social Imagination of Fourteenth-century Texts*, Princeton (NJ), 1992, especially 'Hochon's arrow' and 'The textual environment of Chaucer's "Lak of Stedfastnesse"', pp. 11–31 and 57–74. London was the chosen seat of foreign traders, whose work is interestingly described in Helen Bradley, 'The Datini factors in London, 1380–1410', in *Trade, Devotion and Governance: Papers in Later Medieval History*, ed. Dorothy J. Clayton, Richard G. Davies and Peter McNiven, Stroud, 1994, pp. 55–79; also Derek Pearsall, 'Strangers in fourteenth-century London', in *The Stranger in Medieval Society*, ed. F. R. P. Akehurst and Stephanie Cain Van d'Elden, Medieval Cultures 12, Minneapolis (MN), 1997, pp. 46–62.

The quintessential London poets are Geoffrey Chaucer – on whom see the historical and literary discussion of Paul Strohm in *Social Chaucer*, Cambridge (MS), 1989 – and the poet of Cornhill, William Langland, who wrote *Piers Plowman*, a dream poem which survives in five versions, and which captures the moral and social unrest of the 1360s and 1370s, and which is available in *Piers Plowman*, Harmondsworth, 1959.

The most recent biography of Richard II is Nigel Saul's *Richard II*, London and New Haven (CT), 1997. For accounts of his deposition a wide range of sources is offered by *Chronicles of the Revolution, 1397–1400: the Reign of Richard II*, trans. and ed. Christopher Given-Wilson, Manchester, 1993. Richard II was the target of criticism from the moment of his succession, a boy unfit to rule, and guided by his elders in a royal council. This image of infantile wilfulness stuck to Richard for life, sometimes strangely attached to complaints about his 'tyranny'. Christopher Fletcher analyses some of these images in the political language of the period in 'Ideas of manhood and the practice of politics: the case of Richard II', *Past and Present* (2005). At Richard's side was his formidable uncle, John of Gaunt, with whom the king maintained a variable relationship of trust and suspicion. On Gaunt, see Anthony Goodman, *John of Gaunt: the Exercise of Princely Power in Fourteenth-century Europe*, Harlow, 1992.

Within a decade of Richard's accession a concerted opposition was mounted against his government by magnates who came to be known as 'Appellants', and for a while in 1387 England was in a state of civil war; see Anthony Goodman, *Loyal Conspiracy: the Lords Appellant under Richard II*, London, 1971. The next stage of overt political confrontation opened in 1397; on modes of address in these final years of the reign see Nigel Saul, 'Richard II and the vocabulary of kingship', *English Historical Review* 110 (1995), pp. 854–77.

By 1397 Richard II had created a safe haven for his court in Cheshire and Wales, as shown in R. R. Davies, 'Richard II and the principality of Chester 1397–9', in *The Reign of Richard II: Essays in Honour of May McKisack*, ed. F. R. H. du Boulay and Caroline Barron, London, 1971, pp. 256–79.

Richard II's court attracted comment from home and abroad, high and low.

Philippe de Mezières, French soldier and diplomat, wrote a *Letter to Richard II* in which he advocated peace with France and a vision of future political harmony, which would allow both nations to engage in crusading. Comment about Richard at home never came in stranger form than the petition presented in 1397, which brazenly listed governmental abuse and recommended reform; see Alison McHardy, 'Haxey's case, 1397: the petition and its presenter reconsidered', in *The Age of Richard II*, ed. James L. Gillespie, Stroud, 1997, pp. 93–114.

Ultimately, Richard II was deposed through the challenge and determination of Henry of Derby, who returned from exile in France to demand his inheritance, the Duchy of Lancaster – by force. He was a veteran of warfare in eastern Europe, and had strong connections to other European noble houses, as shown in F. R. H. du Boulay, 'Henry of Derby's expedition to Prussia 1390–1 and 1392', in *The Reign of Richard II: Essays in Honour of May McKisack*, London, 1971, pp. 153–72. *Chronicles of the Revolution* (above, p. 340) tells the stories of these momentous years.

Richard's court was renowned for its patronage of art and poetry. Indeed, the term 'Ricardian' has been used by scholars to describe the explosion of vernacular poetry which was informed by a deep awareness of continental work, of which Geoffrey Chaucer and John Gower are the main examples; see J. A. Burrow, *Ricardian Poetry: Chaucer, Gower, Langland and the Gawain Poet*, London, 1992. On French poetry and music in English aristocratic households and the court, see Ardis Butterfield, 'French culture and the Ricardian court', in *Essays on Ricardian Literature in Honour of J. A. Burrow*, ed. Alastair J. Minnis, Charlotte C. Morse and Thorlac Turville-Petre, Oxford, 1997, pp. 82–120. On the flourishing of Welsh poetry in a variety of genres and metres see D. Simon Evans, *Medieval Religious Literature*, Writers of Wales, Cardiff, 1986. Richard's court attracted the work of skilled writers and artists. The most famous artefact produced in and for it is the Wilton Diptych, the restoration of which has created a new burst of interest, exemplified in Dillian Gordon, *The Wilton Diptych*, London, 1993.

Richard II's reign saw early challenges in the form of the convergent regional political movements which arose in East Anglia and Kent, and which have come to be known as the Peasants' Revolt. The sources have been collected and translated by R. B. Dobson in *The Peasants' Revolt of 1381*, London, second edn, 1983; for seminal articles on the uprising, see *The English Rising of 1381*, ed. T. H. Aston, Oxford, 1981. A number of literary scholars have discussed the surviving political invective, and the conditions which allowed our sources to survive, for example Steven Justice, *Writing and Rebellion: England in 1381*, Berkeley (CA), 1994 and Paul Strohm, ' "A revelle!": chronicle evidence and the rebel voice', in *Hochon's Arrow* (above, p. 340), pp. 33–56. Regional studies which track the aftermath of the events have also added depth and variation to the movement, studies such as Herbert Eiden, 'Norfolk,

1382: a sequel to the Peasants' Revolt', *English Historical Review* 114 (1999), pp. 370–77, and Andrew Prescott, 'London in the Peasants' Revolt: a portrait gallery', *London Journal* 7 (1981), pp. 125–43. Political activism and polemic were also displayed in less spectacular ways, but were noticeable none the less on the public buildings of London – in bills and images defaming public figures – and are studied in Wendy Scase, ' "Strange and wonderful bills": bill-casting and political discourse in late medieval England', *New Medieval Literatures* 2 (1998), pp. 225–47.

The social unrest which coalesced into these political movements was linked by contemporaries and by historians to the level and shape of taxation in the 1370s, particularly the poll tax, imposed from 1377. On this type of taxation, see Caroline M. Barron, 'The fourteenth century poll tax returns for Worcester', *Midland History* 14 (1989), pp. 1–29. The rebels were animated by popular expectations of the king as a fount of justice. On the social context of the common law see Paul Brand, 'The making of the Common Law', and 'The early history of the legal profession in the lordship of Ireland' in *Courtroom and Classroom: the Education of Lawyers in England Prior to 1400*, London and Rio Grande, 1992, pp. 57–75 and 21–56.

Another challenging area which demanded a public official response was the figure of John Wyclif and the teaching of his Oxford theology, together with the related dissenting positions which spread through preaching and writing in the vernacular. On his life and times see *Wyclif in his Times*, ed. Anthony Kenny, Oxford, 1986; and on the world of writing which claimed his views as inspiration, and incorporated other critiques, see Anne Hudson's many articles, such as those collected in *Lollards and their Books*, London, 1985, as well as her *The Premature Reformation* (above, p. 329). The social context of religious debate is given in articles in the collection *Lollardy and the Gentry in the Later Middle Ages*, ed. Margaret Aston and Colin Richmond, Stroud, 1997.

The complaints habitually voiced by or imputed to dissenters and heretics touched upon the value of the many common practices of religious life – particularly those which heightened or 'spiced up' routine parish worship: the cults of saints' relics, prayers to sacred images, pilgrimages to shrines, dramatic preaching. The life of parishes and dioceses continued to unfold in thousands of acts of administration, appointment of priests, provision of spaces and trappings, and ritual, recorded in churchwardens' accounts and in bishops' registers.

CHAPTER 4 USURPATION AND THE CHALLENGES TO ORDER, 1399–1422

On dynastic change and the difficulties of establishing rule, see Paul Strohm, *England's Empty Throne: Usurpation and the Language of Legitimation, 1399–1422*, London, 1998. The first decade of the fifteenth century saw a great deal of turmoil and experimentation which reshaped the politics of the British Isles. The sense of insecurity, distrust and suspicion which arises from so many sources is well captured in Simon Walker, 'Rumour, sedition and popular protest in the reign of Henry IV', *Past and Present* 166 (2000), pp. 31–65. The greatest challenge of them all was the Welsh revolt, studied with elegance and wisdom in R. R. Davies, *The Revolt of Owain Glyn Dŵr*, Oxford, 1995. Other challenges arose from magnates, whose aspirations are studied in Alastair Dunn, *The Politics of Magnate Power in England and Wales, 1389–1413*, Oxford, 2003; and some astute comments on the development of this group over the long term are offered in J. A. Tuck, 'The emergence of a northern nobility 1250–1400', in *Northern History* 22 (1986), pp. 1–17. On the rising in Yorkshire which led to the execution of Archbishop Scrope, see the detailed source analysis in Simon Walker, 'The Yorkshire risings of 1405: texts and contexts', in *Henry IV: the Establishment of the Regime, 1399–1406*, ed. Gwilym Dodd and Douglas Biggs, Woodbridge, 2003, pp. 161–84.

Parliament had been the forum in which Richard II was deposed, it gave the new king Henry IV his crown, and also aimed to determine the remit of his powers. On Henry IV's title, see Gaillard Lapsley, 'The parliamentary title of Henry IV', *English Historical Review* 49 (1934), pp. 577–606; and on a confrontation between king and parliament, A. J. Pollard, 'The Lancastrian experiment revisited: Henry IV, Sir John Tiptoft and the parliament of 1406', *Parliamentary History* 14 (1995), pp. 103–19.

One of the areas in which royal authority aimed to assert itself was in the persecution of heresy. A remarkable working relationship developed between Henry IV and Archbishop Thomas Arundel; his biography offers crucial insights into the chemistry between these men: Margaret Aston, *Thomas Arundel: a Study of Church Life in the Reign of Richard II*, Oxford, 1967. One of the initiatives against perceived heterodoxy was the publication of the Constitutions of 1407 and then 1409, which defined areas and modes of religious instruction and debate; on these see Nicholas Watson, 'Censorship and cultural change in late-medieval England: vernacular theology, the Oxford translation debate, and Arundel's Constitutions of 1409', *Speculum* 70 (1995), pp. 822–64. Peter McNiven, *Heresy and Politics in the Reign of Henry IV: the Burning of John Badby*, Woodbridge, 1987, examines the whole reign through the engagement with religious dissent. The burning of Badby was witnessed by the Prince of Wales, who as king was no less committed to orthodoxy; see Jeremy

Catto, 'Religious change under Henry V', in *Henry V: the Practice of Kingship*, ed. G. L. Harriss, Oxford, 1985, pp. 97–115. The labelling and in some cases persecution of suspected heretics took several forms, and resulted in stereotypes like those studied in Derek Pearsall, ' "Lunatyk Lollares" in *Piers Plowman*', in *Religion in the Poetry and Drama of the Late Middle Ages in England*, ed. Piero Botani and Anna Torti, Cambridge, 1990, pp. 163–78. Yet Wycliffite and dissenting writing continued to explore familiar genres and formats; some examples are available in *The Piers Plowman Tradition: a Critical Edition of Pierce the Ploughman's Crede, Richard the Redeless, Mum and Sothsegger, and the Crowned King*, ed. Helen Barr, London, 1993. It was easy to fail official standards of orthodoxy not only by open critique but through excessive conventional piety. A remarkable character was Margery Kempe of King's Lynn, who dictated her autobiography in English, and in it recounted the transformation of her life from mother and wife in a prosperous mercantile family, to a perpetual pilgrim, visionary, and absorbed enthusiast for religious experiences in Europe and the Near East: *The Book of Margery Kempe: Annotated Edition*, ed. Barry Windeatt, Woodbridge, 2004.

One way in which the new dynasty aimed to bolster its image and win hearts was through poetry which celebrated national achievements. Already in the late years of Henry IV the poet Thomas Hoccleve, Clerk of the Privy Seal, wrote for the Prince of Wales a poem in the genre of Mirrors for Princes, his *Regiment of Princes*, in English. Hoccleve continued to comment when the prince became Henry V, as in his *Remonstrance against Oldcastle*, which chastised the eponymous knight-turned-dissenter. See Nicholas Perkins, *Hoccleve's Regiment of Princes: Counsel and Constraint*, Cambridge, 2001; on bureaucracy and writing see Ethan Knapp, *The Bureaucratic Muse: Thomas Hoccleve and the Literature of Late Medieval England*, University Park (PA), 2001. The most authoritative biography of Henry V is C. T. Allmand, *Henry V: the Practice of Kingship*, ed. G. L. Harriss, Oxford, 1985, and, for an almost contemporary view, see *The Deeds of Henry V (Gesta Henrici Quinti)*, trans. and ed. Frank Taylor and John S. Roskell, Oxford, 1975.

The provision of law and administration, together with effective collection of taxes and recruitment to the royal armies, were the preconditions of successful invasion, conquest and maintenance of French lands. On the efforts invested in enforcement of the rule of law at home see Edward Powell, *Kingship, Law and Society: Criminal Justice in the Reign of Henry V*, Oxford, 1989.

An event which touched only a few thousand men from England and Wales far across the channel became one of the most celebrated moments of British history, remembered in monument, song and film: the Battle of Agincourt. One of the most moving accounts is John Keegan's *The Face of Battle: a Study of Agincourt (France), Waterloo and Somme*, London, 1976. On the defence and management of Normandy the authority is C. T. Allmand, *Lancastrian Normandy, 1415–1450: the History of a Mediaeval Occupation*, Oxford, 1983.

Many interesting aspects of life in towns and garrisons arise from the essays in *Arms, Armies and Fortifications in the Hundred Years War*, ed. Anne Curry and Michael Hughes, Woodbridge, 1994, and, more recently, Anne Curry, 'Isolated or integrated? The English soldier in Lancastrian Normandy', in *Courts and Regions in Medieval Europe*, ed. Sarah Rees Jones, Richard Marks and A. J. Minnis, York, 2000, pp. 191–210.

The economy of these decades was characterized by many different trends, and saw the persistence of diversification of manorial production and a growing array of services and goods on sale. On management of the economy see David Stone, 'The productivity of sheep in late medieval England', *Agricultural History Review*, 5 (2003), pp. 1–22, and Andrew K. G. Jones, 'Bedfordshire: the fifteenth century', in *The Peasant Land Market in Medieval England*, ed. P. D. A. Harvey, Oxford, 1984, pp. 178–251.

A number of studies explore the aristocratic and gentry households based on the minute detail of household accounts – for example, ffiona Swabey, 'The household of Alice de Bryene, 1412–14', in *Food and Eating in Medieval Europe*, ed. Martha Carlin and Joel T. Rosenthal, London, 1998, pp. 133–44; and Christopher Woolgar, 'Fasts and feast: conspicuous consumption and the diet of the nobility in the fifteenth century', in *Revolution and Consumption in Medieval England*, ed. Michael Hicks, Woodbridge, 2001, pp. 7–25.

CHAPTER 5 'FOR THE WORLD WAS THAT TIME SO STRANGE', 1422–1461

For biographies of Henry VI and Margaret of Anjou, see Ralph A. Griffiths, *The Reign of Henry VI*, second edn, Stroud, 1998, and Helen E. Maurer, *Margaret of Anjou: Queenship and Power in Late Medieval England*, Woodbridge, 2003. For a subtle and authoritative analysis of the politics of the reign, see John Watts, *Henry VI and the Politics of Kingship*, Cambridge, 1996. The major political figures of the king's minority were Humphrey Duke of Gloucester, John Duke of Bedford, and Henry Cardinal Beaufort. On Gloucester's bibliophilia and involvement in contemporary Italian letters see Susanne Saygin, *Humphrey, Duke of Gloucester (1390–1447) and the Italian Humanists*, Leiden, 2000; on Bedford's European network of patronage and collection see Jenny Stratford, *The Bedford Inventories: the Worldly Goods of John, Duke of Bedford, Regent of France (1389–1435)*, Oxford, 1993; on Beaufort, see G. L. Harriss, *Cardinal Beaufort: a Study in Lancastrian Ascendancy and Decline*, Oxford, 1988.

The political, military and cultural legacy of Henry V's years continued to occupy the talent, resources and administrative efforts of the state. The court continued to produce poetry and pronouncements in support of these, and around particularly challenging moments of state: John Lydgate led here as a poet 'laureate', for whom see Derek Pearsall, *John Lydgate*, London, 1970. On 'propaganda' see J. A. Doig, 'Propaganda, public opinion and the siege of Calais in 1436', in *Crown, Government and People in the Fifteenth Century*, ed. Rowena E. Archer, Stroud, 1995, pp. 79–106.

The king was surrounded by several proactive administrators, such as Henry Chichele, Archbishop of Canterbury, who continued to invigilate over persecution of heresy and reform of the clergy: E. F. Jacob, *Henry Chichele and the Ecclesiastical Politics of his Age*, London, 1952. The legal emphasis in ecclesiastical formation is evident in this period, with a growing number of bishops with legal, rather than theological, training, and with an interest in legal thought. University became the training ground for future high-level administrators, in institutions like All Souls College, which was founded in 1438 as a memorial to the dead in the French wars, but became a powerhouse for training future bishops and high-ranking administrators. See Jeremy Catto, 'The world of Henry Chichele and the foundation of All Souls', in *Unarmed Soldiery: Studies in the Early History of All Souls College*, Oxford, 1996, pp. 1–13.

Henry VI's own taste and preferences were expressed in the interlocked spheres of education and religion. His foundation at Eton (1440) was a feeder school for King's College, Cambridge (founded 1441), in which cadres of royal servants were to be formed. On educational thinking and initiatives in this period, see Virginia Davis, *William Waynflete, Bishop and Educationalist*, Woodbridge, 1993. Henry VI favoured a group of scholars/teachers from these institutions who became his confidants and confessors, one of whom, John Blacman, ultimately even wrote a hagiographical account of the king's life. The circle is discussed in detail and with sympathy by Roger Lovatt, 'John Blacman: biographer of Henry VI', in *The Writing of History in the Middle Ages: Essays Presented to Richard William Southern*, ed. R. H. C. Davis and J. M. Wallace-Hadrill, Oxford, 1981, pp. 415–44.

The patronage of royals and other magnates and the support lent by academic colleges brought to England books, scholars and scholarship which had for a generation or two become the staple of Tuscan schools. Humphrey Duke of Gloucester was an important motivator, and much of his library reached Oxford University. For some examples, see David Rundle, 'Two unnoticed manuscripts from the collection of Humfrey, Duke of Gloucester', *Bodleian Library Record* 16 (1988), pp. 211–24 and pp. 299–313; see also Susanne Saygin, *Humphrey, Duke of Gloucester* (above, p. 345).

Vernacular writing also addressed the matter of politics with vigour; leading administrators and soldiers debated the complex choices which faced government, as John Fastolf did in his report on France: Malcolm Vale, 'Sir John Fastolf's "report" of 1435: a new interpretation reconsidered', *Nottingham Medieval Studies* 17 (1973), pp. 78–84. A similar case was the programme for national renewal based on economic and political reorientation, which was put forward in *The Libelle of Englysche Polycye*, ed. G. Warner, Oxford, 1926. A great deal of writing on the making of politics and on the nature of social obligation within the ruling elite, was produced, in poetry or tracts such as the *Book of Noblesse* by William Worcester, or the advice offered by a member of the landed gentry to his son, *Peter Idley's Instructions to his Son*, ed. Charlotte d'Evelyn, Boston and London, 1935; or from mother to daughter, as in Felicity Riddy, 'Mother knows best: reading social change in a courtesy text', *Speculum* 71 (1996), pp. 66–86. For an archive of documents collected by a London grocer alert to London and national politics, see the edition in *The Politics of Fifteenth-century England: John Vale's Book*, ed. Margaret L. Kekewich, Stroud, 1995.

To the political challenges at home and abroad were added the pressures of a period of slump, which was experienced in most regions between the 1430s and the 1450s. On the economic crisis of the mid-century, useful articles are John Hatcher, 'The great slump of the mid-fifteenth century', in *Progress and Problems in Medieval England: Essays in Honour of Edward Miller*, ed. Richard Britnell and John Hatcher, Cambridge, 1996, pp. 237–72; Edmund Fryde, 'Economic depression in England in the second and third quarters of the fifteenth century: effective resistances of tenants to landlords as one of its consequences. Defiances and rent strikes', in *Violence in Medieval Society*, ed. Richard W. Kaeuper, Woodbridge, 2000, pp. 215–26; and Mavis Mate, 'The economic and social roots of medieval popular rebellion: Sussex in 1450–1451', *Economic History Review* 45 (1992), pp. 661–76. On the trends in serfdom see Diarmaid MacCulloch, 'Bondmen under the Tudors', in *Law and Government under the Tudors. Essays Presented to Sir Geoffrey Elton Regius Professor of Modern History in the University of Cambridge on the Occasion of his Retirement*, ed. Claire Cross, David Loades and J. J. Scarisbrick, Cambridge, 1988, pp. 91–109.

The decline in income affected landowners of modest estates, members of the parish gentry. See the issues arising from the need to secure inheritance and engage in protracted litigation, often led by widows, in *The Amburgh Papers. The Brokholes Inheritance in Warwickshire, Hertfordshire and Essex c.1417–c.1453. Chetham's Manuscript Mun. E6 10 (4)*, ed. Christine Carpenter, Woodbridge, 1998. Magnates were still able to make grand gestures of social obligation and for the well-being of their souls, such as the foundation by the Earl and Countess of Suffolk of God's House at Ewelme studied in John A. A. Goodall, *God's House at Ewelme: Life, Devotion and Architecture in a Fifteenth-century Almshouse*, Aldershot, 2001. On the lifestyle of a comfortable clerical household, see the evidence in *A Small Household of the XVth Century, Being the Account Book of Munden's Chantry, Bridport*, ed. Kathleen L. Wood-Legh, Manchester, 1956.

The parish remained an important focus for local experience and social activity. In areas which benefited from the still buoyant wool trade some magnificent buildings were erected. Urban parishes in particular accumulated books which sometimes circulated as libraries: John Shinners, 'Parish libraries in medieval England', in *A Distinct Voice: Medieval Studies in Honor of Leonard E. Boyle*, ed. Jacqueline Brown and William P. Stoneman, Notre Dame (IN), 1997, pp. 207–30; and Wendy Scase, 'Reginald Pecock, John Carpenter and John Colop's "common profit" books: aspects of book owner-ship and circulation in fifteenth-century London', *Medium Aevum* 61 (1992), pp. 261–74. On participation in parish enterprises see Katherine French, 'Parochial fundraising in late medieval Somerset', in *The Parish in English Life 1400–1600*, ed. Katherine L. French, Gary G. Gibbs and Beat A. Kumin, Manchester, 1997, pp. 115–32; Clive Burgess, 'London parishioners in times of change: St Andrew Hubbard, Eastcheap, c. 1450–1570', *Journal of Ecclesiastical History* 53 (2002), pp. 38–63.

Towns attempted to enhance their competitive advantages: see J. J. Kermode, *Medieval Merchants: York, Beverley and Hull in the Later Middle Ages*, Cambridge, 1998. They attempted to control disruptive behaviour, often through coercive regulation: see David R. Carr, 'From pollution to prostitution: supervising the citizens of fifteenth-century Salisbury', *Southern History* 19 (1997), pp. 24–41; Jessica Freeman, 'Middlesex in the fifteenth century', in *Revolution and Consumption in Late Medieval England*, ed. Michael Hicks, Woodbridge, 2001, pp. 89–103; and on brothels, see Ruth Karras, *Common Women: Prostitution and Sexuality in Medieval England*, New York, 1996. On the tensions surrounding ethnic identity in northern towns, see Cynthia J. Neville, 'Local sentiment and the "national" enemy in northern England in the later Middle Ages', *Journal of British Studies* 35 (1996), pp. 419–37, and Judy Ann Ford, 'The assimilation of foreigners in the lay parish community: the case of Sandwich', in *The Parish in English Life 1400–1600*, ed. French, Gibbs, and Kumin (see above), pp. 203–16.

London politics saw pressure for greater inclusion from middling crafts, as discussed in Caroline Barron, *London in the Later Middle Ages* (above, p. 339). Mercantile well-being and military hegemony were so closely linked that London merchants were involved in politics more than ever before, and developed instruments for record and reference, such as the Chronicles of London discussed in Mary-Rose McLaren, *The London Chronicles of the Fifteenth Century: a Revolution in English Writing*, Woodbridge, 2002.

Mid-century saw great activity in the translation into English of the lives of martyrs, and especially of female martyrs for female patrons. The most impor-tant resulting collection was Osbern Bokenham, *Legendys of Hooly Wummen*, ed. Mary S. Sarjeantson, Early English Text Society 206, London, 1938. On this work see A. S. G. Edwards, 'The transmission and audience of *Osbern Bockenham's Legendys of Hooly Wummen*', in *Late Medieval Religious Texts and their Transmission: Essays in Honour of A. I. Doyle*, Cambridge, 1994. On the interest in female martyrs, attributed to women's choices, see Eamon

Duffy, 'Holy maydens, holy wyfes: the cult of women saints in fifteenth- and sixteenth-century England', in *Studies in Church History* 27 (1990), pp. 175–96.

By the late 1440s the crown was bankrupt (G. L. Harriss, 'Marmaduke Lumley and the Exchequer crisis of 1446–1449', in *Aspects of Late Medieval Government and Society: Essays Presented to J. R. Lander*, ed. John G. Rowe, Toronto, 1986, pp. 143–78) and was ceding land in France; the royal project was in tatters. The political challenges to the king took several forms: popular movements on London, such as the Cade Rebellion (I. M. W. Harvey, *Cade's Rebellion of 1450*, Oxford, 1991); and for the challenges from Richard Duke of York, who demanded greater say and was ultimately named Henry VI's heir, see Michael A. Hicks, 'From megaphone to microscope: the correspondence of Richard Duke of York with Henry VI in 1450 revisited', *Journal of Medieval History* 25 (1999), pp. 243–56; and Ralph A. Griffiths, 'Richard, Duke of York, and the royal household in Wales, 1449–50', *Welsh History Review* 8 (1976), pp. 14–25.

The years 1449 and 1450 saw a purge of royal officials and courtiers, such as the Duke of Suffolk and Bishop Adam Moleyns. For the effect of such instability in the counties, see Helen Castor, ' "Walter Blount has gone to serve traytours": the sack of Elvaston and the politics of the northern Midlands in 1454', *Midland History* 19 (1994), pp. 21–39.

CHAPTER 6 LITTLE ENGLAND AND A LITTLE PEACE, 1461–1485

The political dramas of the reigns of Edward IV saw the contest between a crowned king – Henry VI – and a ruler who had seized the throne, been crowned and ruled during the 1460s while Henry VI was alive, in exile. Not surprisingly, Lancastrian partisans believed that this reality could be overturned, and were led in this hope by Margaret of Anjou from France, and a court of able, albeit impoverished exiles around her. For the political formations, see Christine Carpenter, *The Wars of the Roses: Politics and the Constitution in England, c.1437–1509*, Cambridge, 1997. On the human price, Joel T. Rosenthal, 'Other victims: peeresses as war widows, 1450–1500', in *Upon my Husband's Death: Widows in the Literature and Histories of Medieval Europe*, ed. Louise Mirrer, Ann Arbor (MI), 1992, pp. 131–52.

French, Lancastrian and Yorkist writers were involved in a war of words during the years of waiting. The language of politics is discussed in the introduction to *Four English Political Tracts of the Later Middle Ages*, ed. Jean-Philippe Genêt, Camden fourth series 18, London, 1977, and in Jean-Philippe Genêt, 'New politics or new language? The words of politics in Yorkist and Tudor England', in *The End of the Middle Ages? England in the Fifteenth and Sixteenth Centuries*, ed. Benjamin Thompson, Thrupp, 1998, pp. 23–64.

On polemical writing from France see Craig Taylor, 'Sir John Fortescue and the French polemical treatises of the Hundred Years War', *English Historical Review* 114 (1999), pp. 112–29, and on Fortescue see also Strohm, *The Language of Politics*, Chapter 2 (above, p. 332). For a biography of Edward IV see Charles Ross, *Edward IV*, London, 1974.

Lancastrian attempts to re-establish rule succeeded for a while in 1469–71, when Henry VI was nominal king, and Edward IV was in exile in Flanders. On Edward's host in Flanders and the cultural contact which developed alongside the political, see Malcolm Vale, 'An Anglo-Burgundian nobleman and art patron: Louis de Bruges, Lord of La Gruthuyse and Earl of Winchester', in *England and the Low Countries in the Late Middle Ages*, ed. Caroline Barron and Nigel Saul, Stroud, 1995, pp. 115–31. Edward returned triumphantly in spring 1471, a story told by a member of his entourage in *The Arrivall of Edward IV*, on which see illuminating comments in Wendy Scase, 'Writing the "poetics of spectacle": political epiphanies in *The Arrivall of Edward IV* and some contemporary Lancastrian and Yorkist texts', in *Images, Idolatry and Iconoclasm in Late Medieval England: Textuality and the Visual Image*, ed. Jeremy Dimmick, James Simpson and Nicolette Zeeman, Oxford, 2002, pp. 172–84. For a survey of the politics of the second stage see Anthony Goodman, *New Monarchy: England 1471–1534*, Oxford, 1988.

The first decade of Edward IV's rule saw the re-establishment of domestic administration and a certain buoyancy in trade, and above all required fewer exactions than the 1440s and 1450s. Prominent parish and county gentry settled down to rebuild estates, often buying a great deal of land, like the Townshends, the Sulyards and the Pastons, studied respectively in C. E. Moreton, *The Townshends and Their World: Gentry, Law, and Land in Norfolk c. 1450–1551*, Oxford, 1992; Colin Richmond, *The Paston Family* (above, p. 330) and Colin Richmond, 'The Sulyard papers: the rewards of a small family archive', in *England in the Fifteenth Century. Proceedings of the 1986 Harlaxton Symposium*, ed. Daniel Williams, Woodbridge, 1987, pp. 199–228.

Religious institutions similarly benefited from the stability and economic recovery and mounted projects of expansion and building. Norwich Cathedral was able to begin to rebuild and redecorate practically on the morrow of the fire which struck it in 1468. Parish gentry and substantial tenants contributed to the adornment of churches, as shown in many instances in Eamon Duffy's *The Stripping of the Altars*, London and New Haven, CT, 1992 and in Christine Peters, *Patterns of Piety: Women, Gender and Religion in Late Medieval and Renaissance England*, Cambridge, 2003, as well as, for London society, in Clive Burgess, 'London parishioners in times of change' (above, p. 348). London ecclesiastical courts were busy with cases of marriage litigation, defamation, and sometimes heresy, as analysed in Richard M. Wunderli, *London Church Courts and Society on the Eve of the Reformation*, Cambridge (MS), 1981. Continental forms of piety were not unknown, such as the devotion to the

Name of Jesus and to the Five Wounds, as well as the cult of St Anne; these were incorporated into the elaborate devotional routines of the privileged (such as Lady Margaret Beaufort), but were most frequently adopted in more modest forms in parishes. On these new devotions and related new feasts, see Richard W. Pfaff, *New Liturgical Feasts in Late Medieval England*, Oxford, 1970. These politically troubled times also saw women from landed families, in their widowhood, choosing to remain unmarried in a consecrated religious lifestyle; they came to be known as 'vowesses', and are discussed in Pat H. Cullum, 'Vowesses and female lay piety in the province of York, 1300–1530', *Northern History* 32 (1996), pp. 21–41, and Mary Erler, 'English vowed women at the end of the Middle Ages', *Mediaeval Studies* 57 (1995), pp. 155–203.

English and Welsh parishes were much-adorned, colourful places, a reality which is hard to envisage within the spaces currently in modern, Protestant use. On images in the parish see Kamerick, *Popular Piety and Art* (above, p. 329); for a regional type, the octagonal font, and its meanings, see Ann E. Nichols, *Seeable Signs: the Iconography of the Seven Sacraments, 1350–1544*, Woodbridge, 1994, and Judy Ann Ford, 'Art and identity in the parish communities of late medieval England', *Studies in Church History* 28 (1992), pp. 225–37, as well as Christine Peters, *Patterns of Piety*, Chapter 2 (above, p. 350) Music enters into more common use in urban churches in these decades, inspired by the practices of religious houses and noble households. This emerges clearly from the pioneering work summarized in Clive Burgess and Andrew Wathey, 'Mapping the soundscape: church music in English towns 1450–1500', *Early Music History* 19 (2000), pp. 1–46. Collective enterprises produced elaborate cycles of biblical drama in cities, and brought plays to the rural areas too. The distinctive type of biblical cycle associated in England with the summer feast of Corpus Christi has been evocatively studied in V. A. Kolve, *The Play called Corpus Christi*, London, 1966. On social relations and religious understanding of late medieval drama, see Sarah Beckwith, *Signifying God: Social Relation and Symbolic Act in the York Corpus Christi Plays*, Chicago and London, 2001; and on parish drama, A. F. Johnston, ' "What revels are in hand?": dramatic activities sponsored by the parishes of the Thames valley', in *English Parish Drama*, ed. Alexandra F. Johnston and Wim Hüsken, Amsterdam, 1996, pp. 95–104. Parish games emerge as a subject of collective village organization but also as a subject for criticism, like the game of 'camp-ball', described by David Dymond in 'A lost social institution: the camping close', *Rural History* 1 (1990), pp. 165–92.

The parish became an important site for the provision of basic education in reading and writing. Parish clerks often used rooms around the church as schoolrooms. On education for members of the social elite, see Nicholas Orme, *From Childhood to Chivalry: the Education of the English Kings and Aristocracy 1066–1530*, London, 1984; for some teaching matter from the period see Nicholas Orme, 'A grammatical miscellany of 1427–1465 from

Bristol and Wiltshire', *Traditio* 38 (1982), pp 301–26; for provision in the province of York, J. Hoepner Moran Cruz, 'Education, economy, and clerical mobility in late medieval northern England', in *Universities and Schooling in Medieval Society*, ed. W J. Courtenay and Jürgen Miethke, Leiden, 2000, pp. 182–207; for teaching to girls at home, Patricia Cullum and Jeremy Goldberg, 'How Margaret Blackburn taught her daughters: reading devotional instruction in a Book of Hours', in *Medieval Women: Texts and Contexts in Late Medieval Britain: Essays for Felicity Riddy*, ed. Jocelyn Wogan-Browne, Rosalynn Voaden, Arlyn Diamond, Ann Hutchison, Carol Meale and Lesley Johnson, Turnhout, 2000, pp. 217–36; and for girls' training at work, Caroline M. Barron, 'The education and training of girls in fifteenth-century London', in *Courts, Counties and the Capital in the Later Middle Ages*, ed. Diana E. S. Dunn, The Fifteenth Century, Series 4, Stroud, 1996, pp. 139–53. On childhood experiences more generally, see Nicholas Orme, *Medieval Children*, London, 2001.

Print reached England from the Low Countries, and through the master printer William Caxton, who set up his shop in Westminster. The impact of print was felt in the shape and price of prayer and service books, for which an enormous market existed. On the first decades of print, see the early chapters of David McKitterick, *Print, Manuscript and the Search for Order 1450–1830*, Cambridge, 2004; on the illuminations of such early books see Kathleen L. Scott, *The Master Caxton and his Patrons*, Cambridge, 1976.

Edward IV invested effort in securing the peace which underpinned trade. These decades see the completion of the long-term trend towards the primacy of cloth exports. For interesting evidence on control of training within textile guilds, see *Indentures of Weavers' Apprentices in York, 1450–1505*, ed. Heather Swanson and Philip Stell, York, 2000. Great landlords and religious institutions were still buoyant consumers of diverse luxury goods (see, on food consumption, Christopher Woolgar, 'Fasts and feast: conspicuous consumption and the diet of the nobility in the fifteenth century', in *Revolution and Consumption in Medieval England*, ed. Michael Hicks, Woodbridge, 2001, pp. 7–25), although the mid-century had seen in all, and especially among the more modest landholders, a cut in expenditure. Such choices are discussed in Miranda Threlfall-Holmes, 'Durham Cathedral Priory's consumption of imported goods: wine and spices, 1464–1520', in *Revolution and Consumption in Late Medieval England*, ed. Michael Hicks, Woodbridge, 2001, pp. 141–58. By this stage Portuguese navigators and merchants were settled on the west coast of Africa, and new horizons for British shipping became apparent. 'Rutters', route-books for sea-captains, survive from this period; see D. W. Waters, *The Rutters of the Sea: the Sailing Directions of Pierre Garcie. A Study of the First English and French Printed Sailing Directions*, New Haven (CT), 1967.

Legal services were required for securing title to land, purchase of land by rich merchants, or to secure the loans which underpinned trade, and lawyers were familiar members in households of magnates and gentry in towns, and even lent their services to more modest communities and individuals. On profit and social advancement through legal work, see Mark Beilby, 'The profits of expertise: the rise of the civil lawyers and chancery equity', in *Profit, Piety and the Professions in Later Medieval England*, ed. Michael Hicks, Gloucester, 1990, pp. 72–90. Landlords aimed to secure their legal rights over serfs by drawing up genealogies of servile families: see L. R. Poos, 'Peasant "biographies" from medieval England', in *Medieval Lives and the Historian: Studies in Medieval Prosopography*, ed. Niethard Bulst and Jean-Philippe Genêt, Kalamazoo (MI), 1986, pp. 201–14.

Political strife did not end with the defeat of the Lancastrians in 1471, for within the Yorkist family discontent and competition developed between Edward IV's brothers, and between them and the queen and her kin. All this came to a head at the king's death in 1483. On relations between the brothers, see Christine Carpenter, 'The Duke of Clarence and the Midlands: a study in the interplay of local and national politics', *Midland History* 11 (1986), pp. 23–48, as well as Christine Carpenter, *The Wars of the Roses*, Chapters 8–9 (above, p. 349). On Yorkist endeavours for the richly documented and closely planned event of the reburial of Richard Duke of York, see *The Reburial of Richard, Duke of York, 21–30 July 1476*, ed. Anne F. Sutton and Livia Visser-Fuchs with P. W. Hammond, London, 1996.

The literature on Richard III's reign is vast; on his court and administration see Rosemary Horrox, *Richard III: a Study of Service*, Cambridge, 1989; for interesting documentation on his notorious coronation see *The Coronation of Richard III: the Extant Documents*, ed. Anne F. Sutton and P. W. Hammond, Gloucester, 1983. Richard III collected a great number of history books and prayer books, some of which are discussed and edited in *The Hours of Richard III*, ed. Anne F. Sutton and Livia Visser-Fuchs, Stroud, 1990. Richard's ascent to the throne was followed by a rebellion led by the Duke of Buckingham, on which see Louise Gill, *Richard III and Buckingham's Rebellion*, Stroud, 1999.

On 1485 see Michael Bennett, *The Battle of Bosworth*, new edn, Stroud, 2000; and on the new dynasty see Michael K. Jones and Malcolm Underwood, *The King's Mother: Lady Margaret Beaufort, Countess of Richmond and Derby*, Cambridge, 1992; on political ideas see John Watts, ' "A new ffundacion of is Crowne": monarchy in the age of Henry VII', in *The Reign of Henry VII: Proceedings of the 1993 Harlaxton Symposium*, ed. Benjamin Thompson, Stamford, 1995, pp. 31–53.

Index

Abbots Ripton (Huntingdonshire) 201
Aberystwyth 176, 178
Acle (Norfolk) 290, 294
Act of Accord (1460) 273
Acts of Attainder 273, 278, 314
Adam Davy's Dream of Edward II 29
Adam de Brome 37
Adam of Weil, Sir 82
Adams, Thomas 200
Adderbury, Sir Richard 85
Adderbury (Oxfordshire) 257
Adisham (Kent) 102
administration 14, 49–50, 82, 97–9, 168,
    301
Agincourt 213, 217–19, 228, 234, 344
Agnes, widow of John, son of Nicholas 20
agriculture 334
    before 1300 1, 2
    after 1348 59, 64–5, 66
    crops 18–19, 200–202, 241, 242, 270,
        309
    harvest 131, 132
    livestock 18, 64, 199–200, 202, 241–2,
        248, 256, 270–71
    regulation 19
Albrecht of Bavaria 169
alchemy 290
Alcock, John, Bishop of Rochester 304
Aldborough (Knaresborough) 252–3
Aldred, Peter 134
ale 64–5, 134–5, 209, 295
Alexander the Great 53
Algeciras, siege of 82
Alice de Reymes 46
Alice of Kirkbride 101
aliens
    1300–1400 87–8, 137, 138–9, 157
    1400–1461 178, 183, 204, 243, 246, 247,
        248
All Hallows church, York 234

All Saints church, Bristol 287
All Saints church, Fulham 245
All Saints church, Tilney (Norfolk) 289
All Souls College, Oxford 226, 257, 346
almshouses 9, 197, 212, 252, 303–4, 308
Alnwick (Northumberland) 3, 24, 74
Ambrosden (Oxfordshire) 253
Amburgh, Joan 256
Amburgh family 255–6
Amory, Roger 38
Ampney Crucis (Gloucestershire) 288
Ampthill Castle (Bedfordshire) 202
Andover (Hampshire) 246
Andrew, Dr Richard 257
Anglesey 121, 141
Anglo-Hanseatic treaty 210
Anglo-Irish
    army 29, 285
    culture 8, 9, 107
    identity 8, 106, 108
    politics 29, 106, 108, 284
    settlement 28, 59
Angoulême, Jean d' 218, 227
Anne, Alexander 244
Anne, St 282, 289
Anne of Bohemia (Queen of Richard II)
    113, 128, 155
Antwerp 210
Appellants 130, 131, 161, 340
Appleby (Cumbria) 104
Aquitaine 37, 89, 114, 159, 221
Arbre des batailles 164
Archbishops of Canterbury 50, 51, 261,
    274; *see also* Arundel, Thomas;
    Chichele, Henry; Peckham, John;
    Stratford, John; Sudbury
Archbishops of York 27, 51, 58, 284; *see
    also* Bouvel; Neville, Alexander;
    Neville, George; Scrope, Richard;
    Thoresby, John

Argenteyn, John 313
Argyll, Earl of 25
Aristotle 53, 149
armies
    Anglo-Irish 29, 285
    composition 81, 86, 87, 96, 217, 221, 305
    Irish retinues 106–7, 167
    recruitment 222–3
    retaining 217
    Wales 27, 108, 269
    see also tournaments; war
Arras 229
Arrivall of Edward IV, The 282
Ars notoria 234
art 41, 44, 45, 101–2, 143, 190, 289, 326, 333
Art of Love (Ars amatoria) 303
Arthur, Prince (son of Henry VII) 313
Arthurian imagery 30, 55, 110–11, 113, 176, 260
Arundel, Earls of 32, 80, 130, 144; see also Fitzallan, John; Fitzallan, Richard
Arundel, Sir William 184
Arundel, Thomas, Archbishop of Canterbury 168, 179, 186, 188, 189, 194–6, 199, 213, 222, 260, 343
Ashburton (Devon) 8
Ashton church (Somerset) 289
associations 8–9, 122, 132
Asteley of Nailstone, Sir John 278
Astwick (Hertfordshire) 93
Attepond, Reginald 20
Audelay, John 230
Audley, Hugh the Younger 38
Augustine, St 153
Austen, Jane 258
Auxerre 83
Avignon 39
Ayenbite of Inwyt 157

Bache, Alexander, Bishop of St Asaph 169
Badby, William 188
Ball, John 6, 124
Balliol, Edward 73
Balliol College, Oxford 149, 240
Banbury (Northamptonshire) 280
Bannockburn, Battle of 23, 24, 25, 34, 47, 48
Barber, Henry 27
Baret, John 245
Barnard Castle (co. Durham) 293
barns 18, 132
barons 31–2, 34, 49
Basin, Thomas, Bishop of Lisieux 280

Basset, Ralph, Lord 169
Bassingbourn (Cambridgeshire) 8
Bassingbourne, Sir Stephen 93
Bastard of Burgundy 278
Bateman, William, Bishop of Norwich 97
Battle of Agincourt, The (ballad) 219
Bayeux 269
Baynard Castle 190
Beauchamp, Henry, Duke of Warwick 240, 283
Beauchamp, John 130
Beauchamp, Richard 91
Beauchamp, Richard, Earl of Warwick 234
Beauchamp, Sir William 163
Beaufort, Edmund, Duke of Somerset 272, 300
Beaufort, Henry, Bishop of Winchester 213, 219, 222, 224, 226, 236, 247
Beaufort, Lady Margaret 300, 301, 315, 317
Beaumaris (Anglesey) 121
Beccaria, Antonio 238
Becket, Thomas 104, 174
Beckington, Thomas 237, 292
Beckwith family 160, 167
Bedford, John, Duke of 215, 216, 224–5, 228, 229, 238
Bedfordshire 45, 59, 177, 200, 202, 203, 262
Bek, Archbishop 24
Benedict XII, Pope 83
Bere Regis (Salisbury diocese) 196
Bergavenny, Admiral Thomas, Lord 144
Bergavenny, Joan, Lady 240
Bergavenny, Mary 144
Berkeley, Lord 67
Berkeley, Thomas 54
Berkeley Castle 54
Berkshire 89, 142, 196
Bernwood Forest (Buckinghamshire) 3, 21, 253–4
Berwick 24, 25, 26, 29, 105, 311
Bessarion, Cardinal 303
Beuno of Clynnog Fawr 259
Beverley Minster 30, 155
Bibles 12, 141, 150, 151, 153, 188, 194–5, 260
Bildeston, Nicholas 238
Bingham, John, Lord of Louth 107
bishops
    Armagh 59
    Bangor 221
    Bath and Wells 58, 71, 237, 261
    Carlisle (see Kirkby, John)
    Chichester 261, 265

Durham 18, 74, 80
Ely 36, 42, 98–9, 208, 240
Exeter 275
Hereford 22, 102, 141, 154
Lincoln 42, 150, 151, 154, 189, 260, 294
Lisieux 280
Llandaff 169
Norwich 37, 41, 68, 97, 127, 129, 163, 216, 260
Ossory 29
Rochester (*see* Alcock, John; Brinton, Thomas)
Salisbury 131, 152, 203
St Asaph 169, 261
St David's 208
Wales 169
Whithorn 27
Winchester 13, 47, 64, 78, 236, 257; *see also* Beaufort, Henry
Worcester 132, 189, 236, 238, 271
criticisms of 149
education 264
peerage 92–3
residences 22
roles 7–8, 41–2, 51, 88, 97, 100, 141, 150, 151–2, 260, 261
suffragan bishops 286
visitations 42, 142
Black Book 277, 301–2
Black Death 57–60, 337
aftermath 63–70, 116, 134–5, 148, 339
Blackburne, Henry 87
Blackfriars Council 150
Blackthorn (Oxfordshire) 253
Blacman, John 236–7, 284
Blanche Duchess of Lancaster 110, 114, 155
Blocking, John 232
Blount, Sir Thomas 87
Blunt, John 216
Blythburgh (Suffolk) 207–8, 250, 262
Boarstall (Buckinghamshire) 252, 253–4, 303
Bodiam (Kent) 121
Bohemia 261
Bohemia, King of 76
Bohun, Humphrey, Earl of Hereford and Essex 24, 30, 32, 35, 38, 46, 47, 73, 110
Bohun, William, Earl of Hereford and Northampton 87, 91, 110
Bokenham, Osbern 258, 272
Boleyn family 309
Bolingbroke, Henry *see* Henry IV

Bolingbroke (clerk) 233–4
Bolton Priory (Yorkshire) 18, 20, 21
Book of Noblesse 238, 311
Book of the Duchess, The 155
books 333
antiquarian 239–40
for children 303
circulation 46, 194
commonplace 294
illumination 192, 240–41, 260, 277, 303, 310
libraries 262, 348
manuscript 190, 192, 285, 303, 333
pocket-books 259
print 285, 302–3, 352
regulation 304
religious 15, 45–6, 140–41, 190, 192, 194–5, 216, 222, 259, 260, 261–2, 285, 302–3
secular 194, 303
self-help 237–9, 254
see also Bibles; Books of Hours
Books of Hours 45, 216, 240–41, 284, 290, 302–3, 316
Bordeaux 114, 120, 210
borders 49, 122
northern 23, 92, 130, 173, 179
see also Marches
Boroughbridge, Battle of 35, 39
Boston (Lincolnshire) 189, 308
Bosworth, Battle of 317, 353
Botiller, Sir Andrew 184
Botwright, Dr Jon 295–6
Boucicault, Marshal 217
Boulers, Reginald 265
Bourchier, Isabel 258
Bourchier, John, Lord 184
Bourchier, Thomas 261
Bourg-en-Bresse (Normandy) 269–70
Bouvel, Archbishop of York 189
Bouvet, Honoré 164
Bouzon, Thomas 21–2
Boxford (Suffolk) 8
Bozon, Nicholas 44
Brabant, Dukes of 32, 81, 121
Brabant, Jan III, Count of 77
Bracciolini, Poggio 238, 240
Bradeston, Thomas 91
Bradmore, John 178
Brancaster (Norfolk) 67
Breage (Cornwall) 288
Breckland (East Anglia) 21, 64
Brecon 68
Brecon, Lord of 24

Bredon (Worcestershire) 132
brehon law 10
Brembre, Nicholas 136–7
Bren, Llewellyn 25
Brentford (Warwickshire) 3
Brentford End (Middlesex) 243
Brian, Guy 91
Bridget of Sweden, St 234
Bridgwater (Somerset) 265, 293
Bridlington prophecies 279
Bridport (Dorset) 95, 258
Brigge tomb (Salle) 292
Brill (Buckinghamshire) 3, 21, 253
Brinton, Thomas, Bishop of Rochester 86, 118, 150, 339
Britain 8, 25, 180, 319, 326, 334
Brittany 85
Brittany, François II, Duke of 276, 315, 316
Brixworth (Northamptonshire) 11
Brogeam, John 255
Brotherhood of Arms of St George 285
Broughton (Buckinghamshire) 288
Broxbourne church (Hertfordshire) 289
Bruce, David II, King of Scotland 45, 58, 73, 74
Bruce, Edward 23, 25, 26
Bruce, Robert, King of Scotland 23–4, 25, 27, 28, 36, 38, 73
Bruges 281, 303
Bruges, Louis of, Lord of Gruthuye 281–2
Brugge, John 294
Brut, Walter 151, 153–4
Brut chronicle 35, 302
Bruton Priory 270
Bryene, Alice de 204
Bryn Glas 177
Buchan, Earl of 25
Buckingham, Bishop of Lincoln 154
Buckingham, Dukes of 204, 313, 314
Buckingham, Earl of 128
Buckinghamshire 3, 21, 59, 135, 252, 253–4, 288, 303
Buntingford (Suffolk) 245
Burford (Oxfordshire) 138, 251
Burgh (Norfolk) 90
Burgundy 88, 185, 213, 228, 229, 278, 280
Burgundy, Dukes of *see* Charles the Bold; John the Fearless; Philip the Good
Burleigh, William 198
Burley, Simon 110, 169
Burmington (Worcestershire) 287
Burnell, Hugh, Lord 184
Bury St Edmunds 87, 234, 308
Abbey 20, 29, 126, 235

Busseby, Peter 183
Butler, Lady Eleanor 312
Butlers, Earls of Ormond 107, 110
Byland Abbey (Yorkshire) 174, 194
Byron, Sir John 240

Cade, Jack 267, 271
Caen 80, 269
Caernarfon 141, 178
Caister Castle 284
Calais 130, 171, 218, 229, 248, 273
siege 80–81, 87
Staple 114, 227
Treaty 113
Caldicot Manor (Gwent) 68
Cambraisis 83
Cambridge 45, 49, 71, 247, 304, 307
Cambridge, Richard, Earl of 214, 276
Cambridge University 42, 97, 126, 150, 233, 264
colleges 9, 37, 60, 97, 207, 290, 295
see also King's College, Cambridge
Cambridgeshire 3, 8, 43, 49, 90, 132, 251, 252, 261; *see also* Wisbech
canon law 44–5, 98, 99, 101, 117–18, 207, 208, 255, 339
Canterbury 54, 64, 104, 270
Cathedral 19, 114, 124, 212
Canterbury Tales 138–9, 163–4
Cantilupe, Nicholas 101
Cantref Mawr (Carmarthenshire) 104
Capgrave, John 259, 261
Carlisle 24, 29, 101, 102, 123
Carmarthenshire 89, 104, 178, 214
Carpenter, Christine 47–8
Carpenter, John, Bishop of Worcester 236
Carrick, Earl of 129
Carter, Richard 147
Castell, Thomas 242
Castelnau-de-Cernès 269
Castile 85, 105, 114, 130
Castillon, battle of 268, 270
Castle Acre (Norfolk) 144, 154, 191
Castle Combe (Wiltshire) 249
Castle Rising (Norfolk) 56
cathedrals 41, 42, 71, 118, 191, 192–3, 291; *see also by name of city*
Caxton, William 302, 303, 316
Ceuta 82
Chalgrove (Oxfordshire) 102
Chalvington estate (Sussex) 202
Chamberlain, Sir William 278
Chancery 96–7, 111, 119, 158, 205–6, 227–8, 278, 298

Chandler, John, Dean of Salisbury 196
Chandos, Sir John 83, 89
Channel Islands 224
chantries 9, 46, 146–7, 289, 291, 293, 300
Chapel Royal 37, 216, 236, 291
chaplains 146, 286, 300
Chapman, John 294
charity 9, 197–8, 201, 261–2
Charles IV, King of France 38
Charles V, King of France 89
Charles VI, King of France 89, 164, 175,
    178, 215, 216, 231, 280
Charles VII, King of France 225, 265
Charles of Blois, Duke of Brittany 110
Charles the Bold, Duke of Burgundy 280
Charter of Christ, The 8, 190–91
Chaucer, Geoffrey 9, 111, 138, 139, 140,
    155–6, 157, 158, 163–4, 254, 260, 340
Chedder, Richard 183
Chedworth, Bishop of Lincoln 260
Cherneys, Joanna 232
Cherry Hinton (Cambridgeshire) 43
Chertsey Abbey (Surrey) 284
Cheshire 167, 169, 170
Cheshunt 206
Chester Cathedral 12
Cheynne, Sir John 187
Chichele, Henry, Archbishop of
    Canterbury 189, 195, 208, 226, 227,
    260, 346
children 62
Chippenham (Wiltshire) 91
chivalry 76, 82, 86, 91, 109–13, 238,
    277–8, 330, 338
Chobham (Surrey) 142
Chocke, Margaret 289
Chocke, Sir Richard 289, 293
Christ Church, Canterbury 64, 270
Christ of Sundays 288
Christianity 10, 186–7, 222
Christina of Markyate, St 288
Christine de Pizan 231, 303
Christmas carols 263
chronicles
    Anonimalle 126
    Brut 35, 302
    Crowland 315
    Eulogium historiarum 85
    Froissart 111
    Kilkenny 106, 107
    London 122, 246, 267, 274, 304
    monastic 84–5, 273
    Paris 277
    regional 85, 185, 246

Walsingham 125, 156
    see also genealogies
Chronicles of London 211
churches
    building 11, 193–4, 245–6, 249–52, 288,
        289
    chancels 12, 143
    functions 143–4, 145
    furnishings and fittings 144, 145, 191,
        245, 250, 284, 287–8, 292–3, 351
    maintenance 43, 101–2, 142, 144, 190,
        287–8
    music 193, 263, 291, 351
    paintings 41, 44, 101–2, 143, 190, 289
    patronage 11–12
    pews 145, 288
    sculpture 41, 143, 251, 288
    services and worship 44, 103, 143, 146
    social celebrations 143
    stained glass 9, 101, 190, 285, 289
    symbolism 12, 143, 144, 145, 146, 190,
        262, 285, 288
    see also commemoration of the dead;
        names of churches; parishes
churchwardens
    accounts 144, 263, 288, 289, 294, 325
    election of 250, 294
    responsibilities 144, 190, 194, 250,
        251–2, 291, 294, 295
    skills 294
cities 2, 70, 71, 193, 211
civil war 130, 320–21
Clanvowe, Sir John 155, 164
Clare (Suffolk) 13, 43, 258
Clare Roll 272
Clarence, Dukes of *see* George Duke of
    Clarence; Lionel Duke of Clarence;
    Thomas Duke of Clarence
Claverham estate 202
Claydon, John 190
Clement VI, Pope 98
clergy
    accountability 98
    administration 97–9, 103
    Black Death 58
    chaplains 146, 286, 300
    criticisms of 88, 124, 149, 195–6, 287
    education 97, 100, 103, 142, 285, 298
    income 286
    leave 42
    parliament 50, 51, 92
    personal life 99, 102, 142–3
    responsibilities 101–3, 141–2, 145–7,
        263, 286–7

Clifford, Elizabeth 255
Clifford, Sir Lewis 163
Clifford, Thomas, Lord 255
Clinton, William, Earl of Huntingdon 90, 91
Clopton, John 258
Clyne, John 106, 107
Cobbes, John 293
Cobham, Eleanor 231, 233–4
Cobham, John, Lord 121
Cockermouth (Cumberland) 26
Codrington, John 293
Cokayn, John 214
Colchester 71, 94, 182, 209, 210
Coleshill (Warwickshire) 246
Colet, Laurence 225
Colet, William 142
College of St William, York Minster 293
Collinson, Robert 249
commemoration of the dead 46–7, 60, 104, 146–7, 192, 212, 289, 292, 293
communication 1–2, 40, 72, 83, 105
Confessio Amantis 131, 163, 175
Coningsby Castle 214
Connacht 28
Constitutions of Thomas Arundel 194–6, 222, 260
Conway Castle 171
Cooke, Philip 296
Cooling Castle (Kent) 199
Copeland, John 90
Cornhill (London) 135
Cornwall 3, 13, 20, 141, 168, 203, 246, 288
coroners 119, 214
Corpus Christi College, Cambridge 60, 295
Corpus Christi cycle 292
Corpus Christi feast 4, 102, 126, 147, 308
Corpus Christi guild (York) 299
corruption 98, 119, 197
Corveser, Philip 266
Coryngham, John 152–3
Cotswolds 4, 18, 138, 210, 245, 249, 252
Council of Constance (1415) 187
Council of Pisa (1409) 187
Court of Arches, St Mary-le-Bow 298
Courtenay, Stephen 216
Coventry 2, 36, 71, 204, 247
craft groupings 15; see also guilds
Crécy, Battle of (1346) 80, 84, 87, 105
Creke, Alyne 49
Creke, Sir John 49
Cressy, Sir John 268–9
Croft, Richard 315

Crosby, John 184
Croughton (Northamptonshire) 44
crusades 129, 160, 163–4, 185, 230
Cryfield (Warwickshire) 65
Culblean (Deeside), Battle of 73
culture 8, 9, 107, 155, 216, 237, 239–41; see also art; drama; literature; music
Cumberland/Cumbria 4, 19, 26–7, 67, 78, 104
Cursor mundi 157
Cydewain lordship (Powys) 252

Dafydd ap Gwilym 152
Dafydd ap Llewellyn ap Gruffydd of Mathafarn 313, 317
Dagworth, Thomas 85, 90, 110
Dallingbridge, Edward 121
Danby, Robert 233
Dartmouth (Devon) 121, 123
Dassel, Arndt von 185
d'Aubernoun, Sir John the Younger 49
Dauphins 88, 89, 228, 311
Daventry church (Northamptonshire) 282
Davi, Howel 176
Ddu, Robin 259
de Audeley, Hugh 90–91
de heretico comburendo ('On Burning Heretics') 187
de la Mare, Peter 114
de la Pole, Michael, Earl of Suffolk 130
de la Pole, William, Earl of Suffolk 9, 230, 238, 265, 266–7
De Lisle Psalter 45
De nobilitatibus, sapientiis et prudentiis regum 53
de Vere, John, Earl of Oxford 280, 317
de Vere, Robert, Earl of Oxford 130
de Warennes, Earls of Surrey 144, 191
death 46, 292–3; see also commemoration of the dead
Declaration of Arbroath 27–8
Deeds of Henry V (Gesta Henrici Quinti) 220
demography 1–2, 17–18, 57–9; see also families
Denbigh 68, 89, 176
Denbigh, Lord of see Thomas of Lancaster
Denmark 215
Denmark, Kings of 210, 276
Denton, Katherine 258
Derby, Earl of see Henry IV
Derbyshire 40, 89, 90, 214, 307
Deschamps, Eustache 83, 156

Despenser, Edward, Lord of Glamorgan and Morgannwg 147
Despenser, Henry, Bishop of Norwich 129, 163
Despenser, Hugh 33, 34, 163
Despenser, Margaret 89
Despenser, Thomas, Lord 169, 180, 184
Despenser family 5, 33, 34, 35, 36, 52, 53, 54, 283
Devereux, John 163
Devon 3, 8, 19, 40, 71, 121, 123, 127, 173, 242
Devon, Earl of 221
Dictes and Sayings of Philosophers 303
Diddington (Huntingdon) 152–3
Disce mori (*Learn to Die*) 262
Disendowment Bill (1410) 197–8
Dives et pauper (*Rich and poor*) 181
Dixon, Nicholas 206
Doctors' Chambers 298
domestic service 122–3, 134, 147–8
Domnal O'Neill, King of the Irish 25
Don, Griffith 269
Donal, son of Art MacMurdharha 107
Doncaster 134, 160
Dormer, Geoffrey 308
Dorset 41, 57, 95, 248, 251
Douglas, James 73
Douglas, Sir Archibald 74
Douglas, William 73
drama 141, 146, 151, 235, 259, 291–2, 351
Drayton, Thomas 195
Dream of the Old Pilgrim, The (*Le songe du vieil pèlerin*) 160
drovers 40
du Berry, Duc 171
du Clercq, Jacques 231–2
Dublin 28, 95, 105, 106, 107, 271
Dunstable, John 193, 263
Dunwich (Suffolk) 207–8
Dupplin Muir 74
Durham 26, 66, 97, 118, 134, 194, 293, 306
Dyffryn Clwyd 62, 65
dykes and ditches 19, 65, 68, 253, 309
Dymmock, Roger 154
dynasties 13, 146–7, 299, 300, 306, 321

Earl Soham (Suffolk) 210
East Anglia
  churches 9, 41, 43, 58, 245, 249, 250
  economy 21, 62, 64
  manors 18, 200
  politics 181
  tournaments 87
  towns 70, 296

East Raynham (Norfolk) 297
Easter 146, 291–2
Eaton Bishop (Herefordshire) 102
ecclesiastical courts 14, 99, 101, 117–18, 188, 247, 255, 275, 295, 296, 332, 339; *see also* canon law
Eckington (Derbyshire) 90, 91
economy 78–9, 241, 242, 270–71, 281, 327–8, 339, 345, 347; *see also* agriculture; cities; finance; rural life; towns; trade; work and craft
Edgcote, battle of 280, 281
Edlyngton, John 261
Edmund Duke of Holland 184
Edmund King of East Anglia 41
Edmund of Langley, Duke of York 109, 323
Edmund of Woodstock, Earl of Kent 55
education 346, 351–2
  books 237–8
  cathedral schools 291
  of clergy 97, 100, 103, 142, 285, 298
  foundations 36–7, 235–6
  grammar schools 9, 100, 263–4, 297, 299, 304
  see also Cambridge University; Oxford University; St Andrews University
Edward I
  court 34
  family 75
  finance 37, 338
  grievances against 32, 36
  heraldry 23
  rule 24–5, 27, 29
Edward II 335
  abdication 54
  birth 29
  canonization 159
  character 72
  children 30, 45
  coronation 28, 30, 31
  court 38–9
  death and burial 36, 54–5, 91, 335
  deposition 52, 53, 54, 55
  famine years 17, 18–19
  finance 37, 55
  and France 8, 37–8, 39
  and Gaveston 12, 31, 32, 33
  grievances against 30–32, 34, 35, 36, 48, 93, 335
  Irish policy 28–9
  knighting ceremony 29–30
  marriage 30
  parliament 25, 32, 35, 50–52

Edward II – *cont.*
   religious institutions 36–7, 97
   residences 22
   rule 39, 95
   Scottish wars 23, 25, 27–8, 33–4, 35–6, 38
   Welsh policy 25–6, 36, 52
Edward III
   birth 30
   challenges 72
   character 72–3
   chivalry 82, 109–13
   coronation 53, 54
   court 109–13, 114
   death and burial 115
   defences 70–71
   family 8, 77, 110, 113–14
   finance 77, 78–80, 90–91, 114, 166, 302
   and France 8, 72, 73, 74–7, 80–81,
     83–5, 87, 89, 113–14, 221, 338
   grievances 32, 93
   guards 112
   Irish policy 106, 108
   marriage 72
   mistress 114
   parliament and government 79, 80,
     92–7, 114–15, 338
   patronage 72, 89–91, 109–10, 120, 338
   as prince 52–3
   religious institutions 37
   Scottish wars 54, 73–4
Edward IV
   accession 274
   chivalry 238, 277–8
   claim to the throne 274, 275, 279, 280
   coronations 275–6, 305
   court 277, 278, 279, 290–91, 314
   culture 290–91, 303
   death 312
   as Earl of March 273, 274
   exile 281–2, 350
   family 285, 311
   finance 277, 279, 291, 301–2, 307
   and France 279, 280, 305, 311
   grievances against 281, 283
   imprisonment 281
   Irish policy 278–9, 284–5
   marriages 276, 313
   patronage 277, 278, 281, 284, 308
   religion 289–90, 303, 310
   restoration 282, 350
   rule 278, 280, 304–5
Edward V 290, 299, 312, 313, 314
Edward Duke of York 183, 184
Edward Prince of Wales, 'the Black Prince'

chivalry 91
companions 89–90, 110, 120
death 114
destiny 73, 113
   French wars 80, 81, 84–5, 86, 87
Edward Prince of Wales (son of Henry VI)
   232, 273, 274, 275, 283
Edward Prince of Wales (son of Richard
   III) 314, 315
Edward the Confessor 41, 159, 160
Egmere (Norfolk) 66
Eleanor of Northampton 110
Eleanor of Provence 75
Elizabeth, St 287
Elizabeth Countess of Shrewsbury 306
Elizabeth I 145
Elizabeth of Clare 97
Elizabeth of York (Queen of Henry VII)
   13, 311, 315, 317
Elizabeth Woodville (Queen of Edward IV)
   12, 276–7, 278, 290, 299, 312, 313, 314
Elmham, Thomas 218, 220
Elsworth (Cambridgeshire) 252
Eltham (Kent) 301
Elwyn, John 264
Ely Cathedral 12, 41, 101, 256
Epiphany Plot (1400) 180–81, 184
Eric, King of Sweden, Norway and
   Denmark 210
Erpingham, Sir Thomas 184, 213
Eryri, Rhys Goch 259
espionage 88
Esplechin treaty 77
esquires 81, 82
Essex 123, 124, 125, 131, 135, 246, 249,
   253, 295
estates
   food production 133–4, 135
   management 13, 19–20, 66–7, 78,
     135–6, 162, 199–202, 300, 303, 309
   rights 68
   see also land-holding
Estonia 82
ethnicity 87–8, 116, 241, 246–7
Eton College 192, 236, 284
Eulogium historiarum 85
Everard, Robert 251
Everard, Simon 27
Ewelme (Oxfordshire) 9, 289
Exchequer 206, 210, 265
Exeter 121, 247, 314
Exeter, Duke of 272; *see also* Holland,
   John
Exeter College, Oxford 37, 196

Fais d'armes 231
families 10, 62–3, 67, 123, 139, 147, 254
famine 5, 17–20, 334
Fanhope, Lord 239
Farringdon 196
Farringdon, Sir William 212
fashion 112, 187, 307
Fastolf, Sir John 226, 229, 238, 346
Fauquemont, Jean de 83
Fawkner, Margaret 303–4
Fawkner, Roger 304
Fayreford, Thomas 242
Fécamp, Abbey of 91
Felbrigg, Simon 184
Felbrigg (Norfolk) 201
Felton, John 263
Fenham Castle (Northumbria) 32
festivals 4, 102, 111–12, 257–8
Ffynnon Gybi (Caernarfonshire) 141
Ffynnon Seiriol (Anglesey) 141
Fichet, Guillaume 303
field names 13, 203
Fiennes, Sir Roger 269
Filippo Borromei and Co. 269
finance
    clergy 286
    Edward I 37, 338
    Edward II 37, 55
    Edward III 77, 78–80, 90–91, 114, 166, 302
    Edward IV 277, 279, 291, 301–2, 307
    gentry 21
    Henry IV 183, 210, 211
    Henry V 210–11, 220, 307
    Henry VI 265, 266, 349
    Ireland 105, 106
    parishes 42–3, 190, 197, 286
    Richard II 120, 130, 166–7, 168
    usury 249
Fishburn, Thomas 152
fishing 20, 40, 65, 134, 242, 254
Fitzallan, John, Earl of Arundel 212, 213, 268
Fitzallan, Richard, Earl of Arundel 130, 165
FitzHugh, Henry, Lord 215, 217
FitzRalph, Archbishop of Armagh 59
Flamendeau, Thenein 86
Flanders 75, 77, 129, 139, 163, 280
Flanders, Count of 129
Flaxall, John 289
Fledborough (Nottinghamshire) 99
Flintshire 170
food and drink

1307–1400 21, 64, 65, 132–5
1400–1483 64, 203–4, 209, 241–2, 270, 300
fools 112
foreigners *see* aliens
forest officials 3, 253–4, 301
forests 3, 21, 26, 253–4
Fortescue, John 279–80, 297, 302, 305
Forwich (Kent) 295
Fotheringay, John 86
Fotheringhay (Northamptonshire) 310
Foulden (Norfolk) 97
Foxholes, Margaret 101
France 337–8
    artillery 269–70
    benefits and rewards 81, 82–3, 85, 268–9
    brutalization 86
    chevauchées 74, 80, 83–4, 85, 86
    chivalry 76, 82, 86, 109
    criticism of 76
    distrust and prejudice 87–8
    Edward II 8, 37–8, 39
    Edward III 8, 72, 73, 74–7, 80–81, 83–5, 87, 91, 113–14, 221, 338
    Edward IV 279, 280, 305, 311
    English claim to throne 74–5, 91, 216, 221, 222, 225, 305
    espionage 88
    finance 78–80
    garrisons 222, 268, 269, 270, 345
    Henry V 215, 216, 217–20, 221–3, 225
    Henry VI 8, 225, 228, 229, 266–7, 268, 269, 280
    heraldry 91
    loss of life 268
    poetry 83, 111, 158, 225
    prisoners 86
    Richard II 280
    surgery 87
    truces 73, 77, 86
    wars 38, 72, 73, 74–7, 80–81, 83–5, 87, 91, 113–14, 217–20, 221–2, 229, 269, 311
    women 86
François II Duke of Brittany 276, 315, 316
French–Flemish alliance 121
Fressingfield (Suffolk) 288
friars 151, 182, 189, 191, 265, 283, 293
    Augustinian 11, 43, 258
Friesthorpe (Lincolnshire) 101
Frisby, Roger 173
Froissart, Jean 31, 111, 113, 167
Frulovisi, Tito Livio 238

Fryg family 132
Fulham, Richard 69
Furnivall's Inn 207, 298

Gaelic law 117
Galopes, Jean 222
Game and Play of Chess, The 303
Garonne 84
Gascony 37–8, 39, 52, 75, 84, 89, 120, 224, 335
Gateley church (Norfolk) 284, 287–8
Gaveston, Piers 12, 31, 32–3, 36
Gawain and the Green Knight 157
genealogies 275, 297, 300
  royal 175, 225, 275, 305, 318, 321, 323
gentry 329–30, 350
  Act of Attainder 278
  archives 240
  definition 245, 300
  finance 21
  fortifications 121
  genealogies 275
  household management 203–4, 345
  language 259
  and 'Peasants' Revolt' 125
  pursuits 258, 303
  roles 49, 82, 86–7, 94, 162
  social aspirations 85, 162–3, 239, 301
  Wales 239
  wealth 309
Geoffrey de Bolton 104
Geoffrey of Monmouth 316
George Duke of Clarence 275, 278, 280, 281, 283, 284
George (son of Edward IV) 285
Gerard, Robert 69
Ghent 77, 129, 130, 132
ghosts 174
Gilbert (canon of Malton Priory) 187
Gilbert de Middleton 48
Glamorgan 25, 52, 178–9
Glayster, William 251
Glentham (Lincolnshire) 68
Gloucester 55, 91, 117, 128, 314
Gloucester, Earls of 2; *see also* Audeley, Hugh; Despenser, Thomas
Gloucester, Humphrey, Duke of
  books 237, 238, 240, 241
  Calais 229
  death 231–2
  patronage 240, 242, 244, 346
  Protector 224, 225, 226, 228, 233
  see also Cobham, Eleanor

Gloucester, Richard, Duke of *see* Richard III
Gloucester, Thomas, Duke of *see* Woodstock, Thomas
Gloucestershire 144, 178, 252, 262, 271, 288
Glyn Dŵr, Owain 176–7, 178, 343
Goch, Iolo 107, 126, 176
Godemar de Fay 76
Golden Legend 303
Goldcliff (Gwent) 265
Golein, Jean 75
Gonville, Edmund, Bishop of Norwich 41, 97
Gonville and Caius College, Cambridge 37
Gonville Hall 97
Gough brothers 39
Gough Map 40
Governance of England, The 279–80
Gower, John 119, 120, 131, 158, 163, 165, 175, 303
Grantham, Hugh 204
Graunson, Oton de 158
Gravesend (Kent) 90
Gray, William, Bishop of Ely 240
Gray's Inn 299
Greasley Castle (Nottinghamshire) 101
Great Coxwell (Cotswolds) 18
Great Wishford (Wiltshire) 142
Great Yarmouth 91
Greene, Sir Ralph 6
Gregory XI, Pope 150
Grey, John 216
Grey, Lord Edmund 202
Grey, Sir John 276
Grey of Ruthin, Lords 177, 200, 226, 239
Grocers' Company of London 243
Grosmont, Henry of, Duke of Lancaster 82, 90, 110
Gruffydd, Llewellyn 108
Gruffydd ap Llewellyn ap Phylip ap Trahaearn 104
Gryg, Gruffydd 141
Guild of Luton 277
guildhalls 249
guilds 15, 325, 328
  courts 118
  towns 204, 243–4, 249
  women 61, 249
  writers and stationers 136, 137, 302
'Gwidw and the prior' 46–7
Gwilym ap Sefnyn 58

Haddington (East Lothian) 129
Hainault, William, Count of 52, 77

Hales (Treasurer) 125
Halesowen (Worcestershire) 3, 20
Halidon Hill, battle of 73, 74
Hampshire 19, 89, 130, 246
Handerby, Robert 147
Hanseatic League 167
Hardley (Norfolk) 251
Hardy, Thomas 18
Hardyng, John 112
Hardyng, William 112, 196
Harfleur 216, 217, 221
Harlech Castle 176
Harleston 200
Harpham, John 294
Harrington, William 216
Harrington of Brierley, Sir Thomas 231
Harston church (Cambridgeshire) 251
Hart, Emma 62
Hartlepool 25
Harvey de Stanton 37
Haseley, Thomas 199
Hastings, William, Lord 278, 280
Haukeston, John 170
Havering Manor (Essex) 131, 253
Haxey, Thomas 168–9
Haysand, William 242
health and medicine 62, 87, 112, 158,
    242–3, 308
Hedgeley Moor 276
Helen, St 288
Hemingford (Huntingdon) 27
Hend, John 140
Henry IV
    attempts to unseat 173
    coronation 171, 174
    court 175, 183–5, 211
    death and burial 211, 212
    as Earl of Derby 82, 109, 130, 158, 162,
        163, 165, 166, 170–71, 185, 341
    family 185, 210, 211, 213
    finance 183, 210, 211
    friendship 184
    marriage 212
    patronage 183–4
    religion 8, 180, 182, 186–98, 215, 264,
        343
    resistance to 175, 176–8, 180–81, 185,
        212
    rift with Prince of Wales 185
    rule 173, 174, 179–82, 207
    Scottish campaigns 177, 179
    usurpation of Richard II 170–71, 172,
        173–5, 181, 343
    Welsh resistance 176–7, 178–9, 184

Henry V
    court 213
    culture 216, 237
    death and commemoration 224, 226
    finance 210–11, 220, 307
    and France 216, 217–20, 221–3, 225
    friendships 216
    language 205
    law 205, 206
    marriage 215, 216
    patronage 183, 216
    politics 219
    popularity 175, 219
    as Prince of Wales 177, 178, 180, 181,
        184, 185, 188, 198
    religion 199, 215, 219, 222, 234, 264,
        343–4
    rift with Henry IV 185
    rule 212–14, 215–16, 219–20
    ships 220–21
    Southampton Plot 214, 276
    will 225, 227
Henry V 83, 213, 218
Henry VI 345
    birth 224
    challenges to 271, 272, 273, 274
    coronations 225, 277
    court 232, 236, 277, 345
    criticisms of 227, 230
    cult of 283–4, 287
    death and burial 282, 283
    deposition 274
    exile 274, 276, 279, 305
    finance 265, 266, 349
    and France 8, 225, 228, 229, 266–7, 268,
        269, 280
    genealogy 225
    health 232, 272
    law 206
    marriage 230–31, 232
    minority 224–30
    patronage 226, 230
    religion and learning 216, 235–7, 238,
        264, 284, 346
    restoration 281, 304
    rule 232, 266
Henry VI 275, 282
Henry VII
    coronation 317
    court 312
    family 301, 317
    as Henry Tudor 8, 299, 315–16, 317
    marriage 13, 317
    rule 317–18, 322, 353

Henry VIII 236
Henry of Lancaster 54, 111
Henry Tudor *see* Henry VII
heraldry 23, 75, 91, 119, 300
herbals 4
Hereford, Earls of *see* Bohun, Humphrey;
     Bohun, William
Hereford Cathedral 47, 57, 150, 151
Herefordshire 40, 41, 102, 141, 178, 248,
     252, 326
hermits and anchorites 47, 104, 151, 154,
     189, 234
Herstmonceaux (Sussex) 269
Hert, Walter 112
Hertfordshire 11, 69, 93, 125, 135, 174,
     289
Hexham 276
Higham (Sussex) 90
Higham Ferrers (Northamptonshire) 21
Hildegard of Bingen 153
Hilton, Rodney 325
Hilton, Roger 88
Hinderclay (Suffolk) 199, 201
Hingham (Norfolk) 291
historical sources 14–15
History of the Kings of Britain 316
Hoccleve, Thomas 185, 196, 212, 215, 216,
     226, 259, 344
Holland, Edmund, Duke of 184
Holland, John, Earl of Huntingdon 140,
     163, 180, 184
Holland, Ralph 243–4
Holland, Thomas, Duke of Surrey 184
Holland (Lincolnshire) 5
Holme, Robert 145
Holy Trinity, London 211
Holy Trinity church, Bristol 195
holy wells 141
Honfleur 221
Honingham (Norfolk) 68
Hook Norton (Oxfordshire) 288–9
Horn, Andrew 22
Hornby (North Riding) 263
Horsham St Faith (Norfolk) 127
Horsley Manor (Gloucestershire) 270
Horsley (Somerset) 190
Horstead (Norfolk) 284
hospitals 9, 133, 169, 198, 243, 308
Hothum, Bishop of Ely 37
House of Fame, The 156
houses 203, 232
Hovyngham, John, Archdeacon of
     Durham 194
Howard, John, Duke of Norfolk 300, 317

Howard Psalter 41
Howes, Robert 204
Hull 25, 123, 248, 304, 308
Humbleton Hill 177
Huns, Mabina 255
hunting 3, 131, 301
Huntingdon, Earls of *see* Clinton,
     William; Holland, John
Huntingdonshire 27, 90, 98, 134, 201
Huntington, Agnes 101
Hurley, Master John 238
Hustings court 118

Iberia 75, 82
Iceland 242
Ickham manor (Kent) 64
identity 8–10, 29, 106, 108, 112, 116,
     146
Idley, Peter 238–9
Idley, Thomas 238
Imperial, Janus 137
inheritance 347
     land 18, 62, 200, 281
     law 117
     property 146–7
     women 10, 74, 255–6
inns 204–5, 246, 256
Inns of Court 49, 119, 124, 206–7, 297–8,
     299, 309
Instructions of Parish Priests 194
Iorwerth ap Gruffydd 26
Iorwerth ap Llywarch Lleweni 24
Ipswich School 299
Ireland
     administration 28, 106, 167–8, 271–2
     army 106–7, 167
     Edward II 28–9
     Edward III 106, 108
     Edward IV 278–9, 284–5
     English conquest 28
     finance 105, 106
     hobelars 28–9
     land-holding 4, 5, 278
     law 108, 116–17
     marriage 254, 255
     parliament 95
     people 106, 107
     retinues 106–7, 167
     Scottish invasion 25, 26, 334–5
     stereotypes 167
     warfare 28–9, 335
     see also Anglo-Irish
Ireland, Duke of 130
Ireland, Lieutenants of 29, 31, 285

Irthlingborough College
(Northamptonshire) 189
Isabella of France (Queen of Edward II)
ambitions and power 30, 35, 38, 39, 52,
54, 73
Arthurian invention 55
childhood 30
death and burial 56
fall and exile 55, 56, 89, 90, 111
marriage 30
and Roger Mortimer 52, 55–6, 73
Isabella of France (Queen of Richard II)
161, 167
Isle of Sheppey (Kent) 130
Isle of Wight 45, 88

Jacqueline of Hainault 233
Jacquetta of Luxembourg 276
Jan III, Count of Brabant 77
Jean de Rubeis 220
Jeanne of Valois, Countess of Hainault 77
Jedburgh Castle 179
Jesus College, Oxford 8
Jeurbers, Guillaume 86
Jews 39, 71–2
Joan, Queen of Scotland 45, 111
Joan ate Enges 147
Joan of Arc 225, 228
Joan of Kent 126
Joan of Navarre (Queen of Henry IV) 212
John, King of England 38
John, son of Reginald Attepond 20
John de Newby 88
John II, King of France 84, 85, 90, 111, 112
John of Arderne 87
John of Avence 88
John of Beverley, St 23
John of Bridlington, St 73, 241
John of Bristol 101
John of Fauquemont 76
John of Gaddesden 87
John of Gaunt, Duke of Lancaster
birth 77
campaigns against 128
Castilian wars 85, 105, 114
counsellor to Richard II 115, 120,
128–9, 131, 159–60
crusades 163
death 166
invasion of Scotland 129
marriages 110, 114, 161
Order of the Garter 109
patronage 149, 150, 158, 163, 165, 184
'Peasants' Revolt' 122, 125, 126, 127
and Portugal 139
wealth 173
John of St Mary 72
John of Trevisa 157
John of Trokelowe 24, 33
John the Fearless, Duke of Burgundy 216,
220
John the Scot 39
John the Spencer of Upton 99
John XXII, Pope 28
Joliff, John 101
Jourdemayne, Margery 233, 234
justices 49, 51, 94, 95, 96, 214, 298, 309

Katherine de Valois (Queen of Henry V)
215, 216, 227
Kellaw, Richard, Bishop of Durham 18
Kembald, William 21
Kempe, Margery 189–90, 344
Kempley (Gloucestershire) 262
Kendall, Robert 178
Kenett, William 294
Kenilworth Castle 54
Kent
agriculture 64, 309
churches 42, 102, 293
French attacks 121, 130
houses 301
land 5, 89
law 101, 295
plays 259
towns 62, 71, 90, 121, 135, 246
uprisings 54, 124, 125, 314
Kent, Earl of 55
kerns 107
Ketel, Roger 200
Kibworth Harcourt (Leicestershire) 63,
123, 252
Kidwelly (Carmarthenshire) 178
Kilchief (co. Down) 271
Kilkenny (Ireland) 106, 107
Kilmallock (Limerick) 271
Kilpeck, Alan, Lord of 47
Kilpeck, Joan, Lady 47
Kilpeck (Herefordshire) 11
Kimbolton (Cambridgeshire) 3
King's College, Cambridge 192, 236, 290,
313
King's Hall, Cambridge 37
King's Langley (Hertfordshire) 174
King's Lynn (Norfolk) 71, 95, 211, 259,
308
Kings Ripton (Huntingdonshire) 201
Kingsden, Nicholas 297

kingship 52–3, 275, 321, 335
Kingsholme marshes (Suffolk) 207
Kingsthorpe (Northamptonshire) 65
Kingston Lacy (Dorset) 41, 42
Kirby Ravensworth (Yorkshire) 262
Kirkby, John, Bishop of Carlisle 93, 102,
   104
Kirkby-in-Ashfield (Nottinghamshire) 90
Kirton (Lincolnshire) 90
Knighton, Henry 55, 57, 150, 151
knights 162
   crusades 163–4
   Edward II 29–30
   legal business 95, 118
   pursuits 6, 81, 87, 95, 96, 164, 309
   see also chivalry; tournaments
Knights Hospitaller, Clerkenwell 211
Knolle, Robert 83, 86
Knyvet, John 114
Kydde, Jane 296

La Roche Derrien 110
labour legislation 69–70, 131, 337
Lambeth Palace 126
Lancashire 19, 26, 256
Lancaster, Dukes of see Grosmont, Henry;
   John of Gaunt
Lancaster, Earls of 31; see also Henry of
   Lancaster; Thomas of Lancaster
land-holding
   demesne lands 4, 200
   enclosure 239–40
   inheritance 18, 62, 200, 281
   Ireland 4, 5, 278
   leases 200, 202
   politics 5
   tenancies 4, 14, 20, 59–60, 61, 62–3,
     65–6, 67–8, 202, 252–3
   Wales 5, 179
   see also estates
landscape 2, 4, 65, 67, 202–3
Langland, William 115, 120, 133, 134, 135,
   136, 157, 158, 340
Langlays, Isabel 104
Langley, Henry and Katherine 302
Langton, John 233
language
   dialects 8–9, 43, 157
   English 128, 155, 156, 157–8, 194, 205,
     259–60, 262, 294
   French 8, 44, 45, 53, 155, 158
   Latin 14, 45, 53, 100, 155, 157–8, 240,
     263–4, 294–5
Lantern of Light, The 190

Lantoft, Peter 30
Latimer, William, Lord 114
Laughton (Sussex) 253
Laurencz, John 142
law and order 330–31
   1307–30 48–52
   1330–99 83, 116–19, 131; see also
     'Peasants' Revolt'
   1399–1421 205–8, 214, 344
   1422–61 247, 252
   1461–83 295–6, 352–3
   assizes 96
   in the community 7, 118, 252, 257,
     295–6
   criminal cases 117, 214
   equity 206
   family law 13, 99, 254, 257
   food legislation 133, 135
   forensic antiquarianism 239–40
   guilds 118
   Ireland 108, 116–17
   jury system 117
   legal training 49, 119, 206, 297–9
   litigation 68–9
   London 118, 296, 298
   miscarriage of justice 118–19
   oaths and oath helpers 116, 118
   royal commissions 95
   royal courts 117
   sumptuary legislation 70, 307
   trailbastons 95, 96
   Wales 10
   women 10, 14, 255–6
   see also canon law; Chancery; justices;
     labour legislation; manorial courts;
     Roman law; statute law
lawyers 165
Lay Folks' Catechism 102
Lay Folks' Mass Book 102
le Baker, Geoffrey 81
le Bel, Jehan 81, 111
le Geyte, Ralph 112
le Marescal, Robert 36
Leake Treaty (1318) 34
leather industry 242
Leeds 43
Legend of Good Women 155
Legendys of Hooly Wummen 258
Leicester 95, 151, 182
Leicestershire 63, 123, 150, 200–201, 214,
   252
Leinster 28, 107, 167
leisure activities 295, 303
Lengleys, Sir Thomas 101

Lewis, Emperor of Bavaria 77
Libelle of English Policy 241, 248
libraries 262, 348
Life of Edward IV 310
Life of Henry VI 284
Life of Our Lady 222, 260
Lilleshall Abbey 140
Lincoln 25, 101, 314
Lincoln's Inn 297, 299, 309
Lincolnshire 65
   agriculture 248, 249
   associations 132
   churches 285
   land 5, 65
   law 101, 214
   manors 68, 90
   serfs 296, 297
   see also Boston
Lindsey (Lincolnshire) 65, 249
Lionel Duke of Clarence 106, 108, 109,
   110, 272, 275
Litcham (East Anglia) 250
literacy 44, 141, 151, 294, 302
literature 15, 155–9, 258, 259, 302, 333;
   see also books; poetry
Lithuania 8, 82
Little Melton church (Norfolk) 262
Little Wenham (Suffolk) 2
livery 38, 109, 112, 165, 168
Livre du Corps de Policie 303
Llanddewi-Brefi 104
Llantrisant Castle 52
Llewellyn ap Madog 108
Llwyd, Sir Gruffydd 25, 26, 108
Llwyd ab Ieuan, Ieuan 156
local government 48–9, 136–40, 308–9,
   336
'Lollardy' 148, 150–54, 186, 187, 188–91,
   195, 196–7, 198, 342
London 339–40
   1399–1421 208
   1461–83 308–9, 350
   associations 121–2, 132
   Black Death 58
   chronicles 122, 211, 246, 267, 274, 304
   churches 22, 193, 211, 212, 245, 263,
     287, 288, 289, 291, 294
   Court of Hustings 207
   food and drink 132, 133, 135
   fuel and timber 135–6
   government 136–40, 308–9
   guilds 243–4
   law and order 118, 296, 298
   mayors 243–4

   migrant workers 70
   'Peasants' Revolt' 121–7
   politics 128, 243–4, 348
   population 2, 71–2, 244, 308, 339
   residences 22
   trade 22, 308
   water 135
London Bridge 304
London Chronicle 178
Longthorpe Tower, Bedford 45
Louis, Count of Nevers 77
Louis IX, King of France 225
Louis XI, King of France 276, 311
Louis de Beaumont 48
Louis of Flanders 76
Louis of Orléans 216
Love, Nicholas 189, 261
Lovel Lectionary 192–3
Lovel of Titmarsh, John, Lord 119, 192
Lovelich, Henry 260
Lowick (Northamptonshire) 5
Ludlow 12, 55, 256, 262
Lutterworth (Leicestershire) 150
Luttrell, Agnes 82, 99
Luttrell, Andrew 82
Luttrell, Geoffrey 82, 99
Luttrell, James 273
Luttrell, Sir Hugh 203
Luttrell Psalter 59, 82
Lydgate, John 156, 220, 222, 225, 226, 235,
   259, 260, 303, 345
Lyndwood, William 208
Lynton, Robert 246
Lyons, Richard 114, 133

MacCeabhaill, Maolruanaidh 107
Macclesfield, John 169
Madingley (Cambridgeshire) 49
magic 101, 181, 212, 234, 276, 283
magnates 329, 347
   Acts of Attainder 278, 314
   Anglo-Irish 284
   Appellants 130, 131, 161, 340
   crusades 163–4
   culture 239–41
   and Edward II 31–2, 34
   and Edward IV 281
   fortifications 121
   'maintaining' 165
   marriage 161
   parliament 92
   and 'Peasants' Revolt' 125
   pursuits 164–5
   residences 22, 161, 162

magnates – *cont.*
  and the Scottish wars 24
  wealth and power 5–6, 7, 127, 161, 162,
    239, 300–301
  see also estates
Maidstone (Kent) 124, 135
maintenance agreements 63
Maldon (Essex) 246
Maleverer, Sir Halnath 217
Malle, Count Louis de 129
Malory, Sir Thomas 254, 259
Malton Priory (Yorkshire) 187
Maltravers, John 54
Mancini, Domenico 313
Mannini (jeweller) 139
manorial court rolls 14–15, 62, 325
manorial courts 14, 18, 58, 117, 122, 252,
    253, 297
manors 2, 5, 21, 45, 63, 67, 199, 204,
    252–3, 309
  Wales 68, 178
Manuel II Palaeologus 185
maps 57
March, Earls of *see* Edward IV; Mortimer,
    Edmund, third Earl; Mortimer,
    Edmund, fifth Earl; Mortimer, Roger
March Day 122
Marches 5, 7, 9, 24, 68, 92
Maredudd ap Madog ap Llewellyn 62
Margaret of Anjou (Queen of Henry VI)
    345
  court 232–3, 241
  diplomacy 231
  exile 12, 274, 276, 279, 280, 304, 305
  marriage 230–31
  pageants 230, 246
  political power 232, 313
  and Richard Duke of York 273, 275
Margaret of Burgundy 169
Margaret of Clare 31
Margaret of York 280
Marie de St Pol, Countess of Pembroke 97
markets 3, 21–2, 79, 117, 133, 134, 179,
    203, 209, 210
Marner, Robert 181
marriage 332
  age at 123
  alimony 99
  breakdown 147
  ceremonies 100, 147–8
  clandestine 254, 255
  dowry and land 20, 62
  Ireland 254, 255
  law 99, 100–101, 254, 255, 296, 313

magnates 161
  parental choice 13, 147, 255
  violence 147, 254
  Wales 117
Martin V, Pope 207
Mascal, John 202
Mascy, Sir Geoffrey 240
material culture 3, 307, 325–6; *see also*
    fashion; food and drink
Maurice, son of Thomas, Earl of
    Desmond 107
Maynard, John 128
mayors 135, 136, 137, 140, 243–4, 307, 308
medicine 158, 233, 242
Meditations on the Life of Christ 222
Memoriale Credencium 194, 261
memory 11, 12
Merchant Adventurers 210
merchants 210, 307–8, 309
Merioneth 214
Merton College, Oxford 133, 252, 287
Metcalfe, Miles 299
Mezières, Philippe de 160, 230, 340–41
Michael of Kildare 47
Michaelhouse 37
Middleham College (Yorkshire) 293
Middleham Jewel 290
Middlesex 135, 243
migrant workers 62, 67, 70, 128, 204–5,
    208
migration 15, 17, 21, 208–9
mills 1, 19, 65, 68, 249, 253
Milmete, Walter 226
minstrels 111–12, 176
miracles 104, 284
Mirk, John 140, 194
Mirk's Festial 140
Mirror of the Blessed Life of Christ 189,
    261
Misterton, Alice 99
Mitford, Richard, Bishop of Salisbury 203
Modus tenendi Parliamentum 50–51
Molyens, Adam, Bishop of Chichester 265
Molyneux, Nicholas 164
monks and monasteries 11, 97, 99, 141,
    191, 193, 204, 222, 263, 265
  Benedictine 11, 97, 197, 240
  Dominican 41, 155, 192
  education 97
Montague, John, Earl of Salisbury 180,
    184
Montague, William 89
Moray 25
Moray, Earl of 73

Morgannwg (Glamorgan) 18
Morley, Robert 87, 291
Morley, Thomas, Lord 119
Morris, William 18
Morte d'Arthur 254, 259, 316
Mortimer, Anne 214, 272
Mortimer, Catherine 177
Mortimer, Edmund, fifth Earl of March
  213, 214
Mortimer, Edmund, third Earl of March
  133, 176, 177
Mortimer, Roger, first Earl of March 38,
  46, 52, 54, 55–6, 73, 89, 90
Mortimer family 5, 35
Mortimer of Chirk, Roger, Earl of March
  90
Mortimer's Cross 275
Morton, Dr John 298
Motram, John 291
Mounchessy, Richard 93
Moundsmere (Hampshire) 19
Mowbray, John, Lord 35
Mowbray, Thomas, Duke of Norfolk 130,
  163
Mowbray, Thomas, Earl Marshal 181
Moxby nunnery (Yorkshire) 27
Munster (Ireland) 107
murage 25
murrain 18, 248
Murray, Andrew 73, 74, 93
music 158, 193, 263, 291, 333, 351
Mutford (Norfolk) 97
Myntling, Laurence 297

Nájera, battle of 85, 105
names *see* personal names; place names
Navarre, King of 114
Netter, Thomas 195
Neville, Alexander, Archbishop of York
  128
Neville, Anne (Queen of Richard III) 283,
  315
Neville, Cicely, Duchess of York 12, 273
Neville, George, Archbishop of
  Canterbury 298
Neville, George, Archbishop of York 240,
  275, 280
Neville, Isabel 283
Neville, John, Lord 114
Neville, Richard, Earl of Warwick 225,
  274, 280, 281, 283, 284, 300
Neville, Robert 24
Neville, Sir William 164
Neville family 24, 74, 272, 299

Neville's Cross 74
New College, Oxford 236, 257
New Romney (Kent) 259
Newburgh (Staffordshire) 3
Newbury 314
Newcastle-upon-Tyne 24, 134, 242, 306,
  308
Newchurch (Kent) 293
Newgate School, Bristol 263–4
Newton, Sir John 124
Norfolk
  agriculture 19, 40, 64, 65
  churches and parishes 97, 250, 251, 262,
    284, 286, 288, 295
  estates 64, 68, 89, 201
  insurrection 127
  people 64, 65, 66, 67, 131–2, 223, 245,
    296
  see also Castle Acre; King's Lynn
Norfolk, Dukes of 242, 284; *see also*
  Howard, John; Mowbray, Thomas
Normandy
  1330–77 19, 75, 85, 88, 114, 121
  1412–21 185, 213, 221
  1422–50 224, 265, 268, 269–70
Northampton 34, 82, 123, 153, 306
Northampton, Earl of *see* Bohun, William
Northampton, John 136
Northamptonshire
  battles 280
  churches 5, 11, 44, 251, 310
  housing 253
  law 214
  markets 21–2
  population 65
northern England 23–4, 26–7, 33–4, 70,
  74, 334
Northleach (Gloucestershire) 138, 210
Northumberland, Duke of 214
Northumberland, Earl of *see* Percy, Henry
Northumberland/Northumbria 3, 17, 24,
  26, 32, 74, 157
Norwich 2, 17, 41, 58, 204, 211, 247, 250
  Cathedral 251, 287, 350
Nottingham 130, 182
Nottinghamshire 4, 90, 99, 101, 118, 214
Nuneaton 182
nuns and nunneries 27, 63, 192, 215, 259,
  264–5
Nun's Priest's Tale, The 138–9

Ogmore, Lordship of 179
O'Kennedy family of Ormond 107
Oldcastle, Sir John 198–9, 212–13

Ollingwick (Herefordshire) 141
O'Neill, Domnal, King of the Irish 25
O'Neill family 272
Opus arduum (Hard work) 151
Order of the Garter 109–10, 113, 169, 184,
216, 225, 226, 231, 277–8
Ordinance and Form of Fighting 164
Ordinance of Provisions (1343) 88
Ordinances 31–2, 120, 206
Oriel College, Oxford 37
Orléans 228
Orléans, Charles, Duke of 218, 227, 241
Ormond, Earls of 278
Oseney Abbey (Oxfordshire) 271
Ottery, Roger 102
Ovid 303
Oxford 173, 263
Oxford, Earls of *see* de Vere, John; de
Vere, Robert
Oxford University 9, 42, 97, 148, 149, 150,
195, 238, 240, 264, 314
colleges 8, 37, 97, 133, 149, 207, 226,
236, 238
Oxfordshire 9, 102, 130, 138, 190, 251,
252, 253, 257, 271, 288–9
Oxnead (Norfolk) 286

Paddesley, John 244
Pageant of Concord 159
pageants 231, 246, 292
Pancio de Controne 78
Pannal, Emmot 256
Papal Schism 140
Paris 84, 225, 268
parishes 99–100, 328–9, 347–8, 351
charity 197–8, 200–201
finance 43, 190, 197, 286
patronage 11
politics 190
poor relief 9, 145, 197
roles 44–5, 143–4, 263
parkland 67
Parles, John 94
parliament 331, 338
1307–30 25, 33, 36, 50–52, 53
1330–77 79, 80, 92–7, 114–15, 338
1377–99 120, 128, 130, 131–2
1399–1421 173, 175, 179, 182–3, 184,
187, 197, 210–11, 213, 219, 220, 221,
343
1422–1461 226–7, 239, 245, 267, 272,
273
1461–83 276, 300, 304–6, 312–13
clergy 50, 51, 92
Commons 50, 71, 88, 92, 93–4, 96, 126,
171, 198, 305
elected representatives 93–4, 183, 184,
226, 245, 305
functions 50–51, 92, 94, 210
Irish policy 94–5
Lords 50, 92
petitions 51, 94, 95, 165, 168, 197–8,
248, 272
Welsh policy 179
see also statute law
parliamentary rolls 14
Paston, Agnes 286
Paston, John 284, 303
Paston, Margaret 286
Paston, Walter 286
Paston family 259, 271, 298, 330
Patay, battle of 269
patronage 333
churches 11–12
Edward III 72, 89–91, 109–10, 120, 338
Edward IV 277, 278, 281, 284, 308
Henry IV 183–4
Henry V 183, 216
Henry VI 226, 230
Humphrey Duke of Gloucester 240, 242,
244, 346
John of Gaunt 149, 150, 158, 163, 165,
184
Richard II 128–9, 169–70, 184
Richard III 308
Wales 8, 89
women 326, 336
Paxton-on-Tweed 26–7
Paynell, Katherine 101
Paynell, Sir Ralph 101
Pearl (poem) 158
peasantry 2, 4, 118, 253, 257
'Peasants' Revolt' 121–7, 137, 138, 341–2
Peckham, John, Archbishop of
Canterbury 43, 261
Pecock, Reginald, Bishop of St Asaph and
Chichester 236, 261, 264
Pedro the Cruel 85
Pembroke, Countesses of 43, 97
Pembroke, Duchess of 90
Pembroke, Earls of 32, 158
Pembroke College, Cambridge 97
Penhow, Chepstow 178
Percy, Henry, Earl of Northumberland
169, 170, 177, 181
Percy, Henry 'Hotspur' 178, 181
Percy, Sir Henry 317
Percy family 24, 74, 166

Perrers, Alice 115
personal names 21, 67, 301
Peter of Florence 112
Peterborough Abbey 201, 202
Petrarch 84
Petworth Park 59
Peverel, Bishop of Worcester 189
Peyl, Joan 189
Philip IV, King of France 30, 32, 38, 74
Philip V, King of France 37
Philip VI, King of France 75, 77, 80, 110
Philip the Good, Duke of Burgundy 276, 278, 280
Philippa (daughter of Henry IV) 210, 215
Philippa (daughter of Lionel Duke of Clarence) 275
Philippa of Hainault (Queen of Edward III)
    at court 110, 111–12
    death and burial 113
    family 128
    fashion 112
    and French wars 76, 81
    marriage 72
    symbolism 155
Philpot, John 137
Pickering, Thomas, Abbot of Whitby 297
Pierce the Ploughman's Crede 191
Piers Plowman 8, 115, 120, 133, 135, 191, 195, 197, 344
pigs 241–2, 256
pilgrimages 99, 104, 141, 151, 189, 193, 259
piracy 210
place names 3, 13, 203
plague 12, 199, 270, 320; *see also* Black Death
Plouden, Thomas 157
Plumpton, Robert 255
Plumpton, Sir Robert 217
Plumpton, Sir William 255
Plumpton, William 255
Plumpton Hall (Yorkshire) 217
Plymouth 121
Podington (Bedfordshire) 202
poetry 341
    English 259
    French 83, 111, 158, 225
    Gaelic 107, 125–6, 157
    political 76, 158, 179, 185, 196–7, 216, 219, 237, 279, 310–11, 347
    Ricardian 158
    vernacular 9, 36, 156, 157
    Welsh 141, 156–7, 176, 258–9, 279

see also Chaucer, Geoffrey; Gower, John; Langland, William; Lydgate, John; Shakespeare, William
Poitiers 84, 89, 105
political culture 5, 6–7, 9–10, 149, 232, 279–80, 320–1, 331–2, 346–7, 349–50
poll-tax 14, 120, 123, 150, 342
Polton, Thomas, Bishop of Worcester 238
Pontefract 35, 122, 172, 174, 273, 310
Pontoise 268, 269
Ponynges, Lady 242
popes 151; *see also* popes by name
population
    1300–1330 1, 2, 4–5, 20
    after Black Death 57–9, 65, 66
    1377 115
    London 2, 71–2, 244, 308, 339
    towns 2, 244, 246–7
Pore Caitif (Poor Captive) 153
ports 2, 39, 70–71, 120, 207
Portsmouth 47, 130
Portugal 139, 307
Portugal, King of 114
Postan, Michael 325
poverty 9, 134, 145, 197
Powderham, John 34–5
Power, Arnold 29
Power, Leonel 193
priests *see* clergy
Priests's Eye, The (Oculus sacerdotis) 100
Prior of Coventry 36
Privy Seal 96
Prophet, Adam 20
prostitution 86, 247, 296
Prussia 163, 209
psalters 17, 41, 45, 59, 82
Pudding Norton (Norfolk) 66
Pulham Hall 309
Pyamour, John 193
Pykanham, William 286
Pym, John 50

Queen Mary Psalter 17
Queen's College, Oxford 97

rabbit warrens 21, 59, 64
Radcot Bridge (Oxfordshire) 130
Raglan Castle (Monmouthshire) 67
Rainham (Kent) 102
Ralph of Shrewsbury, Bishop of Bath and Wells 58
Ramesbury, William 152
Ramsay, Ralph 184
Ramsey 201, 252

Randolf, John 246
Ranulf of Otterburn 20
Rawghton, Emma 234
Raymond of Peñaforte 140
reconquista 82
Redgrave (Suffolk) 20
Reed, Edmund 303
reeves 132, 135–6
Reformation 321
Regiment of Princes 185
Reginald de Cobham 91
regionalization 180, 241
Reims 89, 225, 228, 305
religion 329, 336, 342
   1307–30 40–47
   1377–99 140–46
   1399–1421 180, 182, 186–99, 264, 343–4
   1422–61 258–9, 260–61, 264–5
   1461–83 285–95
   artefacts 46
   books 15, 45–6, 141–2, 190, 192, 194–5,
     216, 222, 259, 260, 261–2, 285, 302–3
   Christianity 10, 186–7, 222
   drama 141, 146, 151, 235, 259, 291–2, 351
   heresy 117, 186, 260
   indulgences 289, 302
   institutions 36–7, 40–41, 71, 97, 247,
     346, 350–51
   instruction 43–4, 99–100, 103, 141,
     151–2, 285, 336, 338
   local and vernacular 258–9, 260–62, 279
   'Lollardy' 148, 150–54, 186, 187,
     188–91, 195, 196–7, 198, 342
   'radical orthodoxy' 148–9
   royal writs 187
   and social order 148, 197–8
   and the state 187, 227
   'traditional religion' 148, 149
   women 196, 228, 234–5, 258, 259, 261,
     264, 289–90, 294, 306, 348–9
   worship 44, 45, 103–4, 141, 189, 262,
     289–90
   Wycliffism 150, 153, 156, 194, 195
   see also Archbishops of Canterbury;
     Archbishops of York; bishops; canon
     law; cathedrals; chantries; churches;
     clergy; ecclesiastical courts; hermits
     and anchorites; magic; monks and
     monasteries; nuns and nunneries;
     parishes; pilgrimages; religious houses
religious houses
   archives 240
   finance 11, 41, 91, 103, 197, 249, 307
   foreign houses 91, 211

   medical care 308
   in old age 63
   and parishes 11, 43, 103, 197
   see also monks and monasteries; nuns
     and nunneries
Remonstrance against Oldcastle 196–7,
   212–13
Rempson, Sir Thomas 269
René II of Anjou 230, 279
Repyngdon, Bishop of Lincoln 189
Reydon Hours 46
Reynes, Robert 290, 294–5
Reynold, Joan 294
Rhos 89
Rhufoniog 89
Rhys ap Hywel 24
Rhys ap Thomas 316
Richard II 340
   birth 114, 121
   complaints against 119, 130–31, 167,
     168, 179
   counsellors 115, 120, 130, 131, 160
   court 140, 156, 158–9, 163, 341
   crusades 129, 160
   death and burial 171, 173, 175, 215
   deposition 171–2, 280, 340, 341
   family 8, 126, 169
   finance 120, 130, 166–7, 168
   marriages 113, 129, 161
   maturity 159–61
   minority 109, 115, 120–21, 128–32
   patronage 128–9, 169–70, 184
   'Peasants' Revolt' 124–5, 126, 137, 138,
     341–2
   rule 120, 128–32, 140, 167–8, 180
   rumours of survival 172, 174, 182
   Scotland 129–30, 174
   usurpation of 170–71, 172, 173–4, 181,
     343
Richard II 171
Richard III 353
   coronation 313–14
   court 315
   as Duke of Gloucester 8, 275, 278, 280,
     282, 283, 290, 293, 308, 310, 311–12
   and Edward V 312–13
   foundations 293
   government 316
   marriage 283, 315
   patronage 308
   religion and learning 316
   royal progress 314
   uprisings against 314–15, 316–17
Richard III 313

Richard de Burgh, 'Red Earl of Ulster' 107
Richard Duke of York 232, 252, 258, 267,
    269, 271–4, 275, 310
Richard of Pembridge 109
Richard of York (son of Edward IV) 311,
    312, 313
Richard the Redeless 179
Richmond, Earl of 37
Ripon (Yorkshire) 144
Robbessart, Louis 216
Robert II, King of Scotland 129
Robert de Lisle 45
Robert de Reydon, Sir 46
Robert de Stuteville 90
Robert of Adderbury 50
Robert of Ardern 245
Robert of Artois 76
Robert of Eglesfield 97
Robert of Madingley 49–50
Robin Hood 301
Rochester (Kent) 54, 101, 124
Rodin, Auguste 81
Roger de Elmerugge 39
Roger de Mar 99
Roger de Salkeld 67
Rolle, Richard 165
'rolls of Ninths' (*Nonae*) 79
Roman law 206, 298
Romford (Essex) 295
Roos, Lord William de 211
Roos, Mary 211
Roos, Thomas Lord 268
Rosa medicinae 87
Ross, Earl of 25
Rouen 222, 225
Rougge, Gilbert 123
Rous, John 239–40, 300, 315
Roxburgh (Borders) 82, 179
royal Maundy 38
rural deans 99
rural life 327
    during famine 18–19
    during Black Death 59
    1399–1421 199–204, 208–9
    1422–61 252–4, 256–7
    work 20–21, 61–2, 63, 66, 122, 256
Russel, Philip 101
Russell, John (bishop) 315
Ruthin 177
    Lords Grey of 200
Rutland 123, 214
Rutland (son of Richard Duke of York)
    273, 310
Rye (Kent) 90, 121

Sackville family 202
St Albans 185, 272, 276, 288
St Albans Abbey 13–14, 24, 126, 184, 192,
    240, 273
St Andrew Hubbard, Eastcheap (London)
    294
St Andrews University 264
St Anthony's Hospital, London 169
St Bartholomew Priory 211
St Benet Hulme Abbey 127
St Benet's church, Cambridge 60
St Botolph's, Hadstock (Essex) 11
St Botolph's, London 211
St Brelade's, Jersey 190
St Catharine's College, Cambridge 290
St Crux, York 103
St George's Chapel, Windsor 109, 113,
    169, 263, 292
St George's Day 109, 110, 111
St James Garlickehithe, London 291
St John Maddermarket church, Norwich
    250
St John the Evangelist Hospital,
    Cambridge 133
St John Walbrook 194
St John's, Colchester 182
St Just in Penwith (Cornwall) 288
St Lawrence's church, Ludlow 256
St Margaret's, York 144
St Margaret's church, Westminster 291
St Martin, Harfleur 164
St Martin's church, York 251
St Mary, Carlisle 102
St Mary at Hill, London 194, 212, 288, 291
St Mary Magdalen, Oxford 263
St Mary Munthaw, London 22
St Mary's Abbey, Leicester 151
St Mary's church, Sandwich 246
St Mary's parish, Cambridge 304
St Mawes (Cornwall) 141
St Michael Cornhill, London 287, 288
St Michael Paternoster 212
St Michael's church, Wood Street
    (London) 245
St Mildred's Poultry, London 245, 287
St Olave's Jewry 245
St Omer 76
St Paul's Cathedral 128, 188, 291, 310
St Peter's church, Wenhaston (Suffolk) 293
St Sepulchre church, London 287
St Stephen's, Coleman Street (London) 263
St Stephen's chapel, Westminster 289
St Swithin's Priory, Winchester 202, 307
Saint-Julien-du-Sault 86

Saint-Sardos 38
Saint-Sauveur-le-Vicomte 85, 114
saints 104, 141, 151, 154, 234
Salisbury 119, 192, 196, 314
Salisbury, Earls of 76, 79, 272, 273; see also Montague, John
Salle Kirkhall (Norfolk) 296
salt 65
Salve regina 303
Sandwich (Kent) 90, 246
Santiago de Compostela 99, 141
Santon Downham (Suffolk) 288
Sapiti, Andrea 39
Sarnesfield, Nicholas 110
Sarum Hours 303
Savage, John 183
Savage, Sir Arnold 182
Savernake, William 257–8
Savoy Palace 125, 126
Saxtead (Suffolk) 296
Saxthorpe (Norfolk) 97
Say, Sir John 289
Scales, Anthony, Lord see Woodville, Anthony
Scales, Thomas, Lord 226
Scales family 299
Schort, Thomas 263
Scotland 334
    Declaration of Arbroath 27–8
    invasion of Ireland 25, 26, 334–5
    invasions of 129–30, 177
    parliament 119
    and Richard II 129–30, 174
    sovereignty 26–7
    see also borders: northern
Scottish wars 22–4, 26–8, 29, 35–6, 37, 54, 73–4, 121, 334
Scrope, Beatrice 82
Scrope, Henry, Lord 184
Scrope, John, Lord 278
Scrope, Richard, Archbishop of York 175, 181, 310, 343
Scrope, Thomas 265
Scrope family 177
sculpture 4, 41
scutage 105, 106
sea defences 130
Seagram, Ralph 250
Sedgeford (Norfolk) 64
Seman, Isabel 142
Seman, Robert 251
serfs and serfdom 4, 15, 62, 66, 68–9, 123–4, 202, 252, 253, 296
Serle, William 194

Serpent of Division, The 226
Sever, Henry 236
Shakespeare, William 10–11, 12, 306
    Henry V 83, 213, 218
    Henry VI 275, 282
    Richard II 171
    Richard III 313
    Twelfth Night 298
Shapey (Cumbria) 104
Shardelowe, Sir Thomas 103
Sharnebourne, Thomas 232–3
Shaw, Edmund 313
Sheen Palace 113, 115
sheep 1, 18, 64, 200, 203, 248, 249, 270, 271, 307, 309
Shelford Abbey (Nottinghamshire) 99
Sherborne Missal 192, 193
sheriffs 96, 117, 118, 124, 168
ships 77, 84, 209–10, 220–21
shipwrecks 45, 138, 168
Shirley, John 260
Shirley family 301
Shoreham, William 43
Shrewsbury 130, 178, 181
Shrewsbury, Earl of see Talbot, John
Shrewsbury, Elizabeth, Countess of 306
Shrewsbury Manifesto 272
Shropshire 9, 124, 252
Siege of Thebes, The 220, 303
Siferwas, John 192
Sigismund, Emperor 220, 223
Signet 96
Simon atte Style 27
Simon de Drayton, Sir 5–6
Sizewell (Suffolk) 134
Skenfrith church (Gwent) 146
Sluys, Battle of (1340) 76–7, 93, 105, 130
smallholdings 2–3, 4, 17, 254
Smith, Joan 254
Smyth, William 142
social mobility 67, 123, 128, 131, 139, 298–9
social relations/status 245, 257, 300, 332
social support 61, 63
Solace of Pilgrims, The 259, 261
Somerset 5, 20, 190, 203, 242, 250, 265, 289, 293
Somerset, Duke of see Beaufort, Edmund
Somerset, John 233, 243
Song against the King's Taxes 78
Southampton 267
Southampton Plot 214, 276
Southwark 22, 134, 247
Southwell Minster (Nottinghamshire) 4

Southwell (physician) 233, 234
Spain 163; *see also* Castile
Spain, King of 114
Spalding (Lincolnshire) 296, 297
Spicer, William 127
spices 133, 138, 204, 306
Spileman, Alice 21
Spore, Jack 86
sport and games 295–6
Stackallan (co. Meath) 255
Stafford, Hugh, Lord 216
Stafford, Humphrey, Earl of 214
Stafford, John, Bishop of Bath and Wells 261
Stafford, Sir Henry 300
Staffordshire 3, 67, 248, 289
Standish, Henry 269
Standish family 269
Stanley, Sir William 317
Stanley, Thomas Lord 317
statecraft 219–20
statute law 28, 69, 70, 94, 95, 117, 207, 297
Statute of Additions (1413) 245
Statute of Labourers (1350) 69, 96, 124
Statute of Treason (1352) 70
Statute of Winchester (1285) 28
Statutes of Kilkenny (1366) 106
Stillington, Robert 304
Stirling Castle 23
Stoke d'Abernon 49
Stonor family 259
Stowmarket (Suffolk) 296
Strange, Sir John 184
Stratford, John, Archbishop of
    Canterbury 79, 93, 98
Strathbogie, David 73
Stubbs, John 256
Sturmer (Essex) 123
Sudbury, Archbishop of Canterbury 124,
    125, 138
Sudeley, Lord 281
Suffolk
    associations 131
    churches 8, 41, 249, 250, 258, 262, 288,
        289, 293
    estates 199, 201, 299
    food 134, 204
    law 20, 21, 207
    manors 2, 201, 309
    parliament 184
    towns 210, 244, 296
Suffolk, Duke of *see* de la Pole, William
Suffolk, Earls of 76, 80, 288–9; *see also* de
    la Pole, Michael; de la Pole, William

Sulyard, Sir John 299, 309–10, 350
sumptuary legislation 70, 307
Surrey 135, 142, 283–4
Surrey, Earls of 144, 169, 191
Surrey, Thomas Holland, Duke of 184
Sussex 21, 90, 130, 135, 201–2, 253, 256,
    269, 288
Swaffham (Norfolk) 295
Swanscombe (Kent) 43
Swell, John 142
Swillington, Sir Robert 207–8
Swinbrook (Cotswolds) 4
Swinderby, William 151, 153, 154
Sword of Solomon, The 261
Sycharth (Denbighshire) 176

Talbot, Gilbert Lord 184, 316, 317
Talbot, John, Earl of Shrewsbury 226,
    231, 268, 269–70, 306
Talbot, Sir Thomas 167
Tale of Melibee 139
Talmache, John and Alice 193
Tancarville 269
Tatterford church (Norfolk) 288
Tattershall (Lincolnshire) 285
Taunton (Somerset) 20
taverns 134
taxation 342
    1330–77 7, 71, 78–80, 82, 92
    1377–99 120, 166, 342
    1399–1461 208, 265
    1461–83 280, 304, 307
    exemptions 27, 78, 108, 150, 210
    levies 211
    poll-tax 14, 120, 123, 150, 342
    tallages 50, 210
    tithes 45
    see also 'Peasants' Revolt'
Taylor, William 195
Taymouth Hours 45–6
Tegeingl (Flintshire and Denbighshire) 68
Temple of Glass, The 303
Tendering Hall, Stoke-on-Nayland
    (Suffolk) 299
Testament of Love 136, 155
Tetzel, Gabriel 278
Tewkesbury 132, 147, 282, 284, 311
textile industry 242
    labour 62, 63, 123, 249
    regional variation 40, 209
    sumptuary legislation 70, 307
    trade 1, 140, 166–7, 209, 248, 270
    see also wool
Thame 291–2, 294, 308

Thames Valley 278
Thetford (Suffolk) 41, 87
Thomas, Lord Wake of Liddell 98
Thomas de Lisle, Bishop of Ely 98
Thomas Duke of Clarence 185, 213, 214, 221
Thomas Marquess of Dorset 314–15
Thomas of Ingoldisthorp 19
Thomas of Lancaster 22, 24, 30, 32–3, 34, 35, 38–9
Thomas of St Albans 99
Thomas of Walsingham 127
Thomas (son of Henry IV) 211
Thoresby, John, Archbishop of York 100, 103
Thornbury Manor 2
Thorney Abbey (Cambridgeshire) 261
Thornham Parva retable 41
Thornwerk, William and Elizabeth 246
Thorpe, Robert 45
Thorpp, Richard 256
Tideman of Winchecombe 169
timber 3–4, 136, 309
tin-mining 20, 65, 307
Tipperary (Ireland) 107
Tiptoft, John, Lord 238
Tiptoft, Sir John 182
Toddington church (Bedfordshire) 262
Tommes, Richard 202
Topsfield Hall, Crouch End 275
Totnes (Devon) 71
Tournai 76, 77
tournaments 81–2, 87, 113, 140, 163, 277, 278
Tower of London 124–5, 126, 199
Towneley Plays 292
towns 327–8, 348
  before 1300 1, 2, 3, 15
  1307–99 21, 66, 70–72, 79, 117
  1399–1421 204, 208–9, 210–12
  1422–83 243–7, 270, 300–301, 307
  hygiene 132–3, 133, 247
  population 2, 244, 246–7
  see also cities; London
Townshend, John 299
Townshend, Roger 297, 298, 299, 307
Towton, Battle of 275, 297, 310
trade 328, 336
  1300–1400 22, 39–40, 75, 137–8, 139, 166–7
  1400–1483 209, 224, 242, 244, 270, 304, 306–8, 352
  books 304
  textile industry 1, 140, 166–7, 209, 248, 270

see also markets; wool trade
trades and skills see work and craft
trailbastons 95, 96
travel 2, 40, 241, 308
Treatise on the Astrolabe 155
Treatise on the Coronation 75
Treaty of Brétigny (1360) 73, 85, 113–14
Treaty of Calais (1360) 114
Treaty of Edinburgh (1328) 45
Treaty of Piquigny (1475) 307, 311
Treaty of Troyes (1420) 220, 221, 222, 225, 229
Treaty of Utrecht (1474) 307
Treatyse of Fysshynge with an Angle 254
Tree of Battles, The 231
Trefenant, Bishop of Hereford 154
Tretower Court (Powys) 214
Trinity College, Cambridge 37
Trinity Hall 97
Troilus and Criseyde 260
Trollope, Anthony 9
Troy Book 156
Truce of Leulingham 166
Truro (Cornwall) 246
Twelfth Night 298
Twelve Conclusions 151, 154, 156
Tyes, John 193
Tyler, Wat 122, 124, 125

Ufford, Maud Countess of Oxford 181
Ufford, Robert 90
Ulster, Earls of 107, 110
University College, Oxford 238
Urban VI, Pope 140
Usk, Thomas 136, 155
Uthred of Boldon 97–8

Vagrancy Act 131
Valence Mary Hall, Cambridge 97
valets 81
van Artevelde, Jacob 77
Ventour, William 140
Vergil, Polydore 317
Vienne, Jean de 80, 81
villages 4, 7, 65, 66, 123, 249; see also parishes
villeins 65
violence 5–6, 62, 135, 138, 147, 254, 320–21
vowesses 306
Vows of the Heron 76

Wainfleet St Mary 104
Wakefield, Battle of 273, 310

Walberswick (Suffolk) 250, 284, 289
Wales 326
    allegiances 24, 108
    castles 26
    discontent 266
    Edward II 25–6, 36, 52
    families 62–3
    gentry 239
    and Henry IV 176–7, 178–9, 184
    holy wells 141
    land-holding 5, 179
    law 10
    manors 68, 178
    marriage 116
    military 27, 108, 269
    patronage 8, 90
    poetry 141, 156–7, 176, 258–9, 279
    and Richard II 169–70
    and Richard III 314, 316
    taxation 108
    towns 70
    see also Marches
Walsall Manor (Staffordshire) 67
Walsham-le-Willows (Suffolk) 21
Walsingham 104
Walsingham, Thomas 125, 156
Walston, Walter 194
Walter de Godeston 45
Walter de Mauny 76
Walter de Stapledon 37
Walter of Kirkbride 101
Walter of Milmete 53
Waltham, John, Bishop of Salisbury 131
Walthamstead, John 240, 273
Walworth, William 137
Wantage (Berkshire) 196
war 164–5, 166, 228, 231, 305–6, 330; see
    also armies; crusades; France: wars;
    Ireland: warfare; Scottish wars;
    tournaments
wardmotes 118
warlords 180
Wars of the Roses 306, 310–11, 314–18,
    349, 353
Warwick, Duke of see Beauchamp, Henry
Warwick, Earls of 30, 32, 34, 130, 184
    see also Beauchamp, Richard; Neville,
    Richard
Warwick Castle 32, 281
Warwickshire 3, 65, 204, 214, 240, 245,
    246
water 135, 247
Waterton, Robert, Lord of Methley 223
waterways 40, 65

Watford (Northamptonshire) 253
Waynflete, William, Bishop of Winchester
    236
Webbs, Emma 196
Wedgenock Park (Warwickshire) 204
Welford, John 204
Welland marshes (Kent) 5
Welle, William 91
Wells Cathedral 237, 291, 292
Welsh Newton (Herefordshire) 41, 326
Wensleydale 299, 301
Weobley Castle (Herefordshire) 178
West Chiltington (Sussex) 288
West Raynton (co. Durham) 66
Westley Waterless, Cambridge 49
Westminster Abbey 19, 155, 170, 193, 226,
    246, 302, 314
Westminster Hall 97, 154, 206, 314
Westminster Palace 112, 128
Weston, John 212
Weston, Richard 228
Wetherden (Suffolk) 309–10
Weymouth (Dorset) 57
Whalley church (Lancashire) 256
Wharfedale 26
Whas, John 192
Whitby Abbey 275, 297, 300
White, John 201
White Book (Liber albus) 135
White Waltham (Berkshire) 142
Whittington, Alice 212
Whittington, Dick 212
Wickham Market (Suffolk) 210
widowhood 20, 47, 105, 127, 207, 235,
    255–6, 256, 306, 333, 351
Wiggenhall (Norfolk) 19
'wild man' 12
Wilhelm Duke of Guelders 184
William de Laken 170
William del Clay of Markham 99
William of Erlakar 189
William of Norwich 250
William of Ostrevant 169
William of Pagula 100
William the Conqueror 24
Willoughby, Lady Johanna 211
Willoughby, Sir Richard 95
Willoughby, William, Lord 211, 216
wills
    bequests 82, 100, 188–9, 240, 250, 251,
        256, 262, 291, 294
    endowments 289, 293–4
    executors 250
    Henry V 225, 227

wills – *cont.*
  instructions 194, 249
  probate 117, 255, 275
Wilton Diptych 155, 160–61, 326
Wilton (Norfolk) 97
Wiltshire 90, 142, 249
Wimborne Minster (Dorset) 251
Winchelsea (Kent) 71, 90, 121
Winchester 202, 253, 307
Winchester Cathedral 192, 193, 225, 291
Winchester College 236, 257
Windsor 69, 109, 110, 112, 113, 284, 314
Winfleet (Lincolnshire) 189
Winter, John 164
Wisbech (Cambridgeshire) 68, 200, 286–7, 295, 296
Wisdom (play) 235
witchcraft 212, 228, 231, 233, 295
women
  anchoresses 47–8, 234
  community life 256
  at court 155
  denunciations of 233, 295
  inheritance 10, 74–5, 255–6
  law 10, 14, 255–6
  and 'Lollardy' 154
  patronage 326, 336
  poverty 134
  religion 196, 228, 234–5, 258, 259, 261, 264, 289–90, 294, 306, 348–9
  representations of 256, 288
  vowesses 306
  work 60–62, 122, 123, 249, 256, 328, 332–3
  see also widowhood
Wood, Sir John 315
Woodeaton (Oxfordshire) 190
Woodford (Northamptonshire) 21
woodland 67, 135–6
Woodstock, Edmund of, Earl of Kent 55
Woodstock, Thomas, Duke of Gloucester 110, 128, 130, 162, 164
Woodville, Anthony, Lord Scales 278, 280, 303
Woodville, Elizabeth *see* Elizabeth Woodville (Queen of Edward IV)
Woodville family 278, 299
wool trade 1, 18, 39–40, 78, 129, 137, 138, 139, 210, 244, 248, 249, 306–7, 308; *see also* sheep; textile industry
Woolaston (Gloucestershire) 178
Worcester 12, 123, 178
Worcester, Earl of 238

Worcester, William of 238, 311
Worcestershire 3, 20, 132, 287
work and craft 328n
  apprenticeship 61
  domestic service 122–3, 134, 147–8
  legislation 69–70, 131, 337
  rural 20–21, 61–2, 63, 66, 122
  textile industry 62, 63, 123, 249
  unemployment 131
  urban 58, 60–61, 193, 204, 208
  women 60–62, 122, 123, 249, 256, 328, 332–3
  see also guilds
Wotton-under-Edge (Gloucestershire) 144
writers 136–7; *see also* books; literature; poetry
Wulley, Thomas 296
Wyclif, John 148, 149–50, 151, 187, 197, 198, 236, 342
Wycliffism 150, 153, 156, 195
Wye 34, 142
Wyllys, James 260
Wymeswold (Leicestershire) 200–201
Wymondham (Norfolk) 250

Yedingham nunnery (Yorkshire) 63
yeomen 202, 301
York
  churches 103, 144, 234, 251
  drama 292, 314
  education 304
  guilds 299
  Henry V 211
  mayoral elections 307
  population 2, 67, 205, 256
  religious institutions 46, 118, 293
  Richard III and 311–12, 314
York, Dukes of *see* Edmund of Langley; Edward Duke of York; Richard Duke of York
York Minster 291, 293
Yorkshire 4
  court 33, 168
  insurrection 160
  North Riding 118, 144, 262
  religion 63, 100, 118, 250
  Scots invasion 27
  West Riding 26, 118, 167, 222–3, 292
  wool trade 40, 123, 249
Young, Thomas 272
Ypres, siege of 129